EVALUATION

METHODS FOR STUDYING PROGRAMS AND POLICIES

SECOND EDITION

Carol H. Weiss
Harvard University

Prentice Hall, Upper Saddle River, New Jersey 07458

Library of Congress Cataloging-in-Publication Data

WEISS, CAROL H.
    Evaluation/Carol H. Weiss—2nd ed.
      p. cm.
    Rev. ed. of: Evaluation research. 1972.
    Includes bibliographical references and index.
    ISBN 0-13-309725-0
      1. Evaluation research (Social action programs) I. Weiss, Carol H.
    Evaluation research. II. Title.
    H62.W3962 1997
    001.4'33—dc21   97-44749
                                            CIP

Editorial director: Charlyce Jones Owen
Acquisitions editor: Nancy Roberts
Editorial assistant: Maureen Diana
Marketing manager: Christopher DeJohn
Editorial/production supervision
  and electronic page makeup: Kari Callaghan Mazzola
Interior design and electronic art creation: John P. Mazzola
Cover director: Jayne Conte
Buyer: Mary Ann Gloriande

This book was set in 10/11.5 Times by Big Sky Composition
and was printed and bound by Courier Companies, Inc.
The cover was printed by Phoenix Color Corp.

© 1998, 1972 by Prentice-Hall, Inc.
Simon & Schuster/A Viacom Company
Upper Saddle River, New Jersey 07458

Previously published under the title of *Evaluation Research:
Methods of Assessing Program Effectiveness.*

Printed in the United States of America
10 9 8 7 6 5

ISBN 0-13-309725-0

PRENTICE-HALL INTERNATIONAL (UK) LIMITED, *London*
PRENTICE-HALL OF AUSTRALIA PTY. LIMITED, *Sydney*
PRENTICE-HALL CANADA INC., *Toronto*
PRENTICE-HALL HISPANOAMERICANA, S.A., *Mexico*
PRENTICE-HALL OF INDIA PRIVATE LIMITED, *New Delhi*
PRENTICE-HALL OF JAPAN, INC., *Tokyo*
SIMON & SCHUSTER ASIA PTE. LTD., *Singapore*
EDITORA PRENTICE-HALL DO BRASIL, LTDA., *Rio de Janeiro*

To Benjamin, Samuel, Jacob, and Delilah

CONTENTS

Chapter 6   Developing Measures   **114**

Chapter 7   Collecting Data   **152**

Chapter 8   Design of the Evaluation   **180**

Chapter 9   The Randomized Experiment   **215**

*P*REFACE

Evaluation was a new kid on the research block when my first book, *Evaluation Research*, was published in 1972. A generation of experience has piled up in the meantime. Many types of programs that were just undergoing their first serious reviews then have now been the subject of scores, hundreds, even thousands of evaluations, and we know a lot more about how programs work. We also know more about evaluative methods, statistical techniques, and qualitative approaches to evaluation.

We have learned that solving social problems is difficult and exacting and calls for large resources of money, time, will, and ideas. Most social problems that this nation and other nations face are beyond the reach of easy solutions. No magic bullet is going to end crime, poverty, illness, or the degradation of the environment. People will continue to worry about education, violence, and community cohesiveness. Progress will be made in gradual stages, by incremental improvements, and it will take careful, systematic evaluation to identify which modes of intervention have better outcomes. With the information and insight that evaluation brings, organizations and societies will be better able to improve policy and programming for the well-being of all.

This book is directed at three main audiences. It is intended primarily for graduate and undergraduate students who are gaining their first introduction to evaluation. It is a nontechnical book, requiring no knowledge of statistics, written in easy and accessible prose. I write with the novice in mind, introducing research and statistical concepts in everyday language. Still, students find it useful to know something ahead of time about basic social science research methods.

The second audience is experienced evaluators. The book has much to say about the philosophy, principles, and procedures of evaluation that will make special sense to those who have already been exposed to (and jousted on) the field.

A third audience is administrators, program directors, policymakers, and government and foundation program officers. These people do not intend to do evaluations themselves, but they intend to commission evaluations, review evaluation proposals, and receive evaluation reports. They need to understand what evaluation is, what it can do and what it can't be expected to do, and how to tell a good evaluation proposal and a good report from a poor one. They have to know how to support good evaluation and how much reliance they should place on the evaluations they read about and sponsor.

What's New

This book is a next-generation follow-up to *Evaluation Research*. Much of the discussion is an elaboration of ideas in the earlier book. I still believe, for example, that evaluators must understand the purposes behind an evaluation request and what the various parties want evaluation to accomplish. I believe that good design and measurement are central to the evaluation enterprise. I believe that evaluation has an explicitly political dimension and that evaluators need to understand the politics within the program organization with which they work as well as in the larger policy context.

But I have changed my mind about a few important things. I have learned that evaluation need not be directed exclusively at providing information for decision making. Certainly giving decision makers data on how a program is doing can help them craft wiser programs and policies, but this is not the only function that evaluation serves. From research I have done on how evaluations are used, I have come to realize that the application of evaluation findings to the making of decisions is not simple or easy. Many factors besides evaluative evidence influence decisions. Findings from evaluation are probably most readily applied when they reveal only modest need for change, or when the implied change is congruent with what the organization already wants to do. But evaluation findings have many other important uses. They often have significant impact on agendas, options, and opinions in long-term and indirect ways.

I have also added topics and expanded topics touched on briefly in the earlier book. I include a chapter on the use of qualitative methods in evaluation, and turn the few pages on program theory in the earlier book into a full chapter in this book. I devote more attention to process evaluation—the study of what goes on within the program while it is in operation. I provide an extended discussion of how evaluators can profit from working with program people in collaborative ways. Collaboration can be useful during the planning of the study, periodically during its course, when interpreting results, and in developing plans for using the results. These four topics have considerably more salience in evaluation now than they did a generation ago.

The book also contains a history of social program evaluation and its place in society. It provides detailed guidance on measurement and data collection, and it contains a chapter on analysis—what to do with the data after they are collected. I amplify discussion on meta-analysis and cost-benefit analysis and include material on statistical adjustments to nonexperimental data. Throughout the book I give considerable attention to issues of ethical behavior as they arise before, during, and after the study.

Overview

This book is intended as the primary text for an introductory course in evaluation. It provides practical guidance for the conduct of an evaluation study from its inception, through the planning stage, to research design, data collection, and data analysis, to the reporting, dissemination, and application of conclusions.

Chapter 1 gives a definition of evaluation, provides an example, and discusses the several different kinds of evaluations that can be done. It also traces the history of evaluation back to earlier centuries. Chapter 2 describes the purposes for which participants in program and policy decide to undertake evaluation and the effects of divergent purposes on the ensuing evaluation. It also discusses various procedures by which evaluations are generally commissioned and the importance of the location of the evaluation team in the structure.

In Chapter 3 I discuss the importance of understanding the program. Knowing what the program is, how it works, and how it is expected to reach the desired results helps the evaluator to develop a study that is responsive to key issues. Chapter 4 gives practical advice on the planning of the study. It discusses options available and criteria for selecting among them. It stresses that planning is an iterative process and that the evaluator needs to revise plans as outside conditions intrude. Chapter 5 takes up the matter of stakeholders, the varied groups of people who have a stake in the evaluation and its results, and discusses when it is fruitful to involve them in planning and conducting the study. It considers how evaluators can work productively with stakeholders to make the study relevant to their concerns and to benefit from their knowledge, without sacrificing larger interests or the validity of the work.

Chapters 6 and 7 deal with issues of measurement and data collection in quantitative evaluations. Chapter 6 gives guidance on the selection of measures of program inputs, processes, interim markers of progress, outcomes, and possible unintended consequences. It provides a list of sources of available measures, criteria for the selection of good measures, and detailed advice on constructing new measures. Chapter 7 lays out the array of strategies for collecting data: informal conversations, observations, formal interviews, questionnaires, existing records, data files, available surveys, and a host of others. It gives advice on sampling, data collection through each of the several strategies, and coding of responses, and (as did previous chapters) stresses the ethical considerations involved.

Design is a critical element in evaluation, indicating which units will be studied, how they will be selected, which kinds of comparisons will be drawn, and the timing of the investigation. Chapters 8 and 9 stress that design must fit the questions being asked, and they identify salient concerns that have to be taken into account. Chapter 8 presents a set of designs ranging from the informal study of program participants to the use of comparison groups, including methods for adjusting comparison groups to approximate the group receiving the program. Chapter 9 describes the controlled experiment, based on random assignment of participants to the program and to a control group. It provides guidance for implementing randomized experiments and considers problems that can arise during their course. It also takes account of criticisms that have been leveled against the design and examines which are well founded and which can be remedied. Chapter 10 offers three elaborations of design: replication, meta-analysis, and cost-benefit and cost-effectiveness analysis. It explains what each of these procedures offers and when they are warranted.

Chapter 11 is a description of qualitative evaluation. It describes several styles of qualitative work, and it gives advice on data sources, information gathering, strategies of analysis, and ethical issues that arise in the course of fieldwork. It appreciates the combination of qualitative and quantitative methods and gives advice on using the methods together. Chapter 12 offers guidance for analyzing and interpreting data. It applies the same framework to quantitative and qualitative data, showing the logic of the analytic task.

Chapter 13 focuses on reporting results and disseminating them to relevant audiences. It suggests techniques for reporting and gives tips on satisfying different publics. It puts considerable emphasis on communicating and disseminating results, and it stresses the evaluator's responsibility for encouraging the use of evaluation results and suggests ways to promote their application to issues of program and policy. Chapter 14 sums up the major themes in the book in what I hope is a rousing finale.

Acknowledgments

It is hard to thank all the people whose experience, ideas, encouragement, and criticisms have entered into my knowledge of evaluation. I would have to reproduce the international catalog of evaluation books and articles (at least the ones I've read), list the authors of hundreds of evaluation reports in at least a dozen countries, and name the students in my evaluation courses who shared their interests and puzzlements over many years. I limit myself here to the people who have helped me directly, but I am grateful to hundreds of others.

I had the wonderful fortune to begin writing this book when I was a Fellow at the Center for Advanced Study in the Behavioral Sciences, a place awash in fertile minds and helpful colleagueship. I finished it back at Harvard, an environment with its own brand of nutrients. Two people had the kindness and fortitude to read the whole manuscript and gave excellent critiques: Will Shadish and Janet Weiss, and I am greatly indebted to them. They saw the hidden text as well as the written word, and forced me to clarify what I intended to say. John Willett read the four chapters on design and analysis with great care, taught me, argued with me, and pointed me in the right direction. Robert T. Brennan scrutinized the chapters on measurement and data collection and made detailed suggestions to make them more accurate and complete. Other colleagues who read chapters of the manuscript and helped me improve the text were Joseph Maxwell, Mercer Sullivan, Harris Cooper, and Sharon Rallis. Lee Cronbach, David Fetterman, and Judith Singer offered references, advice, and insight.

Jay Braatz was a great help with the Glossary and the charts. I thank Stuart Yeh, Chris Mazzeo, and Mary Jo Larson for help with library references. I thank Mark Anderson-Wilk and Kathy George for typing drafts of the manuscript.

I am especially grateful to Johanna Birckmayer. Jo has been a steady source of information and advice. She read successive drafts of the manuscript and gave me the benefit of her criticism, sound judgment, and unflagging encouragement over a period of many months.

Whatever flaws remain in the book are the responsibility of this galaxy of advisors. (Not true, but it was fun to say.)

Carol Hirschon Weiss

1

SETTING THE SCENE

"Begin at the beginning," the King said gravely, "and go on till you come to the end: then stop."

—Lewis Carroll (1865)

The emerging federal system for social science research reflects recognition of the need for planning and for the close relationship of knowledge to the formulation and execution of social programs.

—Gene Lyons (1969, p. 240)

Instead of trivial tokens or new Federal programs launched at full scale, [the President] could initiate a set of bold research trials.... Though large-scale problems would not be solved immediately, pilot tests would proliferate, and through evaluation of them, learning would grow.

—Richard Darman (1996, p. 117)[1]

What does an evaluation study look like? Let's start with an easy example, a program to help people stop smoking. One such program enrolls about 100 people each month and gives them three sessions of group activities. After the program has been operating for about a year, staff members ask themselves how well they are doing. They don't see the people after the program ends, and they have no way of knowing if they are successful. Do the people that they serve actually stop smoking and stay off cigarettes?

Staff decide to do an evaluation. Their aim is to find out whether the goals of the program are met: Do participants stop smoking? This is a relatively simple evaluation because there is one clear indicator of success. If a person stops smoking, that's success. You don't have to look any further, because biomedical research has conclusively shown that smoking cessation improves people's health and longevity. The staff go through the lists of people who attended the session that ended the week

---

[1]From Richard Darman, "Riverboat Gambling with Government," *New York Times Magazine*, December 1, 1996, pp. 116–117. Copyright © 1996 by The New York Times Company. Reprinted by permission.

before and call them up. They ask: "Have you stopped smoking?" Answers show that 47% say yes, they have stopped.

But several of the staff say that one week is too short a time interval. It's not so hard to quit for a week. The real question is whether participants stay off cigarettes. So they pull out the names of those who attended sessions during the first three months of the program, almost a year before, and call them up. They ask: "Have you stopped smoking?" The results show that 39% say yes, they have stopped. The staff look at one another in puzzlement and ask, "Is that good?" They had hoped that 100% would have stopped, but 39% is batting .390 (a terrific batting average in baseball) and that is probably 39% more than would have stopped without the program. Or is it?

One staff member reminds his colleagues that many people stop smoking without any program at all. Maybe these people would have done fine without the program. So the staff decides to call smokers they know who didn't attend the program and ask them the same question: "Have you stopped smoking?" Results show that only 2% of these people have stopped. One person says, "See? Our program *did* make a difference."

But another person says, "No, that's not a fair comparison. The people who came to the program were *motivated* to stop, and the others weren't." The problem: How do they find people to compare with their participants, people who were motivated to stop and didn't attend the program? One person suggests looking at the attendees of another stop-smoking program. "That," he says, "would be a fair comparison." But others say that such a study would only compare their program to another program, and that's not what they are really interested in. They want to know if they're doing a good job, not whether they're better or worse than somebody else. Both programs might be poor or both might be wonderful, and the comparison wouldn't be able to show this.

So one staff person with research training suggests that they construct a randomized control group. They need people who are similarly motivated to stop smoking. So from the next 200 applicants to the program (people with similar levels of motivation) they will randomly accept 100 into the program and tell the others that they have no room. ("That's not unethical," she explains, because the program receives many more applications than they have room for, and instead of accepting applicants on a first-come, first-served basis, they will accept them by lottery, which is a technique of random selection.) Random selection does not mean haphazard selection; it means following very strict procedures that take advantage of the laws of probability. If each person has an even chance of falling into the program group, the likelihood is high that people accepted into the program group and people not accepted (the control group) will be very much alike on all dimensions, such as age, length of time smoking, extent of family support for stopping, and just about everything else.

So that's what they do. Out of the next 200 applicants, they randomly take 100 into the program and tell the others that they'll have to wait for the next month's session. After a month they call both sets of people. (They can't wait any longer, because they now feel duty bound to accept the control group into the program.) Answers to the telephone interviews show that 46% of the program group say they have stopped smoking compared to 15% of the control group.

Now staff believe that they have demonstrated the unequivocal success of their program. Nonparticipants with the same level of motivation did not make it on their own.

"Wait a minute," says one of the staff. "We told them that they would be accepted into the program in a month. Why would they try to stop on their own? They're waiting for the program, enjoying their last month of nicotine. That would keep the number of stoppers low." His colleagues look at him in annoyance and say, "Why didn't you think of that before?" Another staff person says, "Or if they were really motivated, maybe they didn't want to wait and went to another program. That might push the numbers up."

Another staff person says, "There's another problem. What does it mean when someone says he has stopped smoking? Did he stop the day before we called, or has he been off cigarettes since he left the program? A lot of people probably stop and start again and then stop again. We probably should have asked a lot more questions about how much each person has smoked since leaving the program." "Yes," agrees another person. "Even if someone just reduced the number of cigarettes he smoked every day, that would be a good result, and we didn't ask questions that would find that out."

At this point staff were almost ready to chuck the whole evaluation. They were even more dispirited when the head of the agency asked: "What makes you think that people are telling you the truth? You were the people who ran the program, and some participants who are still smoking might lie to you and say they'd quit just to avoid hurting your feelings. You should check with a relative or friend or perhaps have them take a saliva test that detects nicotine."

"But we don't have the time or money for such an elaborate study," one person wailed. "Isn't there anything we can do now?"

By the time you have finished the book, I hope you can help them make sensible choices about what to do next. If you'd like to pursue this example, here are references to a few of the thousands of evaluations of smoking-cessation programs: Orleans et al., 1991; Ossip-Klein et al., 1991; Viswesvaran & Schmidt, 1992; Zelman, Brandon, Iorenby, & Baker, 1992.

Domain of Evaluation

People evaluate all the time. Listen in on conversations and you will hear: "I loved that television program last night." "He is doing a lousy job." "That car isn't worth the price they charge." "The food at Joe's Cafe is much better now than it used to be." In more formal terms, you hear about a supervisor evaluating an employee's work performance, a teacher evaluating a student's academic progress, or *Consumer Reports'* evaluation of a line of products. Just as Moliere's *bourgeois gentilhomme* finds out that he's been speaking prose all his life without realizing it, we come to realize that we have been evaluating things of various kinds without necessarily calling the procedure evaluation.

Evaluation is an elastic word that stretches to cover judgments of many kinds. What all the uses of the word have in common is the notion of judging merit. Someone is examining and weighing a phenomenon (a person, a thing, an idea) against some explicit or implicit yardstick. The yardsticks can vary widely. One criterion might be aesthetic: Is the entity beautiful and pleasing? Another yardstick is effectiveness: Does it do what it is supposed to be doing? Another is efficiency: Does it provide benefits commensurate with its costs? Other yardsticks can deal with justice and equity, acceptability in terms of community standards, enjoyment and satisfaction, contributions to social harmony, and so on.

The phenomena to be evaluated can also be diverse. In this book I will be talking about evaluation of one particular kind of phenomenon: programs and policies designed to improve the lot of people. The programs and policies are of many kinds: They can deal with education, social welfare, health, housing, mental health, legal services, corrections, economic development, highway construction, and many other fields. They can be governmental programs, run at federal, state, or local levels, or even internationally; they can be run by nonprofit organizations or for-profit firms. They can be aimed to change people's knowledge, attitudes, values, behaviors, the organizations in which they work, institutions with which they deal, or the communities in which they live. Their common characteristic is the goal of making life better and more rewarding for the people they serve.

Furthermore, I am concerned here with a specific method of evaluation—evaluation research. Rather than relying on the judgments of expert observers or periodic reports from staff, the evaluator in this scenario uses the methods of social science research to make the judging process more systematic and accurate. In its research guise, evaluation establishes clear questions for inquiry. It collects evidence systematically from a variety of people involved with the program. It sometimes translates the evidence into quantitative terms (23% of the program participants, grades of 85 or better), and sometimes it crafts the data into telling narratives. It then draws conclusions about the ways the program is run, or its near-term consequences, or its effectiveness in fulfilling the expectations of those who fund the program, manage and staff it, or participate in its activities.

In this chapter, I first offer a definition of evaluation, and then consider the types of phenomena that are usually evaluated in formal ways. Several different genres of evaluation are possible, and I discuss the difference between evaluation of program operations and the evaluation of program outcomes. Next I consider the differences and similarities between evaluation and other kinds of social science research. A subsequent section explores the history of evaluation.

Definition of Evaluation

At this point I can venture a provisional definition of evaluation, which we will elaborate as we make our way through the book. Evaluation is the *systematic assessment* of the *operation* and/or the *outcomes* of a program or policy, compared to a set of *explicit* or *implicit standards*, as a means of contributing to the *improvement* of the program or policy.

Let's take a look at the five key elements in that definition. The first is systematic assessment. The emphasis on system indicates the research nature of evaluation procedures. Whether the research is quantitative or qualitative, it is conducted with formality and rigor, according to accepted social science research canons. The second and third elements in the definition point to the focus of investigation: the operation and outcomes of the program. Some evaluations concentrate on studying process— that is, the way a program is conducted. Such evaluations may be interested in learning the extent to which the program is following prescribed practices (i.e., the fidelity of the program to its design), or they may aim just to learn what is going on. Some evaluations concentrate on the outcomes and effects of the program for its intended beneficiaries. Such evaluations seek to answer the question: Are participants gaining the benefits that they were intended to receive? Or, in more open-ended fashion, what is happening to them because of the program's intervention? Many evaluations look at both the process of the program and its outcomes for recipients.

The fourth element in the definition is standards for comparison. Once having collected evidence on process and outcomes, the evaluation assesses the merit of the program by comparing the evidence to some set of expectations. Whether the evaluation is focusing on the program's process or outcomes, an element of judgment is present. Sometimes the criterion that is applied to make judgments comes from the official statement of goals set for the program or policy when it was enacted. If the program was established to reduce adolescent pregnancies, an explicit standard is likely to be reduction in the frequency with which adolescent program participants become pregnant. But official goals are not the only possible source for the criteria that an evaluation applies. The goals may have changed over the course of program operations, and what the program is now concentrating on may be teaching pregnant adolescents about proper prenatal health practices. If that is where program energies are being spent, then participating adolescents' health practices and the birth weight of their babies may be important criteria. Other standards of judgment can come from the expectations of other actors on the program or policy scene. The objectives of program sponsors, program managers, practitioners, and participants can become criteria for the evaluation. In some cases, evaluation offers systematic evidence about the program in specified domains and leaves it to the reader to draw conclusions about its merit.

The fifth element in the definition of evaluation is the purpose for which it is done: contribution to the improvement of program and policy. Evaluation is a practical craft, designed to help make programs work better and to allocate resources to better programs. Evaluators expect people in authority to use evaluation results to take wise action. They take satisfaction from the chance to contribute to social betterment.

Doing evaluation through a process of research takes more time and costs more money than offhand evaluations that rely on intuition, opinion, or trained sensibility, but it provides a rigor that is missing in these more informal activities. Rigor is apt to be particularly important when (a) the outcomes to be evaluated are complex, hard to observe, made up of many elements reacting in diverse ways; (b) the decisions that will follow are important and expensive; and (c) evidence is needed to convince other people about the validity of the conclusions.

A wide variety of social programs are operated in the United States and other countries, and new needs continually spark the development of further programs. The past decade has seen programs to feed and shelter the homeless, care for AIDS patients, educate young people about the dangers of drugs, reduce the costs of health care, and help victims of disaster around the world take control over their own lives.

Some of the new programs are logical extensions of earlier efforts; some represent radical departures from the past and a plunge into uncharted waters.

Many people want (and need) to know: How is the program being conducted? What is it actually doing? How well is it following the guidelines that were originally set? What kinds of outcomes is it producing? How well is it meeting the purposes for which it was established? Is it worth the money it costs? Should it be continued, expanded, cut back, changed, or abandoned? Should people flock to it, sign up selectively, or stay away in droves? Does it work for everybody or only some kinds of people?

The answers are hard to come by through informal means. The best informed people (the staff running the program) tend toward optimism and in any case have a stake in reporting success. Many programs provide a variety of services and deal with large numbers of participants. A handful of "consumer testimonials" or a quick tour of inspection can hardly gauge their effectiveness. Decisions about future operations will affect the fate of many people and involve sizable sums of money, and people who have a say (legislators, boards of directors, future clients) are sufficiently removed from the program to want cogent information to help them make choices.

When programs are run by private firms, the market generally supplies the judgment. A private firm can supply a computer program or a training course. The evaluation comes when people either buy the product or service or do not. In time, good programs prosper and bad programs go out of business, or at least they do if consumers have sufficient information about their effects. But when the program is run by government or nonprofit agencies, customer satisfaction or dissatisfaction usually has little impact. Sometimes the program is the only game in town, like welfare assistance or the criminal courts and correctional facilities. Sometimes the program is the only one for a particular group of people, like training programs for members of the armed forces, or the only one that is free, like the public schools. Usually these kinds of programs continue no matter what the demand or the level of client satisfaction.

Private firms can run programs of this type, too, for their own employees. Internal programs, like day care for children of employees or safety procedures for workers, also have a captive population and tend to be relatively immune to client satisfaction or dissatisfaction.

Yet they are all obviously costly investments. Governments, businesses, nonprofit agencies, and foundations pay substantial sums to keep them going. A lot of people care whether the programs are doing what they are supposed to be doing and getting the kinds of results they are expected to get. A lot of people worry about whether they could be getting better results or spending less money, or better yet, both. Without some kind of systematic review, it is hard to know. Evaluation is the best way we have found to provide the necessary information.

What Is Evaluated? An Excursus on Terminology

To be sure we are on the same wavelength, let's agree on the meaning of a set of terms that will be cropping up in the following chapters. Some of the definitions are strictly conventional and arbitrary, but if we agree on them, the rest of the book will mean the same thing to all of us.

From now on I will call a national program, like Head Start or Superfund environmental cleanup, a program. The local operations of the program are each projects. Thus, the Head Start that is operated in the Brigham Community Center is a project. An element of the Brigham Head Start project, like involving parents through weekly meetings, is a component. Evaluations can be directed at any of these levels. We can evaluate national programs, local projects, or subproject components, using the same basic methods.

We can also evaluate policies. For our purposes, a policy is an officially accepted statement of objectives tied to a set of activities that are intended to realize the objectives in a particular jurisdiction. Thus, one federal policy is to encourage donations to charity by allowing taxpayers to take deductions for such donations on their income tax form. There's no program there, but the policy can be evaluated. Evaluative question: Does the tax deduction actually promote philanthropic giving? Another federal policy aims to ensure the health and safety of those who use medical appliances (such as heart pacemakers or wheelchairs). The government requires that manufacturers test the safety of devices before they are marketed and again after they are on sale by asking users to report defects while the devices are in use. That policy can be evaluated, too. Evaluative question: Do the testing requirements and reporting procedures increase the safety of devices? Much the same evaluative strategies are used in policy evaluation as in the evaluation of programs.

In fact, the techniques of evaluation are marvelously adaptable. They can be applied not only to social programs and policies but also to environmental policies, mass transit programs, forestry projects, and elements of military procurement. In a number of such fields, the word *evaluation* is not in common use, but under other guises (e.g., social audits, system reviews, performance measurement), evaluative work is undertaken.

To simplify the prose, I will generally talk about the evaluation of programs, but that is a shorthand device. In that phrase I mean to encompass the evaluation of policies, projects, and components as well.

Another convention I adopt here is to call the evaluator *she,* and all other players in the program world *he.* So policymakers, program managers, program staff, and clients of the program all turn up with the masculine pronoun, while I use the feminine pronoun for members of the evaluation team. This is by no means to suggest that all evaluators are, or should be, women. Nor do I mean to suggest that everybody else in the program arena is, or should be, male. It is simply a convention to avoid the awkward *he* or *she* wherever I use the singular form.[2]

There are other words that come into play frequently in evaluation, many of them already familiar to you through your exposure to research. Among these are *qualitative research, quantitative research, experiment, control groups, randomization, validity, reliability, measurement, indicators, variables, sampling, empirical research.* If you are not certain of their meaning, it is probably a good idea to brush up on definitions and come to feel comfortable with the terms. A glossary appears at the end of the book. You might also look in the index for pages on which there is fur-

---

[2]Cronbach and his associates (1980) used this convention, but they did it the other way around, calling evaluators *he* and everybody else *she.* I like it better this way.

ther discussion, and you can refer to other texts on social science research for fuller discussions of the terms. In this and the next chapter I introduce terms that are unique to evaluation: *formative* and *summative evaluation, outcome* and *process evaluation*, and in subsequent chapters we will encounter the rest of the vocabulary.

Outcome and Process Evaluation

What kinds of questions does evaluation ask about programs (policies, projects, components)? From the time it became a recognized activity in the 1930s, on into the 1970s, the main question had to do with outcomes. Evaluations tended to concentrate on the question: Is the program reaching the goals that it was set up to accomplish? Or, more broadly: What are the results of the program? This focus on outcomes is still a hallmark of the evaluation enterprise.

Outcomes refers to the end results of the program for the people it was intended to serve. I use the term *outcomes* interchangeably with *results* and *effects*. Some of the outcomes that are realized are the results that program planners anticipated—the things they wanted to happen. Other outcomes, however, are side effects that nobody expected—often effects that nobody *wanted*. Thus, for example, a program that serves parents who are deemed to be at risk of abusing their young children may have the unintended result of labeling them as potential abusers, even to the parents themselves. Once they accept that label for themselves, they may become more, rather than less, abusive. Or a program that sets up citizens' advisory groups for toxic waste cleanup activities may have the goal of speeding the cleanup process by dint of citizen pressure. However, when citizens are represented, they may introduce a host of other concerns into discussions of cleanup, such as issues of employment and unemployment, and thereby divert activities from cleanup to job maintenance.

Another word that sometimes comes up when people talk about the focus of evaluation is *impact*. Most of the time, the word means the same as outcomes. An impact study looks at what happens to participants as a result of the program. Sometimes *impact* is construed as long-term outcomes. Occasionally, writers use the word *impact* to mean effects of the program on the larger community. For example, the outcomes of a job training program may be studied in terms of the number of *program participants* who get jobs. Its impact, in this larger sense, might be the effect on the unemployment rate in the *whole geographic area* in which the program functions. In other cases, impact comes between program processes and outcomes (Green & Kreuter, 1991).

A further meaning of impact is the *net* effects of the program, after taking account of what would have happened in the absence of the program. In operational terms, this means looking at the outcomes for program participants (say, 9% hold jobs after the training program) and looking at outcomes for an *equivalent* population of nonparticipants (say, 3% hold jobs at the same point). Then, on the assumption that the same proportion (3%) of participants would have held jobs if they hadn't attended the program, the evaluator estimates the impact by subtracting outcomes for nonparticipants from the outcomes for participants. She estimates the impact of the program as a 6 percentage point increase (9%-3%) in job holding. (The trick here is to be sure the two groups are equivalent. I discuss this issue in Chapter 9.)

This last meaning of *impact* is a vital concept in evaluation, but I don't use the word *impact* in the book. I refer to *outcomes,* and in context the word often means "net outcomes"—that is, that part of the outcome that is attributable to the program. This will become clearer as we move along.

Evaluation can look not only at short-term outcomes but also (if it has world enough and time) long-term outcomes. The High/Scope study of the Perry Preschool Program has followed the children who attended preschool as 3- and 4-year-olds for 24 years (Schweinhart, Barnes, & Weikart, 1993). The long-term follow-up has enabled the evaluators to report that at age 27, young people who had attended the preschool program had significantly higher monthly earnings than an equivalent group of people who had not attended, were more likely to own their own home, had fewer arrests, and completed more schooling. These data have been extremely influential in justifying the Head Start Program, which was loosely based upon the Perry Preschool Program, and in generating support for increased funding.

Although outcomes were the original evaluative focus, evaluation questions now deal not only with outcomes but with the process of the program, too—what is going on. Evaluators need to study what the program actually *does.* In the early days they took for granted that the program was doing what its operators said it was doing. But they soon learned that the assumption was often ill founded. Ralph Tyler, one of the pioneer evaluators, wrote in 1942 that his Eight-Year Study of 30 high schools found that in the first year "only two or three were operating the program described in the proposal" (Tyler, 1991: 7). Hyman and Wright (1967: 745), who were evaluating a rural health program in Egypt, found that most of the centers lacked vital categories of personnel and that even personnel on the job were putting in relatively few hours of work. Evaluators had to know what the programs were actually like before they could draw conclusions about whether they were successful or not. It might be that they never really happened.

There are other reasons for studying program process. Sometimes the key questions that the program community has about the program have to do with its process. For example, what kinds of service are participants being given? Is the service following the prescriptions of the program developer? How often are participants (say in a drug treatment program) showing up? What kinds of problems are staff encountering? Are clients happy with the program? There is a need for studies that focus on systematic assessment of what is happening inside the program.

Another reason to study program process is to help understand outcome data. The evaluator may find that some participants in the program did particularly well and others did exceptionally poorly. There are a lot of possible reasons for such a finding, but one possible reason is that people received different kinds of service or different intensity of service. One group may have received services from highly qualified staff, had the same staff person over a long period of time, and attended regularly. Another group may have had a series of different staff members who were poorly trained, and they may have failed to attend very often. If the evaluator is going to be able to analyze what conditions were responsible for different outcomes, she needs data on what went on in the program.

So we have at least three situations that call for process data. One is when the key questions concern process. Evaluation sponsors want to know what is going on.

Another is when key questions concern outcome, but we want to be sure what the outcomes were outcomes *of*? People often look on one project or a handful of projects as representatives of a class of programs, such as short-term psychotherapy or community health centers. The evaluator wants to know whether there actually was a community health center in place, and what kind of program it was, before she concludes that the Community Health Center Program succeeded or failed. The third situation is when the evaluator wants to associate outcomes with specific elements of program process—that is, to find out which particular features of the program were associated with greater or lesser success.

Contributions of Evaluation

Historically, evaluation research has been viewed by its partisans as a way to increase the rationality of policymaking. With objective information on the implementation and outcomes of programs, wise decisions can be made on budget allocations and program planning. The expectation has been programs that yield good results will be expanded; those that make poor showings will be abandoned or drastically modified. A quote from a congressman, made many years ago, is still a fine summary of the rationale for program evaluation:

> It is becoming increasingly clear that much of our investment in such areas as education, health, poverty, jobs, housing, urban development, transportation and the like is not returning adequate dividends in terms of results. Without for a moment lessening our commitment to provide for these pressing human needs, one of Congress' major, though oft-delayed, challenges must be to reassess our multitude of social programs, concentrate (indeed, expand) resources on programs that *work* where the needs are greatest, and reduce or eliminate the remainder. We no longer have the time nor the money to fritter away on nonessentials which won't produce the needed visible impact on problems. (Dwyer, 1970)

In pursuit of the same objectives, in 1993 Congress passed the Government Performance and Results Act, which requires federal agencies to gather program performance data. The act requires that agencies make a strategic plan for their program activities; establish program performance goals in terms that are objective, quantifiable, and measurable; and then collect data that register the extent to which the program is achieving the established goals. Agencies are required to submit an annual report on program performance to the president and the Congress.

History of Evaluation

These recent efforts to institutionalize evaluation in government agencies are the latest in a long series of attempts to use data and evidence in a search for better understanding of social behavior and wiser social policy. If we are to trace evaluation back to its prehistory, we would probably start the story in the 1660s.

Evaluation is rooted in the empirical study of social problems that began in earnest in Britain in that period (Cullen, 1975). Although the intellectual origins of what was once called "political arithmetic" remain a matter of debate, it is clear that the seventeenth century saw the beginnings of a search for social laws comparable to those contemporaneously developing in the physical sciences. Perhaps the first study that can be labeled evaluative came almost two centuries later. A. M. Guerry, a Frenchman, published a statistical study in 1833 that attempted to show that education did not reduce crime (Cullen, 1975, p. 139). Other statisticians marshalled different data in an attempt to refute his findings. In a counterpoint that has remained a continuing feature of evaluation history, these statisticians not only cited different evidence but also criticized Guerry's methods in their zeal to establish that education did in fact lead to reduction in crime.

At about the same time, another Frenchman, Jules Depuit, assessed the usefulness of public works, such as roads and canals. He published a paper in 1844 that measured the value of a canal project through techniques of *calcul economique*. He used the maximum tolls that users would pay as evidence of the worth of the canals, and he examined the drop in demand as tolls went up as a measure of the limits of their utility (Toulemonde & Rochaix, 1994).

Despite some early forays such as these, evaluation as we know it today is a relatively recent development in the history of the world, even in the history of social programming. Early policies to improve social conditions did not include provision for evaluation. When reformers of the late 19th and early 20th centuries used social science research procedures, it was to conduct surveys in order to document the extent of problems and locate people in need (Bulmer, Bales, & Sklar, 1991). They took for granted that the remedies they provided would solve the problems. There was no evaluation of the prison reforms promoted by Dorothea Dix or of the social services provided at Jane Addams's Hull House. Very little study was done on the effects of installing electric street lighting or purification of water. When the United States passed laws in the second decade of the 20th century prohibiting child labor, nobody thought of evaluating the outcome. It was assumed that child labor would end and results would be intrinsically good. When the United States instituted a system of unemployment benefits in 1935, no evaluation accompanied it. Giving money to unemployed workers to tide them over until they found a new job was obviously beneficial.

People working in the fields of education and health were among the first to do systematic studies of the outcomes of their work. In 1912 R. C. Cabot examined 3,000 autopsy reports and compared them to the diagnoses that had been made of each case; he wrote an article in the *Journal of the American Medical Association* that was essentially an evaluation of the quality of medical diagnosis (Flook & Sanazaro, 1973). In 1914 Dr. Ernest Codman, a surgeon at Massachusetts General Hospital, insisted that the way to evaluate surgeons' performance was by measuring how patients fared after they left the hospital. Codman himself collected a great deal of data, but his work was largely ignored by the medical establishment (Vibbert, 1993). In education one of the best-known studies was the Eight-Year Study sponsored by the Progressive Education Association in 1933, and directed by Ralph Tyler, which looked at the outcomes of programs in 15 progressive high schools and 15 traditional high schools. An early evaluation of the effectiveness of school health programs was conducted by George Palmer, chief of the research division of the American Child Health Association; it was released in 1934. At the end of the decade the Commonwealth Fund sponsored a more elaborate evaluation by D. B. Nyswander, which was released in 1942 (Flook & Sanazaro, 1973).

In the 1940s private foundations began funding evaluations of an array of innovative social programs that they sponsored. A famous one was the Cambridge-Somerville youth worker program to prevent delinquency in suburban neighborhoods near Boston (Powers & Witmer, 1951). Early results were promising, but longer-term follow-up showed that at-risk youth who had received program services were barely doing as well as those who had not (McCord & McCord, 1959). One interpretation was that they had grown so dependent on the help of the youth workers that they had not developed the skills necessary for solving their own problems.

By the 1950s the federal government was sponsoring new curriculum efforts, such as Harvard Project Physics, in response to fears of American scientific illiteracy in the wake of the Soviets' launching of the *Sputnik* satellite. Evaluations were funded to find out how successful the curriculums were. In the early 1960s the President's Committee on Juvenile Delinquency funded a series of projects to reduce youth crime around the country, and federal administrators required that each project evaluate the results of its activities.

The War on Poverty in the mid-1960s marked the beginning of large-scale government-funded evaluation. The federal government began funding an array of programs to help the poor, and it started to require systematic evaluation of the results of the money spent. The Elementary and Secondary Education Act of 1965 included a requirement for evaluation in the law. Senator Robert Kennedy was the moving force behind the requirement. He wanted to be sure that the new federal money was not going to support schools' tired old practices but rather would go to help disadvantaged kids in new ways. He wanted poor parents to be well informed about what was taking place in the schools so they could prod educators to serve their children more effectively. He saw evaluation as a tool to provide parents with the necessary information (McLaughlin, 1975).

Other programs of the War on Poverty were also evaluated, including programs that provided legal services, community health services, job training, nutrition supplements for pregnant women and infants, food stamps, housing vouchers, multi-service centers for social services, preschool education, innovations in delinquency prevention and corrections, mental health services, and community action programs that mobilized residents of poor neighborhoods to determine their own priorities and demand the services they needed. Evaluators developed new methods and tools to fit the varied content and settings of the programs. The development of evaluation in this period owes a lot to poverty, just as it earlier owed a lot to illiteracy and crime.

The same period saw the rise of cost-benefit analysis in the RAND Corporation, Department of Defense, and elsewhere. Defense Secretary Robert MacNamara's policy analysts, dubbed the whiz kids, analyzed the relative advantages of weapons systems to see (in the contemporary phrase) "how much bang for the buck" they delivered. Important advances were made in methods of economic analysis.

Evaluation branched out into other areas. With new legislation came evaluation in such areas as environmental protection, energy conservation, military recruiting, and control of immigration. By the end of the 1970s evaluation had become commonplace across federal agencies. Almost every department had its evaluation office, and some had evaluation offices at several levels in the hierarchy—at the level of the secretary of the department, attached to the major program area, and at the operational level.

In the field, a host of small centers and firms were established to undertake federally financed evaluations. University research centers enlarged their charters to encompass evaluation, special centers were set up, new not-for-profit and for-profit research and consulting organizations arrived on the scene, and established ones expanded into the evaluation area. Many researchers re-tooled their skills so as to take advantage of the new streams of money.

A high point in evaluation history came in the 1970s with the inauguration of a series of social experiments to test novel policy and program ideas *prior to* their enactment. The Negative Income Tax experiment was the largest and most widely publicized (Cain & Watts, 1973; Kershaw & Fair, 1976, 1977). It was followed by experiments with housing allowances (Carlson & Heinberg, 1978; Friedman & Weinberg, 1983; Kennedy, 1980), health insurance (Newhouse et al., 1981; Phelps & Newhouse, 1973), performance contracting in education (Rivlin & Timpane, 1975), and other smaller experiments. In these experiments pilot programs were implemented on a large enough scale to simulate actual operating conditions, and experimental results were expected to help policymakers decide whether to move ahead with the policies nationwide. As it turned out, by the time the results of the experiments became available, the political climate had generally changed. The Negative Income Tax study is a case in point. The initial ardor for change had subsided, and the steam had gone out of the reform movement. In the end, few components of the experimental programs were adopted. However, the information remained available for later policymaking. For example, in 1994 when health reform was on the agenda again for a time, results of the health insurance experiments were dusted off, a new book was published (Newhouse & Insurance Experiment Group, 1993), and the findings entered the discussions.

Evaluation continued to be a growth industry until the Reagan administration took office in 1981. At that point funding for new social initiatives was drastically cut. New and innovative programs have always been the most likely candidates for evaluation, and when the stream of new programming dried to a trickle, fewer calls came for evaluation. Nonetheless, evaluation continued at modest levels, not so much with special evaluation money as with money from the operating agencies. Evaluations were undertaken on operating programs for long-term care, teenage parents, dislocated workers, state waivers of federal rules for the Aid to Families with Dependent Children (AFDC) program, supported work, and others.

During the late 1980s and early 1990s, evaluation funding made a partial comeback (U.S. General Accounting Office, 1987). Some agencies and agencies prospered. For example, Ginsburg, McLaughlin, Pusko, and Takai (1992) wrote about the "reinvigoration" of evaluation at the Department of Education. Other agencies remained in the doldrums (Wye & Sonnichsen, 1992). Over all, evaluation held on to its place in the bureaucracy, and important new work was launched. With the Clinton presidency, more social programming and more evaluation were undertaken, but the Republican revolution that began with the 1994 elections called for massive downsizing of the federal government and the shift of much social programming to the states.

In the past, both conservatives and liberals have found evaluation useful. When conservatives are in office, the emphasis for evaluation tends to be on program cost cutting (how does the program stack up on criteria of efficiency and cost reduction?) and elimination of service to ineligible recipients. When liberals are in power, standards tend to be the effectiveness of service in terms of improvement in beneficiaries' life chances.

With all the backing and forthing at the federal level, one of the notable features of recent evaluation history is the growth of evaluation activity at state and even local levels. For example, the Commonwealth of Massachusetts evaluated its education and training program for welfare recipients (Massachusetts Department of Public Welfare, 1986a, 1986b, 1986c); the state of South Carolina evaluated a project integrating human services (South Carolina State Reorganization Commission, 1989); the city of Chicago, along with local universities and citizen reform groups, evaluated the city's major school reform (Bryk & Rollow, 1992, 1993; Bryk, Deabster, Easton, Luppescu, & Thum, 1994; Sebring, Bryk, Luppescu, & Thum, 1995).

Another recent trend is the increasing use of qualitative methods for evaluation. Not too long ago the only kind of evaluation with professional legitimacy, in rhetoric at least, was quantitative evaluation, preferably using a randomized experimental design. (See Chapters 8 and 9 for discussion.) But some evaluators relied more on words than on numbers, collected their data through observation and informal interviewing rather than through structured interview questions or quantitative records, and their analysis probed the meaning of process and outcomes through narrative analysis. (See Chapter 11.) During the late 1970s and 1980s, they burst into the evaluation literature with an outpouring of books and journal articles, heralding the advantages of their approach (e.g., Bogdan & Biklen, 1982; Fetterman, 1988; Guba, 1990; Guba & Lincoln, 1989; Patton, 1980; Stake, 1975, 1995). They provoked a spirited exchange with supporters of quantitative methods, and the fur flew thick and fast.

Hard upon "the paradigm wars," as these sometimes harshly worded critiques and exchanges came to be known, came attempts at rapprochement. Many key figures in evaluation concluded that evaluation was a house of many mansions and had room for a variety of approaches. In fact, qualitative and quantitative methods could complement each other well, and studies using both kinds of procedures began to thrive.

Out of the melee came increased awareness of the advantages of qualitative techniques and a heightened legitimacy for qualitative work. More evaluations are incorporating a qualitative component, especially in education, and textbooks are now including chapters on qualitative approaches to evaluation. (Including this one; see Chapter 11).

Another noteworthy development has been the development of professional associations in evaluation. Professional associations—the American Evaluation Association in the United States and similar associations in Canada, Europe, Great

Britain, Australia and New Zealand, and elsewhere—provide a forum for evaluators to share their work and their concerns. At annual meetings and through publications, they offer opportunities for evaluators to disseminate their findings, keep abreast of new techniques, consider larger issues regarding the role of evaluation in society, propagate standards of professional conduct, and generally advance the state of the field.

Comparison between Evaluation and Other Research

Evaluation applies the methods of social science research, both quantitative and qualitative. Principles and methods that apply to all other types of research apply here as well. Everything we know about design, measurement, and analysis comes into play in planning and conducting an evaluation study. What distinguishes evaluation research is not method or subject matter, but intent—the purpose for which it is done.

Differences

Utility   Evaluation is intended for use. Where basic research puts the emphasis on the production of knowledge and leaves its use to the natural processes of dissemination and application, evaluation starts out with *use* in mind. In its simplest form, evaluation is conducted for a client who has decisions to make and who looks to the evaluation for information on which to base his decisions. Even when use is less direct and immediate, utility of some kind provides the rationale for evaluation.

Program-Derived Questions   The questions that evaluation considers derive from the concerns of the policy and program communities—that is, the array of people involved with, or affected by, the program. Unlike basic researchers who formulate their own hypotheses, the evaluator deals in the currency of program concerns. Of course, she has a good deal of say about the design of the study, and she approaches it from the perspectives of her own knowledge and discipline. She can choose the way the questions are posed, stimulate further questions, and exercise control over how many questions the evaluation can comfortably address. She is usually free to incorporate inquiries on subjects of particular concern to her. But the core of the study represents matters of administrative and programmatic interest.

Judgmental Quality   Evaluation tends to compare "what is" with "what should be." Although the investigator herself usually tries to remain objective, she is typically concerned with phenomena that demonstrate how well the program is functioning and whether it is achieving its intended purposes. Wherever the questions for study are formulated, somewhere in the formulation appears a concern with measuring up to explicit or implicit standards. This element of judgment against criteria is basic to evaluation and differentiates it from many other kinds of research.

Action Setting   Evaluation takes place in an action setting, where the most important thing that is going on is the program. The program is serving people. If there are conflicts in requirements between program and evaluation, priority is likely to go to program. Program staff often control access to the people served in the program. They may control access to records and files. They are in charge of assignment of participants to program activities and locations. Not infrequently, research requirements (for "before" data, for control groups) run up against established program procedures, and there is tension about which is to prevail.

Role Conflicts   Interpersonal frictions are not uncommon between evaluators and practitioners. Practitioners' roles and the norms of their service professions tend to make them unresponsive to research requests and promises. As they see it, the imperative is service; evaluation is not likely to make such contributions to program improvement that it is worth disruptions and delays. Often, practitioners believe strongly in the worth of the program they are providing and see little need for evaluation at all. Furthermore, the judgmental quality of evaluation means that the merit of their activities is being weighed. In a sense, as they see it, they are on trial. If the results of evaluation are negative, if it is found that the program is not accomplishing the desired purposes, then the program—and possibly their jobs—are in jeopardy. The possibilities for friction are obvious.

Publication   Basic research is published. Its dissemination to the research and professional fraternity is essential and unquestioned. In evaluation, probably the majority of study reports go unpublished. Program administrators and staff often believe that the information was generated to answer their questions, and they are not eager to have their linen washed in public. Evaluators are sometimes so pressed for time, or so intent on moving on the next evaluation contract, that they submit the required report to the agency and go on to a new study.

Fortunately, in the past decades new publication channels have opened. Almost a dozen periodicals now publish articles reporting evaluation studies or discussing evaluation methods, philosophy, and uses. Among them are *Evaluation Review, Educational Evaluation and Policy Analysis, Evaluation and the Health Professions, New Directions for Evaluation, Evaluation Practice* (renamed *American Journal of Evaluation*), *Evaluation and Program Planning, Studies in Educational Evaluation,* and *Evaluation: The International Journal of Theory, Research, and Practice.* These journals, and journals in substantive fields such as substance abuse or criminology, provide a place where evaluators can share the results of their work and also discuss innovative developments in their craft.

The journals also make study results visible to people concerned with program and policy. If progress is to be made in understanding how programs should best be conducted and where and when they can be improved, a cumulative information base is essential. Only through publication will results build up.[3] Even when evaluation results show that a program has had little effect, a situation that generally makes authors and editors reluctant to publish, it is important that others learn of the findings so that ineffective programs are not unwittingly duplicated again and again. When program results are mixed, some good, some not so good, people who run programs would profit from learning about the components of the program associated with greater success.

---

[3]In this technologically advancing age, computerized services are being created to supplement journal publication.

Of course, not all evaluation studies are worth publication. Poorly conducted studies are more misleading than useful. Further, if the evaluator has addressed the issues in such concrete and specific terms that the results do not generalize beyond the immediate project, there is little to report to others. To avoid these limitations, evaluators need to keep the needs of broad audiences in mind when they plan their work. Then published reports can add to the stock of program knowledge.

Allegiance   The evaluation researcher has a dual, perhaps a triple, allegiance. She has obligations to the organization that funds her study. She owes it a report of high quality and as much usefulness for action as she can devise. She wants it to be helpful to the interests of policymakers, managers, practitioners, and program participants. Beyond the specific organization, she has responsibilities to contribute to improvement of programming in the field she has studied (science education, firearms regulation). Whether or not the organization supports the study's conclusions, the evaluator often perceives an obligation to work for the application of the conclusions in order to advance program and policy in the field. On both counts, she has commitments in the action arena. She also has an obligation to the development of knowledge and to her profession. As a social scientist, she seeks to advance the frontiers of knowledge about how intervention affects human lives and institutions.

If some of the differences between evaluation research and more academic social research have made the lot of the evaluator look unduly harsh, there are compensations. One of the most rewarding is the opportunity to participate actively in the meeting of scientific knowledge and social action and to contribute to the improvement of societal programs. It is this opportunity that has attracted so many able researchers to the field of evaluation research despite the constraints that attend its practice.

Similarities

There are important similarities, too, between evaluation and other brands of research. Like other research, evaluation attempts (a) to describe, (b) to understand the relationships between variables, and (c) to trace out the causal sequence from one variable to another. Because it is studying a program that intervenes in people's lives with the intention of bringing about change, evaluation can sometimes make direct inferences about the causal links that lead from program to effect.

Evaluators, like other researchers, use the whole gamut of research methods to collect information—interviews, questionnaires, tests of knowledge and skill, attitude inventories, observation, content analysis of documents, records, examination of physical evidence. Ingenious evaluators can find fitting ways of exploring a wide range of processes and effects. The data collection scheme to be used depends on the information needed to answer the specific questions that the evaluation poses.

The classic design for evaluations has been the randomized experiment. This involves measurement of the relevant variables for at least two equivalent groups—one that has been exposed to the program and one that has not. But many other designs are used in evaluation research—case studies, postprogram surveys, time series, correlational studies, and so on.

There is no cut-and-dried formula to offer evaluators for the "best" or most suitable way of pursuing their studies. The programs and agencies with which evaluation deals are so diverse and multi-faceted that the specifics of the particular case exert significant influence. Much depends on the uses to be made of the study: the decisions pending and the information needs of the decision-making community, or the uncertainties in the field and the need for better understanding of how programs work. Much also depends (unfortunately) on the constraints in the program setting—the limits placed on the study by the realities of time, place, and people. Money is an issue, too. Textbooks rarely mention the grubby matter of funding but limited funds impose inevitable restrictions on how much can be studied over how long a period. If the evaluator is on the payroll of the agency running the program, there may be limits on her freedom to explore negative aspects or negative outcomes. Thus, evaluation methods often represent a compromise between the ideal and the feasible.

Evaluation is sometimes regarded as a lower order of research, particularly in academic circles, than "basic" or "pure" research. Evaluators are sometimes seen as the drones of the research fraternity, drudging away on dull issues and compromising their integrity out in the corrupt world. But as any working evaluator will fervently tell you, evaluation calls for a higher level of skills than research that is designed and executed under the researcher's control. It takes skill to make research simultaneously rigorous and useful when it is coping with the complexities of real people in real programs run by real organizations—and it takes some guts.

The evaluator has to know a good deal about the formulation of the research question, study design, sampling, data collection, analysis, and interpretation. She has to know what is in the research methodology texts, and then she has to learn how to apply that knowledge in a setting that is often inhospitable to important features of her knowledge. If she persists in her textbook stance, she runs the risk of doing work irrelevant to the needs of the agency, antagonizing the program personnel with whom she works, and seeing study results ignored—if indeed the work is ever completed. So she sometimes has to find alternative ways of conducting the study, while at the same time she stands ready to defend to the death those elements of the study that cannot be compromised without vitiating the quality of the research. Then she needs finely honed skills in disseminating the results of the study in ways that encourage and support the application of findings to the improvement of policy and program.

Summary

This chapter defines evaluation as the systematic assessment of the operation and/or the outcomes of a program or policy, compared to explicit or implicit standards, in order to help improve the program or policy. Evaluation is undertaken when the program is complex, hard to observe, composed of elements interacting in multiple ways; when the decisions to be made are important and expensive; when evidence is needed to convince others about the merit and/or failings of the program. Evaluation can also be a tool of accountability. Program sponsors and operators can use evaluative evidence to report their operations and outcomes to broader publics.

Evaluation can address the process of the program (i.e., how it is being implemented), and it can examine outcomes of the program (i.e., consequences of the program for its participants).

Evaluation is part of a long-term trend toward scientific rationality in decision making that can be traced back to the 17th century. In the middle of the 19th century, studies were done in France to calculate the effect of education on crime rates and the value of canals and roads. In the early 20th century an American surgeon evaluated surgeons' performance by the health of patients after surgery. A landmark study was the evaluation of the consequences of the Cambridge-Somerville youth worker project for youth at risk of becoming delinquent. The big spurt in evaluation came with the War on Poverty of the 1960s and 1970s. The federal government began funding hundreds of evaluations in education, criminal justice, social services, legal assistance, community organization, health care, international development, mental health services, nutrition, and so on. In the 1970s the government supported several large-scale social experiments to test the viability of policy ideas before adopting them nationwide. The Negative Income Tax experiment was noteworthy.

Evaluation differs from other kinds of research in deriving its central questions from policymakers and practitioners, the intended use of its results to improve programming, its situation in a turbulent action setting, and its reporting to nonresearch audiences. The evaluator has obligations to the organization that funds the study, to the larger field of programming (education, physical rehabilitation), and to the social sciences. Similarities with other types of research include the techniques of inquiry that it employs and the search for understanding and explanation.

2

PURPOSES OF EVALUATION

> The real challenge for evaluation research and policy analysis is to develop methods of assessment that emphasize learning and adaptation rather than expressing summary judgments of pass or fail.
>
> —Giandomenico Majone (1988)

This chapter discusses the purposes, acknowledged and unacknowledged, for which people decide to undertake program evaluation. I suggest that the evaluator find out what the program community really seeks from the study and how they expect to use the results. With this knowledge, she[1] can most effectively tailor the evaluation to provide the kinds of information that people are interested in. The chapter also discusses the procedures used to initiate and contract for an evaluation. The location of the evaluation unit—where it fits in the organizational structure—can make a difference in whether the study has sufficient latitude to be useful.

Who Wants Evaluation?

Many people in many locations have an interest in evaluating programs and policies. An organization that funds programs, such as a philanthropic foundation or a state legislature, wants to know what the local operating agencies are doing with the money they receive and how well they are serving their clients. In the field of international development, for example, it is common for donor agencies to seek evaluations of the work done with the funds they provide to developing nations.

An organization that oversees programs, such as the federal Head Start office or the national Girl Scouts of the USA, wants to find out what is going on

---

[1] If the feminine pronoun is surprising, recall our convention: Evaluators are labeled *she* and all other actors on the scene are labeled *he*—program managers, staff, clients, legislators, and so on.

in the field and how clients are faring in the local units. Situated far from the action, they need a mechanism that will provide unbiased information about what is happening on the ground.

Managers of a local project want evidence on the short- and long-term effects of the activities they run. Although they are close enough to see what is going on, they usually do not know the consequences of the project and whether the clients they serve benefit in expected ways. They also do not generally know whether variations in activities produce differential outcomes. They want to learn, for example, whether some modalities of service are more effective than others, whether staff with certain qualifications have better results than others, whether increases in intensity or length of service would improve outcomes, or whether they could achieve the same results for less money.

In some agencies evaluators themselves have stimulated evaluation. When an evaluation unit exists in the agency, the evaluator can press for periodic study of issues that arise during the conduct of projects. This happens at federal, state, and local levels of government and in direct-service organizations. Evaluators who are not on the staff of the agency (i.e., who work in outside research, evaluation, and consulting firms, institutes, or universities) do not generally have an avenue to promote the use of their evaluation services—at least not directly. But they can use many indirect means to make the conduct of evaluations look like an attractive and responsible thing to do.

For whatever reason an evaluation is originated, note that the people who launch it are likely to be situated at the top of the hierarchy. Funders, directors, managers—they come to the evaluator with a particular set of questions and concerns. An evaluator's initial impulse is to accept the concerns that they articulate as the key questions for the evaluation. After all, they initiated the study; they are paying the bills; they have authority to use evaluation results to make changes in the program.

So far, so good. It is important to know what is on the minds of people in authority. But evaluators should recognize from the start that funders and managers do not represent the whole range of questions that are floating around about the program. Nor, however high their rank, are they the only ones who will make decisions about the program. Many other people will have a say about what happens, not least the staff whose day-to-day actions determine what the program actually is and the clients whose decisions to attend or not attend and how seriously to pay attention set limits to what the program *can do*. Evaluators are often wise not to restrict their attention to questions of those in the upper echelons but, where possible, to consider the questions of other people affected by the program.

Overt and Covert Purposes

In olden times evaluators believed that a study that responded to the questions of the study sponsor would almost automatically be used. They assumed that people funded a study because they needed information in order to make better decisions. In the past decades we have learned that this is not always true. Of course, many people do want to know what evaluation can tell them, and many more can be persuaded that evaluation can tell them things that they want to know. But it is equally true that people decide to have a program evaluated for many different reasons, from the eminently rational to the patently political. Before taking the mission at face value, the evaluator should consider the possibility that people are turning to evaluation for less legitimate reasons.

Evaluation as Subterfuge

Postponement   People in positions of authority may be looking for ways to delay a decision. Instead of resorting to the usual ploy of appointing a committee and waiting for its report, they can commission an evaluation study, which takes even longer.

Ducking Responsibility   Sometimes one faction in the program organization is espousing one course of action and another faction is opposing it. The administrators look to evaluation to get them off the hook by producing dispassionate evidence that will make the decision for them.

Window Dressing   There are cases in which administrators know what the decision will be even before they call in the evaluators, but they want to cloak it in the trappings of research. They use evaluation to provide legitimacy.

Public Relations   Occasionally, evaluation is seen as a way of self-glorification. The manager believes that he has a highly successful program and looks for a way to make it visible. A good study will fill the bill. Copies of the report, favorable of course, can be sent to boards of trustees, members of legislative committees, executives of philanthropic foundations who give large sums to successful programs, and other influential people. Suchman (1967) suggests two related purposes: eyewash and whitewash. In an eyewash evaluation, an attempt is made to justify a weak program by selecting for evaluation only those aspects that look good on the surface. A whitewash attempts to cover up program failure by avoiding any objective appraisal.

The program administrator's motives are not, of course, necessarily crooked or selfish. Often, there is a need to justify the program to the people who pay the bills, and he is seeking support for a concept and a project in which he believes. Generating support for existing programs used to be a fairly common motive for embarking on evaluation, until managers found out that evaluations tend to find flaws in even well-regarded programs. In those cases where the general tenor of evaluation is positive, the study also surfaces the "warts and all." Now only the naive manager turns to evaluation when he seeks to shore up the agency's public relations, or the manager who so stringently limits the questions that are addressed that he can be sure of the findings.

Fulfilling Grant Requirements

Often the decision to evaluate stems from sources outside the program. Many federal agencies and foundations mandate evaluation for each demonstration project and innovative program they fund. An evaluation is conducted merely to fulfill the requirement. Some ongoing projects, long past the demonstration stage, are also required to conduct evaluation to satisfy conditions of the grant. For many years this was true of projects to improve the school performance of disadvantaged pupils funded under Title I of the Elementary and Secondary Education Act.

For policymakers who support large-scale multi-site programs, it is obvious that wise policy and proper management are served by a supply of systematic evidence about the program. For untried innovative projects, it makes sense for funders to require evidence on the extent to which the project is working. But to the operators of a project, the demands of starting up and running the project take priority. Plagued as they often are by immediate problems of staffing, budgets, logistics, community relations, and all the other trials of project life, they tend to look on evaluation as just another burden. They see it mainly as a ritual designed to placate the funding bodies, without any real usefulness to them.

For ongoing projects, routine often sets in. Administrators and staff who have been receiving federal funds for 20 years to run pretty much the same project are no longer experimenting with different techniques or materials. They are operating the project that they have learned how to operate. The demand for evaluation looks to them like another one of those pointless hoops they have to jump through to keep getting the money.

Evaluation, then, is a rational enterprise often undertaken for nonrational, or at least noninformational, reasons. We could continue the catalog of covert purposes (justifying a program to Congress, demonstrating that the administrator is acting in accordance with highly prized procedures of management), but the important point is that such motives have consequences for the evaluation that can be serious and bleak.

An evaluator who is asked to study a particular program usually assumes that she is there because people want answers about what the program is doing, how it is doing it, and what the consequences are. When this is not the case, she may in her naivete become a pawn in an intraorganizational power struggle, a means of delaying action, or the rallying point for one ideology or another. Some evaluators have found only after their study was done that they had unwittingly played a role in a larger political game. They found that nobody was particularly interested in learning from their results, but only in using them (or any quotable piece *of* them) as ammunition to destroy or to justify.

Lesson number one for the evaluator newly arrived on the scene is: Find out who initiated the idea of having an evaluation of the project/program and why. Were there other groups in the organization who questioned or objected to the evaluation? What were their motives? Is there real commitment among practitioners, administrators, and/or funders to paying attention to the results of the evaluation? If the real purposes for the evaluation are not oriented to increased understanding and there is little commitment to considering results, the chances for influence are likely to be small.

The saving grace is that evaluations often prove to be useful even when they were begun without any intention to put the results to use. When the report comes in, funders and managers may find that it gives them direction for improving the way the program is run. They may find that the results give them grounds for doing things they were considering doing anyway. Further, so long as the evaluation report is made public (and all reports to federal agencies have to be made public), evaluation findings reach not only their intended audiences but also percolate into the awareness of other members of the program community. Through a variety of direct and indirect routes, people in many places hear about the findings. The potential for general enlightenment from evaluation helps to overcome some of the unfavorable signals emitted by uninterested study sponsors.

Conditions Unfavorable for Evaluation

Is evaluation always warranted? Should all programs if they are good little programs go out and get themselves evaluated? Heretical as it may seem coming from an evaluator, the answer is probably no. If evaluation results are not going to have any influence on the way people think about the program, it is probably an exercise in futility. Evaluation may not be worthwhile in four kinds of circumstances:

1. *When the program has few routines and little stability.* Program staff improvise activities from day to day, based on little thought and less theory, and the program shifts and changes, wanders around and seeks direction. The program that an evaluator starts studying today will bear little resemblance to the program a year or two from now when the evaluation report is ready. At that point the report will be about a program that is ancient history. If evaluation found out what the effects were on participants, there would be no way of knowing *what* was the program that caused them.

    Even if the program initially adhered to a plan, staff may veer off in other directions, either as individuals or collectively. The initial plan is left behind without being replaced by a coherent alternative. Again it is not clear what the program is, and therefore it would not be clear what the evaluation means.

2. *When people involved in the program cannot agree on what the program is trying to achieve.* If there are vast discrepancies in perceived goals, staff are probably working at cross purposes. Again, the coherence of the program is in doubt. Furthermore, it is not clear what criteria the evaluator should use in evaluating program outcomes. A study of the inner workings (process) of the program might be helpful, but major disagreements about goals should signal a go-slow approach for outcome evaluation.

3. *When the sponsor of the evaluation or program manager sets stringent limits to what the evaluation can study, putting off limits many important issues.* The sponsor or manager wants eyewash or whitewash, and the evaluator is expected to give legitimacy to the enterprise.

4. *When there is not enough money or no staff sufficiently qualified to conduct the evaluation.* Evaluation is a demanding business, calling for time, money, imagination, tenacity, and skill. Without sufficient quantities of all of these, evaluation may produce information that is more misleading than informative.

Of course, we can argue that even in such dismal circumstances, evaluation research can produce something of value, some glimmering of insight that will light a candle for the future. This is a fetching notion, and I sometimes succumb to it. But experience suggests that even good evaluation studies of well-defined programs often wind up as litter in the bureaucratic mill. When conditions are unfavorable, the prospective evaluator should be clear about what she is getting into.

Evaluation for Decision Making

Most program directors and project managers undertake an evaluation for reasons that are more auspicious than those we have just contemplated. They may want to know what is happening in the program so that they can take midcourse corrective action. For example, if the evaluation of program process reveals that staff is discouraging tough cases from persisting in the program, the managers may want to retrain or reorient staff to the importance of serving hard-to-serve people. Policymakers may want to know the consequences of the program for its clients so that they can decide whether or not to expand it to new sites or to new categories of participants. These are the kinds of *evaluation-for-decision* purposes that most people assume evaluation serves.

Midcourse Corrections   An important reason for undertaking evaluation is to find out early in the game what is going on so that changes can be made. Sometimes evaluation is triggered by warning signs that all is not well. But in many other cases, a regular commitment to evaluation is based on the hope that ineffective practices can be identified early before they do lasting harm. Evaluations that focus on program process can yield data on what is happening during the program's course and identify points at which improvement is called for. Perhaps eligibility criteria for clients have to be redefined, or rules have to be enforced more stringently when clients fail to follow directions, or new categories of staff, such as outreach workers, have to be added. Evaluation of program processes can send up early signals that attention is needed and identify the kinds of change that are warranted.

Continuing, Expanding, or Institutionalizing the Program, or Cutting, Ending, or Abandoning It   Evaluation can also be dedicated to finding out the extent to which a program is achieving its goals. Information on this score can be used to decide whether the program should be continued and spread to further locations, or whether investments in it should be cut. Past experience shows that evaluation results are not the only basis on which decisions about the future of the program will be made—and not necessarily the major one. Because programs serve many functions, political and symbolic as well as instrumental, evidence of outcomes is only one of the considerations that are taken into account. Nevertheless, evaluation provides data on what the program accomplishes and fails to accomplish, and for whom, and thus clarifies the trade-offs that decision makers have to make.

Testing a New Program Idea   When an agency comes up with a new programmatic approach to carry out its charge, it can try out the approach in a series of demonstration projects and evaluate effects. For example, a philanthropic foundation can conclude that providing services to poor people individually is not enough to lift them out of poverty. Instead, agencies should work at rebuilding the communities in which poor people live. The foundation then sets up demonstrations of the new approach. If the projects prove successful in lively and important ways, those who make decisions about future programming can adopt the community approach as a basic strategy. Or managers of other programs may incorporate some of the key practices into ongoing programs elsewhere. If the projects have poor or mediocre results, modifications can be made to improve their working. In the end, if evaluation shows that they do less well than activities already in practice, the idea may be abandoned.

Choosing the Best of Several Alternatives   Sometimes several versions of a program are run, such as two or more math curricula or several modalities of health care cost containment. The intent of evaluation is to find out which of the options has the best outcomes, with the expectation that the best one will be adopted. Experience suggests that no one alternative is likely to be dominant on all dimensions. Each version of a program is apt to do better in some ways, worse in others. Still, clarifying what each alternative gains and loses can provide significant learning. Those who make decisions then have to consider which dimensions are most salient to the varied publics concerned.

Deciding Whether to Continue Funding   The funder of a set of projects wants to know which of the agencies currently receiving program funds should continue receiving them. This is a legitimate purpose for evaluation, but it is the kind of purpose that tends to make evaluated projects nervous and hostile. They know that they are being judged and that their continued livelihood may depend on how well they do. To borrow a term from the testing field, these are *high-stakes* evaluations. Under such circumstances, projects may try to influence, subvert, or even sabotage the evaluation. Many evaluators are uneasy about conducting studies that make judgments about individual projects, but experienced evaluators learn how to avoid invidious comparisons and keep the focus on things that matter.

Evaluation as Organizational Learning

The purposes listed so far have all dealt with instrumental action. Evaluation is expected to contribute to wiser choices and improved programming. There are other worthy purposes for evaluation that are less oriented to program decisions, and it is to these I now turn.

Recording of Program History   Someone in the program or project seeks evaluation as a record of program history, perhaps from a belief that epochal things will take place that ought to be documented, perhaps with a vague sense that he or others can learn lessons from history. An evaluator under such circumstances will have some difficulty narrowing down the open-ended charge to record what happens and find an agreed-upon focus for the study, but there are opportunities here to contribute to program understanding and, perhaps, action.

Feedback to Practitioners   Rather than providing information to program managers, sometimes evaluation is expected to feed back information to practitioners as the program goes along. The evaluator in this case is expected to be a sensitive observer who keeps track of events and makes visible to staff what they are doing, how participants are responding, what external conditions are impinging on the program, and so on. When the evaluator and the staff share common assumptions about the program and a common language in which to communicate, this can be a highly useful role. Sometimes the evaluator is expected to go further and give staff advice. If this is the case, it is important that the evaluator be something of an expert about programs of this sort, so that practitioners have confidence that the advice is realistic and competent. Where there is a disjunction in viewpoint between evaluator and staff, extended negotiations may be necessary before the feedback is accepted and stands a chance of having practical effects.

A related purpose for evaluation is to give practitioners a tinge of skepticism about what they are doing. Most staff engaged in program service take for granted that their service is good and will have good effects. They believe in the value of their work. They almost have to believe, so that they can get up and go to work every day. As one program manager said to me long ago, the job of a practitioner is to believe; the job of an evaluator is to doubt. The whole raison d'être of evaluation is to ask whether things that the program assumed were good turn out to be good in fact. A sophisticated program manager may want to transmit to practitioners something of the evaluator's doubt. (He may also hope to give the evaluator a touch of the staff's belief.) It may be good for staff to step back a bit and reflect on the consequences of their work and ways in which they can improve their practice. Although this is rarely a direct purpose for doing evaluation, it is sometimes an outgrowth of the evaluation procedure. As such, a canny administrator may find the encouragement of reflective practice (Schon, 1983) to be a desirable byproduct.

Highlighting Program Goals   Another way in which program managers can use evaluation to influence practitioners' behavior is by using the occasion of evaluation to emphasize program goals. If the evaluator is encouraged to use program goals as the criteria against which outcomes are weighed, the study reinforces staff's concern with the goals that have official sanction. As one program manager told me, this turns the evaluation into a disciplining mechanism, a way to get staff to agree (again) on what they mean to accomplish and attend to objectives that might otherwise slide from the forefront of their minds. When they see the connections between what they are trying to accomplish and their daily activities, they bring their work into line with program priorities.

Accountability   Given the current stringency of budgets, public agencies are urged, sometimes required, to give reports to the public detailing what they have accomplished with public funds. The press for accountability can lead agencies to undertake systematic evaluation. Although accountability reasons for evaluation may seem to be ritualistic, much like the "fulfilling requirements" purpose I sniffed at before, there may be more promise in this situation. When evaluation results are reported to policymakers, funders, *and* the public, they get a wider hearing. By virtue of being public, results may stimulate adaptive action. Knowing that other people will be looking may make practitioners more attentive to the public's expectations.

Understanding Social Intervention   Few evaluations are initiated with the express purpose of acquiring basic knowledge about the kinds of things that work to change social conditions and human behavior. Still, evaluations provide a first-rate opportunity for studying the consequences of social interventions. The study of policies and programs in action presents a chance to study the stimuli that lead to change and the environmental conditions under which change is likely to occur. It provides a chance to develop theory about program initiatives. This kind of purpose for evaluation is sometimes tarred as academic and remote from the practical everyday concerns that should be evaluators' fare. But as the social psychologist Kurt Lewin said, "Nothing is so practical as a good theory." If social scientists really understood what it took to alter people's behavior, the nation would save an enormous amount of waste in trial-and-error programmatic efforts.

Because human beings are so various, and because conditions change at an accelerating rate, the development of theory about human action and reaction is a precarious enterprise. Still, evaluation is an opportune site for investigation. Because it goes on in a setting where somebody is trying to *change* clients' knowledge, attitudes, or behavior, it provides an acid test for old theories of intervention and an opportunity to help construct new ones. The theories it contributes to are apt to be partial, time-bound, and generalizable to only a small subset of interventions, but even modest advances can help improve the efficacy of policy and program design.

The question for the evaluator to keep in mind is: Do the conditions that led to evaluation hold promise that people will give considered attention to the findings, either now or in the future? If there's a chance of it, and the resources are adequate, let's do it.

Intended Uses for Evaluation

Even when evaluation is undertaken for good reasons, people can have widely differing expectations of the kinds of answers that will be produced. If the evaluator is not to be caught unawares, it behooves her to know from the outset what questions her study is expected to answer.

Who Expects What?

Expectations for the evaluation generally vary with a person's position in the system. Top policymakers tend to ask for the kind of information that will help them address broad issues: Should the program be continued or dropped, institutionalized throughout the system or limited to a pilot program, continued with the same strategies of operation or modified? Should more money be allocated to this program or to others? They therefore have an interest in the overall effectiveness of the program. That is the kind of knowledge that enriches their thinking and enables them to proceed with greater conviction. Foundation executives, for example, have the opportunity to move their resources from one field to another with expedition. Legislators can initiate new programs and policies and reform or terminate old ones. Although experience shows that evaluation findings *alone* rarely lead to the abandonment of unsuccessful programs or the expansion of successful ones (many other things have to fall into place), evaluation sponsors usually expect data on the program's overall success.

Project managers tend to be less interested in global assessments of the program's effectiveness. They are not generally engaged by issues of extension or termination or provision of more or fewer resources. They are not in charge of such decisions. They are not authorized to decide whether to move from treatment to prevention, from centralized to decentralized operation, or lower to higher expenditures. They are responsible for the current project. They have to work within the parameters that have been defined. Their concern is how to make the project in its present incarnation work as well as possible.

Overall assessments of program effectiveness are directly useful primarily when the data show substantial success. Such information helps project directors mobilize support for the program and ward off criticism. When overall outcome data show mixed effectiveness or a list toward the negative, the information is useful to them to the extent that it helps them figure out which procedures and techniques are more or less successful, which are achieving results most efficiently and economically, which features of the program are essential and which can be changed or dropped. In other words, they seek the kind of direction from evaluation that helps them to improve the program.

The distinction I draw here between policy-level concerns and program-level concerns is worth making. Policymakers care about overall effects; program managers are more interested in the differential effects of alternative strategies. But the lines between policy and program issues become blurred in operation. Policymakers often get involved in program details. For example, the Congress and many state legislatures have taken on responsibility for specific program and policy provisions. They have become micromanagers. Instead of writing broad prescriptions in 10-page bills, they sometimes write bills that cover hundreds of pages, prescribing minute details of a program's functioning, from the membership on its local advisory committees to the square footage of space it shall occupy. Information on details used to be of interest mainly to staff in executive departments who wrote guidelines and regulations for the program and managers who actually ran the projects. Now such information often finds a ready audience in the halls of Congress.

Direct-service staff deal with individuals and small groups. They have practical day-to-day concerns about techniques. Should they spend more of the time in job training courses trying to develop good work habits and less time on teaching subject matter? Should they put more emphasis on group discussions or films or lectures? Should they accept more younger people (who are not already set in their ways) or more older people (who have greater responsibilities and more need)? Practitioners, who are accustomed to relying on their own experience and intuitive judgment, often challenge evaluation to come up with something practical on topics such as these.

Nor do these three sets of actors—policymakers, program directors, and practitioners—exhaust the list of those with a stake in the evaluation. The funders of evaluation research, particularly when they are outside the direct line of operations, may have an interest in adding to the pool of knowledge in the field. They may want answers less to operating questions than to questions of theory and method. Should efforts to help poor families be concentrated on education or job creation? Does increasing the available career opportunities for low-income youth result in lower rates of juvenile delinquency? If coordination among community health services is increased, will people receive better health care? Here is another purpose for evaluation—to test propositions about the utility of models or theories of service. The public, too, has a stake, as taxpayers, as parents of schoolchildren, as contributors to voluntary organizations. They are concerned that their money is wisely and efficiently spent.

Consumers of services have a particular stake in the program, and therefore in its evaluation. At the outset they want some gauge of a project's effectiveness to help them select a particular school, alcoholism treatment center, or vocational rehabilitation project. Later on, if they are not receiving the kind of help they need and want, they would like the evaluation to reveal the extent of shortcomings and to point the way to more beneficial services. Consumers may seek to use evaluation to ask client-eye questions about the program under study. Is the program serving the objectives that clients value? In some communities, opposition has arisen to traditional formulations of program criteria. Activists not only want to improve school achievement or health care. They are concerned with community participation or community control of programs and institutions as a mechanism to assure that clients' wants get priority attention. When such issues are paramount, evaluative questions derive from a radically different perspective.

A host of interested onlookers are the managers and staff of other similar projects who want to learn as much as they can about what works. The managers of other probation services or nutrition projects want to find out how the project under study was run and with what effects. They expect to learn from the evaluation how they can improve their own project, or if they have not yet started, whether its results are so good that they should undertake something similar.

Finally, there are the designers of policies and programs who look to evaluation studies for guidance about the directions that they should take, or avoid, as they go about designing new policies. There are also social scientists who want to draw conclusions about the whole field of social programming and about the ways that human beings respond to interventions in their social world.

Formative and Summative Evaluation

In discussing potential uses and prospective users, a useful set of terms was introduced by Scriven (1967). He was talking about the evaluation of educational curriculums, and he distinguished between formative and summative evaluation. *Formative evaluation* produces information that is fed back during the development of a curriculum to help improve it. It serves the needs of developers. *Summative evaluation* is done after the curriculum is finished. It provides information about the effectiveness of the curriculum to school decision makers who are considering adopting it in their schools.

Scriven (1991) later simplified the distinction. In a phrase he attributes to Robert Stake, he offers this definition:

> When the cook tastes the soup, that's formative evaluation; when the guest tastes it, that's summative evaluation. (p. 19)

This distinction is not limited to curriculum development but can be applied to other types of programs as well, with obvious advantages for the clarification of purpose. Formative evaluations *are designed to* assist those who are developing projects in the early phases. The emphasis is on feedback to developers with an eye to improving the final product. Summative evaluation is meant for decisions about whether to continue or end a program, extend it to other locations or cut it back.

However, many programs are never "finished" in the sense that a curriculum is finished when it is published and distributed. Programs continue to adapt and transmute in response to conditions inside and outside the program agency. For reasons good and not so good, program practitioners and managers modify what they do over time. Change may come about because they learn better strategies through practice, or because of demands from clients, loss of a charismatic director, hiring of staff with different skills, changing community sentiments, rising staff morale, or any of a dozen other shifts. The need for "formative" information continues—that is, information fed back to program staff on how to improve the program.[2]

When other sites seek to adopt the program, they too need formative information. They never replicate the program exactly but adapt it to suit local conditions (Berman & McLaughlin, 1977, 1978). The perennial pattern of program modification is a reason it has proved so difficult to identify the "ideal program" and then work for its institutionalization systemwide. Programs change in operation, and today's exemplary program is tomorrow's mediocrity. Outside conditions differ, too. The program model that starred in "What Works" in Savannah becomes a dud in Detroit. Hopes that evaluation can be used to define *the* program that works and that agencies can "go to scale" with it have been repeatedly disappointed (Elmore, 1996).

In practice, evaluation is most often called on to help with decisions about

---

[2]Data on outcomes as well as data on program process can be useful for formative purposes.

improving programs, projects, and components. Go/no-go, live-or-die decisions about programs are relatively rare (Kaufman, 1976), and reliance on evaluation data to make those decisions is rarer still. Even when evaluation results show the program to be a failure, the usual use of the information is to patch it up and try again. Rare, too, is the use of evaluation in theory-oriented tests of program approaches and models. Despite considerably more writing about program theory in recent years, only occasionally are evaluations funded by people disinterested enough in current happenings to take a cool theoretical look. It is the search for improvements in components and strategies that supports most evaluation activity.

Decision makers may start out with global questions (Is the program worth continuing?), but they often receive qualified results ("There are these good effects, but …") that lead them to look for ways to modify present practice. They become interested in the likelihood of improved results with different components, a different mix of services, different client groups, different staffing patterns, different organizational structure, different procedures and mechanics. One of the ironies of evaluation practice is that its methods are powerful for assessment of overall impact, suited to the uncommon go/no-go decision, but less well developed for understanding how and why programs achieve the degree of impact observed and how they can be improved.

At many stages people turn to evaluation for information that will help them modify the program. They expect evaluation to point the way to constructive change.

Formative-Summative and Process-Outcome: Different Constructs

At first blush, there seems to be close correspondence between the formative-summative distinction and the process-outcome distinction that I made in Chapter 1. Process evaluations examine what goes on inside the program while it is in progress, with a focus on such things as participant enrollment, activities offered, actions taken, staff practices, and client actions. Outcome evaluations put the emphasis on what happens to clients after their participation in the program as a result of the intervention. *Formative* and *process* come in the early stages and seem to be dedicated to improving the program, whereas *summative* and *outcome* are about what happens to participants at the conclusion.

However, the two pairs of terms have quite different implications. *Formative* and *summative* relate to the *intentions* of the evaluator in undertaking the study—whether to help develop the program or to render judgment on it. *Process* and *outcome* have nothing to do with the evaluator's role but rather relate to the *phase* of the program studied.

Evaluators' intentions can change over the course of a study. Evaluation sponsors who originally requested summative evaluation can realize that they want the information to help improve the program (a formative purpose), or the evaluator may change her intentions when she analyzes what the data say. The important point is that outcome data are often helpful for formative purposes, and process data can help the policy community realize why outcomes came out as they did and therefore understand how much summative guidance they provide for the future. Accordingly, the more useful distinction for many purposes is that between the study of program process (looking at what goes on during the program) and the study of outcomes (looking at consequences for participants at the end).

Compatibility of Purposes

With all the possible uses for evaluation to serve, the evaluator has to make choices. The all-purpose evaluation is a myth. Although a number of different types of questions can be considered within the bounds of a single study, this takes meticulous planning and design. Not even a well-planned study will provide information on all the questions from all the people involved.

In fact, some purposes for evaluation are incompatible with others. Consider the evaluation of a particular educational program for slow learners. The teaching staff wants to use evaluation results to improve the presentations and teaching methods of the course, session by session, in order to maximize student learning. The state college of education wants to know whether the instructional program, based on a particular theory of learning, improves pupil performance. In the first case, the evaluator will have to examine immediate short-term effects (e.g., what students learn after the morning lesson). The teachers are not concerned about generalizing the results to other populations, and so the study needs neither comparison groups nor sophisticated statistics. The teachers care about these students in the here and now. The evaluator will want to maximize feedback of results to the teachers so that they can modify their techniques as they go along.

On the other hand, when evaluation is testing the proposition that a program developed from certain theories of learning will be successful with slow learners, it is concerned with long-range effects. Does learning occur and does it endure? The evaluation requires rigorous design so that observed results can be attributed to the stimulus of the program and not to extraneous events. The results have to be generalizable beyond the specific group of students. The instructional program should be faithful to the principles embodied in the theory of learning from which it derives, and it should be insulated from alterations during its course in order to preserve the clarity of the program that led to the effects observed.

Ideally, it is possible to achieve both an assessment of overall program effectiveness and a test of the effectiveness of component strategies. Textbooks on the design of experiments present methods of factorial design that allow the experimenter to discover both total effect and the effects of each experimental treatment. A combination of qualitative evaluation of program strategies and quantitative-experimental evaluation of outcomes can also serve the dual purpose.

However, in practice, juggling multiple questions is a difficult task. The constraints of the field situation may hobble the evaluation—too few students or too homogeneous a group of students, inadequate funds to support the necessary intensity and diversity of evaluation methods, contamination of the slow-learners groups by receipt of other services, dropouts from the program, lack of access to records and data, and so on. These difficulties can afflict an evaluation addressing one question. When the evaluator is trying to attend to two or three very different orders of questions at the same time, it becomes harder to give the requisite care to each. And sometimes they interfere with one another. For example, putting effort into control groups and long-term follow-up will take away resources from the study of immediate effects of teachers' strategies. Giving quick feedback to teachers may lead them to make adjustments in the program that depart from the original theory. Such adjustment runs counter to the need for program stability in the interest of answers about the long-term viability of the program's theory.

With money, time, evaluation know-how, and determination to raise different orders of questions, the evaluator can satisfy the informational demands of multiple groups. But it is a difficult and time-consuming job. Even when evaluators turn to informal procedures and less-than-elegant designs to accomplish the task, they often encounter frustrations. It is useful for the evaluator to identify the key questions raised by different actors and negotiate priorities among them. Or she may be able to plan a series of studies to be carried out in succession, one building on the findings of the earlier ones, to address additional questions. Whatever the plan turns out to be, it remains useful for the evaluator to know the priority among the purposes for evaluation. If a crunch comes, she can jettison the extra baggage and fight for the essentials.

The decision about whose uses shall be served is sometimes beyond the evaluator's control. The manner in which the study is commissioned may determine whose questions get top billing. Whether the evaluator is inside the program agency or outside in a research organization or consulting firm also influences her access to influence. Either inside or outside, her location in the organizational structure will give her more or less opportunity to shape the study. It is to these issues I now turn.

How Evaluations Are Commissioned

There are three basic ways in which an agency that wants evaluation goes about getting a study done: (a) hiring an evaluator on to the staff of the program agency (or assigning the task to an evaluator already there); (b) hiring an outside research/evaluation or consulting organization to do the evaluation; and (c) opening up bidding for the study to all applicants, through a procedure that is known in government circles as request for proposals (RFP). In the latter case, the commissioning agency sets out its requirements for the study and asks evaluation organizations to submit proposals explaining how they would conduct the study and at what cost. Very occasionally, there is a fourth route to evaluation. A university investigator develops a program on the basis of a theory of intervention and applies for a grant to study the effectiveness of the program and, concurrently, the validity of the theory on which it is based (e.g., Olds, 1988). In such a case, the investigator initiates the evaluation and seeks funding from a research grants agency to conduct the study.

Evaluator on Staff

Many agencies maintain an evaluation staff. Large school districts, mental health centers, colleges, and hospitals are among the agencies that often have a permanent evaluator or evaluation team. One of the main advantages is that the evaluator is there, ready and able to take on the job whenever evaluation is wanted. Another advantage is that the evaluator understands the agency and its programs. There is no need to orient her to the realities of program life and the constraints under which the agency operates. A disadvantage is that cost-conscious agencies do not want to maintain idle evaluation capacity and so usually keep the evaluation staff small— sometimes too small to undertake the complex study they want to have done or to do a needed second study when one is already in progress. Staff evaluators can also be drawn off to do other tasks in the agency. For example, evaluators in school districts are often called upon to administer testing programs. The small number of available evaluators can limit the type of evaluation that can be done.

An agency can also hire an evaluation expert to do the work, as an extension of its own staff. The expert reports directly to the chief, and is for all intents and purposes a part-time adjunct staff member. Agencies also hire experts, often university faculty members, to serve as consultants to advise the staff evaluator or review her work periodically with suggestions for modification or further work.

Hiring an Evaluation Organization

When an agency doesn't have its own evaluation staff, it often seeks an outside evaluation organization to do the study. Several types of organizations are available: for-profit firms, nonprofit organizations, institutes attached to universities, faculty members of a school or department of the university. The program agency may check into which groups are qualified to do the kind of evaluation it wants. Or it may go to one organization that it knows has a good reputation, or whose staff it knows, or whose price is right, or with which it satisfactorily worked on a previous evaluation. Or it can hold a limited competition, asking several organizations to explain how they would go about the task, and then select the one whose plans best fit its needs.

The hiring of an evaluation organization gives the program agency a wider choice than it would have if it were limited to its own staff. It can call on a range of skills, talents, and experience that may be lacking on staff, and it can contract for a larger study than it would be likely to undertake in-house.

Requests for Proposals

For government programs, the law limits the opportunity to choose one research/evaluation organization without competition. In order to prevent nepotism, cronyism, corruption, or sweetheart arrangements (where, e.g., the evaluator promises to find good results in order to get the job), the agency has to open the bidding for the contract[3] to all evaluation organizations on an equal basis. The agency publishes

---

[3]The government has two basic mechanisms for funding research: contracts and grants. With a contract, government sets the parameters of the study and awards the contract to the organization whose proposal to fulfill those parameters best suits its purposes. Contracts thus give the government major control over the content, methods, timing, and reporting of studies. Grants are awarded to researchers who initiate their own study and apply for funding. The applications are reviewed for merit, but there is no competition to do the same work. Most government evaluations are done under contract.

a notice about the availability of the RFP in the *Commerce Business Daily*, a publication that lists notices of all goods and services that the government plans to buy. (Yes, it really appears daily. The government purchases amazing numbers of things.) Any organization that is interested in an evaluation RFP calls, faxes, e-mails, or writes for the full RFP or downloads it from the agency's Web site. The RFP sets out the nature of the desired study. The specification can be extremely detailed in terms of sites, number of cases, design, measures, times for data collection, and so on, or it can be fairly general. It also specifies the criteria on which proposals will be judged and the date on which proposals are due.

Sometimes the agency holds a bidders' meeting to which all prospective applicants are invited. There, agency staff answer questions that are raised about the desired study. Again, the procedure is designed to create a level playing field. No one bidder gets inside information. Word about the agency's intentions is given to all at one time and one place.[4]

The next step is for respondent organizations to submit proposals to do the work. Separately they submit budgets detailing the costs they expect to incur in completing the evaluation—and thus the price of the work. After the proposals have been received, the agency assembles a group of reviewers to judge their adequacy. Reviewers often include outside experts, such as university faculty and consultants, as well as inside staff. The substantive proposals are usually reviewed without reference to the budget statement. Only after the top proposals have been selected as finalists are budgets examined. If organizations submit budgets that are orders of magnitude too high or too low, the staff may conclude that the applicants don't understand the task. In that case, they may jettison the substantive proposal.

Reviewers judge substantive proposals against the standards set by the agency. Criteria will include such things as understanding of the agency's needs, capability of staff who will conduct the evaluation, responsiveness of the proposal to the RFP, organizational resources to be devoted to the study. For large contracts, the top bidders can be invited to make oral presentations of their proposals and answer agency questions. After one or more rounds of review, the winning proposal is selected. Even at that point, the government can still negotiate changes in the organization's proposal (or budget) to make it better suit agency purposes.

The RFP procedure represents a fair contracting method, one that is used in government acquisition of thousands of items, from buttons to fighter aircraft. One advantage is that it opens the bidding to all comers. Another is that it tailors the evaluation to the factors that the agency sees as important. A disadvantage is that, when RFPs are very detailed, the mechanism limits the opportunity for evaluation organizations to exercise much creativity and initiative in the design of the study. Evaluators complain that acquiring evaluations is not like acquiring buttons; they are not standardized or interchangeable. When the government agency exercises overly tight control, it risks losing the quality and ingenuity that an outstanding evaluator can bring to the task. Nevertheless, staff in government evaluation offices are usual-

---

[4]Recently a number of federal agencies have discontinued holding bidders' meetings on the grounds that they have become unproductive. Prospective applicants have reportedly become wary of asking questions at the meetings for fear that they would be disclosing their plans to competitors.

ly competent and experienced, so that requirements generally make sense and ingenious evaluators find ways to propose approaches and techniques that will make the
study even more useful than the original RFP anticipated. Another disadvantage is
that the RFP procedure is onerous and time-consuming for evaluation organizations.
Small or new organizations don't have the resources to absorb the costs of preparing many losing bids.

At the levels of state and local government, simpler versions of the federal
RFP procedure are usually followed. Foundations and nonprofit agencies sometimes
choose to go the RFP route, too. However, they often invite only a few evaluation
groups that they know and trust to understand their issues.

Extent of Influence

The mechanism by which the study is commissioned will affect how much influence
the evaluator will have on defining the questions that the study addresses. An insid-
er can have a good deal of influence, but not if she sits somewhere deep in the bow-
els of the agency. An evaluator called to the task because of her expertise and renown
can help to determine which purposes the study will serve, but not if she is hamstrung by an elaborate and highly specific RFP. The evaluator in each situation has
to learn how to maneuver within the constraints of setting and procedures.

Inside versus Outside Evaluation

Parallel to the issue of the commissioning mechanism is the issue of location.
Whether the evaluator is a member of the agency staff or an outsider affects not only
how much say she has in determining the purposes to which the study is directed;
her location has other consequences as well. There is a long tradition of controversy about whether in-house or outside evaluation is preferable. The answer seems to
be that neither has a monopoly on the advantages. Some of the factors to be considered are administrative confidence, objectivity, understanding of the program, potential for utilization, and autonomy.

Administrative Confidence

Administrators must have confidence in the professional skills of the evaluation
staff. Sometimes agency personnel are impressed only by the credentials and reputations of academic researchers and assume that the research people it has on staff
or can hire are second-raters. Conversely, it may view outside evaluators as too
remote from the realities, too ivory tower and abstract, to produce information of
practical value. Often it is important to ensure public confidence by engaging evaluators who have no stake in the program to be studied. Competence, of course, is a
big factor in ensuring confidence and deserves priority consideration.

Objectivity

Objectivity requires that evaluators be insulated from the possibility of biasing their
data or its interpretation by a desire to make the program look good (or bad). Points
usually go to outsiders on this score. They have no obvious stake in the program and
can afford to let the chips fall where they may. Furthermore, they are seen by others

as impartial. While fine evaluations have been done by staff evaluators of scrupulous integrity, there is a lingering suspicion that they will try to please agency superiors by presenting the program in the best possible light. A wish to get along with colleagues in the program part of the agency may exert a subtle press on the evaluator to downplay negative information. When I was a staff evaluator in a small agency, I didn't want to antagonize my program colleagues and have to eat lunch alone.

But outsiders are not always immune from such pressures. They can get so engaged with practitioners and clients and so involved in the processes of the program that they become almost unwitting advocates for it. It even happens that an outside research firm will try to sweeten the interpretation of program results (by choice of respondents, by selection of data) in order to ingratiate itself with agency managers and be first in line for further contracts.

In all events, safeguarding the study against bias is important. While no researcher, inside or out, is totally objective (we all have our beliefs and values, which inevitably color our methodological choices and interpretations), evaluation sponsors should seek conditions that minimize biases for or against the program. A good test of whether they have succeeded is whether the final report is respected as a valid account by program stakeholders with conflicting interests.

Understanding of the Program

Knowledge of what is going on in the program is vital for an evaluation staff. They need to know both the real issues facing the agency and the real events that are taking place in the program if their evaluation is to be relevant. It is here that in-house staffs chalk up points. Because they usually sit close to the action, they are likely to see and hear a great deal about what goes on. They hear the gossip, they know quickly about any cataclysmic event, and they see the faces of clients and staff. Of course, outsiders, too, can find out about program processes if they make the effort and are given access to sources of information.

Potential for Utilization

Utilization of results often requires that evaluators take an active role in moving from research data to interpretation of the results in a policy context. In-house staff, who report results and perhaps make recommendations on the basis of results, have many opportunities to bring them to attention of practitioners and managers. They attend staff meetings, go to conferences, meet informally with staff, and thus are often better able to get evaluation results a hearing. But sometimes it is outsiders, with their prestige and authority, who are able to induce the agency to pay attention to the evaluation. If need be, they can go around the chain of command and bring findings to the attention of top brass, oversight agencies, client groups, or the media.

Autonomy

Insiders generally take the program's basic assumptions and organizational arrangements as a given and conduct their evaluation within the existing framework. The outsider is able to exercise more autonomy and take a wider perspective. While respecting the formulation of issues set by the program, she may be able to introduce alternatives that are a marked departure from the status quo. The implications she draws from evaluation data may be oriented less to tinkering and more to fundamental restructuring of the program. Such fundamental rethinking of program parameters may be especially valuable for unsuccessful, routinized, tradition-encrusted programs—to help them see a broader horizon and imagine an alternative future. However, evaluation interpretations that look toward major program change are probably not likely to be used in the near term. Old habits and interests keep an agency moored in familiar channels. But in the longer term, especially if reinforced by influential actors, the wider perspective may help to bring fresh air and fresh ideas into the tradition-bound agency.

Even if the evaluator does not challenge customary boundaries, the outsider has the chance to raise issues that would be uncomfortable for an inside evaluator to raise. Based on data and observation, she can question activities and ideas that are dear to program people's hearts, such as the fact that service isn't available on weekends or that staff are giving priority to people with less serious problems. She can proffer recommendations that go beyond the commonplace. She doesn't have to abide by the prevailing conventions.

Balance

All these considerations have to be balanced against each other. Costs are a factor in some cases. Previous commitments may be relevant. There is no one best site for evaluation. The agency must weigh the factors afresh in each case and make an estimate of the side on which the benefits pile up.

Level in the Structure

Another factor that influences the nature of the evaluation performed and the uses to which it can be put is the location of evaluation within the organizational structure. Whoever actually does the evaluation, she is enabled or constrained by the organizational level to which she reports. The inside evaluator is responsible to some level in the hierarchy. The outside evaluator, too, receives her assignment and reports her progress to (and may get intermediate direction from) the holder of a particular organizational position.

The evaluation should be placed within the organizational structure at a level consonant with its mission. If it is directed at answering the policy questions (How good is the program overall?), evaluators should report to the policy level. To have the evaluation under the control of the people who run the program is to invite gross or subtle efforts to make the study come out "right." Program people can put up roadblocks in countless ways, from directing evaluators to sheer away from questions of program effectiveness to cutting off their funds for computer paper and photocopying (a true case). If the evaluator nevertheless perseveres and produces a report that disparages the overall effectiveness of the program, managers are likely to stall the report at the program level so that it never receives consideration in higher councils where something could be done.

Surely there are many program directors who are scrupulously fair and would not dream of interfering with an evaluation. And they can do good things, too—

such as ease access to sites, organize conferences with stakeholders, and make plans to apply evaluation results to the improvement of the program. Still, it is unwise to put too much temptation in their way by giving them the opportunity to exercise full control. Furthermore, when the evaluation is under the control of program personnel, however nobly they behave, the study tends to lose credibility in the eyes of others.

When the basic shape of the program is unquestioned and the evaluation issue centers on processes and program components, the evaluator should probably be responsible to program managers.[5] It is program managers who have authority to institute the kinds of internal changes in programming that would be suggested by the study. They may have the responsibility for selecting local projects and for supervising staff who deliver services in ways that evaluation may find need to be modified or reinforced. They can hire new staff or new categories of staff. So evaluation that is geared to questions about activities and operations fits comfortably at the program management level.

In deciding on appropriate location, two criteria apply. One is who can control what the evaluation does and says. The other is who can put the findings to use. If program managers oversee an evaluation, they may be wary of letting questions be asked or information released that might reflect poorly on their performance. On the other hand, they have almost daily opportunities to put results to use when they bear on the regular operations of the program. In contrast, policymakers, who often have less at stake if evaluation findings are negative, are unlikely to seek to censor the evaluation. But they have fewer opportunities to make the day-to-day modifications in program operation that effective use of evaluation results might involve.

Wherever the evaluation project sits in the structure, it should have the autonomy that all research requires to report objectively on the evidence and to pursue issues, criteria, and analysis beyond the limits set by people pursuing their own or their organization's self-interest. The charge to the evaluator is to report as well and as accurately as she knows how, in order to understand and interpret the phenomena under study. If disputes arise between the evaluators and the evaluation sponsor, there should be a set procedure that specifies how the issue will be resolved. The procedure may involve appeal to a higher level in the organization or to an outside advisory committee, or a mediation process may be established to be staffed by managers from another program unit or a research and planning office. At the outset it may look like a bureaucratic frill to worry about procedures for dispute resolution, and the evaluator may be reluctant to talk about disputes before they happen. But disputes do come up, and by the time they have erupted, it is often too late for sound and sober judgment. Tempers are frayed. The time to set rules and regulations for resolution is at the beginning. It is important that the process is in place, so that if conflict comes up, it can be resolved in an orderly fashion.

---

[5]This rule of thumb applies whether the evaluation is performed by an in-house evaluation unit or by an outside research organization. Either one should report in at the level of decision to which its work is addressed. The outsiders probably have greater latitude in going around the organizational chain of command and finding access to an appropriate ear, but even they will be circumscribed by improper location.

Whose Use Shall Be Served?

This chapter considers a glittering array of possible users of evaluation results. Each of them has his own interests and ideas, his own questions and concerns, and a unique palette of opportunities for putting the results to use. The players in the drama include the following:

Funding organization (government, private foundation)

National agency (governmental, private)

Local agency

Directors of the specific project

Direct-service staff

Clients and prospective clients of the project

Directors and managers of programs with similar purposes elsewhere

Program designers

Program consultants, often academics, who consult for and advise decision makers

Scholars in the disciplines and professions who build knowledge and teach oncoming generations

The public, which, in the form of public opinion, sets the general direction of, and limits to, policy and programming

The array of people with a possible stake in the evaluation are often called *stakeholders*. The term is appropriate, but inexact. Appropriate, because these actors do have a potential stake in what the evaluation does and what it finds out, but inexact, because there is little consensus on who is and is not among the stakeholding elect. A body of current lore holds that the evaluator should enlist stakeholders in the definition and conduct of the evaluation. But some of the groups on our list will not even know that an evaluation is in progress until the final results are reported. This is true, for example, of directors of similar programs elsewhere and scholars in the disciplines. Some groups will know about the evaluation but be uninterested in it, even though they recognize a passionate stake in the program. Such is often the case for client groups (Weiss, 1983a, 1983b). I return to the subject of stakeholders in Chapter 5.

Which purposes shall the evaluation serve and for whom? In some cases, the question is academic. The evaluator is on the staff of the organization—federal department, school system—and she does the job assigned to her. Still even in such a case, when choices are constrained, the evaluator has options. She can make suggestions about central evaluation questions, design, measurement, and possible uses for the data. Since she is the expert on the subject of evaluation, her words will usually carry weight. If she has done a good bit of preparatory exploration, she will be able to offer cogent reasons for her suggestions and ways in which her plans serve the most important needs. But ultimately, if her superiors disagree, she will have to go along with what they choose to do—or leave the job.

When the evaluator works in a private research firm or an academic institute or department, she has wider latitude. In an outside research organization, she and her colleagues have the opportunity to elaborate on the RFP and write into their proposal emphases and methods that they believe are most appropriate. In for-profit research firms and not-for-profit research institutes dependent on contract funds, evaluators often do not want to depart too drastically from the funder's specifications for the study. They want to win the contract and are afraid that too much independence of mind will jeopardize the award. In academic settings, evaluators may be willing to exercise more discretion in proposing the kind of study they believe is suitable. They can take bigger risks because their salary doesn't usually depend on winning the study contract and the academic value system prizes high-quality research and independent judgment. At the same time, academic evaluators may have less motivation to be relevant to the program agency's problems and useful to its purposes.

Wherever the evaluator is located, she can, if she tries, often negotiate some of the terms of the study. Program personnel and funders on occasion display a surprising lack of clarity about what uses the evaluation shall serve. When the issue is squarely raised, different parties in the program system may disagree among themselves. Such confusion offers the evaluator room for maneuver.

If she can help shape the basic focus of the study, the evaluator will consider a number of things. First is probably her own set of values. A summer program for inner-city youth can be evaluated for city officialdom to see if it cools out the kids and prevents riots. The evaluator may want to view the program from the youths' perspective as well and see if it has improved their job prospects, work skills, and life chances. It is important that the evaluator be able to live with the study, its uses, and her conscience at the same time.

Beyond this point, the paramount consideration is who is listening. If there is a decision coming up (e.g., about introducing Web sites for transmitting program information), and people who will be involved in that decision want to know what the evaluation can tell them, the evaluator will take their concerns seriously. In general, the evaluator scouts the terrain to see whether key decisions are pending, who will make them, when they will be made, and on what grounds they are likely to be made. If she finds that evaluation has a chance of influencing decisions, she will give special attention to questions that have potential decisional payoff.

Often there is no decision pending, or people who will have a voice in the decision are not interested in hearing the findings from evaluation. Still there are likely to be potential audiences who want to learn from the study and consider the results, and there will be others who do not. When local program managers are conscientiously seeking better ways to serve their clients while the policymakers at higher levels are looking primarily for program vindicators, the local managers' purposes may deserve more attention. On the other hand, if the locals want a whitewash and the higher levels want to understand how the program is using its resources, the evaluator should place more emphasis on the higher echelon's concerns.

However, even people who intend to use evaluation results for specific purposes do not make their decisions solely on the basis of the evaluation. Although the news is a blow to those who expect the world to run on rational principles, evaluation findings alone rarely determine decisions. Other considerations almost inevitably enter in. Each individual in the program community has a set of values and beliefs that influence his stand—for example, "Poor people deserve access to the same mental health services as everyone else," or "Voluntarism is a better way to go than government-provided services." He also often has interests—self-interest—in promoting one course over another. In addition, he has a stock of information—from his prior experience with the program, reports from staff, the grapevine, and from his professional experience and training. These three *I*'s (ideology, interests, and information) are in place, and the new information that comes from evaluation has to contend with them. Essentially, it interacts with them in influencing the positions that people take (Weiss, 1983).

Moreover, there is a fourth *I,* the institution. Program decisions are made within an organizational context (Weiss, 1993). The organization has a history, a set of operating procedures, and a culture, and these institutional elements exert pressures and set constraints. Evaluation findings that imply a need for major change may run into organizational roadblocks, while findings that support the direction in which the organization is moving can be readily embraced.

Then there are all the practical issues that come up when program people seek to implement big changes based on evaluation. They have to consider such issues as the cost of the changes, support or opposition from important political figures, the interest of program staff in keeping the program going, the prevailing political climate, clients' pressure for continued attention, availability of appropriate staff, and so on. In short, when findings suggest fundamental redirection, evaluation findings will contribute to discussion and debate but rarely single-handedly carry the day.

Accordingly, in recent years evaluators have come to pay more attention to the prospects that evaluation can contribute to organizational learning. Organizational learning is often a slow incremental affair, punctuated with occasional spurts of change. There have been many cases where evaluation results have been ignored in the early months after a study's conclusion only to surface two or three years later as one of the rationales for changes in organization activity. In fact, experience has shown that evaluation findings often have significant influence. They provide new concepts and angles of vision, new ways of making sense of events, new possible directions. They puncture old myths. They show that some issues expected to be important are not important and that unexpected issues have become salient. They sometimes occasion a reordering of priorities and a rethinking of program directions. As they percolate into the consciousness of the program community, they shape the ways in which people think about problems and plan their responses.

This view of evaluation as provider of enlightenment is a far cry from old expectations that evaluation would point the way to big decisions about program and policy. The interpretation here may look like a retreat toward insignificance. On the contrary. It is optimistic to recognize that evaluation influences what people know and believe, and that these ideas have long-lasting importance for the kind of world they create. This view celebrates the importance of information. It avoids succumbing to the disillusionment that some evaluators face when the results of their studies are not immediately put into practice. It treasures the instances when the program and policy communities find a direct way to use evaluative results for improvement. It appreciates the complex processes of democratic decision making that do not give any person (however well informed) the authority to make decisions unilaterally but require the participation of many parties in developing new courses of action. On a practical note, it gives evaluators clues on how to move their studies toward more and more responsible use. If the evaluator can identify people in the organization who are willing to listen, and keep up a dialog with them over an extended period of time, she can perhaps influence the scope and pace of the organization's learning trajectory.

Finding attentive listeners and champions of change can be an effective strategy. But the evaluator should not place too much faith in her ability to locate the key decision maker. In fact, there are almost never one or two decision makers. Decisions in our system, particularly in public agencies, almost always involve a great many people in a variety of different offices. Sometimes the legislature and the judiciary get involved, too. Multiple actors have a say.

Therefore, from the start the evaluator should take account of the questions, complaints, and ideas of the variety of people who will take part in making decisions about the program. If the school principal wants an evaluation of a program for gifted and talented students, remember that any decisions that follow on the evaluation will not be his alone. The school superintendent will need to agree, and probably the school board as well. Nor will much happen on the ground (in the program, in the classrooms) unless the teachers go along with the decision.

So when we think about whose use should be served, let us not think of the single decision maker. As Cronbach and Associates (1980) have written, program decisions are made not in a context of command, where one person has all the power and his word is law, but in a context of accommodation, where many people negotiate to reach a decision. The key implication, then, is that the evaluation needs to consider not only the questions of the project manager or program director but also the concerns of other people who will take part in decision making. Beyond that, there are people who help set the climate of opinion around the program, people who appropriate or contribute the funds to run the program, and people who join up for, or fail to participate in, the program. These widening circles of people who are affected in some way by the program—and potentially by the evaluation of the program—are the stakeholders, and the evaluation needs to be alert to the kinds of use that they may make of evaluation results.

The next task, then, is designing the evaluation to provide the answers that are needed. Based on her best estimate of likely use, the evaluator has to make decisions on the basic plan for the evaluation (Chapter 4), measures to be used (Chapter 6), sources of information (Chapter 7), its design (Chapters 8, 9, 10, and 11), and modes of analysis (Chapter 12). Finally she will have to write the report(s) and get the word out to the people who can use the results (Chapter 13).

Summary

Agencies undertake evaluations for a host of rational and nonrational (or at least, nondecisional) reasons. An evaluator newly arrived on the scene should try to understand the purposes that evaluation is expected to serve and the range of expectations (some of them conflicting or contradictory) held by people in different locations in the program community. Realistically she has to design the study in ways that serve the information needs of those who commission the evaluation, but at the same time she has to be aware of the needs and interests of many others in the environment whose actions will affect what happens during and after the study.

I suggest that the evaluator pay attention to the questions of those who face fairly immediate program decisions, those who are most receptive to learning from the evaluation and conscientiously considering its results, and those (like clients) who have few other avenues to make their interests known. Balancing the competing claims calls for a high order of political, as well as conceptual and methodological, skills. Sometimes it requires re-negotiating the original parameters of the study. Since program and policy decisions are influenced by people in many locations, an evaluation is likely to be most influential when it is responsive to questions from a variety of stakeholders.

The distinction between formative and summative evaluation brings a modicum of clarity to demands upon the evaluation. *Formative evaluation* is designed to help program managers, practitioners, and planners improve the design of the program in its developmental phases. *Summative evaluation* is designed to provide information at the end of (at least one cycle of) the program about whether it should be continued, dismantled, or drastically overhauled. Formative/summative evaluation refers to the intention with which the evaluator works. Process/outcome evaluation refers to the phase in a program's life at which evaluation is carried out: during its course or at its conclusion. The two sets of terms, while overlapping, refer to different constructs. I suggest that most programs are never "finalized" but continue to develop as they go on. Therefore, formative data continue to be needed to help in their improvement. Both process and outcome data can be helpful for formative purposes.

Evaluation can be performed by staff within the program agency or by outsiders. Each location has advantages. Inside evaluators understand the organization, its interests and needs, and the opportunities that exist for putting results to use. Insiders also have multiple opportunities to bring results to attention. Outside evaluators have greater autonomy, greater prestige, often a wider range of skills, and a chance to bypass the agency to get results a hearing.

Whether inside or out, evaluators should report to the level in the agency structure that allows them the most appropriate mix of autonomy and access to both information and influence. Reporting to policy levels of an organization will usually minimize attempts to bias the evaluation; reporting to working levels will allow the evaluator to understand what staff do and why they do it and to establish good working relationships with many of those who can later put findings to use.

Evaluation has traditionally stressed the provision of outcome data as a tool to help in decision making. Recent years have seen increased awareness that evaluation findings almost never determine program decisions alone. Policymakers and program managers have to take many other considerations into account. Evaluators should also be alert to the fact that, although some uses of the study are immediate and obvious, much use will be conceptual and difficult to discern with the naked eye. Organizations and members of the policymaking community do not always apply results directly to an immediate decision. More often they learn from evaluation, and their learning affects program decisions subtly and gradually. Nevertheless, the evaluator has to shape the evaluation to answer important questions, so that what the varied audiences learn will lead to policy and program improvements.

3

UNDERSTANDING THE PROGRAM

Programs have fuzzy borders, so that it is not always plain sailing to determine precisely what the program *was* that required evaluation.

—M. W. McLaughlin and D. C. Phillips (1991, p. x)

We should employ metaphors of process, focused activity, marginal change, cumulative transformation, and above all think more imaginatively in terms of determined models of formative, generative processes.

—Frederik Barth (1990, p. 652)

People in the evaluation world talk about program evaluation, but the textbooks and journals put the emphasis on evaluation rather than on the program. Program is somebody else's business. Evaluators come in to whatever program is on the scene, pull out their methodological bag of tricks, and proceed to do the evaluation.

This chapter recommends that evaluators pay close attention to the program. They should be familiar with the general field very early in the game, and they should learn a good deal about the specific happenings of the program under study as the evaluation moves along. They should also understand exactly how the program expects to bring about required change. There are a number of significant reasons for this advice.

Why Program Knowledge Pays

To Develop a Good Sense of the Issues

When the evaluator is well informed at the outset about the type of programming (e.g., family planning services or energy conservation), she has a better idea of the issues that evaluation should address. She knows the general line of development of programming and the controversies in the field. She can gear the study to issues that are current and pressing.

UNDERSTANDING THE PROGRAM

To Formulate Questions

Knowledge of the program helps the evaluator to make evaluative questions relevant and incisive. She can then collect the appropriate data to answer the questions.

To Understand the Data

As evaluation data start coming in, some of the information may look anomalous. Even well along in the study, unexpected and seemingly incongruous findings sometimes emerge. To make sense of them, it helps if the evaluator understands the way that the program is working and how practitioners interact with clients. Such knowledge enables the evaluator to interpret the information she receives and perhaps strike out into new areas of investigation.

To Interpret the Evidence

Only with a good sense of what the program is and how it has been working can the evaluator interpret the meaning of outcome data. If, for example, the program has switched direction in the middle (say, moving from didactic lectures to small-group work in class), knowing about the change is important for drawing conclusions about what worked and what didn't in the program.

To Make Sound Recommendations

Policymakers and program directors expect good data from an evaluation, but often they want more. At the conclusion of a study they want sage counsel about what to do next. If the evaluator is to come out at the end and say something smart and useful about the program, it helps if she knows something about the program going in. Too often in the past the evaluator's recommendations[1] were afterthoughts, poorly thought through, often just the opposite of whatever condition seemed to be associated with low effectiveness. (If the rehabilitation counselors in a low-effectiveness program had low levels of education, the recommendation might be to hire better educated staff—even though there was no evidence that the education of staff affected client rehabilitation.) The evaluator without program savvy has little way of knowing whether her potential recommendations are practical, feasible to implement, politically acceptable, financially affordable, or stand much chance of making things better. Program knowledge improves the odds.

For Reporting

However carefully the evaluator may specify that she is studying the Southwestern Lagos Water Development Project, readers of the report are likely to think of the study as an evaluation of water development projects in less developed countries generally and to draw conclusions that go far beyond the case at hand. The report should do more than name the project. It should specify what the project did, how it was run, what was in and not in the project, and even something about surrounding

---

[1]Evaluators do not always believe it is their job to develop recommendations from the data. As they see it, they give the evidence and let program specialists decide what to do with it. Other evaluators believe that recommendation giving is an important contribution that evaluators can make and that program people want and expect this kind of help. See Chapter 12 for further discussion of the topic.

conditions. This helps to avoid grandiose generalizations that fail to take into account the unique characteristics of the particular project. The reader can then estimate the extent to which the project is typical of the run of projects, or similar to the one project in which he is interested, and therefore a reasonable or unreasonable basis on which to reach judgments.

For Meta-Analysis

Meta-analysis is the systematic summary of the results from a number of different evaluations of the same kind of program. In recent years evaluators have developed statistical procedures for combining data from different studies in order to reach summary estimates of the extent of success of, say, preschool programs or juvenile delinquency prevention programs. In Chapter 10, I discuss methods of meta-analysis.

Here it is important to note that meta-analysts need a lot of information about what the program actually was and did. Particularly when they try to characterize programs as open classroom programs or mental health counseling programs, they need to understand the reality of the program. Often they have to decide whether a program fits their label, and to do that, they need to know whether it fulfills 5 or 10 or 20 of the criteria of open classrooms (Tyler, 1991/1942) or mental health counseling. More than that, meta-analysts are now trying to understand which specific features of a program are responsible for better or poorer showings (Cook et al., 1992). For this task, specification of the attributes of the program-in-operation are essential.

For all these reasons, evaluators are well advised to understand the larger field of programming and the specifics of the program or project they are studying. Most evaluators are not experts in a particular program field. Only after some years of working in the same domain do they acquire a degree of expertise. But right from the start they can take steps to advance their understanding.

Characterizing the Program

Social programs are complex undertakings. They are an amalgam of dreams and personalities, rooms and theories, paper clips and organizational structure, clients and activities, budgets and photocopies, and great intentions. Evaluators of social programs look with something akin to jealousy at evaluators in agriculture who evaluate a new strain of wheat or evaluators in medicine who evaluate the effects of a new drug. These are physical things you can see, touch, and—above all—replicate. The same stimulus can be produced again, and other researchers can study its consequences—under the same or different conditions, with similar or different subjects, but with some assurance that they are looking at the effects of the same *thing*.

Social programs are not nearly so specific. They incorporate a range of components, styles, people, and procedures. It becomes difficult to describe what the program really is. In special cases, a program can be expressed in terms that are clear and reproducible: for example, a change in highway speed limits or a decrease in the size of probation officers' caseloads. Here the program is the change in speed limits or caseloads, and people want to know how much difference the change in scale makes. Another kind of readily describable program is one that involves an increase or decrease in cash payments or charges. Examples would be an increase in unemployment benefits, a decrease in subsidies to peanut farmers, a change in the minimum wage, a rise in rents charged in public housing.

Fairly easy to characterize, too, are programs that involve a mechanism that is well understood or available for inspection. Mammography is mammography, and to understand a program that makes mammograms available, the evaluator probably needs to know only where and to whom they are offered. A new mathematics curriculum also looks fairly clear. However, teachers may implement the curriculum in vastly different ways, and the evaluator cannot assume that the written curriculum equals the program. She needs to find out how different teachers use the new material in class.

In most social programs, it takes effort to understand the content of the program, what actually goes on. Operations often differ markedly from day to day and from staff member to staff member. With programs as large and amorphous as regional economic development or federal technical assistance for state health planning, it takes a major effort just to describe and analyze what the program is. Process evaluation specializes in comprehending the operations of the program.

In outcome evaluation, an evaluator may question whether she needs to spend much time worrying about program content. If evaluation data show that the program yields the desired results, does it make any difference whether it is using rote drill, psychoanalysis, or black magic? A few evaluators still see the program as a black box, the contents of which do not concern them; they are charged with discovering effects. But if the evaluator has no idea of what the program really is, she may fail to ask the right questions. Perhaps she believes the inflated barrage of program propaganda and expects mountain-moving outcomes from what are really puny efforts. More likely, she looks for the wrong order of effects. She looks for the attainment of the types of outcomes that have been verbalized, when the main resources of the operating program have been invested in a different course of action.

Furthermore, unless there is some reasonably accurate and coherent definition of the program, the evaluator does not know to what to attribute the outcomes she observes. Decision makers need to know what it was that worked or didn't work, what it is that should be adopted throughout the system or modified. In an extreme case, when a program is a smashing success and 40 communities want to adopt it forthwith, what is it that we tell them to adopt?

The evaluator has to discover the reality of the program rather than its illusion. If she accepts the description given in the application for funds or in publicity releases, she may evaluate a phantom program. The study will be attributing effects (or no effects) to a program that never took place at all, or one that operated at so low a level of competence or in such a different manner that it hardly deserves to be called by the program name. For example, a business school is supposed to be introducing consideration of ethics into its courses, but some faculty members do not know how to go about this kind of teaching and some do not see the new charge as their business. A recreation program for schoolchildren may be closed on weekends when children have free time; it may be closed erratically so that the children get discouraged from attending; it may be offering activities that fail to attract participants. It will hardly be necessary to collect data on the effects of these programs, because there is little or no program in operation.

Getting to Know the Program

Evaluators can take a number of steps to familiarize themselves with the program area and with the specific program they will be studying. The first and most obvious way is to read about the field. Read what people have written about traffic safety or vocational guidance or whatever the program area may be. Find a good overview book or journal article, perhaps with the help of a reference librarian, and pursue citations in that source that sound interesting. There may be an annual review in the field or an informative overview in an entry in a specialty encyclopedia.

A special resource is previous evaluations. Find as many reports on similar programs as possible, whether they are published or unpublished. The prospective evaluator will learn a good deal about the problematics of the program, and along the way will pick up tips about methodology—the kinds of methods that others have used and how well these methods worked to yield relevant information. Prior evaluations are full of information and object lessons, good and bad. It is worth taking full advantage of the program knowledge they provide. In fact, a required first step in conducting an evaluation should be to read previous evaluation reports on programs of the same and similar kind. Reviews of the literature may exist that summarize a spectrum of past results and identify key issues and problems.

Another source of program information about the generic field is people, particularly people who work in programs of the type the evaluator will study. Talking to program directors and practitioners will give the evaluator insights that "book larnin" may not divulge.

Next the evaluator needs to learn about the immediate program at hand. Her approach can vary from an informal and unstructured look-around all the way to systematic, data-based inquiry. At the informal level, observation is much on the order of what writers on organizational management call "management by walking around" (Peters & Waterman, 1982). You walk around, look, and chat. When visits are unscheduled, the observer has a sense that she is getting an inside view of the program. A few meetings with selected groups (staff, administrators, clients) can yield additional information. In a more formal way, a qualitative pilot study can contribute systematic information.

What the observer finds out depends in large measure on where she looks, whom she talks to, and how much prior programmatic knowledge she has. Prior knowledge is important so that the observer knows *where* to look and *whom* to talk to. If she is a novice and uninformed about the extent of possible variation from site to site, or unaware of the kinds of misfeasance and nonfeasance that program folks might like to keep under wraps, those who are in charge of the tour can, if they choose, direct her to places that will give the picture they want to paint. But with a little program savvy, the observer can find out a great deal through informal observation and conversation. She just needs to be sure to touch a variety of bases and ask probing questions.

A more systematic procedure is monitoring. Monitoring is similar to process evaluation but usually somewhat less formal and intended for a different purpose. Monitoring is generally undertaken by the funding agency that provides the financial support for the program or the oversight agency responsible for program standards. These agencies want to know what is happening in the program for account-ability purposes (and perhaps as a guide to the kinds of technical assistance the project needs). They have a responsibility to be sure that local projects are doing what they are supposed to do. Legislators want to know whether the intent of the legislation they passed is being carried out.

Monitoring, as Rossi and Freeman (1993) write, is frequently directed at finding out (a) how well the program is reaching the target population it is intended to serve, (b) its fidelity to the original design for activities, and (c) the appropriateness of its expenditure of money and other resources. Learning these things about the program—whether it is serving the right people, delivering the right kind of services, or spending its money in the right ways—gives funders and oversight agencies the information to oversee the appropriateness of local operations.

Note that under the usual definition, monitoring starts with a standard in view. It knows which categories of people are supposed to be served, which kinds of activities should be carried out, and how money should be spent, and it measures what the program does against these yardsticks. The criteria that monitoring applies generally come from the initial charter for the program and the rules of the funding agency. While these existing standards give the monitoring process a clear focus, they are also a set of blinders. They direct attention toward a limited scope of conditions and away from all the other things happening in the program and in the environment.

If program staff take a less blinkered view, agencies can learn more from monitoring than merely whether the rules are being followed. If they find widespread deviations from intended ways of work, it is true that the reason may be the shortcomings of the projects. But another reason may be that the original design was not in tune with reality. The program was designed to serve displaced workers whose companies, or whose entire industry, had gone out of business and offer them training for new occupations. But the project may have found few such displaced workers in the area. Most seem to have found employment in other companies or moved away. When monitoring identifies such diversions from intent, and at least provisional explanations for them, it provides important clues for the modification of existing policy—or even the need for new policies.

For the evaluator, monitoring information can be a significant category of data. She can take advantage of whatever monitoring data other people have collected and she can collect her own. The data will orient her to the project and give her a sense of what is going on. If she has the time, resources, and authorization, she can go further and conduct a process evaluation study, gathering systematic data over a period of time about the implementation of program activities.

What Is the Program Trying to Achieve?

A useful way to begin conceptualizing the program is by looking at what it is trying to accomplish. A sensible place to start is with its official goals. Although official goals are only one source of understanding, they represent an entry point into the matter of program intention.

Most programs have some kind of written statement (applications for funding, recruitment announcements, public relations brochures) that describe their activities, and often these statements contain a description of program goals. If the goals are framed in clear and specific terms, they are a good source of information. An energy conservation program aims to reduce the amount of electricity that householders use. A road-building program in a developing country seeks to enable small farmers to transport their produce to the city and thereby increase their income. These kinds of statements shed considerable light on what the program is about.

But some programs lack official statements. If the evaluator asks program staff about goals, they may discuss them in terms of the number of people they intend to serve, the kinds of service they will offer, and similar process information. For program implementers, these are program goals in a real and valid sense, but they are not the primary currency in which the evaluator deals. She is interested in the intended *consequences* of the program.

Other programs have goal statements that are hazy, ambiguous, or hard to pin down. Occasionally, the official goals are merely a long list of pious and partly incompatible platitudes. Goals, either in official documents or in program managers' discussion, can be framed in such terms as *improve education, enhance the quality of life, improve the life chances of children and families, strengthen democratic processes.* Such global goals give little direction for an evaluator who wants to understand the program in detail.

This kind of vague formulation is so commonplace that some writers on evaluation discard the discussion of goals as being too abstract and long term. They prefer to talk about objectives as the near-term down-to-earth effects at which programs set their sights. They say that it is possible for an evaluation to find out the extent to which programs meet their objectives (in this locution), where it would be impossible to tell whether they meet their goals of improving education or enhancing the quality of life. I agree that we should concentrate on specific objectives, but I don't want to abandon the useful word *goals*. Instead, I'll try to bring it down from the stratosphere and use it to mean a program's specific, measurable, near-term aims.

Evaluators wonder why program goals are often stated in fuzzy terms. Part of the explanation probably lies in practitioners' concentration on concrete matters of program functioning and their pragmatic mode of operation. They often have an intuitive rather than an analytic approach to program development and concentrate on formulating activities rather than objectives. But there is also a sense in which ambiguity serves a useful function: It masks underlying divergences in intent. Support from many quarters inside and outside the program agency is required to get a program off the ground, and the glittering generalities that pass for goal statements are meant to satisfy a variety of interests and perspectives. Everyone can agree on improving the neighborhood, where they might come to (verbal) blows over identification of the specific outcomes they have in mind.

Sometimes the divergence in intentions that is papered over through vagueness operates at different levels of the hierarchy. The higher-ups may have one set of purposes—for example, to reduce fraud and overpayment to recipients of public assistance. Direct-service staff may have a different inclination. More sympathetic to the clients with whom they deal, they may want to get them every cent that is legally coming to them and even deliver additional services that improve their lot. If the evaluator listens to official statements, she may learn about the mission of reducing fraud and abuse, but she may not hear about the tension between reducing welfare outlays and maximizing payments and services.

When goals are unclear or ambiguous, more than the evaluation can be affected. Where there is little consensus on what a program is trying to do, the staff may be working at cross-purposes. One side benefit of evaluation is to focus attention on the formulation of goals in terms of the specific behaviors that program practitioners aim to achieve. The effort may force disagreements into the open and lead to conflict. But if differences can be reconciled (and the program may not be viable if they are not), the clarification can hardly help but rationalize program implementation. It may reveal discrepancies between program goals and program content, in which case either the content or the goals should be changed. When a sense of common purpose is reached, the logic and rationality of practice are likely to be enhanced.

A similar kind of problem for the evaluator arises when conditions change. The official goals were fine when the program began and fully descriptive of what the program aimed to do. However, over time, the environment changed, the type of client changed, the staff changed, the budget changed, and the reigning idea of how the program should operate also changed. The program has become considerably different from what it was when the goals were first enunciated. They no longer fit.

When the evaluator recognizes the obsolescence of the goal statement, she can get contemporary information from program managers and staff. They can be a first-rate source and fill her in on intents, as well as on subtle shadings of intention that the official statements rarely mention. However, direct conversations with the people involved do not necessarily solve all problems. Sometimes staff find it difficult to arrive at a clear-cut formulation of the program's goals. Kallen (1966) tells of working with a committee to discuss evaluation of a program for gang youth. Asked to specify the program's goals, the committee members came up with such things as improving the behavior of the youth, helping them become better citizens, and improving their schoolwork. When they tried to be more specific about goals, they felt that behavior and citizenship were too vague to describe what they really were trying to get youth to learn, and they weren't sure that the program actually did anything directly to improve youths' school grades. Kallen reported the discouraging story:

> Finally it turned out that a number of the area residents objected to the young people's use of swear words, and it was decided that one measure of behavioral improvement would be the reduction in swearing, and that this was something the detached worker should aim for in his interaction with the youngsters he was working with. [Was the group identifying program goals or making up new ones?] It was therefore agreed that part of the criteria of success would be a reduction in swearing. I might add that this was the only measure of success upon which the evaluation team and the program advisory committee could agree.

A further complication arises when the program seeks not only to reach official goals but to achieve other things, sometimes in addition, sometimes instead. For example, a social service agency applied for, and received, government funds to run a training program for the unemployed. The goal that it was willing to state up front was that the program would teach the trainees new skills and help them find new jobs. But the agency had other unstated purposes: to improve community relations with people of color in its neighborhood, meet federal regulations against discrimination, encourage members of minority groups to work on its staff, and gain the additional funding that came with the program grant (Meyers, 1981). These are perfectly legitimate objectives. Agencies have to be concerned with more than reaching instrumental goals; they have to maintain the organization in its environment. An exclusive focus on program goals runs the risk of ignoring the system-maintenance goals that are part of organizational life. Being concerned about these other things doesn't mean that the agency is lying about its interest in doing a good job training program for the unemployed, but doing good job training is just one of the items on its list.

Sometimes system-maintenance goals get in the way of attaining program objectives. For example, an agency runs an outpatient mental health program to help troubled people cope with daily living. Helping troubled people is one goal. Another is preventing staff members from burnout, being overwhelmed by the demands of patients. In some cases, the goal of making life easier for staff supersedes the therapeutic goal, and the quality of service deteriorates.

Clients of the program are often worth consulting. They may have different ideas about goals. They may have enrolled in the program to accomplish something different from the things that staff are promulgating. Staff of a methadone maintenance project may discuss their goal of weaning drug abusers from heroin and thereby preventing crimes committed to pay for heroin. The clients may or may not value methadone as a substitute for the highs of illegal drugs, but their expectations from the program may center on its function as a social setting, a hangout, a place to spend time with friends in social activities. To understand what goes on in the program, and the potential conflicts between staff and client expectations, the evaluator may want to hear the goals of other parties besides the staff.

Then, too, many programs have multiple goals. In most cases, the several goals are consistent and represent various facets of a multi-modal program. A program to upgrade a public housing project plans to rehabilitate housing units so that living space is clean, safe, in good working order, and reasonably spacious; it also plans to develop a tenants' organization so that residents will develop a warmer sense of community and take responsibility for maintaining the apartments in reasonable condition; it wants to encourage the tenants' organization to take responsibility for policing the public spaces in order to reduce crime; and so on. These manifold purposes should ideally all be met in a successful program.

However, with complex and ambitious goals, managers and tenants have an opportunity to select that part of the charge that they wish to concentrate on. In some locations people may actively work toward certain of the objectives; in other locations, effort may be going into something quite different. That is one of the risks in programs with complex goals—that people will choose those aspects of the multiple mission that are congenial to them and ignore the rest. To really understand the program, it pays to know which goals are real.

Goals are real to the extent that people are actively devoting time and effort to working toward them. This is not always easy to see in documents or learn from conversations with funders or program managers. From time to time, budget documents give useful clues, at least if they show on which activities money is being spent. (However, many budgets lump staff salaries into one category without indicating what functions these staff are performing.) Watching the program in operation is probably the best way to understand where energies are being spent, and talking to direct-service staff and clients can give further useful clues.

How the Program Works: Surfacing the Program's Theories of Change

For evaluation purposes, it is useful to know not only what the program is expected to achieve but also how it expects to achieve it. As Rein (1981) has written, "A program is a theory and an evaluation is its test" (p. 141). In order to organize the evaluation to provide a responsible test, the evaluator needs to understand the theoretical premises on which the program is based.

The notion of defining program theory has not typically been a component of evaluation. Much evaluation is done by investigating outcomes without much attention to the paths by which they were produced. But evaluation is increasingly being called upon not only to answer the question "Did the program work?" but also "What made it work? Why was it successful or unsuccessful?" and even "How can we make it better?" To make a respectable contribution to such a discussion, it helps if the evaluator understands—and investigates—the program's explicit or implicit theory.

Programs are complicated phenomena, generally born out of experience and professional lore. Teachers, probation officers, social workers, international development specialists, physicians, safety engineers—all develop social programs from a mixture of what they learned in professional school, what they experienced on the job, what stories of other people's experience suggest, and perhaps some social science and evaluation learnings. Programs are not likely to be laid out in rational terms with clear-cut statements of why certain program activities have been selected and which actions are expected to lead to which desired ends.

Yet when the evaluator undertakes to define program theory, those are just the things she wants to know: What ideas and assumptions link the program's inputs to attainment of the desired ends? Getting a purchase on the answer is an even harder task than learning about program goals. Goals are at least a familiar and long-standing concept. The program's theories of change sound strange to many program designers and practitioners.

By theory, I don't mean anything highbrow or multi-syllabic. I mean the set of beliefs that underlie action. The theory doesn't have to be uniformly accepted. *It doesn't have to be right.* It is a set of hypotheses upon which people build their program plans. It is an explanation of the causal links that tie program inputs to expected program outputs, or as Bickman (1987) has put it, "a plausible and sensible model of how a program is supposed to work" (p. 5). Wholey (1987) says that program theory identifies "program resources, program activities, and intended program outcomes, and specifies a chain of causal assumptions linking program resources, activities, intermediate outcomes, and ultimate goals" (p. 78).

Let's take a simple example. Let's say the program (or policy) is an increase in teachers' salaries, and the increase is justified on grounds that it will increase students' achievement. What is the theory that links higher teacher pay to increased student achievement? I can think of a number of possibilities (see Figure 3-1).

One theory might be that higher pay will improve teacher morale; higher morale will lead teachers to work harder at teaching; they will put more effort into preparation and pedagogy, and this will improve students' understanding of material. The mechanisms here are assumed to be first an increase in morale and then an improvement in pedagogy. A variant of this theory would be that with higher morale comes a more pleasant social climate. Teachers develop more congenial relationships with students, which leads students to seek to maintain good relations with the teachers, so students work harder and therefore learn more. Here the mechanism would be better interpersonal relations.

Another theory would be that higher pay allows teachers to give up their second jobs. Teachers who used to moonlight in order to earn enough money can now put their full energies into teaching. Greater energy and attention lead to more thorough preparation of lessons, greater variety in strategies of pedagogy, more effective teaching, and thus better student learning.

FIGURE 3-1 PROGRAM THEORY MODEL: SOME MECHANISMS BY WHICH HIGHER TEACHER PAY MAY BE LINKED TO INCREASED STUDENT ACHIEVEMENT

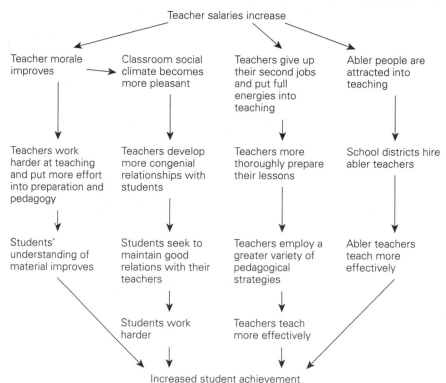

A quite different explanation would be that higher salaries attract abler people into teaching. Because college students learn that they will be better paid in the teaching profession, brighter college students prepare for teaching. Because brighter students become qualified as teachers, school districts hire abler teachers, abler teachers then teach better, and better teaching leads to greater student learning. This program theory has an entirely different time dimension. Evaluation might not be able to locate effects for four to seven years, because it will take time for word of higher salaries to get around, a different caliber of college student to prepare for teaching and be hired, and for the expected "better teaching" to take place and have effects. If the expectation is that the school district offering higher salaries will lure good teachers away from other districts, the time scale would be shorter. But at least one school district relying on such an expectation found that higher salaries induced current teachers to stay on the job longer, thus preventing vacancies from opening up.

One can think of other program theories as well. Higher salaries would, in another formulation, lead to higher social status for teachers, which would lead to greater respect from parents. Greater respect would translate into greater parental support for school demands, such as helping children with homework, encouraging more regular student attendance, support for school disciplinary actions, and more parental participation in school activities. Such increased parent-teacher cooperation would give students greater respect for school and teacher, cause them to behave more properly and study more conscientiously, which would lead to better student achievement.

A final program theory might posit a chain of negative consequences. Higher teacher salaries might provoke parental resentment of the higher taxes they have to pay, which would lead to subtle acts of sabotage against teachers (such as allowing students to get away with truancy, disrespect of teachers, and disruption in the classroom), which would lead to greater classroom discontinuity and disorder, which would reduce opportunities for learning, which would reduce student achievement. To locate such counter assumptions, the evaluator can talk to opponents of the program who have theories about why the program is apt to be a dud—or worse.

Program theory, as I use the term, refers to the *mechanisms* that mediate between the delivery (and receipt) of the program and the emergence of the outcomes of interest. The operative mechanism of change isn't the program activities per se but the response that the activities generate. For example, contraceptive counseling is expected to reduce the incidence of pregnancy, but the mechanism is not the counseling itself. It might be the knowledge that participants absorb from the counseling. Or it might be the confidence that women develop to assert themselves in sexual relationships, the undermining of cultural taboos against family planning, or the signal of a shift in power relations between men and women. These or any of several other cognitive/affective/social/cultural responses would be the mechanisms leading to desired outcomes.

Program Theory and Implementation Theory

Program theory puts the emphasis on the responses of people to program activities. But there is another kind of assumption in programming, one that program people are more likely to articulate: that if the program does all the things it intends to do, good things will happen. Take the example of a job training program whose goal is to enable poor youth to get jobs and become productive earners. The program's activities are to teach craft skills and job readiness skills, such as regular attendance and appropriate dress. Staff's assumptions might be that the program has to take the following steps: publicize the program widely, enroll youth who meet eligibility criteria, provide good training for attractive occupations in accessible locations, give stipends, provide child care, give supportive counsel, refer youth to available jobs. If the program does all those things, the expectation is that youth will be employed.

Moving from intentions and plans to sound program activities is the major challenge that agency managers face. Much of their energy is concentrated on ensuring that the program works smoothly and well. Implementation implicitly incorporates a theory about what is required to translate objectives into ongoing service delivery and program operation. Such a theory is what I call implementation theory. The assumption is that if the activities are conducted as planned, with sufficient quality, intensity, and fidelity to plan, the desired results will be forthcoming. A number of evaluations examine implementation theories of this kind (e.g., McGraw et al., 1996; Pentz et al., 1990). Implementation theory does not deal with the processes that mediate between program services and achievement of program goals but focuses on the delivery of program services.

The two kinds of theory, program theory and implementation theory, intertwine in the evolution of the program. As Figure 3-2 shows, each stage of activity assumes an appropriate response from participants, and responses of participants condition the next stages of the program. Unless the agency carries out the scheduled activities well, it is not likely that participants will make progress toward the goal. And if the participants are uninterested, unmotivated, irregular in attendance, unwilling or unable to learn, or resistant to taking jobs, not much progress will be made. The two streams of activity have to interact to produce desired outcomes.

I call the combination of program theory and implementation theory the program's theories of change.

Organizing the Evaluation to Investigate Program Theories

A big advantage of understanding the program's theories of change is that they can provide the basis for the evaluation. The evaluator can organize the evaluation to trace the unfolding of the assumptions. The evaluation can collect data on the interim markers that are expected to appear. In Figure 3-1, does teachers' morale improve? Do they put more effort into preparation? If so, the evaluator can follow the chain further and find out whether teachers are in fact improving the caliber of their instruction. If morale rises but teachers are not doing anything different in the classroom, the evaluation can identify the point at which the posited theory breaks down.

In the job training program in Figure 3-2, does information about the program's availability reach the target audience? Do young people sign up? Does the staff provide state-of-the-art training for occupations for which there is local demand? Do youth attend regularly? Do they learn? Do they develop more positive attitudes toward work? Does the program provide support and assistance? The evaluation traces each step along the route to see whether the stages appear as anticipat-

FIGURE 3-2 THEORIES OF CHANGE: IMPLEMENTATION THEORY
AND PROGRAM THEORY IN A JOB TRAINING PROGRAM

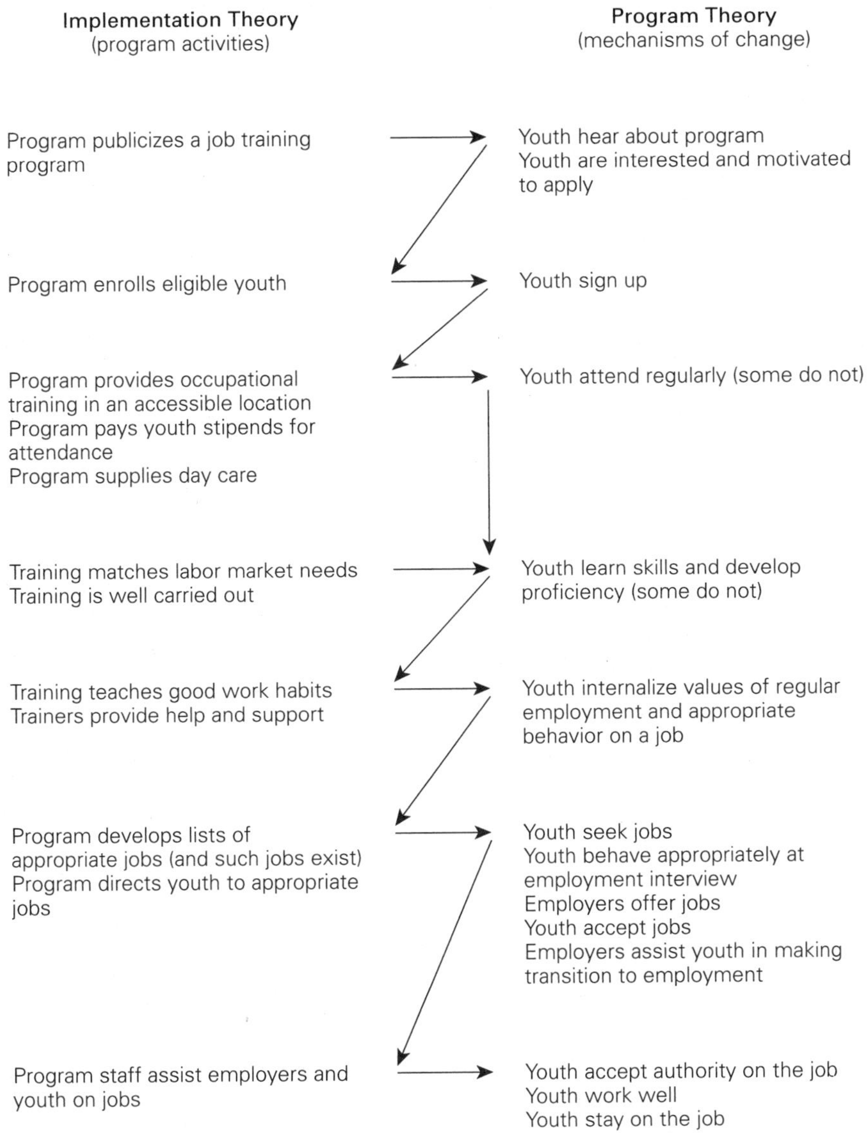

Implementation Theory
(program activities)

Program Theory
(mechanisms of change)

Program publicizes a job training
program

Youth hear about program
Youth are interested and motivated
to apply

Program enrolls eligible youth

Youth sign up

Program provides occupational
training in an accessible location
Program pays youth stipends for
attendance
Program supplies day care

Youth attend regularly (some do not)

Training matches labor market needs
Training is well carried out

Youth learn skills and develop
proficiency (some do not)

Training teaches good work habits
Trainers provide help and support

Youth internalize values of regular
employment and appropriate
behavior on a job

Program develops lists of
appropriate jobs (and such jobs exist)
Program directs youth to appropriate
jobs

Youth seek jobs
Youth behave appropriately at
employment interview
Employers offer jobs
Youth accept jobs
Employers assist youth in making
transition to employment

Program staff assist employers and
youth on jobs

Youth accept authority on the job
Youth work well
Youth stay on the job

ed. If things go as expected, the evaluation can tell *how* the program worked in achieving its goals; it can explain the steps and processes that led to desired results. If data do not confirm some of the steps (e.g., if staff do not locate job openings for trained youth), the evaluation can show where the program goes off the tracks.

The evaluator uses program theories to plan points for data collection. (As we will note in later chapters, the evaluator can use other techniques to plan which data to collect as well.) She can collect data to find out if the program carried out each step of the plan of activities and if each step led to the next step and to expected responses from participants. (An excellent example is Holder, 1997.)

It is also wise to build in theories of unintended consequences, unplanned and unwanted chains of events that the program may set in motion. Evaluators have learned that unanticipated consequences are all around us. When legislators mandate severe sentences for certain classes of crimes, a frequent consequence is that juries become less likely to convict defendants of those crimes. Evidently a jury can believe that the mandatory sentence is too harsh for the person and/or the circumstances and thus refuse to convict. Instead of increasing the severity of punishment, the new law in actuality reduces the severity of punishment. Or a school system that wants to reduce truancy among high school students adopts a policy that refuses class credit to any student with more than 10 unexcused absences in a class during the semester. Some students thereupon attend more regularly, the goal of the policy, but for those who have exceeded the 10-day maximum, there is no incentive to do the classwork, take tests seriously, or even show up.

Theory, or better still, theories, direct the evaluator's attention to likely types of near-term and longer-term effects. The two big advantages of developing the evaluation on the basis of program theories are as follows:

First, the evaluation provides early indications of program effectiveness. It need not wait until final outcomes appear (or fail to appear). It examines the intermediate stages between the initiation of the program and its long-term effects, and in that way gets early clues about what is going well and where anomalies are showing up. If breakdown occurs in the premises about implementation, the implications are immediate and direct: Fix the way the program is being run. If breakdown occurs in markers of early participant progress, the conceptual basis on which the program is predicated may need to be reexamined.

Early data on measures relevant to the program's long-term success are especially useful when the program has an extended time line. For example, a program that aims to revitalize an inner-city neighborhood will take a decade or more to achieve results. Theory-based evaluation calls for the collection and reporting of data on early phases that are conceptually linked to the program's ability to produce long-term success. That is, the data are not just desired interim outcomes; they are the interim outcomes that are considered to be paths to long-term effects. They are part of the assumed causal chain.

The other big advantage of theory-based evaluation is that it helps to explain how and why effects occurred. If events work out as expected, the evaluator can say with a fair degree of confidence how the effects were generated. By following the sequence of stages, it shows the microsteps that led from program inputs through to outcomes. Where several different theoretical assumptions are being tracked, the evaluator can show which of them has the better empirical support.

Such detailed tracking gives a sense of whether the program was responsible for observed changes. That is a big issue in evaluation, whether the program is responsible for whatever outcomes are observed. Many things other than the program might give rise to desired outcomes. The usual way to tell whether the program was responsible is to compare units that received the program with equivalent units that did not. In many programs, such as the neighborhood revitalization program, it is not feasible to use comparison units; similar neighborhoods are too few and too different from each other to provide sensible comparisons. In order to get any purchase on the question of whether the program was the responsible agent, the tracing of program theory can help. A careful tracing of the unfolding of stages of theory provides indications of how well the theories explain what happens and therefore of how implicated the program was in events and outcomes. As Chen and Rossi (1987) state, theory-based evaluation helps to assure that the results identified are firmly connected to what the program has been doing and that they are *due to* program activities.

A side advantage of setting down the expected paths of change is that it sensitizes the evaluator to shifts in program strategy that make her evaluation design irrelevant. Suppose the job training program has had difficulties in operation, and to overcome them the managers have shifted course. They have found that trainees do not have transportation to the suburbs where good jobs are located. To maintain the viability of the program, managers have shifted to providing subsidized transportation. The original process model is obsolete and must be modified to reflect the new conditions. Some new processes are hypothesized and some old ones discarded; new items and directional lines are added and old ones dropped. The model is adapted to current realities, and measurements and analyses follow the new course. The evaluator, alerted early to the changes in program operations and assumptions, keeps her study flexible enough to be relevant.

In a review of social experiments, Cook and Shadish (1994) discuss the need for generalizing the causal relationships discovered through social experiments. They conclude with a call for "identifying the micro-mediating processes that causally connect a treatment to an outcome, usually through a process of theoretical specification, measurement, and data analysis" (p. 576). That is a good description of basing evaluation on program theory.

Building Program Theory

It is not necessary to come up with a single program theory that seeks to explain how the program will obtain the happy consequences expected from it. As in our teacher salary example, it is often useful to have a set of alternative theories for the evaluation study to examine. If one theory does not work out as hypothesized, there are alternative pathways to explore.

How does the evaluator go about constructing a program theory or theories? Usually she doesn't construct theories so much as help the program people to surface their own latent theories. They have some ideas in their mind about how program inputs are supposed to lead to program outcomes, and the evaluator can ask and probe and question until they articulate their assumptions. The evaluator may find that different people on the program staff have different assumptions. That's all right. The evaluator can work with multiple theories. She may find that some of the assumptions sound unpersuasive and overly optimistic. In such a case, she should ask additional questions to see whether the practitioners have something further in mind, such an intermediate step or a picture of outside conditions that would foster the linkage they are positing. That information should be included in the theory, too. The evaluator should keep probing until she is sure that she has uncovered all the assumptions and expectations that program people hold.

If program people draw a blank, or find the exercise unappealing, the evaluator can send up a few trial balloons. She can offer hypotheses based on her own understanding of what the program is and does. Her knowledge may come from watching the program in operation, from acquaintance with similar programs, from social science, or from logical reasoning. Common sense is not a bad guide. Drawing on her analysis of what the program expects to achieve and how it is going about its work, she can offer speculations about the underlying assumptions. For example, if a job training program brings in local business people to teach the sessions, she may hazard guesses that the strategy is based on the businessmen's expertise, on their willingness to donate their time free of charge, or on the hope that they will offer the trainees jobs after the program. She tries these hypotheses with program personnel. With this kind of prod, they are likely to be able to elaborate further.

Who shall settle on the final version of program theory is a matter of contention among evaluation authors. Wholey (1987) and Patton (1989) emphasize the role of program personnel and other stakeholders. Chen and Rossi (1980, 1983) put their faith in social science knowledge and theory, and therefore give the evaluator a bigger say. Chen (1990) suggests that it is possible to follow both courses and generate several theories. Then the final synthesis can be done either by the evaluator alone using her professional judgment or by the evaluator working with key stakeholders (Weiss, 1995, 1997). Inasmuch as one of the benefits of constructing program theory is the enhanced communication it generates between practitioners and evaluators (Chen, 1990; McClintock, 1990), it seems sensible to involve a number of people in the final choice.

Use of program theory as a map for evaluation doesn't necessarily imply that every step of every possible theory has to be studied. Once the theories are in hand, the evaluator can work with funders, program managers, and others to decide which of the several lines of thinking is most central to their concerns. Choices always have to be made in designing an evaluation about which lines of inquiry to pursue. The theory map provides a picture of the whole intellectual landscape so that people can make choices with full awareness of what they are ignoring as well as what they are choosing to study.

Using Theories of Change as a Guide to Evaluation

A program theory usually includes (a) program inputs, such as resources and organizational auspices; (b) program activities, which represent the manner in which the program is implemented; (c) interim outcomes—that is, the chain of responses the activities elicit, which are expected to lead on to (d) desired end results.

Let's look at how an evaluator can use program theory to guide an evaluation. Figure 3-3 presents a program of teacher visits to students' homes (Weiss, 1972). The intent of the program is to improve students' achievement in reading. The home

FIGURE 3-3 PROGRAM THEORY MODEL: TEACHER VISITS TO STUDENTS' HOMES

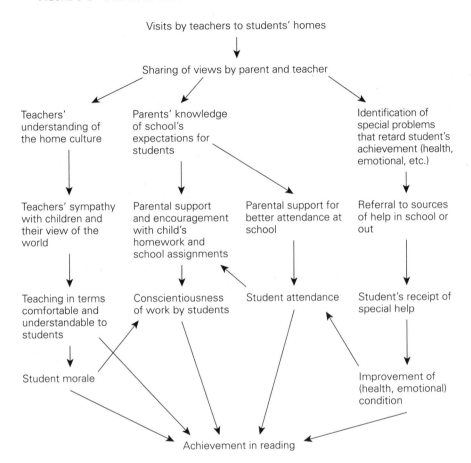

visits may serve several functions. One assumption may be that teachers provide the parents with knowledge about the school's expectations for their child's performance (attendance, homework, and so on). As a consequence of such knowledge, parents may monitor the student's attendance and help him do assigned work more conscientiously. The student will then do better work and his reading achievement will improve. Another theory could be that the visits give the teacher the opportunity to understand parents and the culture of the home. With better knowledge and understanding, teachers have greater sympathy with student's worldview and adapt lessons to fit. Students feel appreciated and respected and their reading achievement improves. A third theory would hold that teachers and parents share knowledge about any special problems that impede the student's achievement, such as dyslexia, emotional problems, or poor eyesight. With this conversation, parents and teachers cooperate to see that the student receives the necessary assistance, and when the problem is ameliorated, the student's achievement increases.

How did I arrive at these theories? I started with the program of teacher visits and the expected outcome of improved student reading performance. Then I filled in the space between with guesses about how one might get from (a) to (d). I used a single outcome, but one can easily use two or more outcomes. (It might take a separate analysis for each one.) As more evaluations develop and test program theories, the hope is that less guesswork will be involved and more knowledge, at least provisional knowledge.

One can also include contingencies in the theory—that is, conditions under which one thing will happen and conditions under which something else will happen. For example, contingencies might come into play in the job training program in Figure 3-2. In communities where the economy is good and jobs are available, the theory might state that trainees go out looking for jobs and find them. However, in communities in recession or with high unemployment, trainees seek jobs but do not necessarily get them.

Similarly, one can envision a theory that makes distinctions among subgroups of people. For example, delinquents assigned to a community service program may respond to the program differently depending on whether they are first-time offenders or repeaters.[2] First-time offenders may absorb the lessons of the program and view their work in the community as atonement for violation of the law. Delinquents with a longer record may regard their hours of community service as punishment and scoff at efforts to redirect their beliefs and values. This illustration suggests the possibilities of elaborating program theories as the evaluator and program staff gain experience, knowledge, and confidence.

Again, it is useful to posit some theories that produce unintended effects, or in the lilting words of a cultural anthropologist, "seek to distinguish actors' purposes from the unsought entailments of their acts" (Barth, 1990: 650). Discussion about what might go astray can be useful on several counts. It can help program staff try to foresee unwanted side effects and guard against them, and it can call such possible effects to the attention of the evaluator, so that she can study them. If there is a likelihood that negative effects can ensue, the evaluator can trace them with the same care devoted to the chains of desirable effects.

The evaluator uses the diagram in Figure 3-3 to decide what data to collect. If she pursues all the chains, she will need data on the subject of the conversations between teachers and parents. She will also need to collect data before and after the home visits about parents' knowledge of school expectations, parental support and encouragement for the student, the conscientiousness of student work, pupil attendance, teachers' knowledge of students' home culture, teachers' style of teaching, and pupils' feelings of being heard and respected. After the visits, the evaluator will have to find out about the identification of any physical or emotional problem, referrals for care, help received, and improvement of the problem.

Suppose that after home visits, student reading achievement improves significantly more than that of a control group of students who did not have the visits. The

---

[2]A variable that distinguishes between subgroups that have different outcomes is called a moderator variable. The moderator variable, such as number of prior arrests, sex of participants, or ethnicity, divides the study population into subgroups that respond differently to the program (Baron & Kenny, 1986).

usual conclusion would be that the visits (and all the assumptions and expectations surrounding them) were justified. But suppose also that records of teachers' visits showed that all the measures of interaction, communication, and understanding between parent and teacher were at very low levels. Teachers and parents were really not communicating. The source of the student's improved reading ability must be sought elsewhere. (One explanation might be that the students misperceived the intent of the teachers' visits; they may have thought teachers were complaining about their work and trying to persuade parents to punish poor achievers. Improved schoolwork could have been a response to the perceived threat.)

If the predicted sequence of events does not work out, further investigation is needed. But when the theory proves to be a reasonable picture of how things happen, it gives some notion of the reasons why. However, even with the best and most supportive data, theories are never proved. At best, they are not disconfirmed by the data. There may be alternative theories that would provide equally plausible or better interpretations of the available facts. Scientific generalizations are built up by developing hypotheses and then submitting them to successive tests in an effort to disprove them or find the limits of their applicability.

In undertaking theory-based evaluation, it is probably best to start with a relatively simple theory. In the evaluation of a community education program to reduce cardiovascular disease (Farquhar et al., 1990), the focus was on reducing cholesterol intake and smoking. One theory that underlay the program was that intensive communication would increase residents' knowledge of risk factors, and increased knowledge about risk factors would lead to changes in behavior (such as reduced intake of cholesterol). With more healthful behaviors, residents would improve in blood pressure, weight, and pulse rate.

So one part of the theory was that communication leads to knowledge, which leads to behavior change. That is the theory of many programs. Sometimes it is assumed that communication leads to knowledge, which leads to attitude change, which leads to behavior change. The evaluator can elaborate the theory with more detail and design the evaluation to investigate each of the several links. The important point is that the theory gives guidance to the evaluation about where to look and what to find out.

When a program is very complex and multi-faceted, like the introduction of case managers to integrate the delivery of social services to multi-problem families, the evaluator may find it impossible to follow every branch of every subtheory underlying the program. Sheer limitations on time and resources will prevent an effort to test each link. Choices will have to be made about which causal pathways to pursue. How should an evaluator decide?

Possible criteria are the following:

1. *Uncertainty*. Some linkages between program service and client progress are more problematic than others. Sometimes no knowledge exists on the viability of the assumptions. Sometimes available knowledge from social science research or previous evaluations suggests that the assumption is unwarranted. This may be a good set of linkages for the evaluator to study, preferably early in the evaluation. If it does not hold up, the program can find out about failings quickly and modify what it is doing.

2. *Volume*. Some services are more frequently offered and the theories underlying them are therefore of higher salience. If many elements in a program rely on the supposition that referring a client to other services is sufficient to get the other service provided, this assumption may be a good candidate for study.

3. *Centrality*. Some pathways carry a heavier burden than others for the likelihood of the program's overall success. The evaluator should give high priority to those pathways that represent indispensable assumptions of the program.

4. *Purpose*. The choice of pathways to pursue is linked to the overall purpose of the evaluation and the questions it addresses. (There will be more about choosing among possible questions in Chapter 4.)

Comparing Program Theory to Actual Developments

Once the data are in hand, the intent of the analysis is to see how well the theory describes what actually happened. Which parts of the theory are supported, and which parts did not turn out as expected? This is important information for the directors and staff of the program under study, so that they can rethink the understandings and replan the activities that did not work out as anticipated. It is important information for people engaged in other programs so that they can take stock of what they are doing in light of the theoretical understandings generated. On a broader scale, it is important for the growth of social knowledge. If, for example, evaluations of programs in many different fields show that the supposed link between change in knowledge and change in behavior is weak or nonexistent, then policymakers and program designers have to develop other theories (and the activities to implement them) when they seek to bring about behavior change. For social scientists, too, this kind of knowledge is grist to the mill of better understanding of human behavior.

The mere construction of such a theory can expose naive and simplistic expectations. Do program developers, for example, believe that those parents who do not have the values, the background experience, or the skills to help their children with academic studies can be persuaded to do so by one or two visits from a teacher? Certainly, more must be built into a program with such great expectations—training for the teachers, for one thing, and reinforcements, rewards, and possibly skill training for the parents. The evaluation theory can be a learning tool long before the evaluation begins.

During the conduct of the home visit program, it may turn out that few teachers actually make the home visits. They may try and fail to find parents at home, or they may shy away from the effort entirely. In that case, it makes little sense to continue to study the effects of what is now known to be a phantom program. Or evidence may show that teachers make the visits, and the evaluator follows along the hypothesized chain of events. She finds out teachers do indeed show enhanced understanding of the culture of students' home, they have more sympathy with the students, but they continue teaching in the old traditional ways without attempting to suit instruction to the pupils' subculture. If the students' reading performance does not improve, we have some clue about the why of it. We can tell where the projected chain has foundered. Similarly, if some parents do learn about the school's expectations for their children's behavior and performance and do try to encourage them to do better homework and schoolwork, yet their children's work is no better done than that of other students, we have a place to look for further insight into the break-down of the expected chain of events.

How does one analyze the viability of program theory? Writers on evaluation have offered several methods of statistical analysis (Chen & Rossi, 1987; Lipsey, 1989). But even without sophisticated statistical techniques, it is possible to learn a great deal through what Campbell (1966) has called "pattern matching."[3] As the words imply, the evaluator compares the expectations generated by theory with empirical data to see how well they fit. Riggin's (1990) evaluation of a mandatory job search program for welfare recipients shows a simple manner in which evalua-tors can use program theory as a basis for recommendations to program managers. The study found that the program wasn't doing what its own theory demanded; its implementation theory was not being realized. The evaluators' recommendations centered on bringing the program into compliance with its theory—for example, applying sanctions where clients were not following the rules and hiring more coun-selors to perform necessary activities going unfulfilled.

Advantages of Explicating Theories of Change

Mapping the theories of change inherent in a program has advantages not just for evaluators but also for the other players in the program world.

Program Designers

During the period when the program is first being developed, program designers can profit from the disciplined thinking that this approach stimulates. The theories-of-change model forces them to make their assumptions explicit, and in doing so, it gives them an opportunity to examine the logic of their ideas. Are they making too many leaps of faith? In Figure 3-1, is it reasonable, based on past experience and research findings, to expect that a few thousand dollars of additional pay will lead teachers to transform their styles of teaching? Thinking through the logic of their expectations may help program designers to consider more powerful or comprehen-sive interventions to achieve the goals they seek, or it may lead them to scale back their expectations for what they can accomplish with the means at hand. It might lead them to call on different categories of personnel or different organizational structures. In short, by asking them to make implicit assumptions explicit, it encour-ages them to think harder and deeper about the programs they design.

Practitioners

During the implementation of programs, practitioners, too, are asked to confront their theories about how the program will lead to change. It may turn out in conver-sation that members of the same staff have different ideas about how the program

---

[3]Campbell (1966) defines pattern matching as "the over-all relationship between a formal scien-tific theory and the relevant accumulations of empirical data" (p. 96). He goes on to say, "The data are not required to have an analytical coherence among themselves, and indeed cannot really be assembled as a total except upon the skeleton of theory" (p. 97). Growth in knowledge comes through "selective retention of theories in competition with other theories" (p. 102). Which theories win out? "It is the absence of plausible rival hypotheses that establishes one theory as 'correct.' In cases where there are rival theories, it is the relative over-all goodness of fit that leads one to be preferred to another" (p. 102).

will achieve its effects. If that is the case, they may well be working at cross-purposes. If practitioners can work through their differences and agree on a common set of assumptions about what they are doing and why, they can increase the force of the intervention.

Also, practitioners can profit in much the same way as program designers. They are in a sense redesigning the program each day by what they do and how they do it. When they surface their assumptions about how the program will work, they have to face their weak or questionable premises and the leaps of faith embedded in their expectations. This confrontation can help them to improve not only their theories and plans but also their regular practice.

Program Managers

A major advantage for program managers is that the evaluation provides feedback about which chain of reasoning breaks down and where it breaks down. Do trainees who are exposed to the training program fail to attend sessions regularly, or do they attend but fail to learn the work skills, or do they learn the skills but fail to look for a job? This kind of information helps managers determine what specifically needs to be fixed. If the evaluation shows that one whole line of theory receives little support in the data, the manager can reconsider the utility of efforts devoted to this line of work.

Managers and Funders of Similar Programs Elsewhere

Information about the theoretical underpinnings of the program has special importance to those who are running or considering the start of similar programs. Not only do they want to know whether such programs are likely to work, but they also want to know how they work. If they understand the what, how, and why of program success (and failure), they can undertake new ventures better prepared to replicate those elements of the program that are associated with successful progression and to rethink and rework those program elements that do not lead on to the next stage.

Policymakers and the Public

Another side benefit of theory-based evaluation is that it provides explanations, stories of means and ends, that communicate readily to policymakers and the public. Its findings can be encapsulated in morals, like Aesop's fables: Teachers who earn higher salaries feel better appreciated, and they work harder at teaching. These kinds of explanatory stories are often more convincing and memorable than are statistical findings alone. They may stand a better chance of influencing the course of future policy.

Of course, there are limitations in the use of programmatic theories of change as a basis for evaluation. One is that it is data greedy. Because theory-based evaluation seeks to follow many steps of the assumed sequence of events, it demands large quantities of data. Heavy demand for data and, later on, for analysis of the data makes claims not only on the evaluator but also on evaluation resources and on the people in the program who must supply the data. Another limitation is that while some of the data called for may well be quantitative in nature, some will probably be narrative and qualitative. The combination calls for ingenuity in analytic strategy and places additional burdens on the evaluator.

Still, the definition of a program's theories of change is worth attention. Looking at program theories is not the only way to go about deciding on the evaluation focus, but it is a good way to clarify and systematize the factors that are worth examining.

Critiques of Program Theory

Some observers question whether an emphasis on program theory will advance the state of the evaluation art. They doubt that people are good at identifying the causal processes at work (Shadish, Cook, & Leviton, 1991). They are skeptical that program practitioners have any special insight into the processes through which change occurs, and they have little more faith that social scientific knowledge is up to the task. Nor do critics believe that theory-based evaluation will necessarily contribute to a growth in program knowledge. They say that while evaluations of one project at a time can yield information specific to each project, it is not clear that findings will generalize beyond the project studied. They doubt that evaluators will be able to distinguish between program features that are common across a family of programs and those that are unique to the local setting. Programs are too complex to be decomposed into a finite set of variables. Therefore, there is little chance for cumulation of findings.

Many qualitative researchers insist that all truths are local and contingent. Each program is its own world and has to be understood in its own terms. The evaluator, in this argument, has to work within the uniqueness of setting, participants, program operations, and time, and these multiple idiosyncrasies preclude drawing generalizations. They say that efforts to generalize about complex undertakings like social programs are not likely to succeed at any high level of abstraction.

I agree that hopes for accumulation of knowledge through repeated tests of program theory are optimistic. For such a desirable end to occur in a reasonable time span, we should start with strong theory at the outset. Unfortunately, program theory in many fields is at a low stage of development. In those fields, the theories that evaluations are likely to be testing are low-level approximations, riddled with inaccuracies and false paths. To discover their flaws and painstakingly revise and improve them will take multiple iterations. This is an arduous way to generate generalizable knowledge.

But individual studies can be pooled with hundreds of other studies of programs of like kind through meta-analysis. Through analysis of the whole body of studies, it may be possible to discover which intervening processes are most strongly associated with achievement of desired outcomes. Another hope for understanding causal theory is that some effects emerge from particular types of program operations consistently enough to be dependable, even if a larger explanatory system is not fully known (Cook & Shadish, 1994).

Program-theory approaches have the advantage of breaking program experience into a series of small chunks—that is, the links between one step and the next. Because the evaluation focuses on these links (rather than just the global assumption that the program leads to desired outcomes), it can examine linkages across a range of program and implementations. For example, many programs rely on case managers to coordinate the services that a family receives from numerous care providers. Common assumptions are that the case manager increases (a) the number and (b) the appropriateness of services the family receives: Theory-based evaluations can test those assumptions in a variety of settings and thus contribute to generalizations about what case managers do and do not accomplish.

Furthermore, the *local* reasons for basing evaluation on program theory remain compelling. For the evaluator studying a particular program or project, unearthing (or constructing) program theories is a helpful way to figure out what to study, how to allocate evaluation resources, where to concentrate data collection, and how to make sense of findings. And it just may happen that evaluators will learn things of use to others.

With all their complexities and quirks, programs display discernible commonalties. Just as the basic social sciences find patterns of behavior that hold across individuals, organizations, polities, and societies, it should be possible to find features and relationships that characterize programs of various kinds. Human behavior is complex, but it is not random. We ought to be able to make headway in understanding what happens under particular sets of circumstances when interventions work to redress social problems.

The search for better program theory is well worth the pursuit. Given the sorry state of social intervention in some fields and the lack of explicit theorizing to guide program development, even a modest advance would mark significant improvement.

Summary

This chapter has highlighted the importance of understanding the program that is being evaluated. It has pointed to several sources of knowledge about the program, including written information, people, and direct observation. The chapter has stressed the value of reviewing past evaluations of the same or similar programs as a way for the evaluator to orient herself to activities, expectations, past outcomes, and explanations for achievements and shortfalls. As a side benefit, past evaluations also offer useful insights into the research methods that other evaluators have used, the instruments they relied on for collecting data, the modes of analysis they employed, and their occasional suggestions for how to do the study better the next time around.

A good method for formalizing knowledge about the program is to construct an outline of the program's underlying theory (or theories). The evaluator should draw on the implicit and explicit knowledge of program personnel in explicating program theory. A statement of theory should lay out the sequence of assumptions that show how program inputs (staff, resources, activities) translate through a series of intermediate steps to desired program outcomes (improvements in people, organizations, or communities). The microsteps of the theory can then become the framework for the evaluation study. The evaluation tracks developments to find out whether the assumed linkages in fact occur.

By using program theory as one basis for structuring the evaluation, the study allows the evaluator to reach conclusions not only about the processes by which services were delivered and the outcomes that they achieved, but also about the validity of the assumptions that link program processes and outcomes. Thus, theory-based evaluation may help to increase the generalizability of study results from the single case under study to the range of programs that are based on similar assumptions. I acknowledge the optimistic (perhaps overoptimistic) cast of these expectations, but I suggest that the effort is worthwhile for whatever improvement over current practice it provides.

Structuring evaluation around program theory is, of course, only one way to go about evaluating a program. Other approaches are valuable, as we will see in subsequent chapters. Program theory can be a minor part of the evaluation or it can be the central core. In all events, learning enough about the program to develop a statement of program theory (or theories) is a useful exercise. It is useful even when the design of the program does not rely on it, for example when the evaluation design is to compare a randomly selected group of people who were assigned to the program with a randomly selected group who did not receive the program. Even when the focus of the evaluation is the comparison between the two groups, an understanding of program theories can illuminate the findings.

Evaluation based on theories of change can be helpful to program staff because it encourages them to think about why they are doing what they are doing and to consider whether there are ways to do things better. It is useful for the evaluator because it encourages her to learn a great deal about the program and to reflect on what she learns before she launches the study. Whether or not program theory becomes a central part of the evaluation, the effort to develop it alerts the evaluator to vital issues and opportunities.

4

PLANNING THE EVALUATION

The point I am trying to make is that one does not plan and then try to make circumstances fit those plans. One tries to make plans fit the circumstances.

—General George S. Patton (1947, p. 116)[1]

Somewhat paradoxically, theory orientation may have its greatest advantage in the domain of practical research design.... A theory orientation provides a framework within which the researcher can address the fundamental but vexing questions of which controls to implement, which samples to use, which measures to take, and which procedures to follow.

—Mark W. Lipsey (1993)

It is a bad plan that admits of no modification.

—Publilius Syrus (first century B.C.)

The conduct of evaluation is complex. It requires forethought and planning. It involves (a) identifying the key questions for the study; (b) deciding whether to use quantitative methods, qualitative methods, or a combination of the two; (c) developing measures and techniques to answer the key questions; (d) figuring out how to collect the necessary data to operationalize the measures; (e) planning an appropriate research design, with attention to such things as the kinds of comparisons that will be drawn and the timing of data collection; (f) collecting and analyzing the data; (g) writing and disseminating the report(s) of study results; and (h) promoting appropriate use of the results.

Each step of the study affects other steps. For example, an evaluator may define a plausible outcome question, but then not be able to collect data that plausibly answer the question. When evaluating a project that aims to increase coordination between the public housing authority and social service agencies serving public

---

[1]From General George S. Patton, *War as I Knew It*. Copyright © 1947 by Beatrice Patton Walters, Ruth Patton Totten, and George Smith Totten. Copyright © renewed 1975 by Major General George Patton, Ruth Patton Totten, John K. Waters, Jr., and George P. Waters. Reprinted by permission of Houghton Mifflin Co. All rights reserved.

housing tenants, her question is: To what extent has coordination been achieved? But she runs into a problem: How can the extent of coordination be conceptualized and measured? It may turn out that there is no feasible way to develop a reliable measure. Or the agencies involved may be unwilling to give her access to their records, and there is no other way to collect the requisite data. In such cases, the evaluator has to go back to the drawing board and try to craft another question that addresses the aim of the program but is susceptible to measurement.

This chapter provides an introduction to the issues that the evaluator has to address as she gears up for the study. It discusses whether the study will address questions of program implementation and/or program outcomes and how to select the central questions for study. It analyzes the pros and cons of using quantitative and qualitative methods. It makes forays into such practical issues as timing and the appointment of an advisory committee. It concludes with consideration of ethical issues that arise.

Planning is a cyclical process. The right design for the study will depend on the questions to be answered, and the questions that can be answered will depend on which designs are feasible. The evaluator will go back and forth between the phases of the study, adapting and adjusting so that the pieces fit together into a cohesive and convincing evaluation.

In earlier chapters we considered who the main audiences for the evaluation will be and the purposes that the study can serve. We also discussed how the evaluator can decide which of the competing purposes deserve priority. With at least provisional closure on that front, the evaluator can move ahead with planning the study. But she remains aware that she may have to circle back and reconsider the questions in light of constraints and new conditions on the evaluation scene.

The Right Time to Evaluate

Let's say you have been called in to evaluate the ABC program. You have been called in now because money for evaluation just happened to become available. But is the time ripe for evaluation? A systematic way to think about the timing of evaluation is through a procedure called evaluability assessment.

Evaluability assessment is a systematic way to examine the program both theoretically and empirically to determine whether a full evaluation of program outcomes is warranted. Wholey (1979, 1983, 1994), who has written extensively on evaluability assessment, states that a program has to satisfy three criteria: (a) The program should operate as intended; (b) it should be relatively stable; and (c) it should seem to be achieving positive results. The first two of these criteria are much the same as two of those we met in Chapter 2 as important preconditions for evaluation. The third asks for at least a glimmering of success. The evaluator analyzes the likelihood that the program can conceivably have good enough effects to be worth formal (and expensive) study.

Evaluability assessment has two prongs. First, it clarifies the series of assumptions that link what the program does to what it hopes to accomplish. The evaluator works with key actors in and around the program to construct what Wholey (1983) calls program design and I call program theory. Then she subjects the program's theory to logical examination. She analyzes the *plausibility* of the linkages to reach an estimate of whether the anticipated series of steps is likely to achieve desired goals.

Second, she gathers together existing data; consults staff, clients, funders, and observers; and quickly collects new information at the site. The empirical information, too, is pressed into service to test the plausibility of the theory and to examine the likelihood of program success.

With a reasonably well run and stable program, and with at least a whiff of positive results, the evaluator can move to the next phase of evaluation. She can concentrate on designing a study to discover what kinds of good outcomes appear, for which proportion of the participants, under which conditions of program operation.

But evaluability assessment can be more than a filter to screen out programs that are not yet worthy of outcome evaluation. It can be a preliminary evaluation in its own right. If neither program theory nor program data promise successful outcomes, the assessment can tell funders and program staff about obstacles and logical incongruities and where the drawbacks lie. It directs their attention to facets of the program that need shoring up. They need to make improvements so that the program stands a chance of favorable outcomes.

Wholey (1983) also suggests that evaluability assessment provides an occasion for program funders and managers to define how they will use the results from further evaluation. A major reason for undertaking evaluation is to improve program operation, and with the foretaste of evaluability assessment, managers can think through the possibilities (and their intentions) to make use of evaluation data.

Types of Evaluation Questions

Let's assume that you have done a preliminary review and decided that the ABC program is promising enough to warrant a full evaluation. A next step in planning the evaluation is to consider the kinds of information to collect. Of all the hundreds of questions that people might ask about the program, which ones shall the evaluation ask?

It is tempting for novices to want to ask everything. They think, "As long as we're undertaking a study and asking 10 questions, why not ask 100? It doesn't take much more effort." Well, that may look like the case at the start, but data *collection* is only the tip of the iceberg. Once we get into a study, we find that additional questions multiply the burden. For one thing, if the evaluation asks for too much information from staff and clients, it runs the risk of losing their cooperation. When the evaluator comes back for more data, they may not be accommodating. A second reason is that the data have to be analyzed. Many is the evaluator who has collected so much data that she is buried in it and has great difficulty in digging her way out. In quantitative studies, data need to be coded, checked for reliability, entered into the computer (and checked again), and then statistically analyzed, hypothesized about, tested, modeled, and reanalyzed. With qualitative data, narratives have to be read and reread, meanings and themes identified, hypotheses developed and tested, interpretations subjected to disconfirmation, and everywhere everything has to be written up and reported. A third reason for being selective in question asking is that a surfeit of data often leads the evaluator to neglect large piles of the data collected. This is a waste of respondents' time and cooperation, evaluators' energy and ethical pride, and forests of trees. During the planning stage, the evaluator has to make choices.

Questions come in many shapes and flavors. For the sake of this discussion, let's think about potential questions in five categories: (a) program process, (b) program outcome, (c) attributing outcomes to the program, (d) links between processes and outcomes, and (e) explanations.

Program Process

Questions about program process essentially ask what is going on in the program. They may be framed in terms of whether the program is doing what it is supposed to do (Is it attracting homeless clients? For how many of them is it providing hot meals?). The issue here is the fidelity of the program to its designers' intentions. Or questions may be framed in more open terms (Who is coming in to the program? What help is staff giving them?). No judgments are made in advance about what the right activities are. The question is: What is happening? In either case, the emphasis in studies of program process is on the processes of recruitment, service, client response, and program operation.

In some cases, only a few features of program process are problematic. The evaluation sponsor may not want to review the basic underpinnings of the program or the main types of service offered. He may only want to know, for example, whether the training provided to staff is adequate. The evaluation can focus on those elements of program process that are particularly troubling to program people. Or it can try to expand the sponsor's horizon and suggest that the study include other related features in addition to the one or two that have been singled out, such as the ways that staff put into practice the lessons that the training tried to teach or the kind of supervision that staff receive on the job.

Program Outcomes

An emphasis on program outcome would direct the evaluation to the consequences of the intervention for its clients. Here the focus is the change in clients' situations (knowledge, behavior, earnings, health status, drug use, or whatever). A likely source of questions about outcomes is the official statement of program goals: What do funders and sponsors expect the program to achieve? But since goals sometimes change during the course of program operation, another source would be contemporary beliefs about what the program is trying to do. Still another source of questions about outcomes would be hunches of program staff, clients, observers, or others about what the real results are, regardless of the rhetoric of intent.

Attributing Outcomes to the Program

Questions about attributions have to do with figuring out whether any changes that are observed over time are due to the program. The evaluation of a job training program, for example, may find that participants who completed the training increased their earnings over the amount they earned before entering the program. But it is possible that their earnings would have gone up anyway, even if they had not attended the program. The economy might have improved and better paying jobs became available, or the trainees were just older and more savvy, or they had been at a particularly low point in their work history just before they entered the program (which is why they enrolled) and would have rebounded anyway. In all these cases, it would be inappropriate to conclude that the program was responsible for the increase in their earnings. The evaluation may want to devote some questions (as well as features of evaluation design, which we'll get to next) to understanding the extent to which the *program* was responsible for the change.

Links between Process and Outcomes

If we have the right information about process, we can see whether particular features of the program are related to better or poorer outcomes. For example, if we know whether clients received health information in groups or individually, we can analyze whether group discussion leads to better outcomes than the same information given one on one. If we know whether the conveyer of information was a nurse or an adult educator, we can examine the effect of this variable. If we know whether one community running the health promotion program provided supplementary information through the media, while another community did not, we may get hints about which of these conditions had better outcomes. We have to have the necessary data in hand to do analyses of this sort.

Explanations

Evaluators often want to know not only *what* happened but *how* and *why* it happened. This entails a search for explanations. Evaluation sponsors and program managers, as well as policymakers and managers of similar programs at other locations, may want to know *why* results came out as they did. If they want to improve the likelihood of success, it helps to know the reasons for achievements and shortfalls. One way to pursue the why of program success and failure is by tracking the program theory, explicitly or implicitly. The evaluator can seek to specify program theory at the start and track its emergence (as discussed in Chapter 3), or she can collect the data first and try to deduce the theory from the evidence.

Additional Decisions in the Planning Period

Long- or Short-Term Study

The evaluation has to plan how far into the future to conduct inquiries. Often the decision is not the evaluator's to make. Evaluation funders may say, "Here is the money for a two-year study." Or the policymaker may say, "We must have the report in time for hearings on legislation to reauthorize the program." But wherever the evaluator has a voice, it is useful to plan the time dimension of the study. In fact, even when she doesn't appear to have a say, if she makes convincing plans and demonstrates the value of longer term information, she may be able to convince others to extend the length of the study.

By and large, longer is better. A study may show great effects right after an intervention—for example, right after the showing of an educational film. But it is likely that the effects will fade away. If the study collects data a year later, there may be little residue of the benefits. That is important for people to know before they invest money in films of this sort. On the other hand, a program may have little obvious effect at the conclusion of the intervention, but over time the gap widens between recipients and nonrecipients of the program. What looked like small gains at the beginning cumulate and multiply over the years. This is what happened in the Perry Preschool Project for low-income children, where small benefits right after participation in the preschool became significant gains when the youth were 27 years old (Schweinhart et al., 1993). Plans for follow-up need to be made during the planning stage so that right from the start the evaluators devise means to keep track of clients after they disperse at the end of the program.

Questions about Anticipated and Unanticipated Features

When we begin to think about questions, most of us tend to concentrate on asking about phenomena that the program is *intended* to affect. This is true for questions about program processes and program outcomes. The evaluator's tendency is to ask about things that are *supposed* to be there. So, for example, if she is studying the process of a neighborhood policing program, she will think of questions about the frequency with which police officers patrol the neighborhood on foot or their contacts with various neighborhood associations. If she is studying outcomes of a home visiting program for pregnant women, she will consider questions about frequency of home visits and the birth weight of the newborn. But programs also do things other than those they are intended to do. Unintended features may be good, or bad, and evaluation should attend to negative features as well.

How does the evaluator figure out what negative side effects may occur? She has three ready resources: (a) her own knowledge, understanding of social processes, and imagination; (b) the claims of critics of the program; and (c) prior research and evaluations of similar programs. Thus, in the program that increases the number of police on foot patrol, the evaluator might hear from neighborhood residents that a more visible police presence leads to more hostile encounters with teenagers who are doing nothing more than hanging out. The process evaluation might inquire into the frequency of such events. In the home visiting program, prior evaluation might suggest that home visitors convey a good deal of information about possible complications of pregnancy to pregnant women (Villar et al., 1992), and the evaluation might ask to what extent the program frightens women as well as enlightens them.

Why should the evaluation pay attention to unintended processes and consequences? For one thing, if the undesirable events do not appear, the evaluation counters the charges of the program's critics, at least on that score. If undesirable consequences do show up, the information directs people's attention to correcting them (train those police on foot patrol not to hassle groups of idlers) and salvaging the good of the program. A worst case scenario would be the program whose negative side effects are so serious that they overwhelm the good it does. An evaluation that failed to take note of them would be a creature from cloud-cuckoo-land.

How to Decide Which Questions to Pursue

With all the options available, evaluators have to plan which of them to pursue. What criteria should they use to resolve the questions about questions? Eight possibilities are (a) the decisional timetable, (b) the relative clout of interested parties, (c) preferences of stakeholders, (d) uncertainties in the knowledge base, (e) practicalities, (f) assumptions of program theory, (g) the potential for use of the findings, and (h) the evaluator's professional judgment.

Decisional Timetable

One source of information is the schedule for upcoming decisions. If there is a major decision point ahead and evaluation information can contribute to making a more informed decision, then questions can be chosen that provide the most appropriate information for that decision. For example, a sex education project is coming up before the school board next year for review, and critics of the project are known to base their antagonism on their assumption that discussion of sex in the classroom encourages premarital sexual activity. Teachers running the project scoff at the notion. They fail to take the board's objections seriously, and they offer other questions that they want the evaluation to pursue. But the evaluator may decide to emphasize questions having to do with students' sexual behavior. She will also want to give a good deal of attention to whether the program was implicated in students' behavior, perhaps comparing those who did and did not receive the program. Her decision is based on the fact that the school board is going to make a decision that involves the life or death of the project. Whatever the people running the program may want to know, the school board's issue deserves priority.

In many other cases, evaluation sponsors want the evaluation to meet a decisional deadline, but the deadline is arbitrary. The date can be moved without jeopardizing anything consequential, and the delay would give the evaluator time to do a better job.

Clout of Stakeholders

A second basis for making choices is to find out who wants to know what. For example, members of a congressional committee want to know whether a liberal immigration policy is resulting in higher unemployment for U.S. citizens; federal officials in the Immigration and Naturalization Service want to know the extent to which the policy is reducing illegal immigration; ethnic interest groups want to know whether the policy is being implemented impartially or whether migrants from a particular country are having a more difficult time securing entrance. These are all difficult questions, and the evaluation does not have the resources to attack them all. One practical way to resolve the dilemma is to go with the party who has the most clout—usually the party who sponsors the evaluation.

It is sometimes hard to justify such a decision on substantive grounds—for example, if the sponsor is ignoring the interests of persons affected by the policy. But the evaluator may gauge that, otherwise, the evaluation will not receive support. It is always worthwhile to try to convince powerful groups of the importance of widening or modifying their original questions. They might be persuaded that other groups' concerns are vital to successful operation of the program.

Consultation with Stakeholders

Another way to cope with an overload of questions is by consulting with all the parties who have a stake in the program, whether as funders, managers, operators, or clients. The evaluator can canvass their questions and concerns in order to understand what is on their minds. She can then make her own decisions on priorities or try to construct a plan that is satisfactory to all of them. She can even convene a group of stakeholders who represent the major interests and encourage them to work out an accommodation among themselves. The evaluator can be the facilitator of the discussion, but she can try to leave it to the parties to decide what shall be in and out of the study.

Sometimes the way that stakeholders come to agreement is by deciding to include everything that anybody wants, which puts the evaluator back where she started. Nevertheless, stakeholder participation in evaluation planning can work well in certain circumstances, and when it does, it has happy consequences. Chapter 5 discusses methods of securing stakeholder participation in evaluation planning.

Uncertainties in the Knowledge Base

Another way to choose questions and focus in the planning stage is through identifying gaps in knowledge. From social science research and from previous evaluations of similar programs, a good deal of knowledge is likely to have accumulated. Rather than spread the evaluation thin over a range of questions, some of which have been fairly well settled, or resorting to expedient means to satisfy parties at interest, the evaluator can devote major attention to those issues still undecided or in contention. If sponsors assent, the evaluation can fill in chinks in the general knowledge base and at the same time provide information that helps resolve local perplexities.

Practicalities

In planning the evaluation, some options will be foreclosed by the constraints of time, money, capabilities of evaluation staff, and access to information. For example, if no one on the evaluation team has qualitative research skills, it is probably not a good idea to plan a major qualitative component to the study. If program records do not carry information about which variations of the program each client was exposed to, there is little point in planning a retrospective investigation of differential outcomes by treatment type. The evaluator can try to remedy some of the limitations—for example, by seeking consultative help from a qualitative researcher or by encouraging program managers to revamp their record system. But the practicalities of the situation may preclude pursuing some interesting avenues of investigation.

Assumptions of Program Theory

Direction can come from a review of the theories embedded in the program. If the evaluator works with stakeholders to identify which steps in their chain of reasoning are *most critical for program effectiveness* and also *most problematic*, priorities can become clear. (In fact, this is a good way of identifying uncertainties in the knowledge base.) The evaluation can address questions that ask whether the linkages that program people anticipate actually hold, say, the link between increased knowledge about the dangers of drunk driving and drivers' motivation to stop driving drunk. Attention to questions that program theories highlight also helps to specify the kinds of comparisons that are needed, the time period required for study, and the actual measures to be used.

Potential for Use of the Findings

Another basis for setting priorities is the potential that findings will be taken into account. If one set of stakeholders is indifferent to the study and the results that will emerge from it while another set of people exhibit great interest, the latter group is more likely to give the results serious consideration at the end of the study. The attentive group's questions may deserve special notice. Similarly, if some people are open-minded, reflective, and champions of empirical evidence, they will probably pay attention to evaluation results and put them to use. Giving priority to questions of concern to them may make sense. Even if people are not directly consulted, the evaluator can often judge which evaluation questions will serve which audiences and make choices on the basis of likely use.

However, it is difficult to foresee patterns of use. People who are indifferent to the evaluation at the start may get highly engaged by the results and use them to rethink assumptions, reorder their agendas, or alter program emphases or modes of implementation. Some potential users of the findings, enthusiastic at the point of initiation, may face serious distractions or political obstacles by the time results are ready, and proceed to ignore the evaluation. Some may have left their positions and moved on. Still, it is worthwhile for the evaluator to keep the potential for use in mind when choosing which questions the study will address.

Components of programs are easier to change than are whole programs, and so information on the efficacy of components is probably more readily used for program improvement than is information on the program as a whole (Cook et al., 1985; Shadish et al., 1991). Program people may react defensively to outcome data that show shortcomings in their program. They are more likely to accept and use data on the efficacy of components, like methods of recruitment, size of groups served, or modes of communicating with community members. When use of results for decision making is an important consideration, the evaluator might consider focusing the evaluation on questions at the component level.

Sometimes the most important use the evaluator foresees is increasing people's understanding of how the program achieves its effects. When evaluation reveals the mechanisms by which results are obtained, policy actors and program planners are likely to take account of the knowledge and directly or indirectly use it to shape later programming. A concern with maximizing the influence of results thus interacts with other criteria for choosing key questions to study.

Evaluator's Professional Judgment

Evaluators work in an action setting peopled by staff with different priorities, and they conduct a study with the purposes of other people in mind. Nevertheless, they do not abdicate their professional responsibility for either the content or the methods of their study. They know a great deal that other people on the scene do not know, and they have an obligation to exercise their judgment in evaluation planning.

Few managers are interested in longitudinal studies that extend beyond the usual two- or three-year evaluation period, and they are certainly not interested in studies that extend beyond the life of the program. Few policymakers are engaged by the idea of focusing on unanticipated consequences. Yet evaluators know the value of these options. Because of a history of about 40 years of large-scale evaluation activity, as well as their own firsthand experience, evaluators have come to appreciate certain kinds of questions. They should seek to promote these questions in negotiating the study's parameters with evaluation sponsors and others.

Which of these criteria should take precedence? It is hard to give across-the-board advice. Each evaluation situation has its idiosyncrasies. Some cases are highly political, with two or three contending parties looking over the evaluator's shoulder at every step. In other cases, evaluation is being done simply to satisfy external obligations, and *nobody* seems to care what direction is taken. Some studies have generous budgets; others operate on a shoestring. Some evaluations begin while the program is still on the drawing board. In other cases the evaluator is not called in until the program has been operating for several years. The best advice is to consider the range of possibilities, know enough about the program and its context to make judgments about what appears to be wise, negotiate with as many stakeholders as seems advisable, and perhaps consult evaluators with experience in similar situations. Conscientious discussion of the theories underlying the program can usually give a lucid picture of where the key doubts and uncertainties lie. Beyond that, the evaluation team has to exercise its own best judgment.

Specifying the Questions

So far we have been discussing questions in general terms. We have canvassed the spectrum of evaluative questions and considered means to narrow down the almost infinite possibilities to a manageable set. Choice of the bands of questions to concentrate on is a major achievement. But very soon the general type of questions has to become much more specific. As Light, Singer, and Willett (1990) have written: "Well-crafted questions guide the systematic planning of research. Formulating your questions precisely enables you to design a study with a good chance of answering the questions" (p. 13). They go on to say that specific research questions identify the population to be studied, the appropriate level of aggregation (e.g., student, class, department, institution), the number of units to be included in the study, appropriate outcome variables, key predictors, and background variables that should be measured. They do not hedge and say that specific questions help to identify these ingredients of design. They flatly state, and I think they are right, that well-written specific questions identify design parameters. In short, clear and well-articulated questions are the basis for research design.

Take a program that provides mastectomies on an out-patient basis and sends women home shortly after surgery. One possible evaluation question is: Do patients in the program do as well as mastectomy patients who remain in the hospital at least overnight? *Do as well* is defined as having no additional medical complications. Posing the question in this manner obviously identifies the study population; it requires a comparison with an equivalent sample of women who have longer hospital stays. The evaluator will not be able to assign women to receive one or the other form of treatment, because the matter is up to the woman and her doctor, but the form of the question alerts her to the possibility that patients who receive outpatient surgery are easier, less serious cases to start with. She will want to control for the stage of the disease in the two samples (and perhaps age) so that the evaluation is comparing similar groups of patients.

Another possible evaluation question is: How long does recovery take under out-patient conditions? *Recovery* needs to be defined, perhaps as removal of drainage tubes. This form of the question doesn't require an explicit comparison, and if comparison with in-patient surgery is desired later, it is likely that data on in-patient cases are already available; no additional data collection is needed. The design and the outcome measure here are different from the earlier example, and the choice of which background factors to take into account will depend on their relevance to recovery, rather than to equating two samples of patients.

Framing the specific question thus points the evaluator to choices in design, measurement of outcomes, and the background factors that need to be measured and analyzed.

Chapter 6 discusses how to develop good questions about process, outcomes, and background variables. During the planning stage, it is a good idea to have the essentials of that discussion in mind. But evaluation planning is an iterative process. The researcher considers questions, methods, and data sources in constant interaction. She cycles through questions and methods and data sources, circling back when she hits a snag. One question may be a wonderful question, but if there is no place or means to collect the requisite data, it has to be modified. A question may need the kinds of comparisons that require experimental design, but if experimental design is impossible in the particular program setting, both the question and the design will have to be reconsidered.

Quantitative or Qualitative Study

An early issue to be addressed is whether the evaluation should use a quantitative or qualitative approach. Without a sophisticated definition, we all have a sense of what the distinction is: Quantitative evaluation deals in numbers, and qualitative evaluation deals in words. Quantitative evaluation collects data that can be transformed into numerical form, so that analysis can be largely statistical and reports will be based in large part on the size of effects and the significance of statistical relationships. Qualitative evaluation tends to use unstructured interviewing and observational techniques, so that analysis and reporting take the shape of narrative.

If we are to be precise, we will note that qualitative and quantitative are not categories of designs but types of data (Lynch, 1983). It is true that qualitative data are usually collected in case studies, ethnographies, or other nonstandardized designs, and quantitative data are collected in experimental or quasi-experimental designs (Campbell & Stanley, 1966; Cook & Campbell, 1979)—that is, designs with strong controls. Therefore, the conflation of type of data with type of design is understandable. However, I can imagine a classy experimental design, where the evaluator has randomly assigned potential clients to the program group and a control group, that relies solely on qualitative data. I've never seen a study like that, but I can imagine it. Correlatively, I can imagine strictly numerical data being collected by a field investigator who goes out to the program site and abstracts data from records, observes and interviews with highly structured instruments, and codes all the information into pre-set categories. I've never seen a study like that, either.

So although the terminology is not strictly accurate, researchers tend to talk about qualitative and quantitative research designs, and I usually succumb to the common usage.

Quantitative approaches come in many varieties. On the *data* side, their common attribute is that they collect information through the use of standardized instruments. Whether the data come from interviews, questionnaires, program records, or observations, the same information is collected on every case in the same format, and the information is transformed into a series of numerical values. On the *design* side, quantitative evaluations usually enlist one or more comparison groups with whom program participants will be compared. These comparison groups are stand-ins for what the participant group would have been like if they had not entered the program. Such a situation cannot exist, and the purpose of the comparison group is to come as close to it as possible. Data are usually collected before and after the program for all groups. Quantitative evaluators use statistical methods of *analysis*, and they present their results in the form of tables, graphs, and models, along with a verbal text that explains the meaning of the results.

Qualitative approaches are also varied. The *data* can come from long-term ethnographic investigation in the style of the anthropologist who spends a year or more in the field coming to know and understand the culture, mind set, and activities of the natives. At the other extreme, data can be collected on short visits to a program site to ask open-ended questions of staff and participants. There are many variations in between. The watchword is flexibility of inquiry. The qualitative evaluator emphasizes understanding, rather than precise measurement, of events. On the *design* side, little emphasis is given to making comparisons with groups who do not receive the program. The qualitative evaluator tends to rely on detailed knowledge of the processes by which the program takes shape and how these processes affect participants, not on statistical comparisons. In *analysis*, qualitative researchers tend to analyze data as they go along, developing later phases of inquiry in response to the knowledge that they gain. They seek to identify recurrent themes and patterns in the data as they progressively refine their insights into how the program is working.

The advantages of quantitative evaluation are well known. It allows the investigator to reach conclusions with a known degree of confidence about the extent and distribution of the phenomenon. Because the same information has been collected from all units under the same conditions, the evaluator can make fairly precise statements, such as 86% of program participants showed increases in knowledge of geography, with an average gain for the whole group equal to .9 years of schooling. If the sample of study participants has been appropriately selected, the evaluator can generalize results to equivalent populations.

Furthermore, the evaluator has an array of statistical techniques to use, with libraries of books to help her choose the most fitting methods and instruct her in their proper use. Statistical techniques allow the researcher to identify relationships among variables, not only one variable at a time but in complex multi-variate ways. Computers and software packages make even advanced tasks manageable. In contrast, qualitative analysis is a painstaking craft whose steps are only now being systematized. Each qualitative researcher has to handcraft methods to analyze the data from her study, although computer software is now available to help with the task. She identifies trends, themes, and patterns, without being able to set precise parameters to the relationships she finds in the data.

Quantitative methods are assumed to yield more objective data than qualitative methods. The evaluator stands at one remove from the program context, not becoming personally or emotionally entangled with unfolding events. With the measures of interest defined at the outset, data collection is not dependent on emerging occurrences. In contradistinction, the qualitative evaluation develops on site. The evaluator herself is the measuring instrument. Without the aid of standardized instruments or codified statistical techniques, she collects and makes sense of data as things go along through the exercise of her own judgment. Before she starts, and through the life of the study, she decides which aspects of the program to examine and which information to collect. Her presence in the interview or on the program scene may influence what information becomes available. In analyzing the information, she selects which themes to attend to and which to ignore, and she interprets the information by sifting it through her own sense-making apparatus.

But, of course, in their way quantitative studies do much the same. Just because numbers come out of a computer at the end, there is no reason to treat them as though they were untouched by human hands. The quantitative evaluator, too, decides which aspects of the program to concentrate on, which data to collect, which patterns in the data to focus on, and how to make sense of the relationships that she finds. Quantitative conclusions, although constrained by the demands of statistical logic, are the product of the assumptions, understandings, and judgments of the evaluator, too.

And qualitative evaluation is not completely personalistic. Good methodology requires that information from one source be tested against information from other sources. Before accepting data given by an interview respondent, the researcher seeks to verify it by comparing it with responses from other people, program files, meeting minutes, correspondence, and other records of various types. Similarly, once a researcher has located what looks like a relationship in the data, she seeks out all the evidence she can find that will disconfirm the relationship. So the qualitative approach is not so laissez faire or subject to bias as some people believe.

Nevertheless, many audiences find quantitative results more authoritative. Qualitative evaluations can offer vivid vignettes and accounts of real individuals, and these can bring home to people the human meaning of the program. But the precision of quantitative findings usually gives them a high degree of conviction.

Which way, then, shall the evaluator go? Which methods and design make best sense for the study? Shall the study apply qualitative or quantitative approaches, or a combination of the two?

Choice of Approach

The critical feature about data collection is that methods match the central focus of the inquiry. Let's look at questions about program process, program outcomes, the relation of process to outcomes, and the elements that mediate the generation of effects. What kind of approach fits each of these kinds of questions?

When the central questions relate to program process, qualitative methods generally have the edge. The program encompasses scores of activities and "variables," and no one may yet be sure which features are important to study. Or the whole situation may be too volatile to want to tie the evaluation to a few arbitrary measures. The qualitative evaluator can remain open to new information and new ideas about what the program is and does.

On the other hand, when a program is clearly defined with well-specified activities, quantitative methods can be used to characterize program process. This is particularly likely when prior evaluations have been done on substantially similar programs. In a program for pregnant teenagers, for example, the evaluators collected quantitative data about the number of contacts that each participant had with counseling services, health services, job finding services, and so on, and the length of contact with each (Marsh & Wirick, 1991). Within each category, they had data on specific services utilized, such as tests for venereal diseases, assistance with finding child care, entrance into job training programs, enrollment in food stamp programs. Such information for each participant tells a great deal about what the program did.

Let's consider a program by the Department of Energy to establish advisory boards to nuclear waste cleanup sites. The advisory boards are composed of representatives of local citizen groups, environmental organizations, and state regulatory agencies. The advisory boards are to write their own charters. The expectation is that by getting all interested parties together on one legitimate committee, advisory boards will contain conflict over cleanup, reduce delay, advance the cleanup effort, and reduce costs.

How do you evaluate a program like this? A quantitative procedure would be to set outcome criteria, such as reduction in conflict, faster pace of cleanup, and reduction in cost, and then seek to develop indicators of process that would appear to be related to these outcomes. The evaluator would need information and imagination to foresee what activities the different boards would undertake. But even if she guessed right about process, it is not at all obvious how she could collect numerical data on things like nature of discourse, emergence of leadership, or development of consensus. The problem is compounded when advisory boards at different sites construe their task in very different ways.

With an innovative and complex program just getting under way, it makes sense to take a qualitative approach. Qualitative investigation can reveal how such a new entity takes shape, what problems are faced, who takes leadership and how important leadership is in determining the board's direction, how goals are set, and how the hundreds of decisions about its future are made. Before cut-and-dried procedures have been developed or standards imposed for what the program must do, a qualitative approach allows the evaluator to rummage around and peer into all the nooks and crannies in order to characterize the program in action. Over a period of time, it would be possible to analyze the experience of a dozen or so of such boards and see if common patterns begin to emerge.

Moreover, qualitative data give dynamic rather than static information, moving images instead of a few snapshots. They incorporate evidence gathered from multiple perspectives and do not rely on only the evaluator's pre-set categories. They provide a richness of detail.

When the study is addressing program outcomes, the balance of advantages is different. To the extent that evaluation sponsors and potential readers are seeking precise answers to questions about outcomes, quantitative approaches are preferable. Because of systematic sampling of the relevant populations, they can give numerical estimates of the proportion of clients who experience good effects, along with an estimate of the degree of confidence they have in the results. They can explain what good effects means in terms of the specific indicators and data sources used.

Qualitative studies tend to give less precise descriptions of program outcomes. Instead of numbers and statistics, they are likely to use words like *many* or *most,* and discuss associations in the data in general terms. But they may focus on matters that are germane to understanding program effects. Where a quantitative study may give accurate data on the proportion of trainees who find a job after training and the wages they earn, a qualitative study may be able to describe how trainees feel about the job hunting process, the kinds of jobs they look for, and why they quit jobs after a brief time. Of course, not all quantitative studies limit themselves to simple outcome measures, and not all qualitative studies focus on matters that reveal or explain complex outcomes. But the tendency is in those directions.

Evaluation can also be called upon to identify the specific features of the program that make it successful or unsuccessful. Is it the curriculum materials that make a difference? the teachers' enthusiasm? the use of computers? the frequency of instruction? Such an analysis can use quantitative or qualitative data.

In quantitative analysis, the evaluator has measures of participants, of program service, and of outside conditions, and uses statistics to identify those features that show the strongest relationship to measures of outcome. Multi-variate procedures allow the evaluator to look at the relationship among program inputs, program processes, and program outcomes, not only two at a time but all at once. In qualitative analysis, the evidence comes from words. It takes the form of vignettes, histories, or systematic narratives, which can be derived from records, interviews, observations, conversations, or similar sources. The relationship of program processes to participant outcomes is examined through interpretation of the narrative materials over time. Quantitative methods have the edge for developing *specific* answers about the relationship of particular program strategies or events to outcomes, if the evaluator developed measures of salient program process ahead of time and collected the requisite data. Qualitative methods are usually superior for capturing processes that nobody thought to measure at the beginning, for understanding the *meaning* of program processes to people in different positions, and for finding unexpected patterns of association in unexpected data. As qualitative analysts develop more systematic techniques for analysis (e.g., Miles & Huberman, 1994), they can begin to approximate the quantitative analyst's capacity to reach conclusions about relationships.

Studies can also ask questions about how program effects are generated. If the study is planning to track the unfolding of program theories, qualitative and quantitative approaches can each be suitable. Qualitative methods are probably more sensitive for following the chains of theoretical reasoning and for locating and tracing unexpected deviations. But where expected pathways are well marked and measurable, quantitative methods can accomplish the task.

By now readers will have anticipated the next question: Why not combine both strategies? Why not, indeed. Many excellent studies do just that. In Chapter 11, I discuss the use of multiple methods in evaluation.

Design of the Evaluation

The word *design* in social science research doesn't mean "plan" in the broad sense. It refers to the specification of which groups to study, how many units in a group, by what means units are selected, at what time intervals they are studied, and the kinds of comparisons that are planned. As questions refer to the content of the study, design is its structure.

Much of the writing on evaluation begins with types of design. Textbooks refer to designs such as randomized experiments, quasi-experiments, case studies, etc. Many textbook authors present a hierarchy of designs. For Rossi and Freeman (1993), for example, randomized experiments are the "flagship of evaluation" (p. 307), at least for the study of outcomes. Their advice for the planning of design is to start with the "best" design first—that is, the randomized experiment. If that turns out to be impractical, go to the second best, and if problems intrude, retreat down the line until you find a design that can be implemented under existing conditions. In the case of the particular program they describe (pp. 324–325), the hierarchy of design choices was randomized experiment, pre- and postcomparison of program clients, posttreatment comparison of clients who successfully completed the program with those who were rejected for participation or dropped out, comparison of clients with clients of other programs serving the same kind of clientele, and finally, locating people comparable to clients in a large national survey and using them for comparison.

For Guba and Lincoln (1989), qualitative studies that are responsive to stakeholder interests and adopt their multiple perspectives on events are not only the best kinds of studies; they are the only acceptable evaluations. The authors aver that facts have no meaning except in a framework of values, and the evaluator has to work with stakeholders to negotiate the values and the facts. Only then can they, together, reach reasonable evaluation conclusions.

The gist of *this* text is that form follows function, design follows question. Once the evaluator knows which questions the study is going to pursue, she selects the type of design that enables the study to answer them. Some questions are best addressed through randomized experiments. For some evaluation questions, a postprogram survey provides all the information that is needed. Other questions require a full-scale ethnography. Whether before-and-after designs are warranted, and the kinds of comparison groups (if any) that are necessary, depend on the nature of the specific inquiry. The key is the kind of questions raised and therefore the kind of evidence needed to provide answers.

Attribution of Effects to the Intercession of the Program

The reason that design is so central in evaluation is that an enduring issue is whether the events that come after the program are *due to* the program. Were the outcomes caused by the program, or would they have occurred anyway? Many things impinge on people's lives other than the programs they attend, and under some circumstances it is vital to be able to separate out the effects of the program from the rest of the cacophony of living. Evaluators have to be concerned about linking the conditions that they observe after program participation, such as higher birth weights for new-born infants or reduced fear of medical procedures, to the program intervention.

The classical means for attributing effects to the program is the randomized experiment. In this design, which we will discuss in detail in Chapter 9, one group of people receives the program and an *equivalent* group of people does not receive the program. The two groups are much the same at the outset. Then the difference between their status at the end must be due to the intervention, since everything else—their rate of development, the external influences they are exposed to, and so on—has been much the same. The way of ensuring that the two groups are equivalent is by starting with a single population and randomly assigning some units to the program and others to a control group.

Experimental design rules out almost all rival explanations for the outcomes that are observed, but it is not an easy design to implement. Evaluators can seldom gain control over recruitment into the program as the procedure requires. For example, when a program already serves everyone, there are no leftover people to assign to a control group. When clients are recruited based upon need or upon accomplishment (e.g., recipients of fellowships), program staff are loath to allow evaluators to decide who gets into the program; they want to exercise their own professional judgment. But the randomized experiment is a fine way to settle the matter of attribution.

However, in some cases, attribution is not a burning issue. Let's say that generations of farmers in a Peruvian village have lived on the margin of starvation, and then a development project comes in and provides seed and fertilizers. In a year or two the economic situation of the village is vastly improved. No experimental design is necessary to demonstrate that the program caused the change. Or take a school in which third grade classes have consistently done poorly in reading, a new reading curriculum is introduced, and reading comprehension in this year's third grade class shoots up. Few teachers would question that the new curriculum was the agent of change.

The significant point is that the evaluation has to be able to rule out *plausible* rival explanations for the change that appears. Donald Campbell has argued (Campbell & Stanley, 1966; Cook & Campbell, 1979) that ruling out plausible rival explanations is the main function of research design. If no other explanation is plausible, then relatively simple designs are acceptable.

But the evaluator has to stay alert. Sometimes plausible competing explanations exist that the evaluator is not paying attention to. Maybe there was a big shift in the population attending the school with low reading scores, and third graders are now coming from families of higher socioeconomic status. That might account for their better reading performance. Similarly, Lincoln Moses told me of a program for training FBI agents in marksmanship. After participation in the program, the accuracy of agents' shooting improved. When the program claimed credit, an official said, "But they always shoot better in the winter." No data had been collected to refute his contention. (I suspect that the story is apocryphal, but the point is well taken.) Don Schon told me about a nutrition program in a Third World country that appeared to fail, based on a comparison of before and after data. The fact that the country had suffered a severe drought while the program was going on was not taken into account. People's nutritional status might have been much worse without the nutrition program, and the program may actually have been very successful in preventing starvation. So it is well to design studies to examine alternative explanations for the pattern of results.

Where the evaluator does not have sufficient control to assign people (or other units) randomly to the program and to a control group, she can try to approximate experimental design. She can employ designs that have been dubbed quasi-experimental because they contain some of the characteristics that aid interpretation without the full panoply of experimental control. More about such designs in Chapter 8.

One Study or a Fleet of Studies?

Another kind of decision has to be made in the planning period: whether to mount one big study (as big as the budget allows) or several smaller studies. Almost always evaluators opt for one study, usually without giving the matter a first, let alone a second, thought. And there is much to be said for the single study. Not insignificant is the greater ease of managing one study rather than several. Also, there is often barely enough money to do one fairly comprehensive study, and the thought of parceling it out over two or more studies may chill the bones.

But there are good reasons to consider doing a series of studies. As Cronbach (Cronbach & Associates, 1980) has written, a single study, even a huge blockbuster study of the million-dollar dimensions that the federal government was funding in the late 1970s, rarely *settles* the salient questions about a program. Because it proceeds from a single set of assumptions, it is limited by the nature of the assumptions it makes and the perspective it takes. People with different assumptions can doubt the findings. If the study takes the federal agency's perspective and answers its questions, it may well be ignoring the divergent expectations and values of program participants or congressional policymakers. Instead, the evaluator may consider "a fleet of studies" (Cronbach & Associates, 1980), each undertaking evaluation from a different perspective. If the whole set of studies produces similar or complementary conclusions, they have much greater credibility. If they do not, the reasons may be apparent from the nature of the inquiries, but if the reasons are unclear, later studies can inquire further into the source of the differences.

Furthermore, any one study is likely to raise new questions. Another study undertaken later can pursue the new questions. Not every study has to set out from port at the same time. The evaluator can plan a sequence of studies, each picking up on issues disclosed in the preceding investigation.

A sequence of studies can also adapt to changing issues in the policy and program worlds. Not infrequently, while an evaluation is in progress, the questions that program supporters and program critics want answered undergo substantial change. The political winds shift; political actors change; budgets tighten; program staff adopt more currently fashionable aims. The original study is now off course. It is exploring issues that have been bypassed by the tide of events. The capacity to undertake another shorter term study that is responsive to present concerns would be a major advantage.

A series of studies can also adopt different methods. Instead of a single study nailing itself to the mast of quantitative-experimental-statistical or qualitative-responsive-interactive, two or more studies can set forth, probably at different times, to address different issues with appropriately different methods.

The key word is *flexibility*. Putting all the evaluation resources in one basket ("and watching the basket," as financier Bernard Baruch is reported to have said about his philosophy of investing) is one way to go. But another is to hold some resources in reserve so that later studies can be conducted to address new questions or newly visible questions as they arise. I'm afraid that this advice is not likely to appeal to the evaluator who receives a modest grant or contract to conduct a study and doesn't think she has enough money anyway. It may have more appeal to the granting or contracting agency, which can, with less sacrifice, commission a series of studies over a period of time. The idea of a set of sequential studies remains something that should be considered during planning.

Designs for Different Types of Programs

Evaluators sometimes long for rules for the type of design suitable for different types of programs. Suchman (1967), Cronbach and Associates (1980), Rossi and Freeman (1993), and Shadish et al. (1991) have made various attempts in this direction. One distinction that has wide applicability is whether the program is an early demonstration of an innovative program idea or an established ongoing program. In a demonstration project, the purpose is to find out whether the innovation is worth large-scale adoption. Evaluation is central, and validity is essential. The evaluator is generally given authority to arrange conditions that will allow the study to judge how well the program works. She will be able to assign people randomly to program and control groups. She will often plan for a particularly strong and well-executed version of the program in order to find out whether *at its best* it achieves desired results. If it proves to be successful, a useful next step is to run the program under ordinary operating conditions. If it still works when run the routine way most programs are run, without extra resources or especially enthusiastic or well-trained staff, then it becomes a candidate for widespread adoption.

With an ongoing program, on the other hand, a common question is whether there are ways to increase the program's effectiveness. The agency is committed to the program or something very much like it; it is not seeking an overall judgment as a basis for continuation or termination. The evaluator rarely has control over the assignment of participants or the intensity or quality of implementation. She has to make do with conditions that exist—although it is amazing how ingenious evaluators can be in difficult straits.

Shadish et al. (1991, pp. 427–428) bring a few other considerations into the discussion of design, such as the location of the evaluator (whether employed in the public sector, the private sector, or a university), which affects how much independence she is likely to have, how readily she can call together an expert evaluation team, how accustomed she is to meeting short deadlines, and her relative emphasis on theoretical or practical questions. For example, university evaluators should probably do studies that focus on theoretical questions, take a long time, and are likely to be critical of current policy. Over all, evaluation planning still depends heavily on the particular circumstances of the immediate case. Chapters 8, 9, and 11 continue this discussion.

Some Practical Plans

Advisory Committee

As the evaluator goes about making decisions regarding the coming study, she should consider whether to set up an advisory committee to the study. There are two kinds of reasons why an advisory committee is often a useful idea. One is methodological; the other is political. On the methodological side, such a committee can help the evaluator cope with the knottier issues of measurement, design, and analysis. If advisory committee members are methodological experts, they can help tide the study over the technical shoals. They may know of appropriate measurement scales, pitfalls in particular designs and how to avoid them, newer analytic techniques, and recent evaluative evidence from similar programs. Such gurus can also help to give the study greater credibility with study sponsors and other audiences. If they are well-known researchers with established reputations, their imprimatur can later help to protect the evaluation from the criticism of those who are disappointed with the direction of study results, critics who often make their pitch on grounds of inadequate methodology.

An advisory committee can also serve a political function. It can help the evaluator understand the interests of people who are involved in the program and may be affected by the evaluation. It can include policymakers, program managers, and/or program recipients. An advisory committee can alert the evaluator to special sensitivities among the actors, which may have to do with the history of programming in the area, the line-up of supporters and opponents, impending policy changes, budgetary realities, organizational constraints, and the whole array of contextual forces. The program may be dealing with special populations, such as African Americans, young children, the aged, mental patients, gays, people with disabilities, Latinos, patients with chronic diseases, workers recently terminated by their employers, abused spouses, prison inmates, recent widows and widowers, or undocumented aliens. When the nature of the population being served gives rise to sensitive issues in the program context, an advisory committee can help the evaluator understand and deal with the issues. It can help her understand recipients' concerns and assist in making the study responsive to their concerns and credible to them, even as it tries to answer the questions that policymakers raise.

The membership of the two kinds of advisory committee will be different: methodologists in one case and savvy program and constituency people in the other. Evaluators have sometimes mixed the two kinds of experts on one committee, with erratic results. By and large, the mixture is unstable. Prestigious academics usually want to discuss fine points of methodology, which bores program people to tears, and program and constituency people want to discuss the political environments within which the program operates, not usually a matter of significant moment to methodologists. If a study needs both kinds of help, or the protection that both kinds of experts can provide, it may be a good idea to consider two advisory committees.

You can call them by different names, and it is probably just as well if they meet separately.

Time Schedule

The timing of the study needs good planning. Usually the evaluator is working with a fixed deadline. She receives funding for a limited time, and she is expected to deliver a report about results by the time the contract period ends. Within that constraint, the evaluation team needs to develop a timetable for which tasks have to be accomplished by which dates if they are to meet the deadline.

One of the recurrent problems in evaluation is that studies take a long time to collect data and then have insufficient time left for careful analysis and interpretation. Report writing is also time-consuming, especially if the sponsor wants to see a draft report before the final report is prepared. The study schedule has to build in extra time for the later steps in the work plan.

Also, unexpected problems will inevitably crop up. Murphy's law: If something can go wrong, it will. So time has to be left to deal with reluctant program staff who fail to turn in expected files, computers that crash, and all the heartaches and the thousand natural shocks that evaluation is heir to. This suggests a need for flexible scheduling.

For all the importance of the planning phase of the study, it is vital not to let the study be bogged down. It has to move along at a reasonable pace so that the later phases can be accomplished without skimping. When time begins to run out, the evaluation may have to make cuts: perhaps fewer sites, fewer cases, fewer measures, fewer callbacks, fewer data checks, fewer analyses. It is important to think through the pluses and minuses and make a considered decision on what can reasonably be expected within the time frame. True, it may be possible to cajole the sponsor into an extension of the time period, but don't count on it. And even if an extension can be gained, there will be plenty of further tasks that need to be done if the study is to attain a high degree of validity and utility. Make a realistic schedule and try to stick to it.

Ethical Issues

Evaluation deals with real people in real programs, often people in serious need of help. The results of the evaluation may have real consequences for these programs and these people. Therefore, evaluation has an obligation to pay even more attention to ethical questions than most other kinds of social science research have to do. It is no academic issue whether the evaluation report indicates that the program is serving its target population well or ill. All the research decisions that go into reaching that conclusion have to be made with ethical considerations in mind.

Ethical issues come up repeatedly over the life of an evaluation study. Here I discuss the kinds of issues that arise during the planning phase. In subsequent chapters I discuss ethical issues that come up in later phases. I do not want to isolate the discussion of ethics in a ghetto in the text, which readers can skip or forget and thereafter ignore. I bring up the topic whenever it is relevant to the subject of the chapter.

Ethical issues deserve high priority during the planning of the evaluation study. The evaluator will be intruding into the work domain of staff, interrupting their routines, perhaps observing them in action, and asking them many questions about what they do, know, and think. Similarly she will be collecting information about program recipients, and they may be in a more vulnerable state—ill, needy, or at a particularly critical point in their lives. The evaluator will have access to information about them that may show them in a poor light or that may even subject them to sanctions if it ever became known to others. For example, delinquents in a diversion project may reveal episodes of law violation; veterans receiving assistance may give facts about their status that show they are ineligible for benefits; physicians in a community health project may disclose involvement in assisted suicide. Whether evaluators should collect such information and how they deal with it represent significant ethical issues.

Honesty

As a first principle, the evaluator should not lie to respondents. She may sometimes be tempted to cover up the purpose of the study because of fears that the word *evaluation* will set off alarms in respondents' minds. If staff have had bad experience with past evaluations, she may want to pass off her questions, and her presence, as part of an innocuous-sounding study of attitudes or needs, or as a fact-gathering exploration to help the staff. The best advice is: Don't. For one thing, as Blau (1964, p. 28) has noted, it is hard to maintain a fake cover over time. For another, as Whyte (1984, p. 65) notes, discovery of deception will pretty much bring the study to an end. Finally, there is the question of ethics. The evaluator should have respect for respondents and treat them as she would want to be treated, with candor and honesty.

That doesn't mean that she has to tell respondents everything. She doesn't have to use the word *evaluation* if she has reason to suspect that people will clam up. She doesn't have to explain the full ramifications of the study or its potential consequences. But what she does disclose should be true. People should have enough correct information about the study to decide whether they are willing to answer questions and permit observations, and they should understand something about the uses to which the information will be put.

Informed Consent

Nobody should be dragooned to participate in the evaluation. As in any research project, respondents should know enough about the study to be "informed," and they should have enough leeway to decide whether to "consent" or refuse to participate. Evaluators sometimes believe that the social value of evaluation for the agency, the clientele, and the country—to find out how effective a program is and the extent to which it requires modification or support—should override the rights of individuals to refuse to participate. But the rights of the individual cannot be dismissed so readily. It is their right to decide whether and how to contribute information, and it is the obligation of the evaluator to respect their judgments.

Confidentiality and Anonymity

All information collected during a study should be held in strict confidence. No one but the evaluation team should have access to any information about particular individuals. The only information released in reports should refer to aggregates of individuals in large enough chunks so that no single person can be identified. If a report includes quotes from interviews or observations, the identity of the speaker should be carefully masked unless the individual gives specific permission to be identified.

Usually evaluations promise respondents that their responses to questions will be confidential, so that people will feel free to give honest answers, whether or not the answers are socially acceptable. It is critical that such promises be relentlessly kept. Evaluators should not tell one respondent what another respondent has said, nor should they relate good stories or amusing anecdotes from the study during conversation, because it is possible that listeners know the people involved and can piece together their identities.

This actually happened to me during a study in a Chicago school. After a day of interviewing the principal and teachers in one school, I had a drink with a friend who was an administrator in the Chicago school system. I mentioned the study and told him generally what I was doing. Although no issues of confidentiality were involved, I didn't want to divulge the school's identity. With all the high schools in Chicago, I didn't think that mentioning "a high school" could lead to recognition. But later I mentioned that I'd seen a student in a wheelchair in the hall. My friend said, "I know what school that is," and he named the school. It was the only one at the time where students with disabilities were attending a regular high school. I quickly thought over what I had said about the school. The talk was harmless enough, but I was painfully aware that the principal could have been identified.

Saying that confidentiality will be observed is not enough. During the planning period, procedures must be instituted to safeguard confidentiality. All members of the evaluation team should receive training in ethical standards. Plans should be made to remove names from interviews and questionnaires and promptly replace them with code numbers. The key that links respondent names and code numbers should be kept in a locked file. Field notes from an observational study should include pseudonyms rather than people's real names. Arrangements should be made to file away all papers under lock and key, and no documents should be left on desks where stray visitors can scan them. Look at your offices as if you were a spy out to steal information, and then secure the offices from potential break-ins.

High Competence

If there is one unambiguous ethical imperative it is to plan and carry out an evaluation with the highest competence possible. The "Guiding Principles for Evaluators" of the American Evaluation Association (1995) state it this way:

1. Evaluators should possess (or, here and elsewhere as appropriate, ensure that the evaluation team possesses) the education, abilities, skills, and experience appropriate to undertake the tasks proposed in the evaluation.
2. Evaluators should practice within the limits of their professional training and competence and should decline to conduct evaluations that fall substantially outside those limits. When declining the commission or request is not feasible or appropriate, evaluators should make clear any significant limitations on the evaluation that might result. Evaluators should make every effort to gain the competence directly or through the assistance of others who possess the required expertise.

3. Evaluators should continually seek to maintain and improve their competencies, in order to provide the highest level of performance in their evaluations. This continuing professional development might include formal coursework and workshops, self-study, evaluations of one's own practice, and working with other evaluators to learn from their skills and expertise. (pp. 22–23)

Reciprocity

Evaluators ask for people's time and information and sometimes give nothing concrete back to them. All they produce is a report that goes to a program director or a policy office in Washington. Some evaluators believe they have an ethical obligation to feed back study results to the people who contributed information to the study. I agree. For most purposes, reports to respondents can be short and couched in simple terms, but they should cover issues that respondent groups are likely to care about. As I will note in Chapter 13, the consequences of reciprocating respondents' contributions can be happy ones. Respondents who receive an accounting of what the study found out will often be interested in seeing that members of the decision-making community pay attention to the results. In some cases, having realized that they have a stake in the evaluation as well as the program, they will take steps toward implementing reforms that the evaluation suggests.

Summary

Evaluability assessment is a procedure to determine whether a program is worth evaluating. It examines the fidelity of the program to its design, its stability, and whether there is reason to expect positive outcomes. One way to determine whether positive outcomes are likely is to analyze the program's underlying theory to see whether presumed linkages and mediating mechanisms are plausible. Another way is to collect preliminary information from records and people.

If the program is a reasonable candidate for evaluation, a next step is to decide what the key question(s) shall be. Questions may relate to program process, program outcomes, the links between processes and outcomes, or explanations of why the program reaches its observed level of effectiveness. Decisions have to be made, too, about how long the evaluation will continue collecting data. By and large, long-term follow-up is desirable. The evaluator also needs to specify which unintended consequences are possible and should be included in the evaluation. If a program produces negative side effects, these can swamp whatever good effects appear.

Given all the options available for study, the evaluator has to be selective. Some of the bases on which she can select questions are the relative clout of interested parties and their preferences for particular foci of attention, uncertainties in existing knowledge about programming of this sort, and the practicalities of time, money, evaluator's technical proficiencies, and access to information. Program theory provides an incisive set of criteria. It identifies the assumptions that are central to the program's success, and it shows which of the mediating assumptions are most problematic. Analysis of the program's theories of change is a good way to set priorities. With all the contending bases for choosing the focus of study, the evaluator has to exercise her professional judgment. However much she attends to the wishes of the study sponsor and other stakeholders, and however many interests she aims to satisfy (for timely input into decisions, for adding to the stock of knowledge in the field), in the end she has to rely on her own good judgment—and negotiate her priorities with funders and sponsors.

An early step in planning involves the choice of quantitative or qualitative methods for collecting data. Quantitative methods generally have the advantage of comparability of data, data in numerical form, accepted methods of analysis, a known degree of confidence in the extent and distribution of phenomena, and the authority the data carry in the minds of many audiences. Qualitative methods span a wide spectrum. Their common characteristics are flexibility of inquiry, attention to the meanings and perspectives of program participants, and a dynamic account of developments over time. Qualitative data also tend to provide richness of detail and anecdotes or quotations that capture the essence of the phenomena under study. A mixture of quantitative and qualitative methods will often be useful.

The research design of the study has to be planned. Key to choice of design is whether the evaluation should be able unambiguously to attribute participant outcomes to the intervention of the program. When casual attribution is vital, the best choice is random assignment of eligible people to receive or not receive the program. The difference between the two groups at the end represents the effect of the program. But often random assignment is not practicable, either because all eligibles are entitled to participate in the program or because the program has already enrolled participants prior to the evaluator's arrival. In such cases, other designs are available.

The chapter concludes with a discussion of ethical issues that come up during the planning period. Chief among them are the necessity to be honest and respectful to those who cooperate in providing information and the obligation to conduct the evaluation with the highest possible competence.

Perhaps the most important message is the iterative nature of the planning process. Planning begins with clear specification of the questions the study should address, proceeds to choice of design and data collection method, and goes on to sources of data. It then cycles back through questions, design, and data until a sound and practical plan is reached and all the elements of good evaluation are present.

5

ROLES FOR THE EVALUATOR

[Evaluators'] clientele is the entire social network involved in and influenced by the social program, not just some specially empowered managerial hierarchy or elite.

—Lee Sechrest and A. J. Figueredo (1993, p. 649)[1]

Too many cooks spoil the broth.

—Old proverb

As our profession [evaluation] has changed and [is] changing rapidly with the external environment of organizations, I feel that there is a new demand for leadership from evaluators.... Roles such as change agent, reality shaper, collaborator, facilitator, risk taker, learner, teacher, are inherently part of the transformational and moral leadership style.

—Lorraine Marais (1996)

The shoemaker should stick to his last.

—Old proverb

With all the references sprinkled through the last four chapters to sponsors of the evaluation, funders of the program, program managers, staff, and clients, it is obvious that the evaluator works in a crowded environment. Her decisions about the emerging shape of the study cannot be based on theoretical or technical grounds alone. As noted in Chapter 2, usually she negotiates the plans for evaluation with stakeholder groups. Only when she secures their consent and cooperation can she be assured of having the resources—funds, authority to act, access to program sites and program files, information—that a successful evaluation requires.

This chapter discusses the ways in which the evaluator can interact with stakeholders. It also considers the roles the evaluator can take, whether as objective outsider or co-investigator with program staff. As the epigraphs at the head of the chap-

---

[1]From Lee Sechrest and A. J. Figueredo, "Program Evaluation." Reprinted by permission from *Annual Review of Psychology*, vol. 44, © 1993 by Annual Reviews Inc.

ter suggest, there is a tension between detached and participatory stances. In a detached role, the evaluator seeks to stand above the fray and maintain as much autonomy and objectivity as possible. In an engaged role, she tries to be responsive interactively to the concerns and interests of stakeholder groups. Advantages and disadvantages accrue to both positions, and roles intermediate between them are possible. This chapter explores the dimensions of the subject.

The traditional role of the evaluator has been one of detached objective inquiry. The evaluator is seen as a seeker of fact and understanding who aims to produce a valid report on the program—its inputs, processes, and/or outcomes. The evaluator is careful to avoid becoming unduly biased by the views, hopes, or fears of program staff. She puts her trust in methodology. With appropriate research tools and techniques, she expects to develop comprehensive answers to the questions with which she began the study. Her expectation is that these answers will help people make wiser decisions about the future of the program and understand more about what it is and what it does.

In large part, that vision of the evaluator role still holds center stage, especially when the study is a large-scale, multi-site investigation. The view is particularly apt when the study is funded by higher level authorities with the aim of reviewing their commitment to its continuation. The evaluator knows that absolute neutrality is impossible, but she tries to uphold the conventions of scientific research, with special emphasis on good data, sound analysis, and candid reporting. She will make her results known to appropriate audiences, and to the extent that the evaluation can contribute to building better program theory and/or improved methodology, she will report results in the professional literature.

But dissident views on the evaluator's proper role have come to the fore in recent years. Words like *empowerment, justice,* and *emancipation* have appeared in the evaluation prints, as has another set of terms that include *critical friend, co-investigator, facilitator,* and *problem solver.* These words, which suggest a range of different approaches to the evaluator's job, betoken new sets of understandings about what evaluation is and should be. The evaluator who works with one or a few projects, and whose mandate is to help the projects improve their methods of operation, usually sets up closer relationships with the program. In situations where she interacts on a regular basis with one staff, the distinctions between evaluator and practitioner become less air-tight. This is particularly so when the evaluator uses qualitative methods of inquiry that require her to observe, talk informally to people, and spend considerable time on-site. She becomes involved with project staff on intimate terms. Brown (1995) discusses these newer views as moving toward a view of evaluation that is political rather than neutral or value free. She writes:

> In a social science context that acknowledges multiple perspectives and realities, it is easier to discuss the advantages and disadvantages of evaluator as co-learner rather than expert, conveyor of information rather than deliverer of truth ... educator rather than judge. (p. 204)

Brown's implication is that the evaluator is not to conceive her role solely as collecting and reporting data about the program to whoever is concerned; instead, she is to collaborate with program staff in devising ways to improve the program.

Types of Participative Roles

Advocates of participative approaches offer a range of advice, with often subtle nuances of difference between the different forms of relationship they recommend. Rather than try to cover all shades of opinion, I'll describe three stages along a continuum of evaluator roles. All three are on the participative side of the scale, as opposed to the evaluator-in-charge role that has tended to prevail.

Empowerment Evaluation

At one extreme are those who suggest that community members should conduct their own evaluation of their own projects, with the evaluator offering help and advice from the sidelines. Sometimes called empowerment evaluation (Fetterman, Kaftarian, & Wandersman, 1996), this stance puts people involved in planning and running the project securely in control. They not only design the evaluation; they do it. The evaluator can teach them basic evaluative techniques, coach them as they proceed, and provide assistance when asked. But her aim is to give project personnel the ownership of the study. As Fawcett et al. (1996) write, the mission of empowerment evaluation is to "legitimize community members' experiential knowledge, acknowledge the role of values in research, empower community members, democratize research inquiry, and enhance the relevance of evaluation data for communities" (p. 162).

The communities that seem to be empowered in these kinds of studies are the people associated with the project: managers, practitioners, and members of community coalitions and advisory boards. By and large, the main players seem to be the professionals who run the projects; community members who take leadership roles in the projects are sometime participants.

If the project staff and community members do a poor job of evaluation, that is a price that is paid in order to reap the rewards of community self-determination. The evaluator can try to bring the most relevant techniques to their attention, but they decide which advice to heed and what to do.

Collaborative Evaluation

In the middle of the continuum is evaluator as collaborator and co-investigator. No artificial wall separates practitioner from evaluator. They embark on a joint inquiry. The evaluator, in the words of Rossman and Rallis (forthcoming), is a critical friend. She contributes her research skills; they contribute their knowledge of the project and its clients. Together they undertake an empirical investigation. The evaluator doesn't make judgments based on the data. She doesn't render opinions on what is wrong and needs to be changed. Instead, she urges practitioners to reflect on the data and their own knowledge of the project in a process that will move toward better programming.

Stakeholder Evaluation

Probably the least radical of these views of evaluator roles has been called stakeholder evaluation. Here the evaluator acts as convener of the various stakeholders— that is, groups of people who are likely to be affected by the project and those whose decisions can affect the future of the project (Greene, 1988). She engages in a structured effort to learn their concerns, their assumptions, their questions, their data needs, their intentions for the evaluation. She seeks to shape the evaluation to answer their questions and meet their priorities, but she remains in charge of the technical research work. She reports back frequently to be sure that the study is on target. When the data are analyzed, she engages representatives of stakeholders in interpreting the meaning of the data and its implications for program improvement.

Thus, empowerment evaluation shifts not only the direction of the study but its actual conduct to members of the program community. Collaborative evaluation calls for a co-equal sharing of control. The evaluator usually does the more technical tasks, but program people have an equal say in what shall be measured and how, what comparisons should be made and when, and how the data shall be analyzed. Over the course of the study, they may gain considerable expertise in even the technical tasks of evaluation, and the evaluator gains a stake in the advancement of the program.

Stakeholder evaluation leaves the conduct of the study in the hands of the evaluator, but it gives heavy advisory weight to the desires of stakeholders at every stage. The evaluator can conceive of herself as partner and helper, or she can maintain the posture that once other participants have determined the kind of study they want, she has responsibility for the design, measurement, and analysis phases of the study. It is even possible for her to lay claim to the role of objective outsider insofar as the conduct of the study is concerned, but the press is to collaborate with others all along the way.

The terminology of empowerment and stakeholder evaluation is relatively recent, but the ideas behind the terms have a long pedigree. *Action research*, which goes back at least to the 1940s, similarly engaged practitioners with researchers in the process of studying their own organizations and activities. *Self-evaluation*, whose origin is lost in the mists of time, relied solely on organizations and their members to evaluate the outcomes of their work. In the 1950s the national headquarters of many voluntary organizations developed evaluation manuals for their local affiliates to guide them in conducting self-evaluations.[2] The difference between then and now is that there are more professional evaluators working today with better training and a more self-conscious sense of profession. Current calls for participatory evaluation represent a desire to show greater respect for the knowledge and capacity of the practitioners and community members with whom they work without sacrificing high standards of evaluative performance.

Reasons for Alternative Evaluator Roles

The argument for involving evaluators more closely with program people (and other interested parties) has a philosophical basis in constructivist ideas of multiple perspectives and multiple realities. No longer do social scientists believe in the existence of a single truth. Truth is contingent and conditional. People in different loca-

---

[2]Manuals and guidebooks for evaluation continue to be produced. The United Way of America developed guides to outcome evaluation for its local affiliates (*Focusing on Program Outcomes: A Guide for United Ways*, 1996) and for organizations that receive United Way funds (*Measuring Program Outcomes: A Practical Approach*, 1996). The Office of Juvenile Justice and Delinquency Prevention in the U.S. Department of Justice published the *Community Self-Evaluation Workbook* (1995) for communities that received Title V Delinquency Prevention Program grants.

tions in the social system construe knowledge, truth, and relevance in markedly different ways, each of them legitimate and worthy. Evaluation should not privilege one set of beliefs over others. It should not take seriously only the questions and concerns of study sponsors rather than those of staff and clients whose lives may be even more affected by their experiences in the program.

Redefinition of the evaluator role also derives from some sorry confrontational experiences in the past. When higher level officials have sponsored evaluations of projects that they fund or when projects have been required to produce an evaluation in order to qualify for continued program funding, project staff have complied under duress. They felt that the evaluation was foisted on them, and they tended to regard the evaluator with suspicion. At best she intruded on their space, interrupted their work, and looked over their shoulders. At worst she was going to spy for the enemy (whoever the enemy might be), looking for fault, and then write a negative report about what they were doing, with possibly disastrous consequences for the good work in which they were engaged. Thus, their participation was sometimes half-hearted or even obstructionist.

In international development projects, the divergence of perspective between the evaluator and program personnel was often intensified. The evaluator generally came in under the sponsorship of the development agency that was funding the program, and her viewpoint was apt to mirror theirs. She was divided from local project personnel and beneficiaries by a difference in cultural background and often in language, and she occupied a different position in the status hierarchy—that is, she was an agent of the donor while they are recipients. People in the host country may see evaluation as more of a threat—to continuation of donor-agency funding—than as any conceivable help to them. Yet the evaluator needs to talk to them, understand their activities and their views, have access to their records and to the people whom they serve. Unfortunate relationships that developed in the past have led to a reexamination of the role of the evaluator and a reassessment of where her loyalties should lie.

Another factor entering into the discussion was the growing realization that the major use of evaluation results was not in making go or no-go decisions about programs or projects but rather in finding ways to improve them. If program improvement is the actual, factual consequence of evaluations, it is well for the evaluator to recognize that project people will play a major part in improvement decisions. They have to be seen less as subjects of somebody else's evaluation and more as partners in a collective effort of program reform. The evaluator will encourage them to use evaluation data to reflect on ways in which they improve their practice and the effectiveness of the program. When they buy into the evaluation, there is a better chance that they will pay attention to results and use them as a basis for subsequent change.

A further driving force behind the move toward participative approaches is evaluators' discomfort with the power imbalance. Many evaluators have found it disquieting to have so much control in a situation where others feel like helpless victims. They see it as unfair and unjust. They want to shift the inequitable relationship between program staff and evaluator in the direction of greater equality. They believe that evaluation should acknowledge the program staff's experience and wisdom and engage with them in a nonhierarchical search for improvement.

In even deeper ways, some evaluators see evaluation as a tool that can make its own contribution to the welfare of a community. Particularly when a project is community based and engages residents as well as professionals in its work, they believe that evaluation itself can be turned into a collateral "program" that assists in the overall progress of community development. Giving direction of the evaluation over to staff and local residents helps to give them a sense of self-determination and enhances their feelings of efficacy. It is an opportunity for people to assume responsibility and control for something that affects their lives.

Another reason behind the press for closer involvement with the program community is a sense that evaluators will learn much from others about how to make the study better—more relevant to needs, better attuned to options available, steeped in richer awareness of the culture of the project and its administering organization. Without such intimate knowledge, the evaluator is apt to develop an off-the-shelf study, asking routine questions and answering them in routine ways. With input from project people and others, she can take account of local knowledge and local opportunities and tailor the study to the special conditions of the setting. Brandon, Newton, and Herman (1993) say that information from stakeholders makes the study more valid because they know which *questions* are relevant and therefore which *data* need to be collected.

In the same vein, involvement of project staff and other stakeholders helps to overcome a concentration on narrow issues. Evaluators have been known to look at single measures of effectiveness, such as test scores, without recognizing the range of effects that the program may have. They have sometimes ignored issues of program implementation, which project staff are interested in and which they can do something to change. When project people have a say, they can direct the study toward wider issues with greater relevance for the local staff. The study will be better research with more pertinence to local conditions.

An abiding hope is that involvement of stakeholders in evaluation planning will increase the use of evaluation results. Historically, under traditional evaluation practice, policymakers and program managers have managed to ignore many of the findings that evaluations produce. But if people on the scene have had a stake in planning and developing the study and setting its direction, they have acquired ownership in it. The sense of ownership will be even stronger if they have carried out the study themselves. Therefore, when the results are available, they are apt to take a keen interest in applying the hard-won findings to program decisions and program improvement.

This is an impressive catalog of reasons for close involvement of evaluators with project staff and other local people. But it is wise at this point to consider the advantages of the traditional evaluator role: the dispassionate outsider who gives a candid accounting of what the program is and does. In that role, she has the major advantage of widespread credibility. Her results will be credible to policymakers, to program recipients, to managers of other programs, and to all the varied groups who become interested in the study. When she has become enmeshed in relationships on the local scene, the findings do not have the same aura of objectivity. She can be suspected of having gone native and adopting the values and viewpoints of one interest group or another, unable to give a fair reading.

The dispassionate outside evaluator can still listen to stakeholders' concerns and information interests. Such conversations alert her to the array of questions, demands, complaints, and hopes. But she need not cede judgment about the shape of the study to others. She can elaborate and refine the questions that stakeholders suggest and give them her own interpretation, and remain as objective about the study and its results as any nonconsultative evaluator would be. When credibility with outside audiences is important, a less involved, more detached role can be advisable without sacrifice of local knowledge.

Implementing a Participatory Evaluation

The definition of appropriate participative roles for evaluators varies with the advocate. Let me give a generic account of what a moderate degree of participation might look like and how it can be put into practice.

A first step is to identify the people who should participate in the evaluation, whom I will call stakeholders. (Even though the term tends to be associated with one particular brand of participation, I use it generically.) In studies that have self-consciously involved stakeholders, the group most often included is composed of program managers and staff. In many participative studies, they are the only group that is represented, and much of the literature on stakeholder evaluation seems to take for granted that they are the group that matters. It is their interests that are being maintained as against the dominance of the study sponsor.

But obviously other groups are interested as well. As we saw in Chapter 2, many people have an interest in the findings of evaluation. If findings become the basis for action, recipients of program service will be affected—women in family planning centers, cancer patients in hospitals, reckless drivers required to attend remedial driver education programs, residents in public housing. If the evaluator defines them as groups to be included in evaluation planning, she may find that their concerns differ from those of program personnel. If she invites policymakers or their representatives to sit around the table, too, the diversity of interest will widen.

The decision on whom to include is a key first step. If the evaluator limits participation to program managers and practitioners, the participative process will be easier to manage, but it will also be less representative of the variety of interests in the larger community. The evaluator needs to think through what she aims to accomplish through the participatory process. Perhaps she can talk to a few members of each potential group to understand the nature of the concerns that exercise them. She should be able to recognize where their interests lie, what their priorities are likely to be, the fears and worries that beset them, and where the evaluation fits into their scheme of things. Forearmed with an understanding of such elements, she will be better able to decide how far to include them in evaluation planning. Even if they do not have a formal role, she can consider their wants and try to avoid stirring up their anxieties.

Not all of the groups identified will want to participate in evaluation planning. They may care about the *program*, but they do not necessarily understand or care about its evaluation. Some client groups (particularly those with serious handicaps, like major illness, and those with low levels of education) often do not want to get involved. Many high-level policymakers are too busy with other issues to spare the time for engagement in the planning process. Managers of agencies running similar programs and academic social scientists are not likely to find the opportunity to help plan somebody else's study a fetching notion. So there is a limit to how many stake-holders can actually be drawn into the planning of the evaluation.

Nevertheless, it is useful to find out what issues are on their minds. The evaluator can also draw on other sources. If the program or policy has a high political profile, the media may have reported the bones of contention and the arguments on each side. A knowledge of the academic literature on the topic can disclose the nature of current discourse. Interviews with former clients can give the flavor of their concerns. Past evaluations are also a useful reference. It is then up to the evaluator to bring the concerns and puzzlements of non-attendees into the stakeholder discussions.

One of the early discussions with stakeholders is likely to be about which matters the evaluation should concentrate on. See Chapter 4 for a description of the kinds of issues that need to be resolved. The evaluator should tell stakeholders what she knows about the study—who wants it, what the initial questions about the program are, how long the evaluation will go on, and whatever else she can ethically tell them. She should indicate her intent to give them a voice in evaluation decisions wherever possible. And she should not behave as if she were more important or more knowledgeable than they, but like a colleague engaged in a mutual endeavor to improve service for people. She is going to be heavily dependent on them for information and understanding, and a little humility would even be in order.

The wider the range of participants, the less likely it is that they can readily reach consensus on the purpose of the evaluation or the questions it should address. Evaluators who have used stakeholder approaches to evaluation planning report that the process can sometimes be highly contentious. Different stakeholders, because they have different stakes, can find it difficult to accommodate one another's ideas. In the evaluation of a transit program, the transportation specialist may be concerned only with the program's efficacy in moving people and goods rapidly at reasonable cost. A safety engineer has a different order of concern in mind—the safety of the travelers and the system's employees.

A skillful leader can cope with an array of argumentative stakeholders around a table, but evaluators are not necessarily chosen for their skills in interpersonal relations. Technical skills in evaluation are not always joined to diplomacy or patience. Some evaluators lack the political talents to elicit the participation of all parties, manage conflict, and encourage resolution of differences. There may come a time to introduce a facilitator, an outsider who is not involved in the evaluation *or* the program but who knows how to lead group discussions on controversial topics without intruding into the substance of discussion.

Because people skills are often not their forte, evaluators have developed an array of technical solutions to stakeholder captiousness. They have developed systematic techniques for eliciting the priorities and interests of participants in evaluation planning. One such technique is *multi-attribute utility methods* (Edwards & Newman, 1982). These are procedures by which participants rank their priorities on a set of dimensions in ways that allow for the combination of results across individuals. Another procedure is *concept mapping* (Trochim, 1989), a technique for obtaining a set of statements and concepts from participants and then using statistical methods to construct a map of the group's collective concepts. The mapping technique can be used to identify goals, theories, measures, priorities, or themes for the evaluation. It leads to a framework for discussion expressed in the language of the participants. The result is a graphic representation, fitted with labels that participants choose, and comprehensible to those who participated in the exercise. The evaluation of a Big Brother/Big Sister program used concept mapping with program staff (Galvin, 1989) to develop a theory about how the program operated.

Some evaluators have instituted formal data collection strategies in lieu of face-to-face meetings (e.g., Brandon et al., 1993; Henry, Dickey, & Areson, 1991; Lawrence, 1989). They have surveyed stakeholders by interview or questionnaire, collecting information about their perceptions of the program being evaluated, the kinds of information they want, and the nature of actions they take that information could usefully inform. The data are analyzed, and sometimes a summary is returned to respondents asking for reactions and further comments. Through iterative inquiry, a priority list is generated about the issues that various groups would like the study to address.

When the evaluator elicits stakeholders' views by interview or questionnaire, the raw responses have to be processed and combined before they are meaningful. Some evaluators have used content analysis of stakeholders' responses to identify common themes across the several groups; some have asked participants to prioritize their own responses and have then analyzed only the top 6 or 10; some have asked respondents to indicate the relative importance of different items and then have weighted responses by the importance rating; others have analyzed the responses themselves in order to understand the range of stakeholder interests (Brandon et al., 1993; Carey & Smith, 1992; Deutsch & Malmborg, 1986; Henry et al., 1991; Palumbo & Hallett, 1993; Salmen, 1989). The usual conclusion is that these kinds of procedures may create some problems but that they are worth using.

Balance of Pros and Cons

On balance, does the engagement of program managers, practitioners, policymakers, and beneficiaries help or hinder the evaluation process? In many ways, it is a help. In fact, in many ways it is essential. Just as advertised, it gives project staff and other groups a voice in directing the study and, in so doing, helps to win their support. They become more likely to cooperate with evaluators' requests for information and for modification of routine procedures. When they not only understand but also support what the evaluation is doing, they care about the quality of information that is being collected and become friends rather than foes to the evaluation process.

The process of participation often helps them understand the *program* better. As they go through discussions of program theory, program philosophy, expected outcomes in the short and long term, and the relation of activities to desired outcomes, they gain insight into what they are doing. Often they learn to implement the program with greater fidelity to its underlying premises. Evaluation becomes a means of staff development on issues of program planning and implementation.

Stakeholders also learn about evaluation. To the extent that they become better informed and more sympathetic to evaluation procedures, some of the learnings are likely to stick. They gain a taste of methods of accountability. They may be more likely to undertake evaluative actions in the future, even if relatively simple ones, that encourage a critical reflection on program activities.

On grounds of justice, participatory evaluations tend to level the playing field. People often ignored in traditional evaluation practice can participate on an equal footing with policymakers and program managers. The food stamp recipient, Asian subsistence farmer, staff member in a shelter for the homeless, parent of a special-needs student—all have a say in what kind of evaluation will be done. In House's (1980, 1990) term, there is more justice. Reports have identified important contributions that powerless participants have made to the definition of evaluation emphases.

On the other hand, sitting together around a conference table, for all its egalitarian atmosphere, does not obliterate the distinctions that obtain outside the door. Still important are distinctions of class, age, race, nationality, occupation, gender, and other statuses relevant to a particular program (e.g., officer/enlisted person, caregiver/care receiver, law enforcer/former law breaker). They inevitably affect the way that different people participate in the planning process. To mitigate such distinctions, evaluators have recommended such things as training for participants in the basics of evaluation, involving stakeholders through work in small groups that crosscut the positions of participants, and cultivation of openness and sensitivity on the part of the evaluator to the expressed and unexpressed concerns of different groups. But overcoming the power and knowledge differentials across different stakeholder groups is not easy. Some studies have worked hard to provide information and training to less privileged groups in order to bring them up to speed, with fitful results. Many evaluations sidestep the issue. They either do not invite in representatives of clients or they invite all groups in with impartial bonhomie, but do nothing to prevent their feelings of inferiority in discussions of evaluation and watch them drop out with a sigh of relief.

Still, proponents claim that stakeholder approaches are valuable in and of themselves. They model the more egalitarian society that many program and evaluation people hope to attain.

For all the rhetoric surrounding the issue, it is well to remember that the evaluation arena is not the center ring. More important decisions are made elsewhere. Most people are interested in the *program*, not the evaluation, and they are reluctant to get bogged down in the uncongenial details of research. They may believe that the evaluation is unlikely to make much difference in the wide world of action. Nor are staff and client groups necessarily interested in, knowledgeable about, or skillful at evaluation tasks. They are often overawed by the professionals and defer to the knowledge of the evaluator. Evaluators do not always give them much encouragement to voice their unique perspectives. In fact, more than one evaluator has written about the involvement of staff and clients as valuable for promoting their "compliance" with the demands of the research.

Representatives of some stakeholder groups that are invited to participate do not do so with great regularity. Irregular attendance at stakeholder meetings is a commonly reported phenomenon. The absentees' interest in the evaluation may have been shallow at the start, or the demands on their time are too constant to allow them the time to attend meetings, or they do not have enough knowledge about evaluation or about the program to believe that they can contribute much. With intermittent attendance, they lose track of what has been going on in the planning process, and their commitment to the study ebbs.

Beyond highlighting key questions for study, it is unclear whether involvement of other groups improves the evaluation design. Some evaluators say that it does. An evaluation of an educational program for homeless children included the parents of the children in planning, and despite a number of problems (such as status differences, time requirements), the evaluators believed that the participation of the parents enhanced the study's validity and relevance (Brandon et al., 1993). A study of HIV patients in the military used a participant advisory panel to meet on a weekly basis and formulate recommendations on issues such as confidentiality and inquiry into drug and alcohol use (Carey & Smith, 1992). The evaluators say that this, coupled with other procedures to ensure feedback from patients, led to high participation in the study and better understanding of the meaning of findings. On balance, it seems possible that inclusionary procedures increase the relevance and feasibility—if not the technical quality—of the evaluation.

If empowerment evaluation turns over the actual conduct of the evaluation to stakeholder groups, the odds are that the professionalism of the study will suffer. Even with coaching from an evaluator, evaluation novices are apt to skimp on the niceties of measurement and design. The rationale for self-evaluation rests on other grounds. The argument is that granting self-determination to local groups is so important for enhancing their pride and development and for fostering the utilization of findings that the quality of the evaluation as research is secondary. How persuasive that argument is depends heavily on the peculiar circumstances of each case.

Much of the case for participatory procedures rests on the promise that people who have participated in a study will be more likely to put the findings to use. But some stakeholders do not make, or even influence, decisions about the program's future. This is usually the case for direct-service staff, like teachers and probation officers, and for recipients of program services. When evaluation results are ready, they don't have the authority to do much about them—except lobby those in charge to heed the evidence and make needed changes. *Their* utilization of results will come about, if at all, through pressure on others to pay attention to the findings. Such action usually takes coherent organization and good leadership.

Some people who were invited into discussions about the shape of the evaluation at the start will participate enthusiastically and become committed to the study. But by the time results are ready, they have moved on and left the scene. The people who replace them have no allegiance to the evaluation. They may welcome it, or they may have a different agenda and different fish to fry. The evaluator's careful strategy of involvement in these cases goes for naught.

Still, evidence suggests that those who participate in evaluation planning do in fact have greater interest and commitment to using results. When staff are evaluation insiders, they are privy to early findings and often want to put them to use quickly. Managers and staff have much to gain from running an effective and efficient program, and when evaluation points the way, they are ready to follow (Behn, 1991). At the very least, those who are involved with the evaluation tend to know more about the results than do bystanders and will have many chances to ponder them. The absorption of evidence and ideas can have long-term consequences for how they think and behave.

Additional Limitations to Participatory Approaches

Some additional limitations need to be taken into account. Including other groups in evaluation planning, for all its advantages, can take an inordinate amount of time (House, 1988; Murray, 1983; Stake, 1986). If the evaluator seeks consensus on the main direction of the study, she will find that people can take a long time to work through the issues and reach substantive agreement. When the timetable for the evaluation calls for quick start-up, she can find it nerve-wracking to wait patiently for consensus to emerge. If she decides to take an active role in resolving differences, she is apt to antagonize one group or another.

Another concern arises when representatives are chosen to speak for stakeholder groups. The evaluator has to decide who the representatives shall be. Who shall speak for the staff? for clients? for members of the higher bureaucracy who will fashion new policy proposals? In international development projects, experience has shown that formal community leaders may lack legitimacy. They hold the formal positions, but they do not hold the trust or allegiance of community members. They are not always effective conduits for information to or from the people in the area (Salmen, 1989).

Similarly, spokespersons for parents, clients, staff, or legislators, may not be able or willing to contribute the ideas of their supposed constituency or report back to them. They may end up representing only themselves. It is the old principal-agent problem, where the agent (in this case the representative of the stakeholder group) acts on his own behalf more than on behalf of the group that he purports to represent, and the principal (the constituency) has no way to hold him accountable. In this case, it is not always clear *which* constituency the stakeholder representative is supposed to represent (parents of all the children in the program? in the school? in the district?). Nor are there always available channels for communicating with the constituency. Talking to many members of stakeholder groups, rather than relying on a few representatives, is often the better course.

In the more radical devolution of authority to stakeholders that enables them to conduct their own study, the evaluator will usually work with one group—probably program staff—and act to devolve more authority but to a narrower group of people.

Much of the discussion of collaboration, stakeholders, and empowerment comes down to the involvement of program staff. It is well to recognize at the outset that their participation in planning the evaluation will usually introduce a large dollop of conservatism. They are likely to see issues in a relatively narrow focus, to veer away from questions that problematize basic features of the program, and to assume that most of what is going on will remain unchanged. From their perspective, the evaluation should focus on those issues about which *they* have questions and avoid issues that they see as peripheral—however important such issues may be to others. They can place staff and managerial issues at the top of the priority list, and give less attention to matters that affect the program's benefits to clients—or ignore such issues entirely.

Because participatory strategies involve program staff in the planning and perhaps in the conduct of the study, the evaluation will probably gain a measure of influence on future directions within the program. It does so, however, by placing some fundamental questions about the program off limits.

Ethical Issues

One of the most important obligations an evaluator has in negotiating with study sponsors, program staff, and other stakeholders is to clarify what the evaluation can and cannot do. People sometimes have unrealistic expectations. On the one hand, they can expect the study to reach comprehensive and authoritative conclusions about the worth of the program, its successes and failures, which will tell them exactly what to do next. On the other, they may expect the study to be the messenger of bad tidings, which will threaten the future of the program and of their own jobs. It is up to the evaluator to explain the extent and the limits of the study's likely contributions.

It is particularly important that she make clear what the study cannot do. Potentially embarrassing as it may appear to pull back from the overoptimistic claims she may have made to get funding for the study, she should describe the limits to the questions the study can answer and to the authoritativeness with which it can answer them. The evaluator needs to be candid about the extent to which the study can hand down clear judgments about the quality of the program's services or the utility of its outcomes or render any other hard and fast judgments. She should acquaint stakeholders with the limits to the study's capacity to show that the program was responsible for changes that occurred and the limits to its generalizability to future conditions, other places, staffs, and projects. It is much better that people know of such limits at the beginning rather than find them out at the end.

She might also explain that in most settings higher level policymakers are not likely to use evaluation results as the single basis for their decisions. Therefore, even though the study may turn up unattractive results here and there, their visibility is not likely to lead to termination or cutback of the program. Historically such results have been more likely to lead to efforts to improve the program, give it assistance and support, and help it do better. Fears of immediate negative consequences from evaluation are usually unwarranted.

Protection of Staff and Client Interests

Through all her dealings with others, the evaluator needs to keep standards of ethical behavior in mind. She should deal fairly and sensitively with people. At the same time, she has a professional and ethical responsibility to report the results of the study fully and honestly. The two imperatives are often in tension. The obligation to protect the interests of people in the program can conflict with responsibility for honest reporting. As the American Evaluation Association's (1995) *Guiding Principles* state:

> Because justified negative or critical conclusions from an evaluation must be explicitly stated, evaluations sometimes produce results that harm client or stakeholder interests. Under this circumstance, evaluators should seek to maximize the benefits and reduce any unnecessary harms that might occur, provided this will not compromise the integrity of the evaluation findings. Evaluators should carefully judge when the benefits from doing the evaluation or in performing certain evaluation procedures should be foregone because of the risks

or harms. Where possible, these issues should be anticipated during the negoti-ation of the evaluation. (p. 24)

Can't you hear the wrangles in the committee room that went into that care-fully worded statement? The point is that the evaluator has to take account of the well-being of the people involved with the program. On the other hand, she can't compromise or soft-pedal or omit information from evaluation reports that shows them in a less than positive light. Her first obligation is the honesty and integrity of her work. As some have said, the evaluator is like a certified public accountant whom the public can trust for honest accounts of social programs.

Nevertheless, given the fact that evaluations are not Truth Writ Large but rea-sonable approximations performed by fallible human beings, the evaluator should not dig in her heels and refuse to consider other people's points of view. I will have more to say on this subject in Chapter 13 on reporting and disseminating evaluation results. For here, it is well to note that the ethical demand on the evaluator is to treat people with consideration. As the Joint Committee on Standards for Educational Evaluation (1994) has written:

> Evaluators should respect human dignity and worth in their interactions with other persons associated with an evaluation, so that participants are not threat-ened or harmed. (p. 81)

Conflict of Interest

Evaluators have a stake of their own in the evaluation. They obviously have a pro-fessional interest in doing a good study and getting professional recognition and appropriate compensation for it. They usually also have an interest in satisfying the study sponsor. If they are on the staff of a government agency, program organization, or research institute, they want to please their boss and colleagues and thus advance their careers. If the study sponsor is an outside funder, the evaluator may be inter-ested in pleasing that organization so that it will send more work and funds her way. These are daily concerns in evaluation practice, and evaluators learn how to recon-cile their own interests with those of ethical and professional practice—or else they don't survive long in this environment.

One of the purposes that statements of standards and guiding principles serve is to alert the evaluator to possible conflicts of interest. She has to take these things seriously. She has to learn to subordinate her personal and professional-advancement interests to the interests of the parties to the evaluation. She cannot, for example, cave in to agency demands that she omit Site Z, which randomly fell into her sam-ple, because investigation there might reveal things that the agency does not like. She cannot avoid collecting some types of relevant and necessary information (say, data on racial antagonisms), because her superiors are wary of political conflict. Even though it might jeopardize her own stake to pursue a full and fair inquiry, the codes of professional behavior enjoin her to persevere. But she should be sure that such data are indeed necessary.

The standards and guiding principles also exist to take the heat—to serve as an excuse in the face of demands to do something unethical or unprincipled. An evalua-tor can say to a study sponsor, "I'd like to do what you ask, but professional standards for evaluators don't allow such actions." Unfortunately, codes of principles have to be worded so generally that it is often difficult to convince an agency official that what he is asking falls outside the allowable zone. It is often a matter of interpretation. Nevertheless, it is important to have such codes to demonstrate to others that evaluation is a profession with strong ethical standards and anything does *not* go.

Sometimes stakeholders have a financial interest in a program—say, owners of nursing homes or firms that sell educational software. Those are obvious stakes, but sometimes the financial interest is more covert. It is important to get all such information out on the table at the start. Others should know which interests are operative. It is the task of the evaluator, with whatever stakeholder group she has convened, to try to ensure that these stakeholders do not receive preferential treatment.

Personal friendships and professional relationships can raise other more subtle conflicts of interest. An evaluator who has her office in the program agency can hardly fail to be sensitive to staff's interests and needs. An evaluator who is doing fieldwork among the homeless may find her allegiances coalescing around their needs. Evaluators have to take frequent stock of their own feelings and commitments so as not to overrepresent the views of stakeholders with whom they have special relationships. They may consider the advisability of reporting their own biases up front in any report they write.

The Joint Committee on Standards (1994) encapsulates the discussion of conflict of interest with this standard: "Conflict of interest should be dealt with openly and honestly, so that it does not compromise the evaluation processes and results" (p. 115). That's as good a guide as you can get.

Openness of Communication

Evaluators can get themselves into tough spots if they are so diplomatic that they fail to describe or explain problematic features of the evaluation. Candor is of the essence. For example, the evaluator may find that information that she had been assured was in the organization's archives is not forthcoming. The archivist says it doesn't exist, and her own limited search has turned up few traces. She doesn't want to blame the person who informed her of data availability at the outset, nor does she want to get the archivist into trouble by complaining about his lack of zeal in searching. However, she has to undertake a whole new set of data collection activities, which means more time, more money, and more demands on people's memories and patience. Without any explanation from her about the reasons for this extra work, the agency's top official becomes outraged at the delay in reporting and the additional expenditure for unplanned investigation.

This episode is relatively benign, as these kinds of things go. Many problems could be avoided by open communication, but evaluators often want to avoid imbroglios and thus choose silence over confrontation. However, confrontation—as diplomatic and gentle a confrontation as possible—is often the wiser course. Put the cards on the table, and people will generally respect the confronter and the argument. The resolution will not always favor the evaluator, but at least the issue will be resolved, and work can proceed.

These kinds of disputes underscore the importance of the advice I offered in Chapter 2 about the structure of evaluation. It is important to have the evaluation's

location and lines of authority clear from the beginning, so that everyone understands where and how disputes will be resolved. Instead of having misunderstand-
ings fester and add to mutual distrust, the air can be fairly rapidly cleared.

Candor is a two-way street. Program people need to communicate with the evaluator, too. Attempts to conceal or mislead are apt to go awry. A savvy evaluator, skilled
in the techniques of inquiry, will find out. It is better for them to be up-front about even
unpleasant conditions than to foment an atmosphere of distrust and suspicion.

When collaboration goes very well, program staff become "reflective practitioners" (Schon, 1983). That is, they combine something of the staff's belief in the
program with the evaluator's doubt. They look at what they are doing with a
thoughtful and questioning glance, and review their successes and failures with an
eye to doing better. With an analytic perspective, they analyze their performance and
incorporate the learnings into their daily practice. Such reflective practitioners find
evaluation an ally and an aid. It helps them to ground their self-reflection in sound
data and join with colleagues in open-minded inquiry about improvement.

Summary

Whereas the traditional role for the evaluator has been that of dispassionate observer and reporter on things as they are, current thinking has introduced a range of possible alternatives. Most evaluators are aware that there is no one single truth. People
in different positions see the world from different perspectives and define their interests in different ways. They even construe knowledge, or what passes for knowledge, differently. The evaluator is therefore advised to gather a range of viewpoints
in planning an evaluation study.

Some advocates go further. They suggest that the evaluator not only listen to
other people but that she give them an authentic place in planning, conducting, and
interpreting the study. She is advised to become a partner in a collaboration. She is
to work with program practitioners in a collective effort to use data to improve the
program. At the extreme, writers on empowerment evaluation urge evaluators to turn
the whole conduct of the evaluation over to practitioners and community people.
The evaluator will train them in evaluation methods and coach from the sidelines.
By so doing, the evaluator rights the imbalance of power that has tended to give
evaluators the authority to judge others and affect their lives and careers. When program and community members conduct their own evaluation, they gain self-determination, justice, and empowerment.

The chapter gives advice on how an evaluator can work productively with
other groups in planning an evaluation study.

Some of the reasons for working with others are practical. When the evaluator
knows how each party defines the problematics surrounding the program, she can
plan a study that has relevance to a broad range of potential users of its findings. But
some of the reasons for canvassing stakeholder opinions and involving them in the
conduct of the study have to do with deeper issues of justice, power relations, and
development of community capacity.

The evaluator should treat others with respect, heed their opinions, and value
their knowledge. With stakeholder participation, she will learn how to make the

study more relevant to the range of concerns that surround the program and make the study more feasible to conduct. She will also help to assure that program people and other interested parties will buy into the study. When they gain a sense of ownership, they are more likely to put the results to use.

An endemic tension exists between protecting the rights of practitioners and program managers on the one hand and reporting fully and honestly on the other. When the study finds shortcomings, program people may wish to soft-pedal them or explain them away. The evaluator's responsibility is to provide a full and candid report. In some cases, the tension is readily resolvable. When the use to be made of findings is solely within the discretion of staff, then there is little point in belaboring failures and shortcomings. The point is to provide cues to improvement. However, when the evaluation is also meant to serve the interests of higher policymakers and funders, candor should not be sacrificed. Nevertheless, the evaluator has to recognize that evaluation is one reading, one fallible reading, of a complex situation. She has an obligation to listen carefully to the views of others. But then she has to exercise her own good judgment in interpretation.

When program people play a major role in the evaluation, their bent is likely to be conservative. They see the world through their own lenses, and they are likely to accept much of the structure and process of the program as given and unchangeable. They will not ask the full range of questions that others might bring to the table. For example, they are likely to ignore some issues that recipients of the program would raise. If only program staff are represented in evaluation planning and conduct, the evaluator may undertake to represent the views of those who are not part of the planning and take their concerns into account.

Participatory evaluation is no panacea. Some people who are asked to cooperate in the study will not do so. Some who helped to define the study in the early days will have left their positions by the time the results are ready. Their early commitment to the study will have no consequences for how the new people will respond. The representation of a few stakeholders in the study will not necessarily convince their colleagues that *their* interests are being represented.

Nevertheless, when participatory evaluation works well, it tends to have positive effects on the nature of the study that is done and on the willingness of potential users to pay attention to the findings. Program managers and practitioners are apt to absorb its lessons into their daily work, and they may also feel strengthened in their capacity to determine the future of the program and the organization.

When the evaluation is carried out for purposes of decisions at higher levels, less entanglement with the program is likely to be advisable. A more detached evaluation is likely to have greater credibility in policymaking communities. It has an aura of objectivity that instills confidence among upper-echelon officials.

6

DEVELOPING MEASURES

When you can measure what you are speaking about, and express it in numbers, you know something about it; but when you cannot measure it, when you cannot express it in numbers, your knowledge is of a meager and unsatisfactory kind; it may be the beginning of knowledge, but you have scarcely, in your thoughts, advanced to the stage of *science.*

—William Thomson, Lord Kelvin (1894)

Since the measuring device has been constructed by the observer ... we have to remember that what we observe is not nature in itself but nature exposed to our method of questioning.

—Werner Heisenberg (1958)

By this time the evaluator has made a great deal of progress. She knows why the evaluation is being done and the environment in which its results are awaited; she knows what the program is like and how it is expected to work; she has assured herself and her team that adequate resources are at hand and an appropriate location in the organizational structure; she has negotiated agreement with program managers, staff, and other stakeholders about what the study will cover and their cooperation with it; and she knows the main questions that the study will address. Now is the time to decide on the specific measures to be developed, the sources from which the data will be derived, and the methods for collecting the data.

For the purposes of this chapter, I will assume that the evaluation is largely quantitative. Quantitative evaluators have to make most of their choices in advance. They are required to craft specific evaluation questions at the outset and figure out where and how to collect the data they will need to answer them. But much of the discussion here is relevant to qualitative work, too. Although qualitative evaluators have more latitude in choosing and changing questions as the study goes along, they, too, need a good sense of where the study is heading.

114

In Chapter 3, I discussed the development of program theory as one way to go about the planning of the evaluation. I suggested ways in which program theory can help to identify a series of variables for the study. These variables have to do with desired program outcomes or goals, possible unintended consequences of the program, components of program implementation, and interim markers of progress. It is often useful to develop measures of program inputs as well. These would be the resources of all kinds that go into conducting the program and the environment within which the program operates. So let us add program inputs to the list.

Of course, the list is all out of order. Chronologically, we would start with inputs, go on to program implementation processes, then to interim markers of progress, and on to desired and unintended outcomes. But the order here follows the logic of backward mapping (Elmore, 1996). One starts with outcomes and maps them backward to their origins.

In this chapter I discuss how to go about measuring this set of variables. I start with a brief definition of what a measure is, and then go on to talk about measuring:

1. Desired outcomes
2. Unintended outcomes
3. Interim markers of progress toward outcomes
4. Components of program implementation—that is, program processes
5. Resources, inputs, and environment

Following that discussion, the chapter considers other decisions that have to be made about measurement: the qualities of good measures, how many measures are enough, and the ways in which measurement prefigures the kinds of analysis that can be done.

Measurement

I use the word *measure* to signify data that can be expressed quantitatively to characterize a particular phenomenon. Or, as Stevens's (1951) classic statement puts it, "In its broadest sense, measurement is the assignment of numerals to objects or events according to rules."

It is vital to distinguish between a measure and a concept. In an evaluation study, the evaluator may be interested in students' gains in knowledge. Knowledge is a concept. The measure of knowledge has to be specific; it may be "scores on the National Assessment of Educational Progress (NAEP) fourth-grade math test." Or the evaluator of a job training project wants to pay attention to program processes, particularly the extent of each participant's exposure to the classroom component of the training. Exposure to the training is a concept; one measure of the concept would be "number of hours spent in classroom training." Another evaluator, looking at a program for former mental patients, wants to study their mental health status. One possible measure is "scores on the Gurin scale of psychological distress" (Kessler & McRae, 1982).

There are four general levels of measurement: nominal, ordinal, interval, and ratio. With a *nominal measure*, numbers are assigned to categories, such as categories of religion (Protestant, Catholic, Jewish, Moslem, etc.), occupation, or political preference. The numbers have no mathematical meaning; they simply stand for different items in the set. The two requirements for nominal measures are that the categories have to be mutually exclusive so that each case fits into only one category, and the categories have to be exhaustive so that there is a place (and a numeral) for every case. In an evaluation, the evaluator may want to look at the differences in projects in different regions of the country; she divides the country into eight regions (*Northeast, Middle West,* etc.) and assigns a number to each region. That gives a nominal measure, and 8 isn't more or better than 1. Dichotomous measures are a special class of nominal measures that have only two possible values, for example male/female, or arrested/not arrested. The advantage of creating nominal measures by assigning numbers is that they can be analyzed statistically. Common uses are to look at the frequencies with which each category appears ("55% of participants were male and 45% female") and to divide other data in the study by these categories ("80% of the males complied with the regimen compared with 55% of the females"). Nominal measures can also be used as predictor and outcome variables. Because these kinds of measures refer to categories, they are also called categorical measures.

An *ordinal measure* represents a hierarchical ordering. Higher numbers go to categories that are greater than lower numbers. An example would be occupation measured in terms of the level of education required for the job. Occupations that require a graduate degree would be highest, followed by those that require college graduation, and so on. The earlier categories receive higher numbers, but the differences between categories are not equal. Another example might be "intensity of staff's commitment to the project," measured by a self-report of commitment on a five-point scale from "very strong" to "very weak." Again, it is likely that the differences between the categories are unequal.

Interval measurement differs by having not only an order from more to less, but also equal intervals between the items. Most indices constructed to measure beliefs, behaviors, intelligence, and aptitude are presumed to be interval measures, although the presumption is often wrong.

Ratio measurement has all the characteristics of the nominal, ordinal, and interval levels, and in addition, the scale is anchored by a true zero. True ratio measures would be number of siblings, years of schooling, frequency of program attendance, wages earned, number of arrests.

Analysts' preference for measures is in the reverse order from the way I've presented them. They like ratio measures, then interval, then ordinal, and will settle for nominal only when there is no better way to handle the data. The reason is that statistical analysis is more powerful and versatile with measures that have ratio-level properties. Evaluators sometimes needlessly categorize data—for example, by collecting age data in 10-year ranges instead of asking for exact age. Not only does such a procedure limit the use of certain statistical tools, but it also reduces the amount of information available for analysis. People in their late 20s may differ in their response to the program from those in their early 20s, but with the categorized data, it will be impossible to find out. The evaluator can always combine ratio and interval data into categories after the fact, but she cannot create interval data from data that were collected in categories.

I will use the word *indicator* to mean much the same as *measure.* The main difference is that an indicator is at least an ordinal measure and has a direction. One end of the scale is more, better, or more intense than the other end. The unemployment rate is an indicator; up is worse. Reading readiness scores are indicators; up is better. In evaluation, we usually know in advance which way we expect the indicator to go. In fact, if we don't know and don't care which way it is expected to move, it's a poor indicator. Indicators generally have policy implications. When there is consensus about which end of the distribution is good or bad, there is frequently a societal interest in intervening to make things better.

Measures can also be composites made up of sets of items. *Scales, indexes, tests,* and *inventories* refer explicitly to composite measures made by combining individual items. All of these terms represent quantitative descriptors that can become variables in the analysis. Variables are values of phenomena that vary across members of a population. They are the stuff that statistical analysis works with. Measures, indicators, and variables overlap in meaning.

Program Outcomes

Let us begin the discussion of measurement with program outcomes. While program outcomes chronologically come last, outcomes represent the anchoring point for the evaluation. Outcomes define what the program intends to achieve. Of course, some evaluations deal exclusively with program process, as, for example, when the evaluation of a new project examines the kinds of clients who are recruited or the kinds of activities that are conducted. But unless exploration of process is its sole purpose, keeping an eye on outcomes makes sense from the start.

Sources of Outcome Measures

When the evaluator is considering the construction of outcome measures, an obvious place to start is with the program's official goals. In Chapter 2 we encountered these goals and recognized their advantages and possible limitations for evaluation purposes. They have the distinct advantages of being official and authoritative, and they usually represent the major objectives that funders and program staff expect the program to accomplish. Possible limitations are that they may be vague or outdated, or that different program actors have different ends in view, or that there are multiple goals with different people devoting their energies to achieving different purposes.

When official goal statements suffer some from these kinds of disabilities, what can an evaluator do? Four courses are open to her:

1. She can pose the question of the program's goals and wait for program personnel and other stakeholders to reach a consensus. But she may be in for a long wait. There will be time to play a lot of computer games in the interim.
2. She can read everything about the program she can find, talk to practitioners at length, observe the program in operation, and then sit down and frame a set of outcome measures herself. Sometimes this is a reasonable procedure, but there are two dangers. One is that she may read her own professional preconceptions into the program and subtly shift the goals (and the ensuing study) in the direction of her own interests. The other risk is that when the study is completed, the program practitioners will dismiss the results with the comment "But that's not

really what we were trying to do at all." Nevertheless, there are occasions when, in lieu of better options, this is a sensible course.

3. She can set up a collaborative effort in goal formulation. This is often the best approach. Sitting with the program people and the evaluation sponsor, and perhaps other stakeholders, the evaluator can offer successive approximations of goal statements. The other people modify them, and the discussion continues until agreement is reached. Note that the evaluation is not seeking agreement on a single goal but on a set of goals for study.

4. If these steps fail to yield a consensual definition, she can table the question of goals, and enter upon an exploratory, open-ended study. If the study's sponsors agree, she can undertake a process evaluation to find out what the program is really doing. When the people who should know what the program is trying to accomplish cannot agree, this can be a useful strategy. It may be particularly useful in complex and uncharted programmatic areas. Rather than trying to browbeat people to formulate arbitrary and superficial goals in order to get on with the study, the evaluator tries to understand significant happenings inside the program that might otherwise go unstudied, unanalyzed, and unsung. Evaluations based on too-specific goals and indicators of success may be premature in a field in which there is little agreement on what constitutes success.

Official goals and consensual agreements are not the only sources that the evaluator can use to define outcomes. An experienced evaluator searches for the hidden agenda, the covert goals of the project that are unlikely to be articulated but whose achievement sometimes determines success or failure no matter what else happens. For example, a project of interdisciplinary studies in a university aims to provide students with knowledge that transcends disciplinary boundaries. That is an important goal for the faculty who have put together the set of course offerings. But another, unstated, goal is to win the support of the departmental faculties and the university administration. If they do not, even consummate educational results may not be enough to keep the project alive. The evaluator, if she wants to understand the project and its evolution over time, is well advised to keep an eye on matters that are of overriding concern in the situation (Do the departments resent the incursion of the interdisciplinary program into what they consider their turf? Is the university administration opposed to granting tenure to interdisciplinary faculty?) as well as the official goals. She will learn much that explains why the project makes the adaptations it does and where the real game is.

There are a number of reasons to scout beyond official goal statements in setting the outcomes by which the program will be evaluated. Sometimes the evaluator believes that official goals are incomplete and neglect an important concern. For example, a state legislature enacted a program of child care for welfare mothers who were in job training courses. The purpose of the legislature was to enable the women to complete training, get a job, and get off welfare. The legislature believed that the purposes of the program would be achieved if the number of women on welfare went down or at least if the women whose children were in day care moved off the welfare rolls. In evaluating the child-care program, the evaluator was concerned about the quality of care given to the children. Although the legislature's purposes had to receive priority (or else the future of the program might be in jeopardy), the evaluator could include some measures relating to the welfare of the children.

If the evaluator focuses exclusively on official goals, she may fail to see other significant elements in the scene. The evaluation may concentrate so hard on what the program staff says is important that it ignores conditions that make much more difference for program participants. In fact, wily staff may purposely try to limit the evaluation to goals on which they know they will look good and fail to discuss goals whose attainment is more problematic for the agency. Scriven (1991) has counseled evaluators not to ask program people about goals at all, because their responses might bias the study. He has advised evaluators to adopt a goal-free approach. Under this rubric the evaluation would forage widely and examine outcomes that are consequential for the lives of program participants.

Goal-free evaluation is a fetching notion, and limiting evaluation to program-sanctioned goals does run the risk of neglecting outcomes of high importance to other stakeholders. But in practice the evaluator cannot ignore the aims the program seeks to achieve. No evaluation can study everything. The evaluator has to make choices about what to look at. If the choices are guided not by program intentions but by the evaluator's assessment of what people need, that gives the evaluator a strong voice in choosing the outcomes that matter for the program. Allowing the evaluator to define program goals also jeopardizes the willingness of program people to pay attention to the results of the study. If it was not studying things that they thought were important, why should they take it seriously? Thoughtful consultation with stakeholders would seem to be in order, and if the evaluator is persuasive enough and has sufficient resources, she may be able to convince them to go beyond their image of desirable accomplishments.

Emphasis on Accountability

For a variety of reasons, evaluators can be reluctant to rely heavily on officially sanctioned statements of goals as the backbone of the evaluation. One instance would be when she is out of sympathy with official goals—for example, if official goals stress cost savings and she cares more about the welfare of clients. But current thinking has reemphasized the legitimacy of taking official goals and objectives as the starting point. Many agencies, both public and private, are facing a press for what has been called results-based accountability. Interest groups, the media, legislatures, and informed publics are demanding that government programs be held accountable for more than the activities they perform, such as treating arthritis patients or inspecting poultry. They should be held accountable for the results they achieve, such as improving the health of patients or ensuring safe and healthful poultry. Their results have to be framed in terms of the goals that society, through its elected representatives, has charged them to accomplish.

In the past, regulation of agencies and programs centered mainly on inputs. Laws regulated the conditions of agency operation and the practices they must follow (preschools must have so many square feet of space per child, teachers must have degrees in education, all high school students must receive two years of instruction in math). Now there is much more concern with what comes out at the end. For example, in 1994 Congress passed a law adopting educational goals for the year 2000, which incorporate such goals as increasing the high school graduation rate to at least 90% and seeing that all students leaving grades 4, 8, and 12 demonstrate competency in challenging subject matter in English, math, science, history, and geography.[1] A commission was established to track the extent to which the goals were being realized, and the National Center for Education Statistics is collecting relevant data. In 1994 Congress passed the Government Performance and Results Act, which mandates that all federal agencies report on the results—that is, the outcomes—of their work.

Agencies are accommodating to the pressure for accountability, sometimes even embracing it, for four kinds of reasons: (a) Requirements for explicit measures of accomplishment have logic and reason on their side. It is fitting that agencies and programs report on what they have actually achieved. (b) Having agreed-upon standards for accomplishment is expected to promote collaboration among staff in the agency. When staff agree about what they aim to do and take joint responsibility for doing it, they may be more likely to develop an organizational culture of enterprise and responsibility. (c) Results-based accountability diminishes the need for centralized micromanagement and rigid rules. Legislatures or executive agencies do not have to mandate the number of hours of instruction in each subject. If the school demonstrates that it is improving mathematics knowledge (or whatever other outcomes are adopted), it can be allowed much more flexibility to generate appropriate and responsive types of service. (d) Agencies have come to accept accountability demands as a way to restore public confidence in their work. They hope to show that programs are accomplishing their purposes and program investments are worth their salt—and the public's support.

An emphasis on goals and accomplishments is in tune with the times. Evaluation can build on this foundation. Official program goals should be one input into the development of outcome measures, and usually an important input, although the evaluator can draw on other sources to round out the array of outcomes she studies.

The Measurement of Outcomes

Whatever program goals are going to form the basis for outcome measures, they must be stated in clear terms. They must give the evaluator guidance on what to look for. In a classroom program, should she look for evidence of enjoyment of the class? Interest in the subject matter? Knowledge of the subject matter? Use of the subject matter in further problem solving?

The goal has to be specific. It must be able to be translated into operational terms and made visible. Somebody has to *do* something differently when the goal is reached. Thus, if the goal is to interest students in science, their interest should be manifested. Perhaps they talk more often in class, raise their hands more often, do more outside reading on the subject, tell their parents about it, or any of several other things. These actions are the kind of thing that can be measured.

---

[1]The national education goals were agreed to by the nation's governors and the president at an education summit in 1989. Five of the six goals are outcome goals like those mentioned in the text, and one is a process goal: "Every school in America will be free of drugs and violence and will offer a disciplined environment conducive to learning." The governors and the president established the National Education Goals Panel to be at the center of a process for "holding the nation and the states accountable for their [the goals'] attainment" (National Education Goals Panel, 1993, p. xiii). The goals panel has issued periodic reports on progress being made in achieving each of the goals. The reports present such data as the high school graduation rates and scores of 4th, 8th, and 12th graders on subject matter tests.

In quantitative evaluation, the goal has to be measurable. This is not as serious a restriction as it may seem at first glance. Once goal statements are clear and unambiguous, skilled researchers can measure all manner of things. They can use the whole arsenal of research techniques—observation, content analysis of documents, testing, search of existing records, interviews, questionnaires, sociometric choices, laboratory experiments, simulation games, physical examinations, measurement of physical evidence, and so on. With attitude inventories and opinion polls, they can measure such seemingly soft goals as improvements in self-esteem or self-reliance. But since few programs set out only to change attitudes, the evaluator will also want to find and measure the behavioral consequences of changed attitudes—the things participants do because they feel different about themselves, other people, or the situation.

For example, an energy conservation program aims to reduce the amount of electricity that householders use. The desired outcome is reduced electricity usage. That translates easily into a reasonable and practicable measure: megawatts of energy consumed by the household. The goals of a road-building program in a developing country are to enable small farmers to transport their produce to the city and thereby increase their income. Here we have a two-step theory: The existence of roads will encourage farmers to carry their crops to the city instead of selling them locally, and transporting crops to the city will increase farmers' incomes. In this case, we might have measures of the frequency with which farmers actually take their produce to the city (or the weight or value of crops so transported), the amount of produce they sell in the city, and the income they earn through these sales. This collection of outcome measures is a little more difficult and perhaps more problematic than the first example. But we are getting close to the nub of the matter.

Measuring Effects on Persons Served Most evaluations concentrate on changes in program participants. They commonly use measures of attitudes, values, knowledge, skills, and behavior. Each of these may be directly relevant to program goals. A vocational education program, for example, may expect to impart basic knowledge, specific skills, values about work, attitudes toward job seeking, and employment in an allied trade.

In some cases, behavioral outcome measures are difficult to find or develop. How, for example, do you observe, record, and quantify the self-sufficiency of residents in an extended-care facility? One procedure is to administer inventories to the respondents that ask them questions about their behavior under a variety of conditions: How often do they dress themselves? Make their bed? Take walks without help? and so on. Another procedure is to turn to expert judgments, asking expert observers to rate the residents on scales from "fully self-sufficient" to "requires constant care."

Participants' opinions about the program are sometimes used as an outcome measure. They are asked whether they liked it, whether it helped them, whether they would recommend it to others, and similar questions. There is some merit in finding out whether the program appealed to its audience. In the extreme case, if it is totally unacceptable, nobody will come. But certainly people may like or dislike a program for reasons unconnected with its goals. They may have hazy or misguided expectations of what the program is intended to accomplish and therefore assess its interest and utility in irrelevant terms. Unless it is a specific goal of the program to interest or entertain or offer expected services to the participants, the popularity contest model for evaluation is woefully incomplete.[2]

Measuring Effects on Agencies   Some programs aim to produce changes in institutions rather than in people. They may seek to make local bureaucracies more responsive to residents, alter the type of clientele served or the composition of governing boards, broaden an agency's concept of its mission. In such cases, indicators of program outcome will be measures of institutional characteristics. Some of these can be aggregated from data about individuals in the organization (e.g., number of daily contacts with local residents), and some can be global measures of the institution (e.g., total budget, proportion of the budget devoted to a particular activity, hours during which facilities are open).

Measuring Effects on Larger Systems   There are an increasing number of programs whose goals are to make changes in a whole network of agencies (increase communication and referral among all agencies dealing with troubled youth in a community) or to change a community or even a national service delivery system (education, mental health, job training). A series of programs, from the Community Action Program of the War on Poverty to the Model Cities Program a few years later, to community development corporations to a current series of foundation-funded comprehensive community-based initiatives, have aimed to revitalize low-income communities. By the mid-1990s a number of major foundations were sponsoring community initiatives designed to build community in poor neighborhoods, increase coordination of agency services, empower the residents, and revitalize the neighborhood (Adams, Aller, Krauth, St. Andre, & Tracy, 1995; Chaskin & Joseph, 1995; Enterprise Foundation, 1993; Kubisch, 1996; Pew Charitable Trust n.d.; Rostow, 1993; Stephens et al., 1994). Several large government programs are now working at the community level in health promotion, substance abuse prevention, prevention of juvenile delinquency, and reduction in violence and sexually transmitted diseases. Experience has shown that programs targeted at individuals have had indifferent success, and program funders now believe that programs need to change the social and cultural context in which behavior occurs. They expect geographically based programs to alter community conditions and community norms (Goodman, Wandersman, Chinman, Imm, & Morrissey, 1996; Thompson & Kinne, 1990; Winett, 1995).

In cases like these, outcome measures have to relate not only to the individuals who live in the communities and the improvements in their life chances, not only to the social agencies serving the community and the increase in coordination and cooperation among them, but also to the community itself. The programs aim to improve the neighborhoods. In some cases, the expected change is in physical facilities—better housing, cleanup of empty lots, better street lighting, less graffiti, more amenities. But there is also expected to be a shift in neighborhood culture. Residents are supposed to take more responsibility for the geographic site and for one anoth-

---

[2]Studies of compensatory education programs find one universal finding: Regardless of the type of program, duration, or actual results, parents are enthusiastic (McDill et al., 1969, pp. 43–44).

er. If the objectives of the programs are realized, there should be more interaction among neighbors—more visiting, more helping behavior, more organization of people to pursue common aims. Residents are expected to feel better about their community and about themselves and their future.

Measures have to be located or devised that relate to such developments. They can relate to individuals in the neighborhood (Do more of them get jobs?), to agencies (Do they share data on the families they serve?), to the community (Is there more sense of empowerment—of the capacity of neighborhood residents to influence what happens?). Data can come from interviews with community leaders; observations within city departments or police precincts or at neighborhood meetings; local-level statistics on agency clientele or services provided, city budgets spent on services to the neighborhood, hospital admissions, high school graduations, housing starts; logs kept by staff; analysis of documents or of news stories; sample surveys of residents; and so on.

One of the problems that evaluators face at this level is the difficulty of defining the geographic area that constitutes the neighborhood to the different groups who live and work there. One man's neighborhood is another man's alien turf, even when they live next door to each other. Another problem is the paucity of available statistics at a neighborhood level (health statistics, crime, employment, and so on). A growing number of evaluations are now directed toward the neighborhood or community level, and opportunities are increasing for cooperative efforts at improved measurement. (See Chapter 7 for ways of collecting data at the neighborhood level.)

Measuring Effects on the Public   If a program seeks to alter public values or attitudes, the appropriate indicator of outcome is obviously the public's views. Cumming and Cumming (1957), for example, administered questionnaires and conducted interviews to determine the effects of a community educational program designed to alter public views about mental illness. They found that the six-month program produced virtually no change in the population's attitudes toward mental illness or the mentally ill. Recent campaigns have often been more successful. Flora, Maccoby, and Farquahar (1989) describe the Stanford studies of community programs to reduce cardiovascular disease. They compared communities with a media campaign, with a media campaign plus individual contact, and no campaign. They found that those who were exposed to the media-only campaign and those who also received the face-to-face intervention improved in knowledge of health practices and changed their behaviors to lower risk of disease. The media-only recipients made smaller improvements than those with the more elaborate intervention, but they had better results than the control communities.

Choice among Measures

When measures of outcomes have been defined, there is often a list of them jostling for attention. A next step is to decide which of them to use in the evaluation. How does the evaluator make the decision? In Chapter 4 on planning, I discussed the choice of central questions and mentioned a number of bases on which the choice can be based: the expectations embedded in program theory, the decisional timetable, the relative clout of interested parties, the preferences of stakeholders, uncertainties in the knowledge base, and practicalities of time, money, and skill. When it comes to choosing among outcome measures, the same kind of decision has to be made, and the same criteria are relevant.

In addition, sometimes a problem arises from incompatibilities among outcome goals. A neighborhood development project, for example, seeks to increase coordination among the public and private agencies serving its run-down neighborhood. It also desires innovation, the contrivance of unusual new approaches to services for residents. Coordination among agencies might be easier around old, established, accepted patterns of service than around new ones. Innovation is likely to weaken coordination, and coordination may dampen the innovating spirit. Which outcome measures shall the evaluator include in the study?

In cases like this, it is usually a good idea to include measures of both outcomes. The evaluator may also be well advised to work out the program theories underlying these expectations with program stakeholders. When they have confronted the assumptions embedded in their expectations, they may be alerted to the probable incompatibilities between the outcomes. They may not change their goals or their activities right away, but they will be more sensitive to the possibility that achievement of both goals simultaneously is unlikely. If early results from the evaluation suggest that one goal is being achieved in locations where the other is not, they may become ready to institute program changes.

Before settling on the final list of outcome measures, the evaluator will want to review them to be sure that the study is being directed at important purposes. She doesn't want to do an elaborate study on the attainment of minor and innocuous goals, while vital outcomes go unexplored.

Short-Term or Long-Term Measures?

Another issue is whether to include short- or long-term measures. Decision makers, who by professional habit respond to the demands of the budget cycle rather than the research cycle, sometimes want quick answers. If they have to make a decision in time for next year's budget, they see little value in inquiring into the durability of effects over 24 months. It is this year's results that count.

But decision makers who have had prior experience with evaluation studies often see the utility of continuing an investigation over several years so that the program's long-term effectiveness becomes manifest. Clearly, it is good to know whether early changes persist or fade out quickly. It is also important to know whether the absence of early change is a mark of failure or just the prelude to the slow building up of consequential changes over time. (This is sometimes called a sleeper effect.) Evaluations, wherever possible, should measure long-term effects, particularly when basic policies or costly facilities are at stake. A comparison of short- *and* long-term effects provides additional information about how, and at what pace, effects take place.

As we saw in Chapter 5, the evaluator is well advised to thrash out the final selection of measures for study with decision makers and program managers. They are all involved. It is she who will have to live with the study and they who will have to live with the study's results.

Yardsticks

Once outcomes that will form the criteria for evaluation are set, the next question is how much progress toward the desired outcome marks success. Suppose a vocational program enrolls 400, graduates 200, places 100 on jobs, of whom 50 are still working three months later. Is this success? Would 100 be success? 200? 25? Without direction on this issue, interpreters can alibi any set of data. A tiny change is better than no change at all. No change is better than (expected) retrogression. Different people looking at the same data can come up with different conclusions in the tradition of the fully-only school of analysis: "Fully 25 percent of the students...," boasts the promoter; "only 25 percent of the students...," sighs the detractor.

Some commentators have suggested that the evaluator require sponsors and/or program staff to set forth their definitions of success at the outset of the evaluation, before the data come in, so that they are not influenced by what the data show. That idea has a plausible ring to it, and it would make sense *if program people had a sound basis for making such judgments*. But sometimes they don't. If they are forced to set standards for what they consider success, they will do it, but the standards may represent little more than guesses—or hopes. When numerical standards are arbitrary (say, 20% of deadbeat dads will pay child support), the advance setting of success markers tells little about reasonable expectations. More likely it distinguishes between optimists, who expect the program to go far toward remedying the ills of the century, and pessimists, who don't—or politicos, who don't want to be held accountable for more than minimal change. With the availability of evaluations in many substantive fields, program staff have a better foundation for setting yardsticks, but often they haven't read the evaluations of other similar programs. The evaluator can bring the evaluations to their attention. Once they are alerted to the general run of results for transportation programs for the disabled or company-supported basic education for hourly workers, they are likely to set more appropriate standards of success. In that case, early attention to standards of judgment—before the data come in—can forestall later wrangling about interpretation.

The question of how much change is enough really makes sense on a comparative basis. How do the results compare with last year's results, with the results for those who did not get the special program, or with the results from programs with similar intent?[3]

The evaluator can draw on past evaluation studies to compare with the results of this evaluation. Such a comparison is easier to make if the studies use the same or similar outcome measures. When deciding on how to measure outcomes (and processes) in the study, the evaluator should keep in mind the utility of using measures that have been used in previous work so that comparison is facilitated.

---

[3]This of course limits the question rather than settles it. How much better must the program be before it is considered a success? Statistically significant differences do not necessarily mean substantive significance. It is important for the evaluation to help the program and policy communities figure out the practical significance of the findings. If the evaluator is not well enough informed about the practice field to venture such an estimate, she should provide enough data to allow experts in the field to judge the significance for practice. Cost-benefit analysis frames the answer in these terms: How much does it cost for each given amount of improvement?

Unanticipated Consequences

The program has desired goals. There is also the possibility that it will have consequences that it did not intend. The discussion of unanticipated results usually carries the gloomy connotation of undesirable results, but there can also be unexpected good results and some that are a mixture of good and bad.

Undesirable effects come about for a variety of reasons. Sometimes the program is poorly conceived and exacerbates the very conditions it aimed to alleviate. A loan program to inefficient small business people may only get them deeper into debt. Or a program can boomerang by bringing to light woes that have long been hidden. Thus, a program on child abuse may bring to light many more cases of child abuse than anyone had ever suspected. By bringing the problem into the open and collecting data about it, the program seems to be increasing the very problem it aimed to prevent. Some programs raise people's expectations. If progress is too slow or if only a few people benefit, the results may be widespread frustration and bitterness. Occasionally, a program that invades the territory of existing agencies generates anger, competition, and a bureaucratic wrangle that lowers the effectiveness of services.

Programs can displace problems rather than solve them. A system of frequent police patrol can reduce crime in the neighborhoods that are being patrolled, but crime may rise in adjacent neighborhoods where police presence is less visible. The total crime rate may be unchanged.

Sometimes programs tackle one aspect of a complex problem. Even if they achieve good results in their area, the more important effect may be to throw the original system out of kilter. Thus, an assistance program to underdeveloped areas introduces a new strain of rice that increases crop yield—the goal of the program. But at the same time, the effect is to make the rich farmers richer (because they can afford the new seed and fertilizer and can afford to take risks), widen the gulf between them and the subsistence farmers, and lead to social and political unrest. Fragmented programs all too often fail to take into account interrelationships between program efforts and the overall system in which people function. What are originally conceived as good results in one sphere may be dysfunctional in the longer view. It is because of such complex interlinkages that one-shot short-term evaluations may miss the most consequential effects of the program they are meant to study.

Good unanticipated consequences are not so usual, because reformers trying to sell a new program are likely to have listed and exhausted all the positive results possible. Nevertheless, there are occasions when a program has a happy spin-off, such as having its successful features taken over by a program in a different field. There can be spillovers of good program results to other aspects of a program participant's life. For example, students who learn reading skills may become more cooperative and less disruptive in school and at home. Contagion effects appear, too. People who never attended the program learn the new ideas or behaviors through contact with those who did.

A wise evaluator brainstorms in advance about all the effects—good, bad, and indifferent—that could flow from the program. Envisioning the worst as well as the best of all possible worlds, she makes plans for keeping tabs on the range of likely outcomes. What were unanticipated consequences are now—if she judged well—

unintended but anticipated. She also has to remain flexible and open enough during the course of the study to spot the emergence of effects that even a sweeping preview had not envisioned.

If she or her evaluation staff is close enough to the scene to observe what goes on, informal observation may be sufficient for a first look at unplanned effects. In more remote or complex situations, she may have to develop measures and data-gathering instruments to pull in the requisite information. One good source of information about possible unintended consequences is the critics of the program. On what grounds are they opposed to it? What do they think might happen that program planners have ignored? Thus, in the late 1990s many political leaders were convinced that welfare programs, instead of aiding the poor, were encouraging them to be permanently dependent on the public dole. These critics believed that the result of public assistance was to reduce recipients' sense of personal responsibility and any expectation they might have had of using their own talents to support themselves and their children. This type of criticism can give evaluators of new state-level welfare programs a lead to the type of effects they might examine.

In like manner, the Negative Income Tax experiments of the 1970s took their cues from opponents of the concept of a guaranteed income (negative income tax) for the poor. Opponents warned that such a plan would produce the unwanted effect of causing recipients to work less or even withdraw from the labor force entirely. Therefore, the researchers devoted a large part of their study to finding out whether this unintended outcome would materialize. (They found small reductions in work effort. White male heads of households reduced their hours of work, but not by a great deal; black and Hispanic males did not. Overall, there was little change among male heads of households but larger reductions among wives, especially white wives [Watts & Rees, 1977].)

Sometimes no one in or around the program has given much thought to possible negative consequences. The evaluator can gain clues from social science knowledge, prior evaluations, exploration on the ground, discussions with experts in the program field, and her own logical thinking. Once possible side effects are identified and seen to be a reasonable possibility, the evaluator will want as valid and precise measures as she can devise of these outcomes—and face the same measurement challenges she faces with measuring intended outcomes.

Interim Markers of Progress

Sometimes the real changes that a program wants to produce lie far in the future and are not so much goals as unanalyzed pious hopes. A management incentive program aims to increase the organization's attraction for executives in the interests of improved long-term managerial effectiveness; an educational program for inner-city children is intended to improve their school performance in order to enhance their social and economic status as adults. It would take years, even decades, to test the program's effectiveness in achieving its long-range expectations. In the interim, proxy measures have to be used that are germane to more immediate goals and presumably linked to desired ultimate outcomes—for example, length of executive tenure, or children's scores on achievement tests. These are the kinds of links that the evaluator has incorporated into the statement of program theory. The theory sets out the expected intermediate stages on the way to the desired long-term outcomes. When the evaluation cannot continue far into the future, as evaluations usually cannot, it attends to these intermediate stages and proximate measures.

Evidence that the purported relationships hold is often feeble—for example, that longer executive tenure is associated with management effectiveness or that school achievement is directly related to the economic and social advancement of poor children. Nor does research knowledge always suggest better proximate measures.

The problem affects not only evaluation; it is also central to program design. Programs have to be designed to produce certain short-term changes on the assumption that they are necessary conditions for achieving long-range ends. As in many other aspects, the evaluation inherits the fallibilities of the program. Often the best that evaluation can do, at least under the usual time constraints and in the absence of better knowledge, is accept the assumptions that the program staff and other stakeholders have agreed to incorporate into their program theory, and proceed to find out how well intermediary outcomes are being met. It is left to further research to explore the relationships between short-term outcomes and long-term consequences. Only when evaluations are funded with long time horizons, 5, 10, 20 years, will evaluation will able to contribute to an understanding of long-term results.

But when desired consequences are not so remote as to outlast the evaluation, there are decided advantages in measuring both the short-term and longer-range effects. Programs attempt to set in motion a sequence of events expected to achieve desired goals. As Suchman (1969, p. 16) noted, if the program is unsuccessful, there are two general categories of reasons. Either it did not activate the causal process that would have culminated in the intended goals (this is a failure of implementation), or it set the presumed causal process in motion but the process did not cause the desired effects (this is a failure of theory). (See Figure 6-1.) Stated another way, program failure is a failure to implement activities that achieve proximate goals; theory failure occurs when the achievement of proximate goals does not lead to final desired outcomes.

When previous research has demonstrated the link between immediate program goals and desired long-term outcomes, there is little need for evaluation to pursue results beyond the first stage. In evaluation of a smokers' clinic, it is enough to discover that the program led participants to stop smoking. It is not necessary to investigate the ultimate incidence of lung cancer, because biomedical research has decisively settled the relationship. But in fields where knowledge is less developed, further investigation is highly desirable.

The best way to conceptualize interim indicators, or benchmarks as some call them, is to consider the program's theory of change. In fact, even if the evaluator hasn't gone through the exercise of eliciting and/or constructing the program's theory, here is a point at which she will have to go through analogous thought processes. She has to figure out what early states are likely to lead on to the ultimate desired effects.

Let's look at a program based on the theory that giving newly released prison inmates 20 weeks of unemployment insurance will prevent their return to a life of

FIGURE 6-1

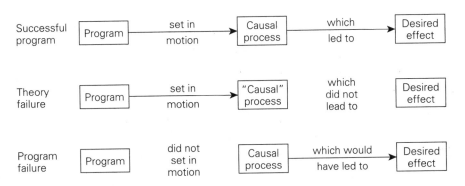

crime. The thinking goes that newly released felons need money, but finding a job is difficult because they lack skills and they have a prison record. Without money, they are tempted to go back to crime. The program provides money for a period long enough so that they can either find jobs or enter formal training programs or otherwise make a prosocial adaptation to life outside the prison (Rossi, Berk, & Lenihan, 1980).

The program mails weekly checks. What is the immediate expectation? The theory assumes that the ex-offenders will look for jobs. So markers of progress might be time spent job hunting, or number of job-related contacts made, or number of applications submitted to potential employers. Another expectation might be that the ex-offenders stay away from criminal contacts. So another interim measure might be the amount of time they spend with bad companions. Similarly, the evaluators can develop measures about efforts to get training and education.

Interim markers are part-way accomplishments on the road to desired outcomes. Examples of items that have been studied are the following:

Number of people who have completed the course

Creation of teams

Rules adopted

Intentions to use contraception

Increase in self-reliance

Linkages established between branches of the firm

The assumption is that such milestones are important for reaching the ultimate objectives.

Incorporating interim markers into the evaluation allows the evaluator to give early feedback to program staff, managers, funders, and policymakers. She can point to linkages that are not working and suggest alternative strategies. For example, if 15 lectures about the dangers of drugs are not increasing adolescents' intentions to refrain from drugs, perhaps the program should consider reinforcement procedures or social supports.

Program Processes

Program processes may sound too flexible and spongy to withstand measurement, and evaluators often choose to study them through qualitative methods. But many elements of implementation are relatively easy to measure. This is all to the good because process evaluation is an important part of the evaluation story. It is especially useful to have *measures* of process, so that they can be entered into the same analyses as outcome measures.

Some process variables, which describe how the program is being carried out, are important to measure because they are expected to lead to desired outcomes. But other program processes, with little casual connection to outcomes, are measured because they allow analysis of how the program operates, for whom, and with what resources. The evaluator measures them because they may help to distinguish between those who do well and those who do not—that is, as control variables. For example, the severity of a patient's illness at the time he enters the program might be measured because there is reason to believe that it will affect the success of treatment.

Patterson et al. (1992) evaluated a program that aimed to increase supermarket shoppers' purchase of healthful foods, such as fruits and vegetables. The supermarkets undertook activities such as setting out displays, distributing educational flyers, placing healthful foods prominently on the shelves, and marking their ingredients. The evaluation kept track of the extent of distribution of monthly flyers, the visibility of displays, the prominence of shelf placement, and so on. Those were the process variables. Interim outcomes were the extent to which shoppers were aware of the information about healthful foods. The longer term outcomes, based on program goals, concerned the purchase of the several categories of nutritionally sanctioned foods.

Which characteristics need to be measured depends on the program. Possible indicators include such things as the following:

1. Type of programmatic activity
2. Characteristics of staff offering the service
3. Frequency of service (strength of treatment)
4. Duration of service
5. Intensity (dosage)
6. Integrity of service to intended (planned) design
7. Size of group receiving service
8. Stability of activity (vs. frequent shift in focus)
9. Quality of service
10. Responsiveness to individual needs

Let's say that the program is a set of radio public service announcements to acquaint mothers of young children with the benefits of an anti-dehydration agent for children suffering from diarrhea. On the list of attributes above, the program can be characterized as (1) a set of radio announcements; (2) created by advertising agency staff, broadcast by professional station announcers; (3) broadcast weekly; (4) over a six-month period; (5) for two minutes; (6) completely consistent with the planners' intent; (7) to a listening area that was part of two rural provinces inhabited by

300,000 people with 104,000 radios; (8) the activity was highly stable, involving repeated broadcast of a set of five announcements; (9) of high quality; (10) that was not responsive to individuals' questions or interaction but that represented good medical advice (Cronbach & Associates, 1980).

Not every program will be usefully described on the same set of variables. The choice of variables for measurement has to be based on the program's expectations and assumptions about what programmatic features will matter.

If the program is well known and coherent, a few measures are usually sufficient. Immunizations of young children are well understood, and the evaluation can be satisfied with description of how many inoculations were given to which kinds of children at which locations against which diseases. But if the program is vague or novel or being developed as it goes along, the evaluator may need to describe what is going on in more detail.

A mental health center is offering mental health counseling to clients, but what exactly does this mean? *Mental health counseling* is too vague a label to communicate much and the evaluator will want to describe the program more explicitly. It may take some digging to find out whether the counseling means referral to psychiatric services, individual psychotherapy of one type or another, group therapy, social support groups, or any of a dozen other things. Procedures for monitoring the program in progress have to be established in order to find out what is going on. These can be relatively simple procedures such as a discussion with the director, a review of staff case records, or attendance at staff meetings. On the other hand, if important categories of information are not forthcoming from such sources, the evaluator may want to conduct regular interviews with staff or even seek to make frequent observations of the counseling program in process. One common procedure is to introduce new record-keeping forms that counselors are asked to fill out.

Smith (1987) claims that monitoring treatment in a mental health center can be done frugally with a limited number of process indicators. Her list includes percentage of staff time devoted to direct service to clients, percentage of intake and therapeutic sessions canceled, changes in clients' level of functioning as measured by therapists' ratings on well-validated scales, and clients' length of stay in the program. Measures like these can provide descriptors of the program in action.

Process variables can also be developed empirically during the course of analysis. Although the evaluator may not have had the foresight at the outset to suspect that they were relevant, she can ask the questions of the data later, and by appropriate analysis find out whether outcomes are affected by such things as qualifications of staff, extent of staff participation in decision making, and frequency of staff turnover. The only requirement is that the data must be there to be analyzed—which means that the evaluator needs a modicum of forethought, knowledge, and luck.

One of the unresolved problems in studying program process is whether and how to measure the *quality* of program activities. It would appear that the quality of program performance will make a difference in how successful the outcomes are. A program can fail not because its services were inappropriate or poorly designed but because they were badly delivered. It's like a film that is brilliantly written and elegantly photographed but poorly acted, so that the result at best is mediocre. An evaluation example is the road built to encourage farmers to take their crops to market in town. It can fail to bring about the desired results not because roads are a poor idea or because farmers will not use them to transport crops but because the road was poorly built and washes away in the first rainstorm. It seems sensible for evaluators to pay attention to how well a project teaches, counsels, trains, treats, publicizes, delivers, organizes, builds, manages, coordinates, facilitates, diagnoses, or whatever else it does.

But how is the evaluator going to assess the quality of program process? Ay, there's the rub. The evaluator is often not qualified to render judgment on the professional performance of staff in different fields. Even if she were an expert, or could bring experts in, developing measures of quality would require extensive work—frequent observation of staff in action, the construction, testing, and revision of rating scales, multiple ratings by different raters and checks to be sure that raters were applying the same standards and reaching the same ratings about the same performance—and even then, project staff might disown the whole operation as uninformed and biased.

The main way that evaluators can go about introducing assessments of quality into their studies is through the use of accepted performance standards. Where a practice field has established a set of criteria for performance, the evaluator can use measures about the extent to which the project meets those standards. In a feeding project for the homeless, for example, the evaluator can collect data on the nutritional adequacy of the menu. In preschool programs, adult-child ratios are an accepted standard of quality care. In newer program areas or areas where standards are changing, the evaluator can use standards being proffered by professional leaders. An example in the field of social services would be the participation of clients in determining the type of services made available; in education, a parallel would be the promulgation of high standards for student achievement. But unless standards are widely accepted, adopting measures of such elements as indicators of program quality can generate controversy.

Program Inputs, Resources, and Environment

Inputs are the resources that go into the program. They tend to be set at the outset. They include the organization under whose auspices the program is run, such as a social service agency, a government department, or a school. There is a budget that specifies the amount of money that the organization can spend on the program. There is a staff with certain credentials and experience, a physical site or a number of sites, and a plan of activities. There is the community (or communities) within which the program functions, with its community history, demography, job opportunities, transportation facilities, relations with higher levels of government, laws, internal conflicts, grudges, and celebrations. These characteristics set the parameters for the program. They are the raw materials with which the program works.

Some of the possible inputs to be considered are the following:

1. Organizational auspices
2. Budgetary amount
3. Nature of staff (number, credentials, experience, gender ratio, etc.)

4. Management (experience of managers, relation to program staff, degree of hierarchy, etc.)
5. Location (e.g., condition of buildings, convenience to public transportation, space)
6. Plan of activities
7. Methods of service
8. Philosophy or principles of operation
9. Purposes
10. Period for which recipients receive service
11. Year(s) of operation
12. Size of program
13. Client eligibility standards
14. Relevant community characteristics

Obviously, not all of these items should be included in any one study. The evaluator has to consider which ones make sense in (a) describing the essentials of the program and (b) helping to explain what happens. She has to be selective.

If the project is run only at one location, inputs are not likely to vary. There is one organizational provider, one staff, one plan of activities, and so on. In that case these items cannot become variables in the analysis. Variables are, by definition, things that vary. Where there are no variations, that characteristic cannot be used to distinguish better and poorer conditions.

Even when inputs are constant, it is nonetheless important to record what the inputs are. Such a record serves several functions:

1. It amplifies the description of the program and makes concrete what it was and what it was not. When people read about the program's outcomes, they will be able to interpret the results with full understanding of the characteristics of the program that brought those results about.
2. If the evaluator, or someone else, later wants to analyze the benefits of the program in relation to its costs, input information comes in extremely handy. Costs are not only financial outlays; they include other resources that were devoted to the program, such as volunteers' time and the use of facilities. An accounting of inputs describes resources that were invested in mounting and running the program.
3. Some time in the future scholars may want to do a meta-analysis. Meta-analysts aggregate the results of evaluations of similar programs in an attempt to understand the general effects of programs of this class (Cooper & Hedges, 1994a). When they search out original evaluations, they often can not tell what the program was really like—for example, whether it was operating on a shoestring or was lavishly funded, whether service was provided by paraprofessionals with no special training or by people with master degrees. They therefore are driven to dump into the same pot all programs that call themselves by similar names, without being able to make important distinctions. When they try to go further and use meta-analysis procedures to try to tease out the factors that were responsible for different outcomes across programs, they frequently lack identifying information about the programs to use in their analysis (Cook et al., 1992). Good data on inputs would solve these problems.

4. Specification of inputs alerts the evaluator to changes that occur over the course of the program. Once having defined the inputs, the evaluator needs to check periodically to see whether the same inputs are in place. If changes have been made, new participants will receive different quantities or quality of some things (activities, budget expenditures) from those who were in the program earlier. It is possible that the changed conditions will influence outcomes. For example, cuts in funding may be responsible for differences in outcome for those served in palmy times and those served under conditions of austerity. It is also possible that the change itself, altering from one kind of service to another, requires re-tooling and slows the program dynamic. The evaluator should keep track and record the information.

When the program operates in multiple sites, many inputs do vary and relevant items can be conceptualized as variables. For example, the program may be run in six different communities that have different services and facilities available, or staff with different capabilities, or differing philosophies and norms of operation. In such cases, the inputs become *input variables*. They can be analyzed in the same way as process variables. In fact, sometimes inputs seem to be indistinguishable from process variables, and evaluators have trouble deciding which bin to put them in. To let you in on a secret of the trade, the good thing is that it doesn't matter. Whether the evaluator calls an item an input or a process variable or a mediating variable makes little difference so long as the item is appropriately handled in the analysis. What is important is that input and process variables be chosen that are known to be related to outcomes, suspected of being related to outcomes, logically related to outcomes, or likely to be cited by critics of the program as the explanation for whatever good outcomes are observed.[4]

Program participants are also a form of input. If there is a single group of program participants, they can be seen as "put in" to the program, and their characteristics can be classified as input variables. One rationale is that the particular mix of participants is a resource with which the program works. The nature of the participant population helps to determine how and how well a program functions. Another reason for considering them as inputs is that the characteristics of the group become the environment that mediates the program for each participant. Think of a new college-level science program introduced into an advanced class and the same program offered in a class composed of students who had previously failed science. Each individual receives the program in the context of the other people in the group, and fellow group members help to determine the repertoire of legitimate responses.

Some of the participant characteristics that may be considered as inputs are the following:

1. Age
2. Sex
3. Socioeconomic status
4. Racial/ethnic background
5. Language spoken at home

---

[4]I thank Robert T. Brennan for this concise statement of criteria for variables.

6. Attitudes toward the program (or toward health, job, leisure, school achievement, or whatever else is relevant)
7. Motivations for participation
8. Severity of problem that the program is trying to change
9. Aspirations
10. Expectations from the program
11. Attitudes of other family members toward the program (toward health, job, marriage, or whatever else matters)
12. Degree of support from family (friends, fellow workers, supervisors, and so on) for the intended goals of the program

Describing participants on these dimensions requires collecting data from individuals and classifying the data along some quantitative dimension. Years of age is easy, as is years of education, but for some of the more subjective items, like aspirations or family support, appropriate scales will have to be located or constructed. Individuals' responses can be arrayed along a scale from "very high" to "very low."

When the *composition of the group* is conceptualized as an input, the data on individual participants are aggregated to characterize the group. Thus, after assigning a value to each individual (0 = male, 1 = female), the whole group is characterized by its gender characteristics (e.g., percentage female). If several different groups are involved in the program, the environment for individuals may differ depending on their group membership, and these kinds of characteristics may become variables in the analysis. That is, the nature of the surrounding group may affect experience in the program, and recipients may have different outcomes depending on which kind of group they were in.

When the recipients of the program are organizations, a different set of characteristics will be in order. Characteristics of participating organizations will differ depending on whether they are schools, hospitals, state employment agencies, or voluntary citizens' groups. Depending on what factors are likely to be relevant to the evaluation, some key features might be the following:

1. Size (number of staff or members)
2. Budget
3. Public, private, or nonprofit
4. Nature of function (e.g., transportation, health)
5. Level in the hierarchy
6. Age of the organization
7. Rate of staff turnover
8. Trends in budget over past five years (e.g., increasing rapidly, increasing slowly, stable, decreasing)

A note of caution is in order here, a caution that applies to all the categories of variables discussed in the chapter. The evaluator can think of many variables that are interesting to study. But most evaluations have limited resources, and it is far more productive to focus on a few relevant variables than to go on a wide-ranging fishing expedition.

Previous studies will give indications of the types of variables that are apt to make a difference for any particular program. If such evidence is lacking, the evaluator usually makes her selection on the basis of program theory, scraps of data, the accumulated wisdom of practitioners, and logical thinking. These are not negligible sources of plausible hypotheses. As a rule, it will be useful for decision purposes to give preference to factors the program can change (manipulable variables such as type of service given or type of client served) over fixed attributes over which the program has little control.

Multiple Measures

Adequate indicators in evaluation, like adequate measures of concepts in all social research, usually entail multiple measurement. Each specific measure is an approximation of the outcome in which we are really interested. Say we are concerned with good driving as the outcome of a course in driver education. Knowledge of traffic rules can be one measure; ratings of driving ability by an observer might be another; records of traffic violations, a third. At best, each is a partial measure encompassing a fraction of the larger concept. Together they give a pretty fair take on good driving.

There are good reasons to use several items to measure a complex concept. The first reason is that no single item is up to the task. It takes a number of items to cover the varied dimensions of mental health or "a learning organization." Another reason is that each measure contains a load of irrelevant superfluities, extra baggage unrelated to the outcome under study. With the use of a number of measures, each contributes its own facet of information and each has its own peculiar irrelevancies. The effect of the extra baggage associated with each item is limited, and the evaluator develops a better rounded and truer picture of program outcomes.

Multiple measures might be useful, for example, in the evaluation of educational curriculums. Evaluators have usually relied on formal tests of pupil achievement. But test scores are influenced by many things other than the cogency of the curriculum, and the curriculum is intended to produce understandings and applications of knowledge that are only partially susceptible to assessment by tests. Outcome measures for a curriculum program can include measures of classroom behavior, attitudes, and the subsequent careers of students.

Separate measures can be combined to form one or more composite measures of program success. Combining separate items requires some assurance that the different measures are complementary and neither repetitions of the same dimension nor measures of unrelated dimensions. Further, it requires decisions on the relative importance of the different measures (Do they deserve equal billing?) and on the statistical procedures to represent the relative values of measures that use different scales (How do you combine reading scores and numbers of books borrowed from the library?). There is also the possibility that a composite index masks the upward and downward movement of the individual indicators. Therefore, before developing a composite measure, the evaluator will explore the statistical properties of the different items. Reporting changes in the separate measures may be preferable in some cases to combining information.

How Many Measures Are Enough?

How many outcome measures should an evaluator collect? That, of course, depends on the nature of the program and the aims of the evaluation. Sometimes a program has one clear and overriding goal, and there is an obvious measure of the extent to which that goal is reached. Chen, Wang, and Lin (1997) evaluated an intervention to reduce the amount of garbage generated in a neighborhood in Taiwan. The intervention was a reduction in the number of days on which garbage was picked up. The outcome measure was the weight of the garbage on the remaining days. That was the single measure of interest.

In other cases a program has multiple goals. The Head Start program hopes to improve children's cognitive skills, but it also expects to improve their health, immunization, nutrition, emotional well-being, social relationships, and family functioning. In this case, multiple measures will be needed to tap into the several dimensions.

Nevertheless, there is a limit to how many measures should be collected. Restraint is definitely in order. The trick is learning how to balance the zeal for comprehensive measurement with the leanness of efficiency.

Measurement of Variables

Once the set of variables has been specified—inputs, processes, interim markers of progress, longer term outcomes, and unintended consequences—the next step is to figure out how to measure them.

Locating Existing Measures

The development of measures, sometimes referred to as instrumentation, is a demanding phase of evaluation. If earlier studies have been done in the field or measures have been created that are suitable for the subject of concern, the task becomes one of locating existing measures. It is worth a large amount of searching to locate measures that have already proved workable, rather than to create new ones.

An advantage of using preexisting measures is that most of the trial-and-error work is done, and there will often have been an analysis of the reliability of the measures. Also, it is generally possible to find out the responses that earlier investigators derived through their use of these measures, and thus to have available some kinds of comparative data from another population. Comparison helps to pinpoint the characteristics of the evaluation group that are special and the extent of their divergence from other groups.

Repeated use of common measures helps to build up a body of knowledge. As different evaluation studies use common indicators of outcome (e.g., scores on the same test), it becomes possible to make comparisons about the relative effectiveness of one program against another. (The important qualification is that other factors have to be taken into account if the comparisons are to be fair.)

Brodsky and Smitherman (1983) compare the development of measures to the making of wine. A good grape, they say, needs the opportunity to flourish and develop:

> As it meets the test of time, its taste provides great reliability. But many new wines, fresh out of the cask without the opportunity to age, may be distasteful....

Research scales work much the same way. Many individuals will develop research scales like a knee jerk, reflexively in response to a need for assessment. These scales have no breeding whatever. Clipped off the vine of the developer's scientific thought, they have no heritage. What they lack in taste, they make up for in pretentiousness. (p. 4)

Thousands of measures have stood the test of time. Even seemingly abstract concepts such as psychological stress and marital satisfaction have been measured successfully for many years.

Sources for Evaluation Measures

One source for well-established measures is previous evaluations of programs similar to the one under study. Some evaluations are reported in journals (such as *Evaluation Review, New Directions for Evaluation, Evaluation and Program Planning*, and *Educational Evaluation and Policy Analysis*); others are available as government documents through clearinghouses (such as Educational Resources Information Center [ERIC] for education) or for sale through the government's National Technical Information Service (NTIS); others can be obtained from the government agencies or foundations sponsoring the evaluation or from the authors of the evaluation report.

Thousands of sources can be searched by computer, whether they are local databases available in libraries, usually on CD-ROM, or in databases accessible through the Internet (such as Medline for articles in medical journals or PsycINFO for articles in journals in psychology and related fields). Computerized searches are notorious for producing mountains of information. The savvy evaluator has to know how to narrow the search with appropriate keywords and good use of the syntax of various search engines. The technology and scope of electronic information retrieval are changing so rapidly that the evaluator may want to consult a reference librarian or other specialist in tapping these resources.

For those who prefer hard copy, several handbooks are available with lists of tried and tested measures that have been used in earlier studies. The distribution of responses from previous research is sometimes included. Among the useful compendia are the following:

Bearden, William O., R. G. Netemeyer, & M. F. Mobley. (1993). *Handbook of marketing scales*. Newbury Park, CA: Sage. This collection contains measures of such things as innovativeness, materialism, "Hispanicness," and sexual identity.

Bowling, Ann. (1991). *Measuring health: A review of quality of life measurement scales*. Philadelphia: Open University Press.

Brodsky, Stanley L., & H. O. Smitherman. (1983). *Handbook of scales for research in crime and delinquency*. New York: Plenum.

Brown, Brett V., & Christopher Botsko. (1996). *A guide to state and local-level indicators of child well-being available through the federal statistical system*. Washington, DC: Child Trends.

Bruner, II, Gordon C., & P. J. Hensel. (1992). *Marketing scales handbook: A compilation of multi-item measures*. Chicago: American Marketing Association. This 1,315-page handbook contains measures on many psychological traits, like dogmatism and self-confidence, and organizational characteristics, like role conflict and leadership style.

Conoley, J. C., & J. C. Impara (Eds.). (1995). *Mental measurements yearbook* (12th ed.). Lincoln, NE: Buros Institute of Mental Measurements.

Jones, Reginald L. (Ed.). (1996). *Handbook of tests and measurements for black populations* (2 vols.). Hampton, VA: Cobb and Henry.

McDowell, I., & C. Newell. (1987). *Measuring health: A guide to rating scales and questionnaires.* Oxford: Oxford University Press.

Mangen, D. J., & W. A. Peterson (Eds.). (1982–84). *Research instruments in social gerontology* (3 vols.). *Clinical and social psychology* (vol. 1, 1982); *Social roles and social participation* (vol. 2, 1982); *Health, program evaluation, and demography* (vol. 3, 1984). Minneapolis: University of Minnesota Press.

Miller, Delbert C. (1991). *Handbook of research design and social measurement* (5th ed.). Newbury Park, CA: Sage.

Orvaschel, H., & G. Walsh. (1984). *The assessment of adaptive functioning in children: A review of existing measures suitable for epidemiological and clinical services research.* Rockville, MD: National Institute of Mental Health.

Price, J. M., & C. W. Mueller. (1986). *Handbook of organizational measures.* Marshfield, MA: Pitman. Although oriented toward business organizations, it contains many measures relevant to other organizations, such as measures of autonomy, communication, satisfaction.

Robinson, John P., Phillip R. Shaver, & L. S. Wrightman. (1991). *Measures of personality and social psychological attitudes.* San Diego: Academic Press.

Strickland, O. L., & C. F. Waltz (Eds.). (1988). *Measurement of nursing outcomes: Measuring nursing performance. Practice, education, and research* (vol. 2). New York: Springer.

Walker, D. K. (1973). *Socioemotional measures for preschool and kindergarten children.* San Francisco: Jossey-Bass.

Waltz, C. F., & O. L. Strickland (Eds.). (1988). *Measurement of nursing outcomes: Measuring client outcomes* (vol. 1). New York: Springer.

Finally, many organizations develop and sell specialized tests and inventories. An example is the Educational Testing Service, which produces a wide range of instruments.

Developing New Measures

The evaluator searches assiduously for available measures directly relevant to the subjects she wants to study, but occasionally she comes up empty handed. She may find some measures that are inferentially related, and if they are easy to collect, long used, or with good reliability and known distributions, she may be tempted to make do with them. But it is wiser to stick to the relevant core of the subject under study than to rely on a string of unproved assumptions that try to link the measure to the concept of interest. For example, an evaluation requires a measure of good citizenship, and the evaluator can find only a measure of participation in voluntary organizations. She can make an argument that volunteering in a community organization is a way of demonstrating good citizenship, but to use this measure as a surrogate for citizenship will probably yield misleading results.

It is better to develop a measure that provides a reading on the exact dimension of interest than to use one that is off the mark. Developing new measures can be difficult and time-consuming, but measures that are off center from the main issue, even when reputable and time honored, are likely to obfuscate rather than enlighten. In some cases the evaluator may choose to include both the well-documented measure that does not fully capture the phenomenon she wants to study, along with a new measure that deals with the exact concept she is interested in but lacks a track record.

Devising questions, test items, and forms often looks so easy that it comes as a shock to find how difficult it is to do. Amazingly often respondents fail to understand or misinterpret even seemingly simple questions. For example, a mother who is asked how many days her son failed to attend school may not include in her answer the days he was sick, evidently because she does not consider those days as "failure to attend." Sometimes items that should hang together do not elicit the same kinds of answers from respondents. Or answers about likely behavior do not predict at all what people actually do. I will have more to say on this subject later in the chapter when I discuss the qualities of good measurement.

Items for Interviews and Questionnaires

The utility of interviews and questionnaires depends on asking good questions. Survey interviews and written questionnaires carefully frame questions and ask all respondents the same questions in the same words in the same order. Most of the questions are usually closed ended, with answer categories given as part of the question. To provide good answer categories, the evaluator has to know what answers the respondents would give if they answered freely. The categories should be right on target, so that respondents get the immediate sense that the evaluator understands them and their situation. The answer categories should be comprehensive, so that they cover the whole range of answers that people want to give. Giving answer categories that are off the mark indicates that the evaluator doesn't understand the story, and discourages people from participating in the survey or from continuing once they have begun.

Interviews and questionnaires can also include open-ended questions that allow the respondent to reply in his own words. Open-ended questions are particularly useful when the evaluator wants respondents to explain why they chose a certain answer, when she wants their suggestions for improvement, or when she doesn't know enough to anticipate what the categories of answers are apt to be. Their disadvantages are that they have to be coded after the data are in, which takes time and money, and they do not yield information that is comparable across respondents. If one person responds to an open-ended question that he entered the program because of parental pressure, the evaluator has no way of knowing how many other people did the same thing—but just neglected to say so. But open-ended questions are certainly preferable to poorly worded closed-ended questions with limp or inept options for response.

In developing the questions for a survey interview or questionnaire, several principles need to be followed. Some of the ABCs of question construction are the following:

1. *Use simple language.* It is vital that all respondents understand the question in the same way.

2. *Ask only about things that the respondents can be expected to know.* That seems like obvious advice, but it is amazing how often evaluators and researchers ask about events and conditions that many people have only vague notions about.

3. *Make the question specific.* Don't ask: Did you attend the program regularly? Instead ask: How many times a week did you attend the program? Or better: How many times did you attend the program last week? When asking for recall of past events, it is good practice to limit the time period being asked about.

4. *Define terms that are in any way unclear.* If you ask "How far do you usually jog?" add in terms of miles or fractions of miles.

5. *Avoid yes-no questions.* They give relatively little information. Instead, give answer categories like: "a great deal," "quite a bit," "some," "a little," "none"; or "agree strongly," "agree somewhat," "disagree somewhat," "disagree strongly." Or ask where the respondent would place himself on a scale from 1 to 10, where 1 means "not at all" and 10 means "completely."

6. *Avoid double negatives.* Don't ask: How much would you dislike the inability to receive service at the same health center? It would take a grammatical wizard to figure out which side is good.

7. *Don't ask double-barreled questions.* Don't ask: Did you use the videos and pamphlets in the sessions you ran? If the respondent says no, does that mean that he used the videos only, the pamphlets only, or neither? Ask about one thing at a time. If you ask: How much do you respect and admire John Jones? the respondent might respect Jones but not admire him at all, or vice versa. The question will confuse him, and/or the answer will confuse you.

8. *Use wording that has been adopted in the field.* Researchers have been asking demographic questions for decades, and a lot of experience has accumulated. For example, for age, ask date of birth. That yields more accurate answers than asking how old a person is. The Census Bureau has developed manuals that show the question wording they use in the dozens of surveys that they run.

9. *Include enough information to jog people's memories or to make them aware of features of a phenomenon they might otherwise overlook.* Questions don't have to be models of brevity. A question can say, "Some ninth graders in the public schools in this district take a health education course that includes a unit on sexual reproduction. Has your child attended such a course this year?"

10. *Look for second-hand opinions or ratings only when first-hand information in unavailable.* Respondents can give more accurate information about themselves than they can give about other people. If accuracy is important, it is better to go directly to the person involved. However, if the evaluation seeks a general sense of scope, awareness, or intensity, the response of another person who is easier to reach may give sufficient information. If the person whom you want to interview is impossible to locate, sometimes a spouse, a parent, another relative, even a neighbor may be able to provide enough data. Sometimes the opinions or ratings of other people are part of the evaluation design. Thus, the evaluator who wants to know how an executive trainee is performing on the job may seek out the opinions of supervisors and co-workers. But if you want to know how the executive trainee sees the situation, you should go to him.

11. *Be sensitive to cultural differences.* Evaluations can involve people from other cultures, as in studies of international assistance programs abroad, or from subcultures in this country. The evaluator can not assume that all people will give accurate information about themselves or their families to a stranger. In some cultures, personal information is not dispensed lightly, and respondents will provide evasive answers—or none at all. In some cultures, a norm of courtesy pre-

vails, and respondents will say what they believe the evaluator wants to hear. When the evaluator appears to represent an outside group of higher status, such as an international assistance agency, respondent bias may be magnified. Neither can the evaluator assume that topics that are part of the ordinary conversation mill in the mainstream culture in this country are acceptable to others, or that words and phrases will have the same meanings to those who grow up under different sets of norms. It is advisable to get advice from indigenous informants and to adapt questions to fit the sensitivities and concerns of the local community. Some questions should not be asked if they violate the norms or beliefs of the program population.

12. *Learn how to deal with difficult respondent groups.* Certain categories of people present particular problems to interviewers, such as young children, the mentally ill, prison inmates, people with critical illnesses, or speakers of foreign languages (for whom translations of interview forms cannot readily be prepared). Researchers have invented ingenious ways of getting information from some of these groups, and you are well advised to look into these specialized techniques.

For advanced advice, there are a number of excellent texts on the market, such as the following:

Berdie, Douglas R. J., F. Anderson, & M. A. Niebuhr. (1986). *Questionnaires: Design and use.* Metuchen, NJ: Scarecrow Press.

Converse, Jean M., & Stanley Presser. (1986). *Survey questions: Handcrafting the standardized questionnaire,* a Sage University Paper. Newbury Park, CA: Sage.

Foddy, William H. (1993). *Constructing questions for interviews and questionnaires: Theory and practice in social research.* New York: Cambridge University Press.

Labaw, Patricia. (1985). *Advanced questionnaire design.* Cambridge, MA: Abt Books. This book is less concerned about the wording of individual questions than the order in which questions are asked, the format in which they are presented, the mix of questions, and the design of the total interview/questionnaire.

Paine, Stanley L. (1951). *The art of asking questions.* Princeton, NJ: Princeton University Press. Still excellent and still in print.

Sudman, Seymour, & Norman Bradburn. (1982). *Asking questions: A practical guide to questionnaire design.* San Francisco: Jossey-Bass.

Many books on methods of survey research pay some attention to the framing of questions.

Pilot Testing Questions

Most of us have the illusion that we can sit down and dash off a good list of questions. Survey researchers have learned that the task is much harder than it looks. The task is to help respondents understand exactly what is being asked of them, enable them to provide appropriate answers honestly, ensure that all respondents are interpreting the same question in the same way, and ensure that the evaluator understands what the answers mean. The job takes thought, critique, pilot testing, revision, further pilot testing, and revision again until the questions capture the explicit kind of information required.

The procedure for developing a set of questions for a survey interview (whether in person or by telephone) or a questionnaire is this:

1. *Look at questionnaires and interview protocols that other evaluators have used in studying similar programs or policies.* You may find some questions that are just what you want to ask. You will also get clues to the language the investigators used (What did they call heroin? What did they call skipping school?). You will see the order of questions they asked, and since it is usually wise to place the most sensitive questions late in the interview, you will see what they thought were difficult questions to ask.

2. *If you don't know much about respondents' situation or their likely pattern of responses, run a small preliminary open-ended survey with a similar population.* By asking questions of people who are similar to the respondents who will be queried, the evaluator can learn the range of answers that are likely to come up and build appropriate answer categories into the questions. To the extent that she can use respondents' own language and turns of phrase, the questionnaire will show the savvy of the study and its match to respondents' situations. A preliminary survey also gives a sense of which questions are totally misunderstood, which bring in large numbers of "don't know" answers, which questions irritate or anger people, and so on.

3. *Write a questionnaire or interview form.* Do it as well as you can. Get advice from colleagues who have done it before.

4. *Seek critiques of your questions.* Ask evaluators and researchers, ask program staff, ask a few members of the target population.

5. *Revise the questions and question order.* Add some questions, drop others.

6. *Do a pilot test with the questionnaire or interview form.* Call on people who are as similar to your target population as possible. If you have a small number of program recipients, you don't want to use them up by having them answer this preliminary version of the form. If there are a very large number of program recipients, you can ask real recipients to perform this function, but then don't include them in the final study. You don't need a large number of people in this phase, but be sure that you select a group that is diverse in age, sex, race/ethnicity, or any other characteristic that you believe might affect responses.

7. *For questionnaires, get people to fill them out in much the same way that you will be asking regular respondents.* But it is acceptable to administer the questionnaire in a central place. Even if you plan a mail survey, you don't need to use the mails for the pilot test. You are not trying to find out anything about response rates at this point. You are trying to improve question wording and placement. After respondents have completed the questionnaire, ask them about any items they had problems with, didn't understand, were reluctant to answer, and so on. Then go over the questions with them (debrief them) and ask them what they meant by each response. You may find out that they are occasionally misinterpreting your words and answering a question that you did not write. This is fodder for the next revision.

8. *In the pilot of an interview survey, go out and interview people.* Don't delegate the interviews to an assistant. Do them yourself. You'll want the tangible sense of how the interviews are going to go. Furthermore, you have the best understanding of what information the study should be netting, and you will be alert to hitches and botches in the responses. Go through the interview in the order you have constructed it. If the respondent asks for more information or clarification before answering a question, don't provide the clarification. Say that he

should answer as well as he can. Note down the places where the respondent asked for clarification, hemmed and hawed, was unable to answer, or became restless or irritated. When the interview has been completed, go through the same debriefing as with the questionnaire, finding out what people meant by their answers. At that point, after they have told you their interpretations, you can explain what the questions meant to ask. You can even ask them to help you frame a better question, one that will communicate better to them and people like them.

9. *Revise the questionnaire or interview.*

10. *Do another pilot test.*

11. *If problems continue to arise, you may have to do another round of revision and pilot testing until the form is ready to use in the regular survey.* At some point it will be ready to go.

If possible, do some analysis of the data from the pilot test. Strange or implausible answers may be a sign that respondents do not understand the questions as you meant them. A lack of relationship between measures that you expected to be related may signal that one or more of the measures needs work. Before spending a lot of money collecting data that prove to be of poor quality, the evaluator may even want to do some preliminary assessments of the validity and reliability of the measures, perhaps with the help of a measurement expert. The next section discusses validity and reliability.

Desirable Characteristics of Measures in Evaluation

Whether the evaluator chooses to use well-established measures, creates her own, or relies on a combination, she wants some assurance that the measures are good ones. Experts on social measurement (sometimes called psychometricians), evaluators, and researchers have developed empirical techniques for assessing the quality of the measures they use. This type of assessment requires specialized skills, some of which the evaluator may not have. In that case, she can call on the advice of an expert. At the least, she should be a savvy consumer.

It helps to think about measures as winding up as variables in analysis. The way a phenomenon is defined and the quality of the data that are collected to measure it will determine the extent to which the resulting variable can carry the load that analysis places on it. To be robust and hearty, a measure should have the following characteristics:

Validity   Validity has to do with the extent to which the indicator captures the concept of interest. An indicator should measure what you intend to measure.

Some phenomena are difficult to measure. A program may be aimed at increasing the self-sufficiency of handicapped adults in a group home. How is self-sufficiency measured? That depends in the first place on what the program intends to do. Is it trying to teach clients to dress and feed themselves, to take care of their living quarters, to work in sheltered workshops, or what? Once the program staff has explained their meaning of *self-sufficiency* in all its dimensions, it is the task of the evaluator to figure out how to operationalize the concept. Let's say that the programmatic meaning is that clients should become able to take care of their daily lives with minimal assistance—dressing, washing, keeping their rooms clean, marketing, preparing simple foods, and getting along with their housemates. Whatever measure the evaluator locates or develops should deal with the clients' capacity to exhibit those behaviors. If the evaluator finds an indicator developed for previous research that measures self-sufficiency in terms of individuals' self-reported *feelings* of sufficiency in different circumstances, it will not provide a valid measure of the concept in this situation.

Validity highlights the centrality of dealing with the right stuff. Measurement experts often point out that a measure is not valid in and of itself; it is valid for certain uses. One way of assessing validity is called *criterion validity*. Evidence for criterion validity is of two types: concurrent and predictive. Concurrent evidence of criterion validity would demonstrate that a particular measure relates well (correlates) with another established measure of the same concept administered at the same time. Predictive evidence of criterion validity relates the measure to some phenomenon in the future. For example, a statewide eighth grade achievement test would show predictive validity if it correlated with students' grades in ninth grade. The correlations between such measures are sometimes called validity coefficients. Like all correlations, they can range from -1 to 1, with a correlation close to 1 suggesting that the measure is valid, while a correlation near 0, or worse a negative correlation, would suggest that the measure is not valid.

Another way of assessing validity is known as *construct validity*. Evidence of construct validity relies heavily on theoretical argument. To produce evidence about construct validity, the evaluator proposes theoretical relationships between the measure of the concept and measures of other, presumably related concepts. For example, if the concept is workplace stress, the evaluator may argue that individuals with high workplace stress would also show signs of sleeplessness, weight gain or loss, and high blood pressure. She might further propose that individuals with high stress would have a lower opinion of their employer and be more likely to consider leaving their job. To provide evidence of construct validity, the evaluator would administer measures of all these concepts and find out whether the expected relationships exist—that is, whether the other indicators correlate positively with the measure of workplace stress.

A third aspect of validity is *content validity*. This is an important concern when the concept being measured is multi-dimensional. A valid measure would range across the full spectrum of the concept. For self-sufficiency, a measure with content validity would cover the whole range of behaviors identified as relevant. Once the measure was devised, its items would be compared to the list of behaviors that constitute the self-sufficiency concept.

Finally, if different measures of one concept are collected by different methods (e.g., some are responses to interview questions, some come from observations of behavior), and if they converge, the evaluator can have confidence that they are likely to be valid. Thus, studies of crime-reduction programs will often use official statistics on crimes reported to the police *and* responses of neighborhood residents to victimization surveys. These data deal with different aspects of crime, officially reported crime and the experience of being victimized by crime, both of which are fallible measures. They are also collected by different methods. When the two sources show similar reductions in neighborhood crime, the data are more convincing.

Sometimes a relationship between two measures is the result of use of the same data collection procedure (e.g., respondents' self-report). In order to show that the measurement method is not responsible for any correlation observed, a measurement expert may demonstrate that other concepts measured by the same method are not correlated—for example, that self-report of workplace stress is not related to self-report of family stress. Such evidence reinforces the validity of the measure of job-related stress.

Reliability Reliability has to do with whether repeated efforts to measure the same phenomenon come up with the same answer. Imagine measuring the length of a room. One way would be to pace off the room, putting one foot in front of the other, calculating how many foot-lengths it takes to reach the end of the room, and estimating the number of inches in your foot. Another way is to use a tape measure. While pacing out the room will yield varying answers depending on how you position your feet at each step, the tape measure is going to come up with consistent answers time after time. It will yield more *reliable* answers. One sobering consequence of using unreliable measures is that they tend to lead to underestimates of relationships in the data—most uncomfortably, underestimates of the effect of the program on outcomes.

When an evaluator uses questionnaires, tests of knowledge, inventories of attitudes or mental states, interviews about feelings or past actions, or agency records, issues of reliability will often arise. In some cases the question is whether the respondent's answers depend on his frame of mind at the time of data collection and whether he would respond differently on another occasion. In other cases the concern is whether the documents or files from which the evaluator is extracting information are accurate and up to date.

A set of techniques have been developed to estimate the reliability of data. Much of the work on reliability has been done in conjunction with testing. The reliability of test instruments has been estimated by test-retest procedures and by internal-consistency checks. Test-retest, as the name implies, examines the consistency of answers given by the same people to the same test items, or a parallel set of items, at two test different administrations. Test-retest reliability is reported as a correlation, where a value of 1 would indicate a test with perfect reliability, and a value of 0 would represent a test with no reliability.

High rest-retest reliability is a desirable quality in a measure, but in practice this is not a simple way to assess an instrument's reliability. From a practical standpoint, if a subject responds to the same (or a closely parallel) instrument twice, particularly if he does so within a short time period, the second responses are likely to be heavily influenced by his recollection of what he said before, thereby inflating the estimate of reliability. On the other hand, if the second administration comes some time after the first, the respondent may have actually changed. For example, a television viewer responding a second time to a questionnaire about viewing habits may give different answers, not because the instrument is unreliable, but because his habits have changed.

When a measure consists of a number of items, internal-consistency checks look at people's responses to different subsets of items in the instrument. Originally, internal consistency measures were a variant of test-retest techniques, but instead of two tests administered at different times, items on one test were divided into two sets. This procedure was known as split-half reliability, and it was derived by estimating the correlation between the two halves. By and large, most methods of estimating the internal consistency of a measure, including split-half, have been supplanted by a global measure of consistency referred to as alpha, or Cronbach's alpha (Cronbach, 1951).

In evaluation the reliability of agency records is often an issue. The reliability of records can be estimated by collecting new data on items in the agency files and seeing how well the two sets of data match. Such a procedure is a variant of the test-retest method.

Another reliability issue that arises in evaluation is the reliability of judgments by program staff. Judgments are sometimes used as indicators of participant outcome, and when this is the case, it is usually advisable to have outsiders, rather than the program staff, do the rating. However objective they may be, staff members can be suspected of bias—often justly—in the direction of seeing improvement where none exists, or placing high value on tiny, subtle shifts that seem trivial to others.

Another precaution is the use of several independent judges. They each rate the same cases, and the evaluator checks to see how much consistency there is across judgments (interrater agreement). Estimates of interrater agreement are interpreted like other reliability estimates, with an estimate near 1 representing very high reliability and estimates near 0 indicating very low agreement.

If interrater reliability is low, the whole procedure is suspect and should be revised. Perhaps smaller chunks of behavior need to be singled out so that raters are concentrating on exactly the same things. Perhaps the raters need more training; perhaps different kinds of instructions need to be given to raters; perhaps benchmarks need to be provided so that all judges have a common frame of reference for what constitutes "unacceptable," "adequate," or "good," or what behavior should be rated 1, 2, 3, 4, or 5. Clear directions and training for raters on which factors to consider and their relative importance can improve interrater agreement. Ratings of particularly complex or fast-paced behaviors may be more reliable if made from audio- or videotapes, which give the raters a chance to review the behavior. Only when each rater is applying the same yardstick, and doing so in terms the evaluator has defined, will their ratings be comparable and have much meaning.

Reliability is not an inherent quality of the measure but a quality of the measure used in a particular context. Even when an existing measure is reported to have high reliability, it may not be very reliable when used by different raters with different clients. Reliability will also be affected by such things as the homogeneity of the sample; the reliability of a measure will be lower when the sample is homogeneous than when it is used with a more diverse sample. If possible, the evaluator should assess the reliability of her measures with her own staff and on her own population. She can estimate the internal consistency of her measurement scales. She can subject a subsample of ratings to a second rating by other judges and calculate interrater agreement. If reliability is low, the information sends a signal to improve the items, the training for raters, procedures for administration, or other characteristics of the instruments and data collection techniques.

Direction   For evaluative purposes, an outcome measure should have direction—that is, a good end and a bad end.[5] Thus, the evaluator knows which direction of change she hopes to see in unemployment rates, birth weights of newborns, history test scores, attitudes of hopelessness, and so on. For measures of program process, there may not be the same conviction about which kinds of service and activity are good, but there can be direction in terms of more or less. Thus, a measure of process might be hours of exposure to program activities, frequency of field trips to cultural institutions, or number of youngsters in preschool group. For some process measures, even this degree of directionality may be absent. Some program activities can be classified only in terms of the content of the activity, such as nutritional counseling or help with budgeting, and the measures are categorical.

Sensitivity to Differences   A measure on which a large block of the cases bunch up on a single value, or on a limited part of the scale, is not going to be very useful in analysis. The evaluator would like values to spread across the measurement space in order to capitalize on the differences among individuals. That is one reason why questions that ask for yes or no answers are less useful than questions that ask for more differentiated responses (e.g., "agree strongly," "agree somewhat," "disagree somewhat," "disagree strongly"). It is also why questions that present categories for respondents to check are less useful than questions that ask for actual numbers. The raw numbers (e.g., on income, age, numbers of persons in the family, or number of years on welfare) allow more differentiation across respondents. In my experience, almost all novices frame questions in terms of preset categories, such as elementary schooling or less, some high school, high school graduation, some college, college degree, or graduate education, instead of asking for actual years of schooling. I did the same thing when working on my first study but fortunately had an experienced mentor to dissuade me. Not only does the open-ended question collect a wider range of responses, but it also protects against the danger that the evaluator has misjudged the range of responses and most of the cases wind up in one category.

Currency   When a measure relies on asking people questions, it is wise to ask about conditions and events in the present and the very recent past. The events should be fresh in their memories so that people haven't forgotten the information or make errors in retrieving it. This means that if the evaluator wants to know about food purchases, she should ask about purchases over the past week, not over a longer period. (If she needs information for a longer period, she may want to ask respondents to keep diaries of their purchases.) Even for high-salience events that one might think people will remember, such as hospitalizations, researchers have found

---

[5]Shadish (1997) reminds me that some scales do not have a good end and a bad end. In a letter he writes, "The MMPI, for example, has scales that you are pathological on if you are too low or too high. In some marital therapy, too much or too little dominance can be dysfunctional.... [The relevant concept might be] absolute departure from the middle."

that people do not give accurate reports over a long period. It pays to frame questions in terms of the present wherever possible. It is particularly unwise to ask people what they thought or how they felt six months or a year ago. Human beings do not remember information on opinions, attitudes, or internal states very well. Their inclination is to report their attitudes in the past as being much closer to what they are now than their attitudes at the time actually were.

Realistically Connected When seeking outcome measures, the evaluator usually thinks of the long-term expectations of the program and then crafts measures that deal with those expectations. However, some programs are only tangentially related to the hoped-for outcomes. For example, a program that gives teachers a stronger voice in school governance has its ultimate justification in expected gains in student achievement. But it is overoptimistic to expect that a change in governance arrangements will lead directly and quickly to gains in student test scores. So many intermediary conditions and events have to take place between the program and the change in achievement test scores that using test scores as a measure is unrealistic. Similarly, it is unrealistic to expect that the introduction of an automated record system in a hospital can be evaluated in terms of more appropriate patient care or shorter hospital stays. Those may be long-term hopes, but the measure has to be more closely connected to what the program can actually achieve.

Unbiased by the Data Collection Method Bias is the systematic distortion of a measure by some irrelevancy. To the extent possible, a measure should not be susceptible to bias because of the way the data are collected. For example, if the evaluator collects information on mother-child interaction by observing them in a laboratory setting, it is possible that they are behaving differently from the way they would in their own home with no one present. When data about participant reactions are collected by the same staff members who conducted the program, it is possible that participants give answers more favorable to the program than they would give if asked by someone else. When questions have a distinct social-desirability tilt ("Have you stolen money from classmates?"), respondents may be tempted to misreport so as to sound more socially desirable than they really are. (In subcultures where being bad is a prized feature of growing up, respondents may overreport their misbehavior.) Because of the possibility that the very act of collecting data influences the nature of the data collected, Webb, Campbell, Schwartz, Sechrest, and Grove (1981) have written an engaging book about nonobtrusive methods of data collection—that is, methods that do not involve asking anybody anything. One example: gauging the popularity of a museum exhibit by measuring the wear in the tile in front of the exhibit. However, even with the ingenuity that Webb et al. display, such methods generate a very narrow band of information.

It is usually impossible to avoid all obtrusiveness when collecting information for evaluation. Fortunately, many respondents appear to be perfectly willing to own up to actions that one might expect them to seek to conceal. Delinquents and ex-offenders usually give detailed information on crimes they commit; alcohol and drug abusers frequently tell about their continued abuse of those substances. With sample checks of self-reports against official records or physical evidence, many evaluators have found that concerns about bias have been overblown. Respondents are likely to report fairly accurately about sexual behavior, crime, drug and alcohol abuse, or receipt of public assistance (although not domestic violence). The subject that gives the greatest trouble these days is probably income. Many people overreport their income level and the rich tend to underreport it. For all the surprising accuracy of reports on many sensitive issues, it is still important to check the possibility that data are biased. The evaluator should also avoid use of collection procedures that tend to encourage distortion.

Accessibility   Sometimes evaluators think of a relevant or clever measure for an activity, but when they go out to get the information, they find that it is not available. This seems to be particularly likely when the measure refers to conditions in a neighborhood or small geographic area, such as the frequency of child abuse and neglect in a neighborhood or the proportion of children in the neighborhood who hold library cards (Coulton, 1995; Coulton, Korbin, & Su, 1995). No matter how ingenious a measure may be in the abstract, unless the data are available, it is not going to be of much use.

System   All measures need to be defined carefully and in full detail. For example, is age defined as age on last birthday or age on nearest birthday? Then information for the measure needs to be collected systematically and consistently, so that all units are comparable. Careful conceptualization and definition are called for, and questions have to be pilot tested and revised (often several times around) until it is clear that they are bringing in the desired information.

Summary

This chapter has discussed the measurement of five categories of variables: program outcomes, unintended consequences of the program, interim measures of progress toward program goals, program processes, and program inputs. Process evaluations will consider only program processes and inputs. Studies of outcome can concentrate on intended and unintended outcomes, but often they will cover all five categories.

Outcome measures are usually the dependent variables in the analysis. Interim markers of progress, which represent intermediate outcomes, can also be used as dependent variables in the middle stages of a study to see how well the program is moving along the designated way stations. Process and input variables can be used to explain differences in outcomes. They also provide useful information in their own right.

Measures can be constructed about individuals, about groups (such as program staff or trainees' co-workers), organizations (such as a hospital), sections of organizations (such as a service within the hospital), neighborhoods, or communities. Wherever possible, the evaluator should identify existing measures that have already been tested and validated. Not only are such measures likely to be more valid and reliable than newly crafted measures, but studies that have already used them provide information about the distribution of responses in known populations. If no existing measures tap the dimension that is required for the evaluation, the evaluator can proceed to develop and refine new measures. It is better to measure the right thing, even if there is some wobble in the measure, than to measure the wrong thing, even if it can be done elegantly.

The development of new measures and interview questions is not a casual activity. It requires a rigorous set of steps, culminating in pilot testing and revision of items until respondents understand their meaning and supply the right kind of data. Many questions in surveys, questionnaires, and attitude inventories include multiple-choice answer categories. The evaluator has to learn enough about the situation to devise answer categories that fit what respondents really want to say.

Measures can be nominal (i.e., simply an assignment of numbers to categories); ordinal (i.e., with an order from less to more); interval (i.e., with equal distances between the points); or ratio (i.e., with all the previous characteristics plus a true zero point). Statisticians prefer to deal with measures in the reverse order from that presented here. Ratio and interval measures are the most robust and versatile in statistical analysis and nominal variables the least.

Evaluators face the temptation to measure everything within sight because all kinds of things might have an influence on how successful the program turns out to be. But they have to exercise restraint. Measurement, and the subsequent data collection and analysis, are expensive and time-consuming. Careful review of earlier evaluations should give good clues about which characteristics of the program and its surroundings are worth measuring. But although I urge restraint on the number of different factors the evaluator measures, it is often necessary to include several different measures of a single factor in order to cover all its facets. For example, if the evaluation needs to include a measure of school safety, several dimensions of safety will need to be measured in order to be sure that the study captures relevant aspects.

Measures should be valid (i.e., they must capture the dimension of interest) and reliable (i.e., they should be consistent from one administration to another). Good outcome measures for evaluation should also have a direction; everyone should know in advance which way the measure is expected to move. Measures should be sensitive to differences, so that the data spread across the whole scale. Outcome measures should be reasonable, not holding the program to unrealistic standards of performance, and undistorted by the data collection method. Accessibility of data is always a consideration. If data are not available for the measure, the evaluator has to craft an alternative measure for which data can be located.

7

COLLECTING DATA

[My master in the land of the Houyhnhnms] argued thus: that the use of speech
was to make us understand one another, and to receive information of facts; now
if anyone *said the thing which was not*, these ends were defeated; because I cannot properly be said to understand him; and I am so far from receiving information, that he leaves me worse than in ignorance, for I am led to believe a thing
black when it is white, and short when it is long.

—Jonathan Swift, *Gulliver's Travels* (1735)

Where Chapter 6 dealt with the development of measures, this chapter considers
how to collect the data needed for the measures. It discusses a variety of data collection techniques. Particular emphasis is placed on the interview, particularly conducting interviews and coding responses.

Sources of Data

Measures can deal with attitudes, values, knowledge, behavior, budgetary allocations,
agency service patterns, productivity, and many other items. Data for evaluation can
come from a gamut of sources and be collected by the whole arsenal of research techniques. The only limits are the ingenuity and imagination of the researcher.

The most common sources of data in evaluation studies are (a) informal discussions and interviews with program managers, staff, and clients, (b) observations,
(c) formal interviews with clients and staff, (d) written questionnaires to clients and
staff, (e) existing records, particularly program records, and (f) available data from
other institutions.

Informal Interviews

Informal discussions are particularly helpful at the beginning, in order to help the
evaluator orient herself and the study to the situation. They come in handy later on
for helping the evaluator understand information she is receiving from more formal

sources. In fact, whether or not the evaluator considers her interchanges with people in the program as data, they provide texture and an almost palpable sense of program reality in which to ground the study.

Some evaluation studies are mainly qualitative in nature. That is, they rely on discussions and observations for their data, and they report results in the form of narrative accounts and illustrative episodes. In qualitative evaluations, informal interviews are a major source of information.

Observations

Observations can be informal, too, embodying a look-around-and-see perspective. The evaluator watches the implementation of the program in a variety of settings over a period of time. She takes notes and records what she sees.

Observations can also be structured. In some cases, the evaluator will develop a protocol for recording specific behaviors during the observation period. For example, a classroom observer can sit through a 50-minute class period and record the number of times that the teacher performed each of the behaviors that the program was meant to include. Observers can also record the number of questions that students raised, the number of students who became engaged in discussion, or any other observable behavior that is relevant to the evaluation.

If the observer does not have a usable protocol for real-time recording of events, she can tape-record sessions and code the events later. Codes can capture the types of interactions that occurred, their order and frequency, and so on. (I say more about procedures for coding a little later on.) Coding from tapes can also capture more subtle and nuanced elements, such as the types of words and phrases that are used in discussion. If physical properties of the situation are important (e.g., movement around the room or facial expressions), the session can be videotaped.

Observations can also generate ratings. An evaluator can watch staff implement a preschool program and rate each staff member's responsiveness to the children's questions. This rating can be one of the measures of program process. Similarly, an evaluator can observe the manner in which trainees perform cardiopulmonary resuscitation and rate each person's competence (Brennan et al., 1996). In this case, the rating provides a measure of program outcomes.

One of the endearing advantages of observation is that it does not involve asking anybody anything, and therefore it does not usually introduce the biases that obtrusive questioning can bring about. When the evaluator's presence in the situation is unobtrusive, people may not expressly tailor their actions and responses to the type of image they want to create. However, observation as a method of data collection remains vulnerable to bias. The observer is the instrument and brings her own set of blinders to the task. She sees what she is looking at, and maybe what she is looking for. And even with the most unobtrusive observer, people who know they are being watched may act differently—at least for a while. But it is unusual for anyone in a real situation to maintain a masquerade for very long.

Webb et al. (1981) collected a book-full of nonreactive measures in which the presence of the researcher does not cause a reaction in the source of the data. A study of the social structure of a city examined burial monuments in the cemetery (Warner, 1959). The investigators found that the father was most often buried in the center of the family plot, and headstones of males were larger than those of females. A study of the diffusion of information among physicians relied on pharmacy records to find out when each doctor began prescribing a new drug for his patients (Coleman, Katz, & Menzel, 1957). In a study of the cultural assimilation of Indians and Eskimos in Canada, the investigators used permanent housing as an indicator of assimilation (Barger & Earl, 1971). They found that more Eskimos lived in permanent housing, and more Indians lived in mobile homes. Although Webb and his colleagues try hard to locate measures that have been useful to researchers, it is obvious that unobtrusive measures relying exclusively on observation (and not on records) are extremely specialized and do not have a wide reach.

Formal Interviews

Formal interviews represent a systematic method for obtaining data. There are two main categories of interviews: open ended and structured. Open-ended interviewing starts with a list of topics to be covered and a clear sense of what kinds of information are wanted. The interviewer then tells the respondent the topics she is interested in and, with more or less guidance, allows the respondent to tell the story as he wishes. She follows up each lead with neutral probes, such as "And then what happened?" or "How come the director did that?" until she obtains complete data on the subjects she is concerned with. Each interview takes shape differently. Some respondents may discuss program content, others will talk about relationships, still others will focus on program history, and some may concentrate on outcomes. Each person answers in his own terms and offers the information that is salient to him. Where possible, the interviewer will tape-record the interviews so that she has a complete record of the answers that she obtained.

When the interviews are open ended and the evaluator wants to generalize across them, she faces the task of combining and interpreting the responses after the fact. One way of doing this is by transcribing the interview tapes and then reading and rereading the responses. The evaluator gathers together narrative answers on the same topic from different respondents, often through use of a computerized text program. In this strategy, she develops a growing awareness of the main themes represented in the responses. The other way of analyzing narrative responses is to code the answers into a set of categories. Then she can count the number of answers that fall into each category.

The second kind of formal interviewing is the structured or survey interview. As discussed in Chapter 6, the evaluator chooses interview questions carefully, and if they are new items, she pilot tests and revises them until she is satisfied that they bring in valid and reliable data. Once the interview form is set, she asks every respondent the same questions with the same wording in the same order. This procedure is designed to ensure that each person is responding to the same stimulus and providing comparable responses.

Interviews can be conducted in person or by telephone. Some questions ask for short answers, like marital status or occupation. Some questions are closed-ended with possible answer categories included, much as in multiple-choice tests. Some questions allow for open narrative responses. The interviewer starts by explaining the purposes of data collection and works through the questions. In the process she takes pains not to give any cues about the answers she prefers. She does not want to bias the respondent's answers or suggest that one category of answers is more desirable than another. In evaluation studies respondents can get the idea that they are expected to say nice things about the program, the staff, or the benefits they have gained from participation. The interviewer has to stress that she wants the straight facts and, where attitudes or opinions are being solicited, she wants the respondent's candid opinions. A key feature of interviewing is to avoid biasing the answers whether by tone of voice, body language, or reactions to the respondent's replies.

Interviewing by telephone is usually less expensive. The interviewer doesn't have to travel to reach the respondent's home, and if the respondent is not at home on the first or second try, the interviewer doesn't have to return again and again. Phone interviewers can call back repeatedly at different times of the day and different days of the week. Phone interviews are a good option in evaluation under several conditions:

1. If respondents are scattered around the city or across a wide geographic area, especially if they live in neighborhoods where few interviewers want to travel
2. If most respondents can be expected to have home phones; this condition rules out populations in many developing countries
3. If it is relatively easy to find out respondents' phone numbers—that is, if non-listed or nonpublished phone numbers are rare in the program population or the evaluator can get the numbers from program records

For most purposes phone interviews are just as satisfactory as in-person interviews. Most people are surprisingly patient in answering questions on the phone, even for relatively long periods. Phone interviews sometimes have an advantage of impersonality. The respondent doesn't have to see the interviewer or worry about her judgment and therefore may find it easier to report unacceptable behaviors. Also, when the respondent and interviewer are different in age, race, or sex, the phone mutes the differences and keeps those issues from potentially distracting the business of the interview—which is the exchange of information.

In-person interviewing is economical when all the people with whom the interviewer wishes to talk are available in one or a few locations. The program site is one such place. If the evaluator can reach the clients at the site, and speak to them in privacy, she can avoid time-consuming travel. However, there is a down side to using the program site. The client may see the evaluator as belonging to the program and being part of the staff, not as an objective third party. If this is so, he may be reluctant to divulge news of actions that run counter to the program's objectives or display views that would displease program staff. If the evaluator can locate space for interviewing in a neutral place off grounds, such a site may encourage greater candor.

Written Questionnaires

When in-person or telephone interviewing is not feasible, mail questionnaires can be sent. Mail questionnaires have several advantages. They allow the evaluator to ask a broad range of questions, some of which can be closed ended and some open ended. The respondent can think about his responses instead of answering off the top of his head. He can look up information, consult records, and give more considered replies. He can answer at his convenience instead of having to schedule time in advance. Mail questionnaires are also more economical than interviews.

A main disadvantage is that not everybody returns questionnaires. Response rates may be low, and those who respond to the questionnaire may be atypical of the program population. No one knows how the nonrespondents would have answered had they returned the questionnaire.[1] With low response rates, it is difficult to have much faith that the data are a good representation of the program situation. In order to raise the likelihood that people will respond, the evaluator has to put a good deal of effort into question wording and formatting in ways that encourage participation. One important thing she can do is ensure that the answer categories represent answers that respondents really want to give. In addition, she will usually want to keep the questionnaire relatively short so that completion is less of a burden. She may also consider offering incentives for questionnaire return, and she will definitely send follow-up mailings to try to increase the rate of response.

Another disadvantage to questionnaires is that they require a certain degree of literacy. For students in the early grades or for poorly educated respondents, even simple questions may be hard to cope with. In other cases, the putative respondent may not fill out the questionnaire himself. Busy executives, for example, or non-English-speakers, sometimes turn questionnaires over to other people to answer for them.

When the program, and therefore the evaluation, deal with people who speak languages other than English, the evaluator has to find out which language is easiest for each respondent to read and then seek translations of the questionnaire into those languages—and see that respondents get the proper version. The translation cannot be a literal word-for-word translation from the English; it has to be phrased in the style and idiom of the native language. A way to check on the adequacy of the translator's version in, say, Spanish, is to have another person who speaks both languages translate the questionnaire back from Spanish into English and see how close the meaning is to the original English-language version. Adjustments may be needed in the wording in both languages to increase the consistency of response.

Since relatively few people are willing to write long narrative responses on questionnaires, questions generally have to be kept simple and in multiple-choice format. Some of the richness of in-person communication is lost. Still there are occasions when mail questionnaires represent the best and most cost-effective way to collect data.

Researchers have developed a variety of ingenious techniques to use questionnaires well and raise response rates. Dillman (1978) lists a sizable number of questionnaire studies that had response rates of over 80%. His book is a very helpful guide to how to run questionnaire studies and telephone surveys in ways that obtain good cooperation and good data.

A variant on the mail questionnaire is the group-administered questionnaire. If the evaluator can collect numbers of participants in one room, she can hand out

---

[1] It is possible to get some idea of the characteristics of nonrespondents by comparing late responses, that came in after several followups, with responses that came in early.

questionnaires and ask each person to fill out the questionnaire on the spot. The procedure is much like group administration of an achievement test, and it is probably most feasible in a classroom-like setting. Group administration overcomes the problem of nonreturn and low response rates. Only people who are absent on the day of the administration fail to respond, and they can be reached by follow-up. The evaluator can read the questions aloud, a useful procedure with young children or with adults whose literacy is low. The procedure also ensures that each person is writing the answers on his own form. Although group-administered questionnaires are appropriate only in special settings, they remain a tool of some utility.

Program Records

Program records and agency files are a natural for evaluation data. Programs usually collect a goodly amount of information about the people who participate. Whether they are students in a university, residents in public housing, or patients in outpatient surgical centers, participants will have provided many kinds of information about themselves and their situations. Now that almost all agencies have computerized their files, the data should be easy to access. An early step that the evaluator can take is to familiarize herself with the system, to understand the items that are included and the definitions and categories that the agency uses in classifying data.

However, the fact that data are on computers is no guarantee that they are up to date or accurate. The evaluator needs to check the record-keeping system to find out who collects the data on clients, which items are collected and at what intervals, when and how the data are entered into the computer, and how frequently the information is updated. Although most record keeping is carried on in professional style, some records can be haphazard, with entries months behind and vital pieces of information missing. When that is the case, the evaluator may want to work with the program managers to upgrade the maintenance of the system. She may have to convince them that improvement in program records works to the benefit not only of the evaluation but also of program management—to help them keep track of what is going on. She may even get involved in training the staff who do the data entry.

Similarly, when the evaluation needs a data item that is not included in standard program records, the evaluator will be tempted to try to persuade the agency powers-that-be to add it to the regular record system. If they do, she will save time and work in data collection. She will have to be sure that the staff understand the reasons for the items and the necessary definitions and recording procedures. She may occasionally have to institute training of data-entry staff so that the data are recorded properly. But before she tries to convince the agency to add items to their data system, she will want to consider whether the item is important enough to the program's ongoing concerns to warrant inclusion. If it is, she can definitely seek to get it adopted. Adoption would relieve the study of a burden and would give the program continuous access to useful information. If the item is not of utility to the program, then the evaluator shouldn't try to foist off on the program the responsibility for collecting it—and collecting it over the long haul, as incorporation of the item into the system would imply. She will have to make plans to collect the data herself. It is not ethical to ask the program to assume responsibility when the data would not do it much direct good.

One shortcoming in program files is usually the status of clients who have dropped out of the program. Programs do not usually follow up on their reasons for dropping out or their subsequent whereabouts and activities. If the evaluation needs this kind of information, the evaluator usually has to take the initiative to go out and get it.

Agency records can contain items on client progress—for example, in counseling programs, which look like ideal fodder for the evaluation. But these ratings are based on the judgments of the staff, and practitioner judgments may be unreliable. For one thing, the program rarely sets a common standard for steps on the rating scale. Each practitioner exercises his own judgment, and their criteria for progress may vary widely. In cases where practitioners' work is assessed on the basis of the progress that their clients make, they may intentionally or unwittingly bias their ratings so that they look more effective.

With all these caveats, program records remain a vital source of information. Using them saves the time and money that original data collection requires. There is also the advantage of continuity. Unlike the one-shot evaluation that collects elegant information for a short period of time and then folds its tents and steals away, the agency reporting system provides continuous data over long periods. If the opportunity arises for a long-term follow-up, much of the necessary data will be there—at least for clients with whom the agency maintains contact. Another advantage is that the evaluator who uses program records avoids bothering clients and staff for additional information. She lessens the intrusiveness of the evaluation and reduces the burden on staff and participants.

Rog (1991) describes a management information system (MIS) used in a program for integrating available services to homeless families. In this case, the evaluators, who worked in nine program cities, designed the MIS. They also designed the five sets of forms that collected the data to be entered. The forms consisted of Intake Application; Comprehensive Family Assessment, conducted by outside interviewers; two monthly forms filled out by case managers—Service Utilization Form about services received and Case Management Activity Record about the amount and nature of case management received; two quarterly forms—Changes in Status Form and Achievement of Goals Form to identify progress toward the goals set by the family, both filled out by the case managers; and Exit Form, completed by the case manager with the family.

With good record systems, agencies can do their own ongoing evaluation of their activities on certain key dimensions. One of the treasures an evaluator can leave behind after the study is an enlightened citizenry of program people who can continue to examine record data with an evaluative perspective. The agency has to retain an interest in evaluation, a commitment to maintain the record-keeping apparatus, and enough people with the requisite skills to keep the enterprise going. When program people are engaged in their own evaluation, they have the opportunity for periodic examination of the program's effectiveness. They can also bring the results of their inquiry directly to the attention of the people who are making decisions about the program's future. When the evaluator leaves behind this kind of heritage, she advances the evaluative perspective.

Agencies sometimes change their systems—the items they collect, the frequency with which they collect them, the procedures for data entry and data checking, and so on. If such changes are introduced while the evaluation is in process, they can undermine the evaluation. The evaluator will not be able to compare features of program activities or program recipients on the same dimensions before, during, and after the program. Rules have to be worked out in advance that alert the evaluator to any pending changes, and she must have a say in when and how changes are introduced.

On the other hand, record systems should not stay intact indefinitely. Programs change. Today's emphases may be tomorrow's irrelevancies. Definitions change. An ossified information system quickly loses relevance to the live issues. There has to be a routine way to adapt data items to the current scene, without at the same time disrupting items in time series that make for continuity and comparability over time. What the statistical agencies of the U.S. government do when they alter an indicator, such as the unemployment rate, is maintain old and new items side by side for an extended period. In that way, enough data accumulate so that statisticians can model the differences between the two series and make compensating adjustments in comparing the old and new series. After a time, the new items can carry on alone without losing the benefits of longitudinal analysis.

Program archives also contain data on staff, budgets, rules and regulations, activities, schedules, attendance, and other such information. These kinds of data can help the evaluation develop measures of program inputs and processes. Where needed, the evaluator can also look at historical accounts of the agency's past—annual reports, recruitment materials, minutes of board meetings, and so on. On occasion, such information proves to be highly informative for evaluation purposes.

Data from Other Institutions

Whenever the program involves activities or outcomes that are recorded by other institutions, the evaluator can draw on the records of those institutions. For example, Roberts-Gray, Simmons, and Sparkman (1989) evaluated a program that taught childcare workers, teachers, and food service personnel about nutrition. The expectation was that these workers would teach children and provide more nutritious meals. Among the records that the evaluators examined were school menus (to see if food service workers were improving the nutrition of the meals they offered children) and library records (to see whether the circulation of materials on nutrition increased).

Evaluators of a bail bond project effectively used court records. The program involved defendants who could not afford bail before trial and instituted procedures to convince the court to release them without bond. The program staff investigated each defendant to see if he had a family, home, job, or other roots in the community, and if he did, arranged to have him released from jail without bail prior to trial. The evaluators looked at data on whether the defendant showed up in court. In the three years that the Vera Institute of Justice ran the experiment, 3,505 persons were released on their own recognizance. By looking at court records of appearance, evaluators found that only 56 failed to appear in court, a proportion not dissimilar to the number of defendants who posted bail and failed to appear (Sturz, 1967).

The evaluation of the Saturation Work Initiative Model (SWIM) in San Diego sought to find out about the employment, earnings, and welfare receipt of program recipients who had received a battery of services aimed at moving them from welfare to jobs. The study drew on data from a variety of sources: the California State Unemployment Insurance (UI) Earnings and Benefits Records, which indicated periods of employment and extent of earnings; the Aid to Families with Dependent Children (AFDC) records maintained by the County of San Diego Department of Social Services, which showed whether the program clients were receiving welfare payments; the San Diego Community College District Student Information System, which provided data on enrollment in college-level and continuing education courses; and the San Diego County JTPA Management Information System, which supplied data on enrollment in training activities funded under the Job Training Partnership Act (JTPA). The study also drew on considerable data that the program itself generated (Hamilton & Friedlander, 1989).

School data are another good source. Depending on school regulations, information on achievement scores, attendance, promotions, and similar items can be retrieved for groups of students. Similarly, there are court records, license bureau records, motor vehicle records, and many other sources of data that are relevant for particular purposes. Automated systems are making data retrieval easier. When the evaluator knows how the records are kept and what requirements have to be met to retrieve data, she can sometimes find items that are directly relevant to the outcomes she is studying.

However, public concerns about protecting confidentiality and privacy have led to the introduction of legal safeguards in many data systems. Federal and state legislation and local ordinances have also restricted access. Evaluators have to find out whether their research falls within the allowable guidelines for release of information and then negotiate access. Sometimes agencies will release data on *groups* of people with all identifiers removed. If the evaluator submits the names and identifying information (addresses, Social Security numbers) for a set of people who have been in the program, the agency will give aggregate information on how the whole group of these people fared, while each individual remains anonymous. This procedure loses something; the evaluator cannot link the data to characteristics of the clients (age, length of time in program, etc.). Nevertheless, the data are often well worth having.

A few caveats are in order about using institutional data. The data were originally collected for purposes that have little to do with the evaluator's concerns and so may be not quite right for the questions she is asking. For example, she wants to know how often students take unexcused absences from school. School records give only total number of absences, failing to distinguish absences due to illness or other excusable reasons from unexcused absences. The evaluator has to make inferences from the data.

Also, different jurisdictions keep records differently. The evaluation of a self-care program for diabetics obtains data on health status from in-patient and out-patient records at hospitals. Different hospitals may keep records in different ways, and any differences that are observed may be due to differences in record-keeping methods at the hospitals rather than actual differences in health status. When members of the program group receive care at one set of hospitals and members of the control group are in another set of hospitals, the data can be especially misleading. One useful approach is to rely on hospital records for only fundamental data items that all hospitals keep, such as length of stay or discharge to the patient's own home versus discharge to another care facility.

Combining data collected by the program with data collected by other organizations on the same items is a way to extend the reach of the evaluation without major effort. But keep in mind that units that provide treatment may become sensitized to the need to upgrade their record keeping, while units without the program may continue with their unreconstructed records. Thus, for example, cities that run a needle exchange program to reduce the spread of AIDS among intravenous (IV) drug users may become more aware of causes of mortality among IV drug users. More attentive, they refine their recording procedures. "As a result, mortality attributed to AIDS may increase in those cities relative to control cities simply because the measures used to gauge mortality have become more accurate" (National Research Council, 1989, p. 336).

As we will see further in the section of this chapter on "Ethics," there are—and should be—limits on the use of records, even for legitimate evaluation and research. Incursions on people's privacy is a matter of growing concern, and evaluators who seek access to official records have a responsibility to limit their requests to essential items and, wherever possible, to use aggregate data (which do not identify individuals) as indicators of outcome.

The major advantages of using records from other organizations lie in the authoritative character of official records and the savings in time, money, and effort that their use permits. The evaluator doesn't have to collect the data herself, with all the problems that such original data collection involves (failure to find respondents, respondents' faulty memories or dissembling answers, etc.). However, using agency data has a cost. It takes considerable energy to locate the appropriate institutions, contact them, secure their agreement to release information, set the terms for data release, learn the organization's data system, definitions, categories, and procedures, adhere to privacy protections, prepare a protocol for which items are needed on which individuals, access the files directly or train a staff member of the institution about the specific items to be collected, and so on. Costs mount up.

Other Sources of Data

Many other sources and methods can provide information for the evaluator's purposes. Among them are the following:

Tests of information, interpretation, skills, application of knowledge
Situational tests presenting the respondent with simulated life situations
Simulation games
Psychometric tests of attitudes, values, personality, preferences, norms, beliefs
Projective tests
Diaries of events, usually kept explicitly at the evaluator's request
Focus groups that bring together 6–12 people to discuss a subject, with the evaluator acting as moderator
Physical evidence
Clinical examinations
Physical tests for nicotine, drugs, alcohol

Review of documents (minutes of board meetings, transcripts of trials)
Analysis of financial records
Content analysis of media stories
Photographs, videotapes, children's artwork (An interesting discussion appears in Harper, 1994.)

Tests of information, achievement, and skill are obviously of major importance in educational and training programs. They provide invaluable data on the level of participants' capacities. Texts on educational evaluation and research devote primary attention to testing and to the special measurement issues that tests raise. Evaluators who are working with a program that aims to raise students' knowledge, critical thinking, reasoning ability, or specific skills should be familiar with the testing literature.

Evaluation can also look at students' behavior, such as raising critical questions in classroom discussion or the repair of an automobile in the shop. Situational tests and simulation games are ways of coming close to behavior when circumstances preclude direct observation of what people do in the natural setting. Evaluators can construct tests that ask girls how they would respond to specific ethical situations (Gilligan, 1982), or they devise simulation games that allow educators who have participated in training workshops to demonstrate how they would allocate resources for education in a developing country.

When the goals of a program are to change people's attitudes, values, or opinions, then attitude inventories and projective tests are appropriate. Data from these tests are also useful when the program's theory of change assumes that modifications in attitudes, values, or opinions are necessary *preconditions* for shifts toward the desired behavior. When that is the prevailing theory, the evaluator finds out the extent to which attitudes change and goes on to see whether change in attitudes is associated with behavioral change.

Earlier I noted that people have fallible memories, so that responses to questions about circumstances in the past are liable to error. Diaries are one way around the problem. Instead of asking questions long after the events of interest have taken place, the evaluator asks participants to record events in a diary as they go along. Diaries have been used in studies of food purchases, hospital care, and television viewing. Evaluators find it useful to collect diaries frequently rather than blithely assume that people are conscientiously maintaining them over long periods of time.

The diary method requires a reasonable degree of literacy and a high degree of motivation on the part of diary keepers. Incentives are useful to maintain their cooperation. Some studies provide a weekly stipend. Another good incentive is the evaluator's appreciation and the sense of being important and helpful in a good cause.

Focus groups are another technique for collecting data (Stewart & Shemdasani, 1993; Vaughn, Schumm, & Sinagub, 1996). They were pioneered in market research. Producers of consumer products and advertisers brought together small groups of consumers to discuss the product under review. The advantage that focus groups offer in evaluation is twofold: (a) They obtain the views of 6–12 people in one place in the same amount of time it would have taken to interview one or two, and more important; (b) the views of each person are bounced off the views of the others, so that there is argument, defense, justification, attack, and learning over the course of the session. It is possible to gauge the strength of people's commitment to their views, the resistance of their views to others' arguments, and the changes that occur when different positions are aired.

Physical examinations provide data for studies of health education, health promotion, and health services. Studies of smoking cessation programs use data from saliva tests for nicotine to verify ex-smokers' reports (Zelman et al., 1992). Tests of blood alcohol levels are used in evaluations of programs for alcoholics. Evaluators of a program to teach asthma patients to manage their illness relied in part on doctors' reports of their condition (Wilson et al., 1993).

Other techniques are also relevant in specialized cases. Financial records can yield information about program inputs (the sum available to the program), program process (which activities were funded at which levels), and outcomes (e.g., in programs dedicated to ending instances of fraud, waste, and abuse of public funds). Other program documents can also yield evidence of the several program phases. Evaluators have undertaken reviews of such materials as curricula, test forms, and textbooks; resolutions passed by boards of directors; correspondence with agencies that refer clients to the program; complaints sent in to police review boards; and so on. In an evaluation of changes in the Food Stamp program, Ohls, Fraker, Martini, and Ponza (1992) used cash register receipts, shopping lists, and menus as back up for information on household food consumption.

Newspaper stories are a special form of document. When a program aims for better public knowledge about some issue (e.g., AIDS), one way of finding out about public knowledge is to do a content analysis of the mass media. (The assumption here is that people learn a great deal about what they know and believe about an issue like AIDS from what appears in the media. This assumption can be tested by following the newspaper analysis with an interview survey with the public.) Other circumstances can also call for media analysis, such as attempts to reconstruct the early phases of a program from contemporaneous newspaper stories.

Evaluators occasionally use newspaper stories as data in their own right (for example, for measures of outcome of a program designed to increase media coverage of environmental issues). In cases like this, the main technique is content analysis. Content analysis involves locating all stories on the subject that appear in specified newspapers, magazines, or on certain television programs, and then coding them on the variables of interest. For example, codes can be developed to categorize stories in terms of their length, nature of the environmental aspect mentioned (air, water, soil, endangered species, etc.), inclusion of pro- and/or anti-environmental positions. The data can then be analyzed by such variables as: the print or electronic media in which they appear (to understand the likely audience), the month and year (to detect changes over time), the page on which the story was placed (to gauge salience of the reporting), and so on.

Sampling

When a program has a limited number of participants, say all the young people arrested in two rural counties who are referred by the court to an outdoor adventure program, the evaluator will probably want to ask questions of all of them. On the other hand, if the evaluator is studying a national program with wide reach, she will have to select some members of the target population for interviews. (What I say in this section applies to in-person and phone interviews and questionnaires, but for the sake of brevity, I will talk about interviews.) How does she choose whom to interview?

The discussion of sampling here deals with how to select individuals from the program population who will be asked to provide data. (In Chapter 9, I take up issues of sampling again for different purposes.)

There are two basic ways to select respondents from the total population of program participants: purposive sampling (picking particular people for particular reasons) or random sampling (allowing the laws of chance to determine who is chosen).

Purposive sampling is useful in evaluation when the evaluator is interested in data not just on average participants but on participants at the extremes—those who received the most and least intensive services, those with less than a grade school education and those who had completed college, those who were forced to attend and those who volunteered early. In order to capture the full range of experience, the evaluator can select people who represent conditions at the tails of distribution. Data from this kind of study probe the extent to which a program is effective with the total range of participants. To put it another way, the evaluation is seeking to establish the limits of the program's effectiveness.

Another circumstance that may call for purposive sampling is a need to address specific policy questions. If the evaluator knows that one of the options being considered for the program's future is a major cut in funding, the study may choose to interview in those sites where minimal amounts of money are being spent. In that way, the evaluation is preparing to answer an important policy question: How will the program work if it is funded at much lower levels? These should not be the only sites that the evaluation studies, but poorly funded sites can receive extra evaluation attention. Other situations where a purposive sample is in order are when lists of participants are not available from which to sample, or when participants' refusals to participate in the evaluation are very frequent and would undermine the randomness of the sample in any event.

Purposive sampling can be based on different criteria. The evaluator may seek to maximize variability so as to discover whether the program succeeds across a whole spectrum of sites. Or she may want to minimize variability and create a set of homogeneous cases that can readily be compared with each other. Certain critical cases may be chosen or cases that hold promise of resolving discrepancies uncovered in earlier studies.

Purposive sampling has the virtue of convenience, but except under special circumstances and for important reasons, it is not generally as justifiable as random sampling. There are such strong statistical advantages in favor of random sampling that the evaluator should make creative efforts to get around obstacles and inconvenience in order to benefit from the representativeness of the random sample. Reading good texts on sampling or calling on a sampling consultant will often be wise.

Random sampling is a procedure that ensures that the units chosen are representative of the population from which they are drawn. To ensure representativeness, every unit has to have a known chance of being selected.[2] Scrupulous care is taken to avoid any biases that would give one unit an unfair edge over any other. *Random* doesn't mean "haphazard" in this procedure. On the contrary, it demands exquisite attention to detail.

Statisticians often refer to random sampling as probability sampling, because the word *random* has several usages in statistics. (We will meet randomization again in a somewhat different guise in Chapter 8.) The use of the phrase *probability sampling* communicates the core meaning—namely, that selection is left to the laws of probability, and chance is the arbiter. Nevertheless, since we are going to touch only the surface of the subject here, I will stay with *random sampling.*

The key advantage of random sampling is that it allows the evaluator to generalize from the responses of the sampled respondents to the entire population from which respondents were drawn. If the sample is drawn from the total population of program participants, study results can be assumed, with a known degree of confidence, to reflect the experiences and views of all the people in the program.

Samples can be drawn from lists of participants. Starting from an accurate and up-to-date list of program participants is usually the most sensible procedure. However, lists can have glitches. In some programs, lists include people who have already dropped out of the program. In other cases, new participants are not listed. Some names on the list have errors in spelling, addresses, phone numbers, and other vital data. Because of these possible problems, it is often wise to oversample—that is, to select 550 names when the study wants 500. The extra names can substitute for those who cannot be found. (But this does not solve the problem of missing names. Ways still have to be found to get as complete and accurate a list as possible at the beginning.)

One way to proceed is to draw every 3rd, 10th, or 100th name on the list. The interval is chosen by dividing the total number of names on the list by the size of the sample desired. If there are 2,200 names on the program list, and the desired sample is 550, then the sampler draws every fourth name. This is called a systematic sample, and it is similar to, but not the same as, a simple random sample. Sometimes it is better, sometimes worse. The danger lies in the possibility that there is something systematic in the list itself that will interact with the sampling procedure to produce a sample unrepresentative of the population.

Because evaluations are interested in conditions before, during, and after the program, they seek to interview the same people repeatedly. Repeated interviewing of the same set of people is called panel interviewing. For the discussion of sampling, the implication is that panel members have several chances to refuse to cooperate. Therefore, there is higher attrition than would be the case in a one-wave study, and the sample needs to be larger than a sheer consideration of statistical power would suggest. Because of the likely losses over time (people move away, die, refuse the interview, enter the armed service, leave no forwarding address, etc.), sample size should be increased in order to compensate. If the study deals with particularly

---

[2]It is sometimes said that each unit should have an *equal* chance of being sampled, but that is not necessarily so. For example, one can sample cities or mental institutions or army bases proportionate to size, giving larger units more chances to fall into the sample than smaller ones.

problematic populations, such as drug abusers or parolees, the increase may need to be especially higher.

A larger sample size does not solve the whole problem of respondent attrition. When people drop out of the study, the original sample is changed; the remnant of the sample is no longer representative of the larger population. For example, those participants who were least helped by a program may have little commitment to the program and refuse second and third interviews, while the program's successful stars consent to all the interviews requested. The evaluation of the remnant then shows a much higher proportion of favorable outcomes than the full sample would have shown. One technique to reduce the problem is to make statistical adjustments based on the characteristics of all first-wave respondents in an attempt to compensate for attrition; such adjustment will help but may not be totally satisfactory. Strong efforts need to be made to reduce attrition all the way along.

Interviewing

Two types of formal interviewing have been mentioned: survey interviewing and open-ended (or unstructured) interviewing. Here I discuss ways of conducting both kinds of interviews. I start with surveys.

In survey interviewing, interviewers need to be trained so that each one is following the same procedures. Critical components in interviewer training include the following:

1. Going over each question to ensure that each interviewer understands its meaning and the kind of information that is responsive. This review is critical for helping interviewers know what they are expected to get.

2. Survey interviewers are expected to read the questions just as written and ask them in the order in which they appear. When the respondent doesn't understand a question, she should repeat it in the same words. If the respondent is still confused, the interviewer says that the question means whatever the respondent thinks it means. Unless the study director says otherwise, the interviewer does not reword the question or give further information.

3. If an answer is not responsive (e.g., if the respondent goes off on a tangent), the interviewer is trained how to probe for the appropriate information. (*Appropriate* means that it answers the question, not that it fits some preconceived notion of what the right answer would be.) Probes should be neutral, giving no cues about what the interviewer wants to or expects to hear. Possible probes are: "Anything else?" or "How come the shop closed?" or simply repeating the respondent's last words with a rising inflection: "Sorry to see it?"

4. Listening carefully is the heart of the interviewing job. Good listening is essential for recording responses properly. It is also essential for knowing whether the respondent is being responsive or whether further probing is needed to elicit the appropriate information.

5. An essential part of the interviewer's job is to record the answers on the form. One reason that surveys are more economical than informal interviewing is that structured answer categories already exist, and the interviewer usually just checks or circles the proper answer. There is no need for the expense of tape-recording and transcribing tapes. But then it becomes essential for the inter-

viewer to check the answer in the right place. Training will give the interviewer an opportunity to practice doing this while she is asking questions, listening carefully to answers, maintaining eye contact, and getting ready for the next question. With computerized interview forms, the interviewer can take a laptop computer to the interview and enter answers directly on the screen.

6. The interviewer is trained not to show surprise, disapproval, joy, shock, or any other emotion upon hearing the respondent's answers, especially on controversial topics like violence or drug use. If the respondent berates the staff, lambastes fellow program participants, or makes rude remarks about the evaluation, this is all just data. The interviewer's attitude is professional, and she acts as though she has heard everything and is surprised at nothing.

7. Novice interviewers often place high stock on establishing rapport with respondents with the expectation that the better their relationship, the more likely is the respondent to give full and accurate answers. It is true that a degree of rapport is needed for the respondent to reveal often intimate details of his life. But too much rapport may not be good. It begins to turn the interchange into a social situation, where the respondent becomes reluctant to divulge unflattering information for fear of disturbing the norms of polite conversation. The interviewer should be engaged in the business of asking questions and recording answers, and her best stance is a businesslike one.

8. If a respondent does not want to participate in the interview, the interviewer tries to convince him to do it. However, one of the ethical obligations in this kind of research is to allow potential respondents to just say no. They have the right to refuse to cooperate, and they should not be browbeaten. Similarly, if they start the interview and then decide to break off, or if they refuse to answer a specific question, that is their right, too. After a gentle effort to persuade, the interviewer should courteously back off.

With unstructured interviewing, the interview starts with a list of topics to be covered but leaves the wording of specific questions to the discretion of the interviewer. The interviewer crafts the questions to suit the particular respondent and the flow of conversation in the interview. (The same thing is true with informal qualitative interviews.) The interviewer develops questions as she maintains the flow of the conversation.

Interviewers generally believe that they do a good job thinking up the questions to ask next during a fast-moving interview. But at the same time that they are thinking up the next questions, they are doing many other things: maintaining rapport with the respondent by giving feedback of nods and "mm-hmm's," listening hard to follow the respondent's story, taking notes (just in case the tape recorder fails). They can give only part of their attention to formulating question wording. When they listen to the tapes of the interview afterward, they often find that they framed questions in unclear or ambiguous ways, so that now they don't understand what the answers mean. Or they asked some of their respondents questions that they forgot to pursue with other respondents, so that now they don't know how widespread a phenomenon is. Or they settled for a fuzzy reply from a respondent without probing further to find out what he actually meant.

The solution to these problems is experience. However, the evaluator doesn't want interviewers (including herself) to gain experience at the expense of failed interviews. So training is in order, often a good deal of training. If the study is being conducted by one or two people, much of the training will be self-training. Training has to cover a number of the subjects discussed above for survey interviewers. Interviewers have to know the purpose of the study and the kinds of information that are needed. They have to understand what kinds of answers are responsive to the study's concerns, and what kind of information is expected from each respondent. They should know when to probe for elaboration of responses and appropriate probing technique to use. They especially need to learn how to listen carefully. Since they are formulating questions as they go, they have to acknowledge the information the respondent has already given while going on to ask for further information. They should not react emotionally to anything the respondent says but go about the business of asking, listening, and recording. Their job is to collect the special brand of information that each respondent is uniquely qualified to contribute.

Interviewer training should include the opportunity to do a number of practice interviews. The videotaping of practice interviews gives the interviewer an opportunity to see what she is doing well and what she is doing poorly. The tapes also allow the evaluator (and other interviewers) to give advice and further coaching. The interviewer shouldn't brave the real world until she is comfortable that she can handle a range of situations, from the hostile respondent, to one who talks at machine-gun speed, to one who is laconic and miserly with words, to one who meanders all around the subject. With experience, interviewers are not fazed by the range of human idiosyncrasy.

Coding Responses

Coding is the practice of taking narrative information and slotting it into a set of categories that capture the essence of their meaning. The narrative information can come from open-ended interviews, from open-ended questions in mainly structured interviews, from documents (such as meeting minutes or agency annual reports), from observers' record of observations, from letters that are received by the program, or from many other sources. The first task in coding is to develop a set of descriptive categories that capture the main themes in the material. For example, an interview question asks, "What are the three most important things that you learned in this program?" The evaluator reads through the answers and recognizes that there are answers that refer to specific content knowledge, some that refer to skills, some about personal relationships, and a number of unique one-of-a-kind answers. She therefore has the beginning of a code: content knowledge, skills, relationships, and other.

The next step is to assign numerical values to each category. With nominal codes, the numbers are arbitrary and one number does not represent something more or better than the other numbers. Then evaluators go through the materials and mark the code value on the responses. (In text programs, this procedure can be done directly on the computer.) The code value for this question is now part of the case record for the individual, and in analysis, the evaluator can associate the type of response given to this question with other characteristics of the respondent. A subsequent step is to tabulate the number of responses that fall into each category of the code, and to analyze these responses against other data in the dataset.

The hardest part of coding is developing the list of code categories. There are two basic ways that codes can be constructed. One is to start with the materials them-selves and see what they say. That is what was done in the example above. The other way is to start with a theoretical set of categories—that is, particular constructs that the evaluator expects on a priori grounds to matter in the study. Thus the evaluator of a preschool program expected that the program would have differential outcomes depending on whether the staff took a cognitive approach (teaching children num-bers, colors, etc.) or a developmental approach (nurturing children's progress along the steps of their own development). Therefore, she coded teachers' responses in terms of whether they showed a cognitive or developmental orientation to working with young children. That distinction was expected to be important in her analysis of the program.

The same data can be coded in more than one way. The evaluator can construct theoretical codes and codes based on the evidence for the same responses. She can code the content of responses, the respondent's expressed degree of certainty, the articulateness of responses, and so on.

Once codes are developed for each question and answer category, the evalua-tor compiles them into a codebook. She often lists examples of answers appropriate for each code category so that coders will interpret responses in the same way and agree on the codes assigned. A check on inter-coder reliability is a good precaution. If reliability is low, more training and more examples may be in order.

How many codes should the evaluator make out of answers to a question that asked why the respondent was not working at a paid job? The answer depends on the purpose of the question. What does the evaluator want to know from these respons-es? If the study is trying to find out the whole range of reasons why respondents say that they are not holding paid jobs so that program staff can deal with these issues, she may want a large array of narrow categories. She may be particularly interested in distinguishing the several different reasons why respondents find available jobs unattractive and count up the number of people who gave each of the reasons (pay, co-workers, travel, etc.). But in another case the evaluator wants to know only whether the reasons given represented choices that the respondents made (could they have taken a job if they had wanted to?) or whether they were conditions beyond the person's control. Only two categories would suffice.

The following are characteristics of good codes:

1. They match the intent of the study.
2. They fit the responses. They describe the main content of the narratives.
3. They surface common themes even though the themes may emerge in different settings or situations.
4. They are exhaustive. That is, they represent all the responses given.
5. They are mutually exclusive. They do not overlap. If a response fits in one code, it does not fit in another code.
6. The codebook gives examples, so that coders can understand which code applies. The codebook indicates the limits of the code by telling what does NOT fit within that category. The codebook helps to train coders in its use.
7. Codes are neither so gross that they lump divergent responses nor so fine that the study ends up with almost as many codes as responses. A ballpark generalization is that for large diverse samples, codes of 5–8 categories usually work well. Plus

the inevitable "other," which is necessary to catch the oddball response but tells the analyst almost nothing.

Some codes are ordinal—that is, they go from less to more. Where open-ended answers allow ordered codes, they are highly desirable. The data can then be treated as an ordinal variable in statistical analysis. But many kinds of responses do not have an intrinsic order. With ingenuity, an order can sometimes be devised. In a study I worked on, we had the names of colleges that respondents had attended. What kind of code would make sense? The study director developed an ordered code based on the quality ratings of the colleges, with community and junior colleges at one end and the Ivy League universities and other elite schools at the other. The variable then became "Quality rating of respondents' college." Codes that are strictly nominal (categorical) are clumsier to work with; there are fewer statistical options.

Existing Statistical Data

Another source of data for evaluation is statistical reports of other (usually governmental) agencies. Usually these data have to do with the problem that the program is supposed to cure. Thus, if a program is designed to reduce illiteracy or highway accidents or infant mortality, the evaluator can turn to available statistical series on the prevalence of these ills and look at changes in the statistics from a time before the program starts through to some later period. If the program is effective, presumably it will tend to push the figures down. Because these kinds of statistical data are collected periodically over long time spans, the study can follow the trends over a lengthy period.

There are two main sources of statistical data: administrative records of government agencies and longitudinal surveys. Let us look at each of them in turn.

Administrative Records

Agencies keep records on thousands of items (Coulton, 1997). Among them are the following:

> Building and demolition permits
> Violations of housing codes
> Tax records
> Birth and death certificates
> Emergency medical service calls
> Immunizations
> Medicaid claims
> Hospital discharge files
> Coroners' reports
> Public assistance files
> Unemployment insurance claims
> Child welfare records
> Day-care licenses
> Homeless shelters

Crime reports
Arrest data
Victim data
Liquor licenses
Auto registrations and licenses
Library usage
Students' school records

There are important restrictions on the availability of most of these data for reasons of privacy and confidentiality. But in some cases, when there is a strong public interest in the evaluation, agencies may make some data available. They may insist on such conditions as removal of names and other identifiers. But even when hedged about with restrictions, the data can be extremely valuable.

The fly in the ointment, the bug in the program, comes when the coverage of the agency's record data is not coterminous with the coverage of the program. The agency collects data for the county and the program serves only two neighborhoods within the county. Fortunately, clever people have developed a way out of the impasse, a geographic information system (GIS). If the agency includes the street addresses of individuals in the records, the investigator can take addresses (e.g., from welfare records or court dockets) and "geocode" them to fit the boundaries of the area(s) in which she is interested. Even when agencies do not release break-downs of their reports to the neighborhood level, the evaluator can essentially construct her own neighborhood-level data. She uses the GIS to select addresses that fall within the boundaries of the neighborhoods served by the program.

There are still problems. Geocoding is likely to be a tedious process, even with new computer software. Agency records may not be completely accurate, up to date, or consistent across jurisdictions. Some data will not be forthcoming. But the data situation is improving.

The main attraction of these records is the capacity to monitor trends over time. If the program is having an impact, the effect presumably will show up in the data. However, I have some caveats to offer, which apply to the next section on longitudinal surveys as well, and so appear following that section.

Longitudinal Surveys

The government supports hundreds of repeated surveys on hundreds of topics. In some cases, the surveys collect data from the same individuals over extended periods of time and become a truly longitudinal database. In other cases, the surveys select new samples of respondents and conduct repeated cross-sectional surveys.

Government-supported surveys that are conducted repeatedly include the following:

National Assessment of Educational Progress
American Housing Survey
Schools and Staffing Survey
Youth Risk Behavior Surveillance System
National Immunization Survey

National Health Interview Survey
National Crime Victimization Survey
National Election Study
Panel Study on Income Dynamics
Survey of Income and Program Participation
National Longitudinal Survey of Youth (NLSY)
Children of the NLSY
High School and Beyond
Current Population Surveys

These data can serve several evaluative purposes. Like data from administrative records, they can provide information on changes in key outcome variables—8th grade reading scores, foster home placements, percentage of families without health insurance coverage, percentage of teenagers who report having thought about suicide within the past 12 months. Many of the survey items are reported at the state level and a considerable number are also available for large local jurisdictions such as cities.

The evaluator can obtain many of the surveys on CD-ROM (and soon on newer devices), and an increasing number are being made available through the World Wide Web. Thus she can break out subsets of respondents and analyze the data in ways suited to the evaluation. If she doesn't have the capacity to deal with large data sets, a number of agencies will do custom analyses for a fee. The Census Bureau, for example, will produce custom tabulations of data from the Current Population Reports on a contract basis. Other public and private organizations also do made-to-order analyses. If given a list of Social Security numbers for all participants, a state university may release information on the number who are still enrolled in the university on a given date. *Kids Count*, a publication published by the Annie E. Casey Foundation, provides a comprehensive guide to surveys about children. The guide lists data items, sources, geographic coverage, frequency with which items are collected, how to get the data, and which groups do custom analyses (Brown & Botsko, 1996).

Considerations in Use of Available Data

Obviously there are significant advantages in using data already collected, but here come the promised caveats as well. The evaluator has to be sure that she knows what she is getting—and getting into.

Scope   Evaluation on the basis of changes in existing indicators is a tempting prospect. With the expansion of data systems and advances in technical capabilities to disaggregate data by census tract, zip code, or other small-area designation, relevant data are often already sitting somewhere in a computer seemingly waiting to be exploited. However, before the evaluator leaps at the chance to use the data, she needs to be sure exactly what is being measured, under what definitions, for what population, and with what frequency. The data will not be very useful if they do not match the expected outcomes of the program. The evaluator should check whether the phenomenon being measured (e.g., adolescent pregnancy) is defined in restrictive or overly expansive terms, or if the population from which the data are collected is much larger, smaller, or somewhat different from the population being served, or if the indicators are collected at intervals that do not match the time schedule of the program (say, the data are collected once a year and the program runs for six weeks). Even if the statistical data do not quite match the evaluator's needs, she may be able to supplement them with surveys or program records that provide additional information and that also allow estimation of the extent to which the statistical series reflects conditions in the program's target population.

Accuracy   Accuracy is likely to be a strong point in official statistical series, particularly when the series has been maintained over a period of time by technically qualified staff. Data collected by the Census Bureau or Bureau of Labor Statistics or by reputable survey organizations are known for careful attention to such matters as completeness of coverage and strict adherence to data standards. But some series, although official, are more problematic. Crime statistics, for example, have been known on occasion to have peculiarities. There have been newsworthy instances when a new chief of police took office, improved the record-keeping system—and was confronted with a big jump in the crime rate. Victimization studies, surveys that ask representative samples of the public about their experiences as victims of crime, show that large numbers of crimes are never reported to the police. Many statistical series reflect administrative actions as well as the pure incidence of the problem. For example, delinquency rates reflect the activity of the police in apprehending juveniles as well as the actual rate of juvenile crime. Rates of the incidence of diseases depend on the health department's case finding as well as on the existence of the cases.

Definition of Terms   Definitions of terms may also fail to accord with the evaluator's needs. Standard unemployment figures do not include the underemployed, people who are working part time but want full-time employment, nor do they count people out of work who have gotten discouraged and are no longer actively looking for a job. Labor Department surveys have found that in poverty neighborhoods, unemployment rates can be substantially understated because of these omissions. If an evaluator wants to use these figures to judge the success of a program for reducing hardcore unemployment, neither the before nor the after figures are ideally suited for her purpose.

Geographic Base   Another problem is that indicators are generally based on geography rather than on people. They include any people who are living in the area at a specific time. In some areas, particularly in urban poverty neighborhoods, residents are highly mobile. The people who lived there and were served in the program last year are no longer around to show up in this year's indicators. It is a whole new batch of people whose status is being measured. If higher income people have moved into the neighborhood, the changes in the indicators may look exceedingly favorable, even though the real target group is not better off—only farther off.

The fact that indicators cover areas, and thus populations larger than the service scope of the program, minimizes a program's capacity to make a dent in the numbers. A city will have figures on the percentage of people who vote city-wide and in each precinct, but not figures on voting by the people who were exposed to a get-out-the-vote campaign. It would require changes of heroic proportions in the exposed group to shift the citywide percentages of voters.

Even when a large-scale program is run, to expect it to shift indicators for a geographic area is expecting a great deal. A job training program for disadvantaged youths would have to be monumentally effective to lower youth unemployment rates for the area. Not only would it have to reach, recruit, train, and retain a very large number of target-group youth, but it would also have to help them find and keep jobs for a long enough period to show up in the youth unemployment rate. And even then, the program would have to be sure that the jobs they were getting were *additional* jobs, so that the trained youth were not simply jumping to the head of the queue and displacing other young people from available jobs—young people who would then become unemployed and keep the unemployment rate relatively stable.

Inexactness   There is a temptation in using indicators to make do with the figures that exist, even if they are not direct measures of program goals. The use of surrogate measures is common in all social research, since one indicator rarely captures the entire concept in which we are interested. For example, we may have a program to improve the quality of housing in an urban neighborhood. There are no available figures on housing quality, but there is a figure on overcrowding—that is, the number of persons per room. The evaluator makes a series of assumptions leading to the conclusion that overcrowding is a reasonable indicator of housing quality, and then draws conclusions about the success of the program on the basis of a measure that at best is only a partial indicator of the true objective.

For some conditions there are no reliable population-based measures. For example, there are no comprehensive indicators on the prevalence of HIV in the population. One reliable population-based measure is the prevalence of AIDS infection in newborn infants in 30 metropolitan areas (National Research Council, 1989). This indicator provides data about the level of HIV-AIDS infection among childbearing women, but obviously this is only a segment of the population of interest. The absence of more complete information is due to the resistance of individuals at risk of AIDS and the awareness of government of the need to protect them from possible negative consequences of being identified. Available data are not only limited in coverage of the population of interest but also insufficiently specific to be useful for measuring the effectiveness of interventions targeted at them.

Manipulation   Some data series, especially administrative records, are susceptible to manipulation. Once data series are established, program personnel—like the teacher who teaches to the test—may work to improve those facets of their operation that they know will show up and be judged, and pay less attention to changing the complex social conditions that indicators only partially reflect.

Expectations   Perhaps the gravest impediment to the use of administrative and statistical data for evaluation is that it expects so much. A program must be *pervasive* enough to reach a significant part of the relevant population and *effective* enough to bring about change sufficient to shift people from one category to another. A little bit of change is not enough; people have to move from hospitalized to not hospitalized, from below grade level to on grade level, from unemployed to employed. Programs generally reach relatively small numbers of participants and make small improvements. Even the poverty program of the 1960s and 1970s, considered to be a massive undertaking at the time, was able to mobilize resources that were scanty in comparison with the size of the problem. It is little wonder that indicators resist dramatic change.

Even if change does come, it is apt to take a while to show up. Indicators are sluggish. They are derived from periodic soundings, usually annual, so that there is a considerable time lapse before trends become apparent. By the time changes appear in the figures, numbers of other influences have been operating on conditions. In fact, so many complex interacting factors affect phenomena like poverty rates and life expectancy that it would be presumptuous to ascribe them to a single program.

Some Reasonable Uses   This all sounds negative and overly cautious. As a matter of happy fact, there are many conditions under which the use of available data for evaluation makes eminent sense. For massive programs, such as public education or Medicare, they can provide longitudinal data on the distribution of resources and outcomes. Even for smaller scale interventions, on the order of get-out-the-vote campaigns or introduction of new medical procedures, they can yield informative data on before-and-after conditions directly relevant to the program's outcomes. They have the advantage for decision purposes of using common criteria and collecting comparable data across projects and across time and, if astutely constructed, dealing in issues of relevance to policymakers. They cannot overcome such inherent limitations as the failure to account for external (nonprogram) influences or the absence of information on causes and dynamics of change. But if supplemented by, and related to, specifically evaluative studies on critical issues, their information can be supportive and important. In lucky cases, they offer evidence to help assess the efficacy of a program—and to do so at low cost and with high accuracy.

Ethical Issues in Collecting Data

Data collection raises important ethical issues. As noted previously, participation in evaluations should be voluntary. Clients should not be railroaded into providing information but should have the opportunity to decline to participate. The evaluator can, of course, use all the arts of persuasion to convince clients of the importance of responding to requests for information and promise them confidentiality of the data they provide. But if they remain adamant, they should not be made to feel that they have forfeited full rights to program participation or the respect of staff.

Asking Questions

Some evaluations have to inquire into private and sensitive matters. In family planning evaluations they ask about sexual behavior; in criminal justice evaluations they ask about criminal acts; in job training evaluations they ask about earnings. When the questions are essential for the purposes of the study, the inquiries are justified.

However, sometimes evaluators add questions that are not essential to the purpose of the evaluation and that intrude into sensitive areas that are beyond its scope. Keep a watchful eye. Take note of any special sensitivities of the populations the study will be dealing with, and try to stay aware of risks that the study may pose to them.

Because evaluations sometimes seek sensitive information, such as illicit activity, researchers have developed ways of collecting such information without jeopardizing the privacy of the respondent. One approach allows respondents to remain anonymous. This, of course, precludes matching the same individual's answers before and after the program and examining change on the individual level. The evaluator has to look at average change in the group and cannot examine characteristics of respondents associated with more or less progress. Another device allows the respondent to use an alias (National Research Council, 1989, p. 342), which the evaluator hopes he will remember and use again in subsequent data collection, so that individual-level change becomes amenable to study. A variety of statistical approaches have been developed that permit the evaluator to collect specific information on behavior and tie it to characteristics of the respondent without identifying the individual, but the procedures are cumbersome and of limited usefulness in many settings (Boruch & Cecil, 1979).

Hearing about Illegal Acts

When the evaluator hears about delinquent acts, drug use, or other crimes that respondents have committed in the past, the usual course is to deal with them just as she deals with any other data. She does not reveal them to project staff or to the police. This rule is sometimes difficult to justify. When the respondent discloses a report of heinous crime, such as sexual abuse of a child, doesn't the evaluator have a responsibility to bring this to the attention of authorities? Here again she has to give serious attention to conflicting ethical demands.

Most evaluators believe that their responsibilities to the study are paramount. Unless the information discloses a clear and present danger to other people, she usually keeps the information confidential. A main exception is when she learns about illegal acts planned for the future. In such a case, her obligation to prevent the commission of a crime outweighs her obligation to avoid intrusion into the program scene.

Some states have laws that mandate the reporting of illegal acts by members of certain professions. For example, Tennessee requires health-care professionals to report suspected cases of child abuse, and other states require teachers to do the same. It is not obvious that such laws apply to evaluators, but it would be a good idea to check out state laws.

Another dilemma arises when the information she stumbles upon shows that program staff are embezzling, or otherwise misusing, program funds. Such information is not accidental or unrelated to the study; it is highly relevant to the process and outcome of the program. Again she faces an ethical dilemma, and ethical people can come down on different sides of the issue. Many people do in fact reveal this kind of information to higher authorities. Still, no one that I know has yet worked out a comprehensive rationale or a hierarchy of ethical claims that unambiguously justifies one course of action over another.

The best advice is to discuss ethical issues of these kinds with knowledgeable colleagues. Without divulging the identities of the people involved or the particulars of the situation, you can ask, "Suppose you were doing an interview and someone revealed child abuse, what do you think your obligations are?"

Giving Help

Because an evaluator works in a setting that often serves people in trouble, program participants sometimes turn to the evaluator for help. This is particularly likely when the evaluator has been asking people questions about their experiences. The participants may be having trouble with a program staff person, or they may have a problem unrelated to the program and don't know where to turn, or they may see the evaluator as an educated person who is not involved in the service end of the program and can give impartial advice.

The usual advice is: don't. The evaluator's job is not to make things better—or worse. Her job is to leave the situation as little changed as possible. Ideally she should be a fly on the wall (unless the program is eradicating flies). If she knows that the person asking for help is in serious need, she can refer his question to program staff, or where program staff are not interested or qualified to help, she might refer him to an appropriate community resource. But the role of the evaluator is to stay out of things to the extent possible. For people engaged in intensive qualitative work, the stricture is sometimes hard to follow because they have developed strong relationships. But even in those cases, the common advice is to try to avoid inserting any interventions of their own into the program arena. Such well-meant intrusions only make it more difficult for the evaluation to isolate the effects of the official program and may muddy the waters by intermixing program effects with the effects of the evaluator's help.

Of course, there are limits to the applicability of such strictures. The evaluator is a human being first and seeks to behave like an ethical human being. When she hears about serious problems that she can help to remedy, she wants to help. Is it more ethical to prevent contamination of the evaluation or to help a person in serious trouble? Often a careful scouting of the terrain will turn up ways to do both with minimal intervention—for example, by alerting the person to sources of help in the community. But when that is impossible, the evaluator may put her human obligations first. But she has to think carefully about the competing claims before she does so.

Confidentiality

Another kind of ethical issue arises when outside bodies seek access to data collected for evaluative purposes. The past decades have seen demands from law enforcement agencies and other governmental bodies for information (e.g., about crime or drug use) that was collected for research and evaluation purposes. Faced with such demands, researchers have usually refused to release the data, on the grounds that they had promised confidentiality to their sources and could not violate those commitments. They have compared themselves to priests who are not required to reveal information obtained in the confessional, or journalists, who in some states are protected by shield laws from revealing information obtained confidentially from informants. In some cases researchers have been brought before the courts, and in a few cases the courts have ordered the researcher to provide the information or face jail. At least one researcher has gone to jail rather than violate promises to respondents.

To prevent such episodes, the Public Health Service (PHS) has obtained legislation (P.L. 91-513) that protects research records on identifiable individuals that are collected by the National Center for Health Statistics or its contractors or the National Center for Health Services Research. A second provision of the act allows the Secretary of the Department of Health and Human Services to award special confidentiality certificates to researchers who do research on mental health topics under PHS funding. Boruch and Cecil (1979) point out that protection provided by such certificates is limited. Certificates are awarded on a discretionary basis, and certain kinds of judicial access to records are excluded from protection (National Research Council, 1989). Nevertheless, evaluators continue to consider the potential benefits, as well as limitations, of extensions of legal protection (e.g., Gray & Melton, 1985, cited in NRC, 1989, p. 343).

Summary

This chapter discusses the many ways in which data can be collected. The most common sources are informal interviews, observation, formal interviews either unstructured or structured, questionnaires, program records, and data from other institutions. In addition, the evaluator can use tests; scales and inventories of attitudes or opinions; judgments of staff, participants, or experts; participant diaries; focus groups; physical examinations; program documents such as minutes of meetings or financial records; newspaper stories; and government statistical series. Each source has significant advantages under specific conditions, and each requires careful consideration of costs and constraints. Existing statistical series, for example, have the advantages of accuracy, the availability of longitudinal data for long periods of time, well-understood definitions of terms, and low cost—since the data have already been collected. They have the disadvantage that the jurisdictions for which they have been collected may not be coterminous with the boundaries of the program's service area. When this is the case, the evaluator can use new techniques that allow her to subdivide the data to the relevant geographic area. Other possible disadvantages are that the items included in the series may not be quite right for the purposes of the evaluation and that change in indicators may be sluggish. Nevertheless, when items fit, longitudinal statistical series represent an excellent source of information.

The interview is the most versatile tool. To make optimal use of interviews, it pays to understand the conditions under which open-ended (unstructured) interviews are appropriate and when the structure of survey interviewing is more suitable. Unstructured interviewing enables the evaluator to hear about the situation from the respondents' perspective without the imposition of the evaluator's frame. It lets the respondent tell the story as he sees it and gives a freer account of events. Survey interviewing has the advantage of asking questions in uniform ways so that every person queried responds to the same stimuli. Surveys give comparable information across all respondents. But the information they elicit is limited by the questions posed, which depend on the evaluator's knowledge and attention.

Interviewers ask the survey questions in the exact words and the exact order in which they are written. If the respondent does not understand the question, the interviewer repeats the question without adding new words or interpretation. When answers are not responsive to the question, the interviewer probes further, using neutral prompts. The interviewer's aim is not to intervene between the question and the respondent. She is the vehicle that carries home the data.

Unstructured interviewing gives the interviewer more latitude in framing questions and tailoring them to the individual's special knowledge and situation. However, this type of interviewing makes demands on the interviewer's ability to ask questions, listen to the answers, record answers, maintain rapport with the respondent, and think about the next question to ask—all at the same time. Training and experience are essential for gathering appropriate and complete information.

When unstructured questions are asked, responses are often coded into categories. Code categories should match the intent of the study and capture the gist of responses. Since coding requires the exercise of judgment, all coders are trained to code the same response in the same way.

Collection of data often poses ethical dilemmas. Despite the need for information, evaluators should not coerce people into supplying data. Cooperation should be voluntary. Questions may have to deal with sensitive issues, like family planning, because that is the substance of the program. But they should be asked in ways that are sensitive to respondents' cultural sensibilities and the risks that answering may pose for them. Unnecessary intrusions into respondents' privacy should be avoided.

Program participants may tell the evaluator about unsavory or illegal activities. They may also ask her help with life crises. In both these circumstances, most evaluators try to keep mum. They don't want their intervention to become entangled with program services, so that participant outcomes are a response not only to the program but also to their meddling. On the other hand, situations can arise where the evaluator is ethically bound to report illegal acts, especially those planned for the future. Similarly, even though she tries to refer request for help to program staff, at some junctures she will feel a human obligation to offer the requested help to a person in dire straits.

8

DESIGN OF THE EVALUATION

> People who write about methodology often forget that it is a matter of strategy, not of morals. There are neither good nor bad methods but only methods that are more or less effective under particular circumstances in reaching objectives on the way to a distant goal.
>
> —George C. Homans (1949, p. 330)[1]

The evaluator's task is to create a study design that fits the questions to be asked. The design indicates which people or units will be studied and how they are to be selected, which kinds of comparisons will be drawn, and the timing of the investigation. This chapter sketches a number of design options. It gives an indication of the requirements for using each design and their advantages and disadvantages.

The designs I discuss should not necessarily be viewed as separate design packages, total entities among which the evaluator picks. Rather, they are bundles of techniques that can be put together in different combinations. The evaluator develops strategies for selecting participants, assigning them to groups, making comparisons, and timing the data collection. The designs in this chapter and the next provide a guide to available and well-tried evaluation practices, but the evaluator uses her judgment in tailoring them to the situation at hand.

The designs in this chapter have been used primarily in quantitative studies. They are geared to the collection of data that can be expressed quantitatively and compared over time, but there is no intrinsic reason why they could not be used when qualitative data are collected. For example, it is not common in qualitative evaluations to choose respondents by random sampling or to include a comparison group that does not receive the program. Yet on occasion there may be plausible reasons for doing so.

---

[1]From George C. Homans, "The Strategy of Industrial Sociology," *American Journal of Sociology, 54* (1949): 330–337. Copyright © 1949 The University of Chicago Press. Reprinted by permission of The University of Chicago Press.

Qualitative evaluators might think more explicitly about some of the design choices they make, just as quantitative evaluators might take into account features that are common in the qualitative world, such as an emphasis on the context within which the program functions and participants' perspectives on their experiences. This chapter can give ideas that make sense in qualitative as well as quantitative evaluations.

Designing the Process Evaluation

The experiment and most of the other designs discussed in this chapter are appropriate for outcome evaluations. For process evaluations, the modes of inquiry are frequently informal, and designs tend to be more casual. In fact, process evaluation is not very different from what is often called monitoring. One key difference is that monitoring is done primarily on behalf of funders and other high-level officials to hold the program to account. They want to know what is going on in the program for purposes of oversight. Evaluations of program process, in contrast, are often conducted for the benefit of the program. Process evaluations help the program understand what it has been doing and how, and lead to reflection on how it might improve its operations. Another difference is that process evaluations are generally more systematic than monitoring and rely more on data and less on intuitive judgments. But monitoring and process evaluation are similar kinds of inquiry.

A process evaluation has to be designed, whether it uses quantitative or qualitative methods of investigation. First, the evaluator has to decide which sites to study. If the project operates at a single site, that decision is made by default. But if there are several sites, or smaller sites embedded within larger ones like classrooms within schools, she has to choose how to allocate energies. She also has to decide which people to query. Such a decision can be made opportunistically, selecting informants informally as chances arise and as people pass her along to other people to talk to. Or she can use systematic sampling strategies to be sure that she covers principals, teachers, guidance counselors, and librarians and, within the teacher group, to represent teachers not only of the core subjects but also the arts, vocational subjects, special education, and bilingual classes. Another decision she has to make, consciously or by the way, is the time periods at which data will be collected—over how long a period, at what intervals, and how intensively.

The notion of *designing* a qualitative inquiry used to be heresy; it was taken for granted that such studies took shape in the field as the investigator figured out what was happening. In recent years, qualitative investigators—at least some qualitative investigators—have become more receptive to the notion of design. A big difference between the first and second editions of Yin's *Case Study Research: Design and Methods* (1984, 1994) is the addition of a 35-page chapter explicitly on design. Where many early books on qualitative approaches scanted the subject, several newer ones make design an integral feature (e.g., Maxwell, 1996; Miles & Huberman, 1994).

A major advantage of qualitative study of program process is the opportunity to find the unexpected. The evaluator can follow the trail wherever it leads. She also learns which aspects of the program matter to staff and to participants, what elements of the program are salient to whom at which times. For example, even if a health maintenance organization is giving important categories of preventive care, clients may grumble over the lengthy spells of waiting time and the obstacles to seeing the same physician at successive visits.

Qualitative study of program process can take account of context. It can lead to awareness of how physicians' time is allocated and why scheduled health-care appointments are always late. It can look into the nature of the setting—physical facilities, neighborhood environment, and financial resources. Only constraints on time and access will limit the range of data that the qualitative evaluator assembles.

When should an evaluator conduct a process evaluation through qualitative methods? (a) When she knows little about the nature of the program and its activities. Qualitative methods allow her to poke around, listen to people, and become familiar with the program staff and participants. (b) When the program represents a marked departure from ordinary methods of service. A truly innovative program may set in motion a stream of developments that no one would have foreseen. (c) When the theories underlying the program—implicitly or explicitly—are dubious, disputable, or problematic. In such a case, the evaluator is uncertain of what to look at and measure in a process evaluation. A wider gauge inquiry is worthwhile.

But the evaluator may already be familiar with this kind of program and the elements that should be watched. She may also want to be sure that the study collects *comparable* data across sites, informants, and time periods. She may, for example, want to have consistent and reliable data on the frequency and intensity of program service and its fidelity to the program's original intent. In that case she can turn to techniques that yield *quantitative* measures of program process.

One procedure is to design forms that staff fill out on a regular basis. The forms can ask them to enter the nature of the problem the client presented, the type of service they provided, dates and times of service, and any special features of the contact. Such information will cumulate over time to provide a running picture of the program in action. Another way to collect data is through interviews with program recipients and/or program staff. The evaluator can develop a survey form that asks structured and unstructured questions about the operation of the program. All respondents can be asked the same questions so that data will be comparable across respondents, or an unstructured survey can be conducted, with a flavor of the ethnographic, to give people an opportunity to tell their story from their own perspective.

Whichever method, or combination of methods, is used for process evaluation, the evaluator has to decide the frequency with which information will be collected. These decisions will depend in part on the specific nature of program processes, such as how routinized they are, and the frequency with which their content and structure are apt to change. Information about characteristics of program participants is not likely to change very often, but information about the services they receive may call for more frequent recording. A plan should be made, too, to capture any big unexpected shift in the way the program operates.

Designing the Outcome Evaluation

The underlying logic of evaluation design for outcome studies is twofold: (a) to compare program participants before they receive the program with their situation afterward in order to see if they have made gains on key outcomes and (b) to com-

FIGURE 8-1 DIAGRAM OF AN EXPERIMENT

		Before	After	
Random assignment	Program participants	a	b	$b - a = y$
	Control group	c	d	$d - c = z$

If y is greater than z, the program has had a positive net outcome.

pare program participants with an *equivalent* group of people who did not receive the program (a randomly assigned control group) in order to see whether participants' gains exceed those made by nonparticipants. In Figure 8-1, the difference between b and a represents the outcomes for participants (let's call the difference y). The difference between d and c represents the outcomes for the control group (let's call that difference z); z is the change that the group in the program would have experienced if they had not received the program. Then y minus z is the *net outcome* of the program. It is the additional advantage that the program produced over whatever gain would have happened anyway.[2]

The next chapter delves more deeply into experimental design and the randomization procedures required to implement it. Here I introduce it as a standard against which other designs are often judged. The experiment is very good at ruling out the possibility that something besides the program led to observed effects (e.g., participants were getting older and would have improved anyway, or conditions outside the program were responsible). Experimental design provides a level of confidence in the internal validity of results that other designs often aspire to.

Despite the acknowledged attractions of the experiment, it is often difficult to implement. As we will see in Chapter 9, it requires that the evaluator have a strong voice in the assignment of eligible people into the program and into the control group. That condition is often difficult to obtain. It also requires constant vigilance to be sure that the groups stay intact, continue to provide data, and do not become contaminated (e.g., by the controls' exposure to program materials). Donald Campbell made a great contribution to the discussion of design when he argued that what is essential is not one particular research design but the ability to rule out rival explanations (other than the program) for any changes in outcome that are observed (Campbell & Stanley, 1966; Cook & Campbell, 1979). He and his collaborators listed a dozen or so "threats to validity"—that is, conditions that could conceivably cause the observed changes—and he advocated designs that guarded against them.

In the absence of experimental design, conditions other than the program can be responsible for observed outcomes. Chief among them are the following:

Selection. Program recipients were different from the people with whom they are being compared from the beginning; therefore, differences at the end may be due

---

[2]Sampling from a population never produces two groups that are absolutely identical. Random fluctuations have to be taken into account. Therefore, the evaluator has to make inferences about whether the difference between y and z is greater than the likelihood of random error. She tests the difference to see whether it is statistically significant.

to the fact that different types of people were selected or selected themselves into the program.

Attrition. The loss of people from the program group was different from loss of people in the comparison group; therefore, even if the two groups were alike at the start, the surviving remnants may be different and outcomes may reflect these differences.

Outside effects. Participants in the program and comparison groups may have been exposed to different experiences and conditions (besides the program) while the program was in session; differential exposure to extraneous events may affect outcome measures.

Maturation. The sheer passage of time, and the processes involved in growing older, may account for observed outcomes. For example, as children age, their cognitive processes develop and mature, and they may learn more even without the help of the program.

Testing. Taking a test once may teach people to be better at test taking the next time around; outcomes may reflect this improved capacity. Similarly, responding to questionnaires and interviews in the beginning may alert people to the subject matter so that they become more conscious of the topics, and increased familiarity can affect outcomes.

Instrumentation. If there is a change in the instrument used to collect data from the preprogram to postprogram time, outcomes may reflect the change in data collection tool or technique. If raters change their standards for rating, this too represents a change in instrumentation.[3]

If there is no reason to suspect that selection or attrition or outside events or any of the other threats are getting in the way, then experimental design is a luxury. If one or another of the threats to valid conclusions *does* exist, then the design needs to guard against that particular condition. Of course, threats to valid conclusions can exist that the evaluator is not aware of, and she has to take scrupulous care to find out what they are. But the evaluator need not try to attain a perfect design for the edification of her research peers and the glorification of her research reputation; she is doing an evaluation to inform the policy community about the program and to help decision makers make wise decisions. Her task is to provide the best information possible. What the evaluator needs to be concerned about is countering *plausible* threats to valid conclusions.

Important Concepts

Validity

Here is a definition that is relevant: validity. Earlier we met the term in discussing measures and recognized that it had to do with the extent to which the indicator actually captured the concept that it aimed to measure. When we discuss validity of study conclusions, there is an analogous meaning. Validity has to do with the reality or truth of conclusions; valid findings describe the way things actually are. These days, when social scientists are conscious of the complexity of the world and the impossibility of

---

[3]Campbell and Stanley (1966) and Cook and Campbell (1979) use different words for two of the concepts. They call attrition "experimental mortality," which has too deadly a sound for me. They call outside events "history."

finding one reality or one truth, the definition of reality is usually understood as meaning approximate truth, or as close as we can come to describing reality.

To understand discussions of design, it helps to appreciate two kinds of validity (Campbell & Stanley, 1966). One is internal validity, which refers to the causal link between independent variables (which, for example, describe the participants or features of the service they receive) and dependent variables (particularly the outcomes of the program).[4] Internal validity is concerned with whether the program is the agent responsible for observed effects, rather than external conditions, artifacts of the methodology, or extraneous factors. It indicates whether the relationship between program inputs and observed outcomes is *causal*.

The other kind of validity is external validity, or generalizability. It is concerned with whether the findings of one evaluation can be generalized to apply to other programs of similar type. If this one AIDS prevention program is successful, can we generalize this to other similar kinds of AIDS prevention programs? How far can we generalize the findings? To which class of AIDS prevention programs will they apply?[5]

Research designs vary in the degree to which they achieve internal and external validity. A randomized experiment, in which units are assigned randomly to program and control groups, leads to high internal validity. When the units (say, work groups or individuals) were very much the same at the beginning (a condition that random assignment generally achieves), and had much the same experiences during the period of the program except for receipt of the program itself, any differences that are observed between the two groups at the end are fairly certainly due to the program.

However, experimental design may not be very good at attaining external validity. Because of the need for careful controls to maintain experimental conditions, the program group in the experiment tends to get hothouse treatment, artificially different from what people in other programs of the same type would be likely to get. So results may not generalize very well to other reading programs, drug crackdowns, or physical rehabilitation efforts (Cronbach & Associates, 1980).

There is often a tradeoff between internal and external validity. Designs that do well on one dimension don't always do well on the other. The evaluator has to know which matters more in the particular case, so that she can choose a research design with confidence that it is appropriate to the situation.

Unit of Analysis

The unit that the program aims to change (say, a school) is not necessarily the same unit that is selected into the program (e.g., a classroom). Either of these—or another unit such as a teacher—may be the unit of analysis, that is, the unit that the evaluation measures and enters into statistical analyses.

---

[4] An independent variable is one which is assumed to be a cause of other variables (dependent variables). In evaluation, independent variables are characteristic of participants, program process, and setting, which are assumed to affect the dependent variable, participant outcomes.

[5] Cook and Campbell list four kinds of validity in their compendium. The two that I do not discuss are statistical conclusion validity, which means that the relationship (or lack of relationship) found between the independent and dependent variables is real (and not an artifact, e.g., of too small a sample size or unreliable measures) and construct validity of cause and effect, which refers to the truth of generalizations about higher order abstractions from the variables used in the study (such as generalizing from a single variable used to measure motivation, to the relation between (presumably all) motivation and effects).

The *unit that receives a program* is usually a person, but it can be a group, an organization, or a community. That is, the program can aim to change *not* the person but the performance of a larger unit—such as an agency (e.g., increased referrals to other service-giving agencies) or a neighborhood (denser networks of friendship and mutual help). Even when such a program works through individual people, it is geared to reforming the behavior and sometimes the norms and beliefs of the larger entity. Measures of process and outcomes, and program theory, reflect this concentration on the supra-individual level.

A program to teach household budgeting to young couples provides services to the couple and is interested in the way the couple behaves. A program to reduce child abuse in at-risk families would sample families and seek to reach conclusions about family behavior. A services integration project attempts to induce social service agencies to coordinate the services they provide to children and families. The agency is the recipient of the program. Agencies are sampled to participate in the evaluation, and appropriate measures of outcomes would be the extent to which agencies make changes in the way they deliver services. As another example, consider a radio campaign to encourage charitable giving. Here the community reached by the radio station receives the program. While the program aims to stimulate individuals to give, it is delivered at the level of the community. Its effectiveness will be judged by how much the entire listening area gives. Therefore, one relevant outcome measure is the total contribution received; another might be the percentage of households that contribute. Similarly a change in highway signs and signals is meant to speed the flow of traffic along the whole highway system. The speed at which traffic moves, or the number of vehicles that exit the system in a given time period, is a possible indicator of effectiveness.

Sometimes the program *does* aim to change the individual, but it cannot reach individuals one by one. The people come in clusters, such as students in classrooms. The program has to be delivered to the whole intact classroom. This would be the case, for example, with a new curriculum or a special training program that gives teachers knowledge and skills that they are expected to implement in the classroom. The students are not independent; they are members of the class. Again, the unit receiving the program is the group—that is, the classroom.

The program can be a change in technology, such as introduction of a new computer networking facility, whose purpose is to change the functioning of the whole organization. The unit receiving the program is the organization, perhaps a state agency or a university. The program in this case is delivered to the organization.

The *unit of sampling* is the entity that is selected into the program. In community collaboratives that attempt to create neighborhood change, the unit selected into the program is the neighborhood. In Patterson et al.'s (1992) study of a nutrition education program carried out in supermarkets, supermarkets were selected. In programs conducted in schools, classrooms are usually the unit sampled. There may be two stages of sampling: First, schools can be sampled, followed by choice of classrooms within the selected schools.

The unit for sampling usually matches the unit to which the program is delivered. In two-stage and three-stage sampling, the last stage is generally the one that receives the program. For example, take the evaluation of a program of pull-out services for children with disabilities in regular classrooms. The first stage of sampling selects schools, the second stage selects classrooms, and the third stage selects individual students with disabilities who are going to receive the special program.

The *unit of analysis* is the unit that figures in data analysis. It is the unit that the measures measure, and in statistical analysis, it is the one that is entered into tables and equations.

Researchers used to worry about the appropriate unit of analysis. When analysis is carried out at a higher level—say, at the level of departments within a hospital—it is not possible to reach sound conclusions about individuals within those departments. That is the ecological fallacy, drawing conclusions at one level of analysis and trying to apply it to another level.

The ecological fallacy used to roil the research waters, but it is of modest concern these days. The reason is the advance in statistical methods. Techniques of multi-level analysis make it possible to analyze data at several levels simultaneously. The analyst need not be stuck with the unit of program delivery or the unit of sampling in analyzing the data. She can examine all levels at once.

A matter that requires continuing care is the unit of measurement. If the evaluator wants to be able to analyze the data at several levels, she has to be sure that the measures are attached to the several units. For example, if she wants to examine student absences at the student and classroom levels, she has to define, collect, and aggregate the data for the student (number of absences for each student) and the class (percentage of absences for the classroom). If she has absence data only for the classroom, she cannot infer it for the students. A 10% absence rate for the class doesn't mean that each student was absent 10% of the time. That is the ecological fallacy.

A community-building program that attempts to build a sense of connection among neighborhood residents and encourage participation in neighborhood affairs can be evaluated at the level of the individual—who gets involved, how much time they spend on neighborhood affairs, etc.—but some people believe that its target is really the neighborhood. If one takes the neighborhood as the unit of analysis, outcome measures have to be aggregated to the neighborhood level—for example, proportion of people who participate, number and density of networks of mutual help, percentage of residents who believe the neighborhood is a desirable place to live.

The evaluator needs to pay attention to the units that she is working with. There will be times when the choice of unit will make a large difference in her ability to draw responsible conclusions. An example is La Prelle, Bauman, and Koch's (1992) evaluation of a mass media campaign to deter initiation of cigarette smoking by adolescents. The study was conducted in six treatment communities and four comparison communities. The evaluators used careful design parameters and selected a sample of youth in each community. They then made statistical adjustments on 10 sociodemographic and personality variables that were correlated with smoking in order to compensate for community differences. Although the unit of sampling was the community, the individual was the unit of analysis, and there was so much variation among communities that even after statistical adjustment, they could not detect effects. Their conclusion was that they should have used a different design, perhaps including more communities and using the community as the unit of analysis.[6] They caution that intercommunity variance is likely to be so high that evaluators will have difficulty drawing conclusions about the effectiveness of an intervention at the level of individual; community differences overwhelm individual differences (La Prelle et al., 1992).

The important thing is that the evaluator think through the phenomena that she wants to study. She will want to consider the level of the unit that is selected to participate in the program (and evaluation), the way the program is operated, whether individuals act independently or whether their actions are strongly constrained by some larger group of which they are members. She also has to attend to the level of the conclusions she wants to be able to provide. Then she develops a rationale for selection of an appropriate unit with which to work.

Designs

The following sections describe a number of designs that evaluators have used, ranging from the simple to the complex. Each of them is useful for some purposes, and each of them has limitations. Many of the strengths and limitations have to do with internal and external validity. You can think of these designs as an available set of options, but don't think of them as prefabricated options that can be taken off the shelf and unthinkingly applied to the situation at hand. Each design incorporates subcomponents that can be stitched together in a variety of ways (Cordray, 1986).

Study design takes place within the context developed in earlier chapters: key questions that have been posed, uses to which the study will be put, the program's theories of change, stakeholders' concerns. To create a design that is responsive to the needs of time and place, the evaluator's good judgment is the divining rod (Trochim, 1986).

As you read the following designs, you might keep in mind two questions: (a) What comparisons are being made, and will these comparisons provide sound conclusions? (b) Will the findings from a study like this be persuasive to potential audiences?

Informal Designs

Self-Evaluation

Perhaps the simplest way to evaluate a program is to ask the people who are involved with it what they think: staff, administrators, and clients. Staff are knowledgeable about what goes on and have day-to-day inside experience with activities and, often, with outcomes. They can render judgments about what is going more and less well and provide important suggestions for how to improve program activities.

Administrators, too, are insiders, and they have considerable knowledge about the program's pluses and minuses. In addition, they often get feedback (wanted and unwanted) from outside about what the press, the community, and other organizations like and dislike about the program.

Those are useful sources of information. When the program agency is collect-

---

[6]Their other suggestions were to use a stratified sampling technique, pairing communities at the outset, assigning one to treatment and one to control, or using time series designs.

ing data to improve its own performance, such information may suffice. Its collection brings together the experience and practitioner wisdom of people who spend their working lives engaged with the program's vicissitudes, and their varied sources of knowledge can shed considerable light on the program.

But when the evaluation is destined for outside eyes as well, this kind of information is often suspect. Staff and administrators have a stake in the program. They may interpret subtle cues as progress where others would see little change at all. When staff members know that the evaluation is going to be reported to sponsors and funders of the program, they will generally seek to show the program in its most favorable light. Even if they don't *purposely* slant their replies to the evaluator's questions, they probably are more alert to the program's successes than they are to its shortcomings.

Clients of the program can also be asked to evaluate the program. They, too, are insiders and know a great deal about program workings. But they may judge the program on criteria different from those that animate the program. Students may judge a class by how entertaining it is rather than on how much they learn; delinquents in an institution may judge the program by how early it allows them to be released rather than on the extent to which it socializes them to lawful norms and behavior. Moreover, clients often have a stake in the program's continuation. Many times they don't want to lose its services, whatever the outcomes, because the program is the only available resource for them. So they may tailor their answers to what they think outsiders want to hear.

Despite the weaknesses, these kinds of judgments have value. Training programs for professionals often ask participants to fill out forms rating the whole program and each session, indicating the extent to which the sessions were interesting, informative, responsive to their needs, and so on. The intent is to use responses to improve the content of the training and the allotment of time to different topics. The participants are presumably the people best qualified to give this kind of guidance.

Evaluation of this type is, in essence, a popularity contest. But often the purpose of evaluation is to find out not only whether people *like* the program; it is also to find out if it is doing them any good. Self-evaluation alone is not likely to fill the bill. But judgments of this kind can be incorporated into designs that include other data as well.

Expert Judgment

A step beyond the judgments of people engaged with the program is the use of a knowledgeable outsider. An expert can be called and asked to examine the program and give his judgment. The judgment can be about any phase of the program, from its recruitment practices or financial accounting to the outcomes for its beneficiaries.

Many assessments are made in this way. When a federal monitor goes out to visit a program that his office funds, he is trying to evaluate the extent to which it is doing what it promised to do in its application for funding, the extent to which it is following rules and guidelines, and/or the extent to which it is producing the kinds of outcomes that society wants and expects. Some programs call in their own expert consultants to review their activities and suggest tactics for improving their work.

A variant of the expert is the connoisseur (Eisner, 1991). Here the analogy is to the art critic or the wine connoisseur. Again a person with wide experience and refined standards of judgment makes the assessment. The connoisseur notices subtleties, experiences nuances, and recognizes import. Taking its warrant from the arts rather than the sciences, connoisseurship conveys its insights through metaphor, poetry, or narrative.

School and college accreditation is done though the use of expert judgments. In this case, not one individual but a team of individuals visits an institution, inspects its records and physical plant, reviews the self-evaluation done by its faculty, and interviews administrators, faculty, and students. The team then makes a judgment about whether to accredit the school or program and whether to affix conditions to the accreditation. Even when accreditation is assured, the team will often make recommendations that the institution take steps to meet accepted standards.

Another area where expert judgments are commonplace is in the evaluation of research and development (R&D) programs. Individual research proposals are commonly judged by experts through a mechanism known as peer review, in which a panel of researchers in the field covered by the proposal reviews its quality and importance. The evaluation of R&D *programs* (i.e., the whole set of studies funded and/or conducted by a unit) poses extraordinary problems. Research studies by their nature are ventures into the unknown, and some proportion of them are bound to come up dry. Even when studies lead to new findings or theory, the value of the results will not be known for a long time. Some will add knowledge or change thinking in the field, but only a subset will lead to measurably valuable inventions.

With an intangible product, vague goals, and long time frame, the worth of R&D programs is hard to assess (Bozeman & Melkers, 1993). The best resource is often the opinions of knowledgeable people who have little or no stake in the program under review.

The basis for experts' judgments is their own prior experience. They have seen many other programs and projects, and in their minds they compare this program or institution to others that they know. They usually have some ideal standards as well, some ideas about what a good program should look like. Therefore, they can base their assessment on both comparative information and normative criteria.

The advantages of a team of experts over a single individual are that no one individual's idiosyncrasies carry the day; no single person can exercise his unique standards of judgment. Decisions have to survive the vetting of the team. Also, the team can call on a wider array of experience and skill. Persons who know a great deal about schools' science curriculums are joined by those who know about physical facilities and library practices.

Experts are probably better at judging the procedures and practices of a program than they are at judging outcomes. In assessing program *process*, they can draw on their wide knowledge of other programs and experiences. But they may have difficulty in judging whether the recipients of program service are doing better or more poorly than people in other programs or even people who get no program at all. Without good data on program outcomes, they have to make arbitrary judgments. If they assume that certain kinds of program activities are necessarily linked to good outcomes, the accuracy of their judgments of outcome hinges on whether the hypothesized link holds true. If they talk to a few clients, they may be drawing conclusions from an unrepresentative subset of the program population.

How convincing an evaluation by expert judgment will be to others depends in large part on the reputation of the expert. A widely acknowledged expert on alcoholism treatment might be widely believed. But almost every field has conflicting schools of thought, and one side's expert may be unacceptable to another side. While he may have no bias for or against the particular program under review, he may well have an ideological preference for a particular mode of program practice, and his judgments about the program will reflect his preference. Even the best qualified expert is using subjective standards, standards that he usually finds hard to articulate and that are open to dispute. If his report fails to satisfy some constituencies, they are apt to question his credentials, his experience, and even his integrity, as the testimony of experts in legal trials demonstrates. Sometimes a respected expert ventures into a program whose cultural and historical characteristics are beyond his experience, as, say, in rural Alaska, and his assumptions fail to take the setting into account. The expert's credibility usually depends on who he is rather than what he knows about the particular program under review. Most evaluations try to use methods that are less vulnerable to the vagaries of individual judgment.

Formal Designs

One-Group Designs

A commonly used set of designs examines a single program. The program may be an individual project or a set of projects or a whole statewide or federal program. With this design, the evaluation does not include any comparison with units (people, communities) that did not receive the program. Evaluations of this sort fall into two categories: those that look at units receiving the program only *after* the program has been in operation for a while or is completed, and those that look at it both *before and after*. The kind of data collected can be qualitative or quantitative.

After-only designs are usually employed when the evaluator isn't called in until the program is well under way and no before data are available. Before-and-after studies require an evaluator to be on the scene at the start. Whether data are collected on the situation prior to the beginning of the program or not, data can be—and often should be—collected on program process during the course of the program.

After Only   Sometimes an evaluator isn't called in until the program is in midstream and there is no possibility of finding out what recipients looked like before. In such a case, the evaluator finds out what the situation is after the program and makes a series of assumptions about what things looked like before. On what can she base these assumptions?

First, she can examine records. For example, schools keep records on students that include much data on their backgrounds, prior school experience, grades, test results, health records, and so on. Hospitals, employment agencies, housing projects, and law enforcement agencies also keep files on clients. If the evaluator is lucky, the files include measures on the variables of interest for those who have been in the program at a prior point in time.

If records are unavailable, the evaluator can use historical comparisons. For example, in evaluating a new history curriculum for ninth graders, the evaluator can compare test results at the end of the semester with history test results of the previous year's ninth graders—or (if last year's class was a bit quirky, and any single class is a bit quirky) the five-year average of ninth graders in the school. This adds useful information. But there are drawbacks if the situation in the school has changed. The school may be drawing its student body from a different population, the tests may be different, the teachers may have changed.

The evaluator can ask people involved with the program what the before situation was. Participants can be expected to recall their alcohol intake, job skills, or parenting practices at the time they entered the program. Relying on such retrospective reports seems reasonable enough, but it doesn't always produce valid data. People's memories are surprisingly unreliable. Usually people will remember the past as closer to the present than it really was or be overly influenced by one or two out-of-the-ordinary cases. Without records, they have real difficulty evoking a reliable baseline. But on certain matters of fact, such as age, number of years of schooling completed, and whether they were employed or unemployed and what kind of work they were doing, responses are fairly trustworthy.

Another way to elicit an estimate of the before situation is through the use of experienced judgment. Estimates can be made by well-informed people, perhaps the evaluator herself, about what participants were like at the outset, based on their own experience or prior research. The evaluator may take account of other evaluations she has done or refer to studies on groups similar to current program clients. Outsiders are likely to question the accuracy of such estimates (as would you and I). Without records on very similar populations, the imputation of preprogram data is shaky.

If at the time of the evaluation there are people in various stages of the program—some nearing the end, some part-way through, some just entering, data on the newcomers can be used to simulate a before measure. Provided that recruitment procedures have not changed and that there has not been a high rate of drop out during the program, the status of new entrants may be a reasonable basis for inference about the "graduates"—at least if numbers are large enough so that the laws of probability kick in.

Marsh and Wirick (1991) used this kind of design in their evaluation of a teenage pregnancy and parenting program at Hull House. See Figure 8-2. Each year a new cohort of young women entered the program at two sites in Chicago, who were described as a "new but basically similar group of clients." The post measures of group 1 were compared to pre measures of group 2, and so on for four years.

In this iterative fashion, if methods of recruiting participants have not changed, information is available to approximate the before-and-after design. Outside events are likely to be different for successive groups, and if the evaluator suspects that such events will influence the incidence of pregnancies, she can add a substudy to investigate this one issue. Similarly, additional measurements can be patched on to test whatever other rival hypotheses challenge the validity of evaluative conclusions.

Before and After   The logic of this design seems clear cut: Look at program recipients before they enter the program and then again at the end. The difference between their condition at Time One (T1) and Time Two (T2) should be the effect

FIGURE 8-2 COMPARISON-GROUP DESIGN WITH SUCCESSIVE COHORTS

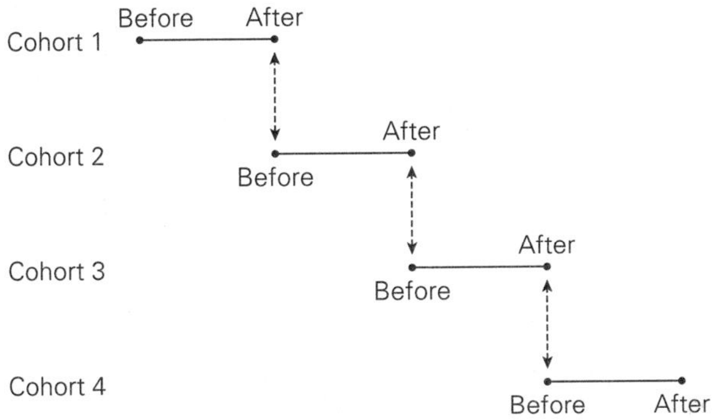

Note: Dotted lines indicate comparisons made between the after data of one cohort and the before data of the succeeding cohort.
Source: Adapted from Marsh & Wirick, 1991.

of the program. Oh, but is it? Only a moment's thought will reveal that many other things happen to program recipients besides their participation in the program. They watch television, get sick, fight with their parents, make new friends, move to a new house, take an evening school course. Was the change in their skills or health or income due to the program? Maybe, but then again, maybe not.

At their best, before-and-after studies can be full of detail, provocative, and rich in insight. If the data are collected with care and system, they offer considerable information about the program and the people who participate in it. When before and after data are supplemented by "during-during-during" data, the evaluation will be able to say much about how the program is working. If the evaluation systematically tracks the assumptions of program theory, it will be able to say much more.

For formative purposes (i.e., for modifying and improving the program), the design may be sufficient. But for summative purposes (i.e., for rendering judgment on how effective the program has been), it is not as authoritative as more rigorous designs. It provides no answer to objections that maturation or outside events were responsible for whatever change occurred. When before-and-after study shows no change, it is possible that outside factors tamped down real changes that would otherwise have been observed. For example, suppose there had been a house-building program for Little Pigs to teach them all how to build brick houses, but after measures taken some time after the conclusion of the program showed that no Little Pigs' houses were still standing. It may be that the program hadn't effectively taught brick-building skills, but it is also possible that the Big Bad Wolf had bought a pile driver that allowed him to level brick houses.

Advantages and Disadvantages of One-Group Designs   As a general rule, one-group designs, while generating important information, leave room for differing interpretations of how much change has occurred and how much of the observed change was due to the operation of the program. Critics can launch effective attacks on the methodology and claim that results are indeterminate. They can point out the threats to validity of conclusions. Still, with all the caveats, there are times when they are worth considering.

A first advantage is that they provide a preliminary look at the effectiveness of a program. If, for example, before-and-after study (with all the contaminating effects of outside events, maturation, and so on) finds little change in participants, and there is no obvious countervailing force, then there is a good chance that the program is having little effect. It may not be worthwhile to invest in more rigorous evaluation now. The program should be strengthened before undertaking further expensive inquiry.

Preliminary reconnaissance is useful because it tends to bring a modicum of realism to people's expectations about the success of the program. When confronted with data that suggest limited success, staff, administrators, and funders may reduce their grandiose assumptions that the program will "restore the sense of community" or "end crime" and begin to engage in realistic planning for the future.

Note that program effects may be *underestimated* if outside events operate to counteract program efforts, or if the evaluator in her mind's eye is comparing participants to groups who can be expected to do better—say, because of higher socioeconomic status or higher ability. If one-group studies do reveal change, and there is serious interest in the extent to which change is attributable to the program, further evaluation can be done under more controlled conditions.

A second reason for considering one-group designs arises from practices of agencies that fund evaluations of social programs. Some agencies demand one-time ex post facto investigation; they are responding to political pressures and short-term needs, and they want quick results. Evaluators will have to exploit every opportunity to supplement and expand the basically inadequate design.

Extending One-Group Designs

One-group designs can be elaborated in two basic directions: collecting more data on what happens during the program and collecting more data on what happens much before and much after the program.

More Data during the Program   One-group evaluation need not be limited only to pretest and posttest measures. There are several ways to extend their reach even without adding a comparison group. One way is to take a "during" measure or a series of "during-during-during" measures. Quantitative or qualitative data can be collected not only on program services but also on participants' progress as they move through the program. These data can be analyzed, either quantitatively or qualitatively, to elaborate the picture of what happens during the program and to identify the association between program events and participant outcomes.

When the sponsor of the evaluation is interested only in the single project under study and not in generalizing to other projects, one-group evaluation can focus on the unique services, events, and people on the scene. It can probe into the relationships among rules, recruitment strategies, modes of organization, auspices, services, leadership, communication, feedback loops, and whatever else people are concerned about. Note that here we are moving in the direction of qualitative investigation.

A further move is to use program theory as the basis for data collection and analysis. Data on participants' progress are laid alongside the assumptions that theory makes about the course of the program's development. To the extent that things work out as posited in the program's theory of change, the evaluation has grounds for confidence that it understands not only what is going on but how program effects are taking shape as well.

When the evaluator designs the study around program theory, she chooses the key nodes of the theory as the content and time points for data collection. For example, a program of tenant participation in the management of a public housing project assumes that such participation will improve resident security. The link between tenant representation and improved security isn't obvious, but the program theory hypothesizes that it will come about through one or more of the claims illustrated in Figure 8-3.

The evaluator then designs methods for collecting data about the extent to which each of these assumptions actually comes to pass. She locates appropriate sources and sets appropriate time intervals. If one or more of the assumptions are borne out, she has a better sense of how the program is working.

Dose-Response Designs With one-group designs, there is no comparison of participant outcomes with people who did not receive the program. Sometimes such comparison is impossible because every eligible person is served. This is the case with Social Security, public schooling, hospital emergency rooms, meat and poultry

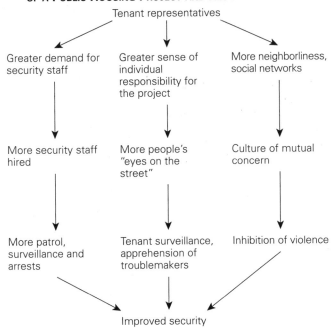

FIGURE 8-3 PROGRAM THEORY MODEL: THE ASSUMED LINKS BETWEEN TENANT PARTICIPATION IN THE MANAGEMENT OF A PUBLIC HOUSING PROJECT AND RESIDENT SECURITY

inspection, Medicare, and many other programs. In such cases, an *internal* comparison can usually be designed. The evaluation can compare participants who received a large quantity of service (a high dose) with those who received a lower dose. The assumption is that, if the program is doing good, more of it will do better. The evaluation examines whether high-dose recipients have better outcomes than their low-dose counterparts.

The notion that more is better may not always be right. One can imagine a program that gives service so sufficient that more of it would not prod outcomes up a single notch. It would reach a ceiling, and a comparison with higher levels of services would unfairly suggest that it was not effective. But such a situation would be rare. Most programs are constrained in resources and struggle to offer service to all those who are eligible. They do not provide *all* the help that they know how to and want to give. On the other hand, if there is reason to believe that a program has approached its ceiling, it might be possible for the evaluator to arrange a lower service level cohort for comparison. The question that such a study would be answering is: Would a reduced level of service, at lower cost, reach equally good results?

With a dose-response design, the evaluator has to take care that those who receive more service are not different on other grounds, too, that they are not more conscientious in attendance, or have higher motivation, or are judged more in need of service by staff. More conscientiousness or motivation would be likely to lead to better outcomes in and of themselves; greater need for service would probably predict poor outcomes. But if the amount of service received is uncorrelated with such other characteristics, the internal comparison can be revealing.

The term *dose response* comes from research on drugs, and in that circumstance the only variation available for study is the amount of the drug received. In social programs, the evaluator can make many other internal comparisons. She can compare: participants who receive service in groups with those who receive individual service; those who receive only job-finding help with those who receive job-finding help plus emotional support; those who see the same physician at each visit with those who see different physicians; and so on. With these varied types of internal comparisons, the limitation of possible ceiling effects does not apply. The evaluation is contrasting alternative kinds of service.

Dose-response is a highly versatile design. It can be used not only in one-group designs but also when the evaluation includes comparison or control groups. We'll meet it again in Chapter 9.

Time-Series Designs   Another kind of extension of one-group designs extends the study both backward and forward in time. This brings us to time-series designs, an attractive option for evaluation. Time series involve a series of measurements on key outcome criteria at periodic intervals before the program begins and continuing measurements after the program ends. It thus becomes possible to learn a great deal about the condition that the program aims to change—for example, unemployment or school drop out. Was the condition stable over the time period before the program began, was it getting worse, or was it getting better even without the intervention of the program? Then after the program, did the condition improve immediately and remain fairly constant at the better level? Did it revert to its original problem status as effects of the program faded out? Or did good results escalate over time, with success generating further success?

Time-series data enable the evaluator to interpret the pre-to-post changes in the light of additional evidence. They show whether the measures immediately before and after the program are a continuation of earlier patterns or whether they mark a decisive change. Figure 8-4 shows five cases in which the same degree of change occurred over the span of the program: The slope of the line from before (B) to after (A) the program is the same. But in these cases the change has different significance. The top line shows a case where things were already improving, and the program doesn't appear to have speeded or slowed down the rate of change. In the second case, the condition is erratic. Improvement seems to occur between B and A, but it is just the same kind of jiggle that happened before without a program and

FIGURE 8-4   FIVE CASES OF TIME-SERIES DATA MEASURING
PROGRAM EFFECTS AT SIX TIME POINTS

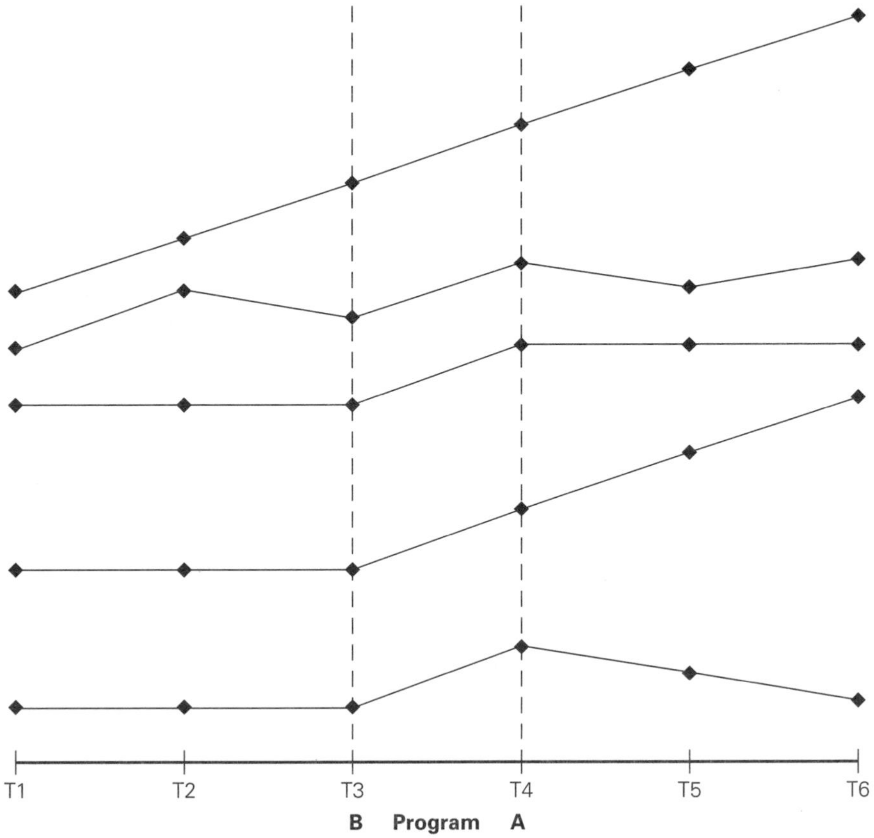

Note: The program was implemented between B, before the program, and A, after.

happened again some time after the program had ended. It is not obvious that the program made any difference.

In the third case, the change from B to A appears to be the result of the program. Things were going along at a consistent level, then escalated after the programs and remained at the higher level. In the fourth case, outcomes improved after the program and continued to improve thereafter. Perhaps the program set off a train of events (improved self-insight, community mobilization) that led to continued development. The final case shows improved outcomes following the program, but the results fade out after the program ends. If the program wants to sustain participants at the higher level of functioning, it will have to institute further intervention.

Time-series data address the question of persistence of effects, an important but often neglected question. Rarely do evaluations go on long enough to follow participants for more than a year or so after their departure from the program. Even when the evaluator plans such long-term follow-up, evaluation funds can run out or be cut off before the long-term data are collected. So there is little information about whether the people who, say, returned to their homes after receiving disaster assistance managed to continue their recovery or fell back into dependency. With a time-series design extending beyond program participation, such information is available.

The requirement for time-series design is the existence of a data set that (a) contains the key evaluative variables (b) on the appropriate population. Rarely will there be enough advance notice of the initiation of a program to enable the evaluator to start collecting the necessary data months or years ahead of the program's start.[7] Fortunately, the government collects considerable data that may be relevant for evaluation purposes, and collects them with sufficient frequency to allow for useful comparisons. As discussed in Chapter 7, there are data series on crime, welfare caseloads, hospital stays, teacher tenure, toxic substance emergencies, medical costs, housing quality, caesarean births, refugee resettlement, consumer fraud litigation, age discrimination charges, violations of occupational safety rules, usage of national parks, defaults on student loans, and hundreds of other topics. Nongovernmental bodies also maintain data series on specialized subjects. Some data sources are more reliable and consistent than others and are collected over longer time periods, but a persistent evaluator can often find some data already in existence. These data indicate the frequency of the problematic condition for extended periods of time before the program begins and after it ends.

The use of existing time series is useful to evaluate changes in policy that affect an entire political subdivision, or public information campaigns, which aim to reach all residents of a geographic area. Time-series data provide evidence about whether and how rapidly conditions change after the new program or policy goes online. Time-series evaluations have been done to evaluate changes in gun control laws (Mauser & Holmes, 1992), traffic enforcement (Campbell, 1969), water conserva-

---

[7]However, even a few months notice can be useful. In the evaluation of an American Friends Service Committee encampment, Dentler (1959) collected data from participants several months prior to the start of the program, again at the beginning of camp, and again at its conclusion. Since the camp ran for less than two months, the additional data point helped to answer questions about whether the camp had an influence or whether the youth were changing anyway.

tion strategies (Maki, Hoffman, & Berk, 1978), seat belt use (Desai & You, 1992; Rock, 1992), and sale of lottery tickets (Reynolds & West, 1978).

Where no data are available that fit the study's needs, the evaluator can *begin* the collection of relevant data. Obviously such a step will not fill in earlier history. "Pre-pre-program" data can be collected only with early warning and long lead time. But the evaluator can plan for "after-after-after" data—that is, for continuing the periodic collection of outcome data for a long period. She makes her respondents into a panel for continued reinterviewing.[8] Panel data fulfill the same functions as time-series data. The main differences are that panel data, being tailor made for the evaluation, are apt to be a more exact match to the needs of the evaluation but, being started for the sake of the evaluation, are apt to be shorter in duration.

The main criticism of the validity of evaluations that rely on time-series (and panel) data is that some outside events coincided with the program and were responsible for whatever change was observed between before and after, or between times 1, 2, 3, and 4. For example, it wasn't necessarily the program that accounted for the decline in smoking; it could have been the television series on the risks of smoking that came along at the same time or the publicity given to a new medical study or the cascading set of restrictions on where smoking is allowed.

There are two main methods of dealing with such a criticism. One is to scout the terrain and see if this kind of event did in fact take place. If there weren't any plausible happenings, then the evaluation is perhaps justified in claiming that the program was responsible for the changes observed. If other rival influences *were* operative, the evaluation will have to look into the possibility that they, rather than the program, affected program recipients. If the evaluation cannot rule out the influence of such outside events, it will have to concede the possibility of an alternative explanation for observed effects.

Another way to cope with the possibility of contamination by outside events is by studying what happened over the same time period to people who did not receive the program but were exposed to the same external influences. If program recipients improved faster than this comparison group, then there is something to be said for the independent effect of the program. This brings us to the next section on design: the addition of comparison groups.

Comparison Groups

All of the one-group designs can be extended by adding another group or groups to the study comprised of people or units (classes, work teams, organizations) that did not receive the program's attention.

When these groups are not selected randomly from the same population as program recipients, I call them comparison groups. (With random selection, they are called control groups.) The main purpose for the comparison is to see whether receiving the program adds something extra that the comparison units do not get. In other words, it is a means to improve internal validity, assurance that the program (and not other things) caused the observed effects. The sine qua non for this comparison to be useful is that the comparison group has to be very much like the program recipients.

---

[8]Where the evaluator collects data from her own panel, the data are usually not called time-series data but panel data.

At the end of the study period, they are going to be the surrogates for what the program recipients *would have been like* if they had not been in the program.

After-Only with Comparison Group   The after-only design can be strengthened by adding a comparison group that is as similar to program recipients as possible. Matching people in the program to similar people who have not participated in the program is a common method of constructing a comparison group in after-only designs. Studies have used next-door neighbors of participants, their older or younger siblings, residents of the same neighborhoods, students in the same schools. In the after-only design, the evaluator has only posttest measures for participants, and she is not sure what their status was at the start of the program. Nor is she sure that next-door neighbors or students in other classrooms were like them at the outset on characteristics that matter. The attributes on which she is likely to match are standard demographic variables, such as age, race, and sex, because these characteristics do not change over the course of the program and they are the easiest to get data about. Sometimes these factors matter. But the evaluator often has scant reason for expecting that they are the ones most likely to affect outcomes.

When records are available on relevant items for the before period (welfare status, school achievement, days of absence from work), these will be eminently useful to fill in the missing before information. If key items can be retrieved for both the program group and the comparison group, this design begins to approximate the "before-and-after with comparison group" design. However, it is unusual for an evaluation to locate all the relevant information in existing records. When factors that influence success in the program are intangibles like motivation or density of social support networks, the likelihood of finding *before* information drops close to nil.

Still, the addition of a comparison group helps to strengthen the ability to make causal inferences. Suppose the recipients of the program do well on an outcome measure (say, released prison inmates are arrested in much lower numbers than expected in the year following the program). Was this showing the result of the program or something else? Adding a group of released inmates who are similar in many ways helps to answer the question. If an equivalent proportion of them are staying clear of the law, perhaps the program shouldn't get the credit. But if they are recidivating at a much higher rate than program recipients, the suggestion that the program is responsible gains credibility.

The comparison group will almost inevitably differ from the participant group in important ways. The sheer fact that participants selected themselves, or were selected by others, into the program is a persuasive indication. Often the evaluator doesn't know which variables are likely to affect outcomes and so doesn't know what kind of comparison group to recruit. Without pretest data, although perhaps with makeshift pretest data, it is especially difficult to disentangle the prior differences from the effects of program service. The best course is usually to extend data collection and move to before-and-after design.

Before-and-After with Comparison Group   This is one of the most commonly used designs in evaluation. The comparison group is selected to be as much like the client group as possible through any of a variety of procedures. But it is not *randomly assigned* from the same population, as would be a true control group in an experimental design.

Often the evaluator can locate a similar site (preschool, university department) serving people much like those in the program that did not operate the program. Then she can compare the status of both groups before the program began and test how similar they were. If there are strong similarities in the pretest on such items as age, socioeconomic status, or whatever items are relevant to the program's purpose, *and* on items assumed to be predictive of success on the outcome indicators, such as motivation and skill, she can proceed with some confidence.

But of course nothing is quite so easy. The comparison group is likely to be different from the program group. For one thing, the program group often selected themselves into the program. They were motivated enough to volunteer. Or staff selected them into the program because of their special need for its services or because of judgments that they would particularly profit from it. People who choose to enter a program are likely to be different from those who do not, and the prior differences (in interest, aspiration, values, initiative, even in the neighborhood in which they live) make postprogram comparisons between served and unserved groups problematic. In job training programs, evaluators have constructed comparison groups from lists of unemployed persons who would have been eligible for the program but had not had contact with it. Others have used unemployed friends of job trainees for comparison. Other evaluators have used people who registered for the program but did not enter (no shows) or those who dropped out (Bell, Orr, Blomquist, & Cain, 1995). Checking often discloses that the groups are not comparable in several respects.

The search for controls who are as like program participants as possible has led to the use of unawares (people who did not hear of the program but might have joined had they heard) and geographic ineligibles (people with characteristics similar to participants but who lived in locations that had no program). Comparison groups have been used in such studies as the evaluation of the supplemental nutrition program for pregnant women, infants, and children (WIC) (Devaney, Bilheimer, & Schore, 1991) and the National School Lunch and Breakfast Programs (Burghardt, Gordon, Chapman, Gleason, & Fraker, 1993).

Each ingenious strategy solves some problems and raises others. What was there about the unawares that blocked their knowledge of the program? What are the effects of community conditions in the different location? The question has been raised whether it is important to eliminate self-selection bias in program evaluation. Since voluntary programs inevitably include self-selected participants, would it be appropriate to evaluate the combined effects of self-selection and program participation? Such a procedure would certainly simplify the comparison group problem and the evaluator's life. Study results would apply to the combination of volunteering and receiving services. It would not be obvious how much of the effect was attributable to the program per se. But if future programs are also going to be available on a voluntary basis, the evaluation results will provide useful information.

Sometimes it is useful to use several comparison groups (students in another community college who are like the program group in the type of educational institution attended and students in a state university who are like the program group in location). Each of these comparisons will shed light on one feature, and each will compensate for differences that the other comparison leaves uncontrolled.

At the least, the evaluator should consider whether program recipients started out as better or poorer risks than the comparison group. Often it is the better risks who were selected or selected themselves in. If they show better outcomes than the comparison group, a plausible explanation is that they would have prospered whether there was a program or not. On the other hand, if the program attracted those most in need, the comparison group started out with an advantage. Even if the program does an admirable job, the program group may not catch up. The change will have to be larger than the initial gap between the two groups before the program registers any effect at all. A more privileged comparison group tends to minimize the observed effects of the program. Initial differences have to be taken into account in analysis and reporting of the data.

Multiple Time Series   A comparison can also be added to the time-series design. If the evaluator can find a similar group or institution and locate periodic measurements of it over the same time span as the program group, she can learn a great deal. This design appears particularly appropriate to evaluations of school programs, since repeated testing goes on normally, and a long series of pre- and postscores are often available.

A well-known example of multiple time series was the evaluation of the Connecticut crackdown on highway speeding. Evaluators collected reports of traffic fatalities for several periods before and after the new program went into effect. They found that fatalities went down after police began strict enforcement of penalties for speeding, but since the series had had an unstable up-and-down pattern for many years, it was not certain that the drop was due to the program. They then compared the statistics with time-series data from four neighboring states, where there had been no changes in traffic enforcement. Those states registered no equivalent drop in fatalities. The comparison lent credence to the conclusion that the crackdown had had some effect (Campbell, 1969; Campbell & Ross, 1968).

Multiple time series are especially useful for evaluating policy changes. When a jurisdiction passes a law altering fire codes, policing practices, or taxation on business, there are opportunities to compare the trends in fire damage, arrest rates, and bankruptcies. Without necessarily mounting a whole new study, officials can examine conditions over a period of time before the new policy was adopted and for a period of time after it went into force, and then make comparisons with similar jurisdictions that did not experience the policy change. One of the advantages of this design is that the localities do not have to be very similar at the outset on many dimensions so long as they were similar on their trends in fire damage, arrest rates, or bankruptcies.

Time-series designs also lend themselves to a number of multiple comparisons. If data are routinely collected, it is probable that they are routinely collected in many places, often under the aegis of higher level governments—new claims for unemployment insurance, admissions to drug rehabilitation programs, and so on. Therefore, the evaluation can draw upon multiple comparisons. Some localities will be similar to the community running the program in size, others will be similar in socioeconomic composition, others in degree of urbanization, and so on. The study can examine how the program community compares to other communities that are similar on different dimensions. It may also become possible to analyze which dimensions are related to the trends in outcomes that are observed. With several series of data, comparisons can take account of these dimensions, singly and in combination, in interpreting program outcomes.

Constructing a Comparison Group A nonequivalent comparison group should be as similar to the program group as human ingenuity can manage. (If the human were ingenious enough to manage random assignment of program and nonprogram groups from the same population, she would have a control group.) Without random selection and assignment, she often resorts to matching. She can try to find a match for each person who is entering the program group on all the variables that are likely to affect that person's performance on outcome measures. For example, in a program that provides self-care instruction for hospital patients, she can try to find a "comparison someone" who is similar to the Asian 45-year-old diabetic woman who receives the program. But matching one to one is often difficult to do. In our heterogeneous polyglot society, there is not a ready match for every program participant. If the evaluator cannot locate a match for the Asian 45-year-old diabetic, she may have to drop the woman from the study. This leads to a loss of cases and a lower sample size, a condition that is bad for the power of statistical comparisons. Losing cases also makes the evaluation less representative of the whole program population. The study will not be generalizable to those like the participants for whom matches could not be found.

Without trying for a one-to-one match, the evaluator can try to find a group of patients whose overall profile is similar to the program group. Afterward, when one group has been exposed to the benefits of the program and the other group has not, the difference in the gain each group has made over the same time period is an estimate of the effect of the program.

Sometimes this is the best that can be done. The comparison group is added to one-group designs or time-series designs to rule out the likelihood that maturation or outside events or simply becoming adept at filling out evaluation protocols was responsible for whatever changes were observed. But matching is less satisfactory than randomized assignment on several counts. Not the least is that the evaluator often cannot define the characteristics on which people should be matched. She doesn't know which characteristics will affect whether the person benefits from the program. She may have matched on age, sex, race, and IQ, when the important factor is parental encouragement. Some wit has said that if we knew the key characteristics for matching, we wouldn't need the study.

In job training programs, where a great deal of evaluation has been done, evaluators have learned that prior work experience is a critical variable. In programs that aim to move families out of poverty, family composition (e.g., the presence of two adults or working-age children) is an important predictor. In education programs, test scores depend to a considerable extent on whether the teacher has covered in class the material that is included on the test. Even when knowledge is available about which variables are implicated in success, data are not always available that allow evaluators to match on that basis. No existing data show which small entre-preneurs have willing family members to call on, and so, however important, this feature cannot become the basis for matching.

Another problem is finding people with the right constellation of characteristics. The woods are not necessarily full of Latino college applicants who are receiving scholarship support. Locating matches for some program groups is complicated by their uniqueness, by the availability of similar services to other people in their situation, and by the perennial difficulty of enlisting the support of comparison group members to whom the program gives nothing. (This latter problem afflicts random-assignment controls as well. The evaluation asks them to cooperate in providing data periodically over a sometimes lengthy period of time, without getting anything in return. Small wonder that attrition rates are sometimes high.)

Matching is sometimes done on the basis of pretest scores. The program serves students who are consistently doing poorly in school. To find a comparison group, the evaluator looks at test scores in other classrooms and selects students whose test scores are very low. This tends to be a poor procedure.[9] It can produce particularly misleading results when program participants and comparisons are drawn from basically different populations. Regression to the mean gets in the way of valid interpretation. Regression to the mean is not intuitively obvious, but it is based on the fact that a person's pretest and posttest measures are not perfectly correlated even without a planned intervention of any kind. Statistically, posttest measures are expected to be closer to the group mean. At a second testing, what look like effects of the program may be artifacts of statistical regression. For example, Figure 8-5 shows a case in which there are no program effects. Each group has simply regressed to its mean. An unwary evaluator may ascribe the shift to the effects of the program when in fact there are no program effects at all.

Regression to the mean can be compounded by measurement error. All measures contain some component of error, and some, such as test scores and attitude measures, contain a sizable amount. On any one testing, some individuals will score artificially high and others artificially low; on a second testing, their scores are likely to be closer to their usual score.

It is better in dealing with nonequivalent controls to compare the measures of natural groups than to select only extreme cases by matching. In Figure 8-5, this would mean using the E_1 and C_1 measures rather than E_2 and C_2.

Comparison groups created by matching can reduce two of the main threats to the validity of study conclusions—outside events and maturation—but they are not an adequate control for selection. As for attrition, when members of either the program or comparison group drop out, the matched pair can be eliminated from the analysis, but in so doing two unhappy events occur. As with the failure to find initial matches in the first place, sample size and subsequent statistical power are reduced, sometimes drastically, and the sample becomes progressively less representative of the total program population. It is usually a better strategy to exploit all

---

[9]Note that we are talking about matching without randomization. If units are matched and then randomly assigned to each group, the procedure increases the statistical precision of the experiment. Matching as a prelude to randomization may even be essential when there are few units, such as cities. But matching as a substitute for randomization can produce pseudoeffects.

FIGURE 8-5   REGRESSION TO THE MEAN: REGRESSION ARTIFACTS IN A MATCHED SAMPLE

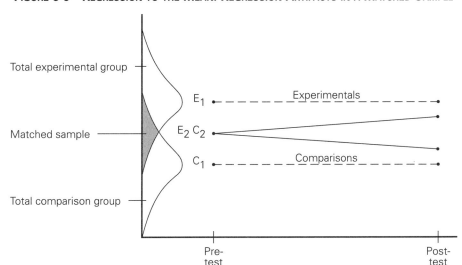

the available data gathered prior to dropout and adjust for differences between program recipients and comparisons that appear at the end.

When members of the comparison group are not very similar to the program group, some inferences can be made if pretest data are available. The evaluator looks at the growth of participants and nonparticipants (Moffitt, 1991). If participants improve at a steeper rate than comparisons, even if their initial status was different, the data may suggest a program effect. But such an inference is uneasy.

In Figure 8-6, we have groups that differed at the start. The program took place between T2 and T3. In 8-6a, the groups grew at the same rate in the period before the program. When the program came along, participants outpaced the comparison group. This data pattern suggests a program effect. But in 8-6b, the two groups continued to grow at their initial rates, suggesting that the program added little. Figure 8-6c shows a case where the two groups were growing at different rates prior to the program and continued at their original rates. Again the program does not appear to have made a difference.

Statisticians have developed a number of ways to adjust nonequivalent comparison group data to avoid or at least reduce the most serious threat to validity: selection bias. I discuss several of these statistical adjustments at the end of the next section. First, I talk about methods for creating comparisons from existing data because such designs evoke the same kinds of problems as matched comparison group designs. The section on statistical corrections comes at the end of the section.

Statistical Techniques in Lieu of Matching

So far we have talked about constructing a comparison group by matching program participants to nonparticipants who share many of the same characteristics. The problem has been where to find similar people and how to ensure that they are as

FIGURE 8-6   THREE TIME-SERIES DESIGNS WITH COMPARISON GROUPS

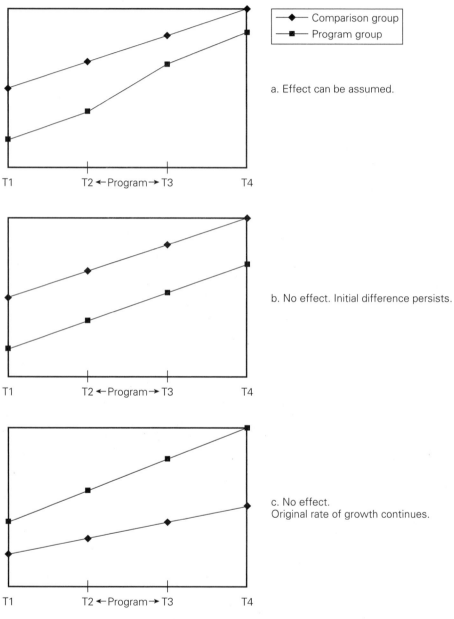

◆ — Comparison group
■ — Program group

a. Effect can be assumed.

b. No effect. Initial difference persists.

c. No effect.
Original rate of growth continues.

T1   T2 ← Program → T3   T4

similar as possible to the participants at the beginning of the program. In large-scale evaluations, matching is often supplanted by use of available data, which are then adjusted statistically. The procedure follows the same logic as matching but makes use of data already collected and adjusts the data to match the participant group.

The use of existing data avoids the necessity of finding, recruiting, and maintaining comparison groups made up of real people. It saves money and time, and it allows statisticians to exercise some of the fancier techniques that they have developed in recent years. In many cases, the techniques have yielded good results. But like all the other designs we have discussed so far, they have their limitations. The evaluator has to decide when and under what conditions they can contribute to the design of the study.

There are four basic ways in which statistical methods can be used in evaluation design. One is by locating a comparison group in an existing data set and then adjusting the data to make the cases as comparable to program participants as possible. A second technique is to predict what the situation (e.g., welfare caseload) would have been in the absence of the program and then compare the actual situation with the predicted situation. The difference between the two should be the effects of the program. A third technique is to try to remove the effects of selection (and attrition) biases in the data on participants through various forms of regression analysis. The final method is to model the likelihood that a person is selected or selects himself into the program (selection bias) and to adjust the measures of outcome to take selection bias into account. This may all sound complicated to nonstatisticians, and it is important that an evaluator understand them very well before trying to put them to use. But the logic is fairly easy to grasp.

Comparison Group in an Existing Data Set In its simplest form, this involves finding a data source that has information on a population roughly similar to the participants in the program. The data may come from such longitudinal series as the National Longitudinal Survey on Youth, Panel Study on Income Dynamics, or High School and Beyond. Evaluations of job training programs often rely on the Census Bureau's Current Population Survey, which has large national samples of individuals, or data from Social Security records (Ashenfelter & Card, 1985; Bloom, 1987; Bryant & Rupp, 1987; Dickinson, Johnson, & West, 1987). Chapter 7 lists a number of national longitudinal data series that have useful data for comparisons.

Once having located a data set, the evaluator should check (a) the population that was surveyed, to see how similar it is to program participants, and (b) the questions asked, to see whether they ask for the information that the evaluation requires in a form that fits the study. If the evaluator has consulted existing surveys early in the game, she may find questions and measures that are suitable for her evaluation, and she can use the identical items to ensure comparability.

When a survey is satisfactory on counts of both population and measures, the evaluator can use data from the total sample as a comparison. Even though the population is not very close to program participants in all respects, the data provide an overall comparison that throws light on the condition of people who did not receive program service.

The evaluator may next want to extract a subset of respondents from the data set who are more similar to the recipients of the program than is the total sample. That means that she has to get the raw data file and manipulate it. Problems can arise even after locating and obtaining the data set: The data are not transferable to the evaluator's computer system without major work in converting and reformatting.

The original database may not be well documented, so that it is not clear what the items mean or how they were collected and coded. The data may be aggregated at a level that doesn't match the unit of analysis being used in the evaluation. Available computer software may be unable to operate on the data as they are formatted (Stewart & Kamins, 1993).

Moreover, data that come from existing data sets are not fresh from the field. They had to be collected months or even years earlier because it takes time to collect, check, code, process, clean, organize, and document the data, and then prepare data tapes or disks for public use. By the time the evaluator receives the data set, it may be several years out of date. Whether or not this is a matter of concern depends on the stability of the information over time and the nature of the comparison the evaluator wants to make.

Many of the large data sets now come on CD-ROMs, which provide quick, accurate, and relatively inexpensive access to the information. They require a CD-ROM player and software designed to retrieve the data on the disk. However, new technology is in the offing, and systems may change relatively soon. They are probably going to keep changing, as electronic wizardry continues to develop.

If the evaluator still wants to go ahead and select a subsample from a relevant data set, she has to identify the variable(s) on which she will choose the subsample, such as education or employment status. She will seek a variable or a very few variables that are associated with the program outcome.

Let us take a dropout prevention program for high school students. The evaluator knows from previous studies that variables associated with dropping out of school include socioeconomic status of students' families (low), school grades (low), and age in grade (older than the average student in that class). She looks at a large national data set and finds individuals with a wide range of values on these variables. She can attempt to select individuals in the data set who are close matches on one or more of these variables. Since she is dealing with several waves of data on the same individuals, she has to decide which year's data to use for selecting the subsample. Unless the evaluator is skilled in analysis of large longitudinal surveys, she should get expert help.

Even when everything goes well, the cases in the dataset subsample may still differ from the program group in their overall distribution. For example, 40% of the dataset cases may show a grade point average lower than 2.0, compared to 55% among program participants. Statistical weights can be introduced to give more weight to each case in the underrepresented category, or differences between participants and comparisons can be reduced through the use of statistical adjustment. See the section on statistical adjustments below.

With all the technical and conceptual problems, the use of existing data to form an artificial comparison group has much to recommend it. Obviously, it saves the time, expense, and psychic wear and tear of recruiting real people to receive no program. It also appeals to the sense of frugality. Here are all these multi-million-dollar longitudinal surveys with opulent quantities of excellent data, collected with conscientiousness and creativity by highly talented researchers available almost for the asking. It feels wasteful to ignore them. Moreover, the datasets provide information on large numbers of people and help to answer a recurrent evaluation question: How do changes in program participants compare to changes in other people in roughly similar circumstances over the same time interval?

Probably the easiest way to make good use of the information is to look at the distribution of responses for the *total survey population* (often from published materials) on data items central to the evaluation over analogous periods of time. Where the survey population differs from the program population, the evaluator should point out the differences and estimate how the differences affect the comparison. For example, if the survey respondents on average come from higher income families, on the basis of past research they can be expected to show faster gains on reading test scores than the program population. The comparison, therefore, will exaggerate the gap between the two groups and tend to underestimate the growth in reading scores of people in the program. When published data, or easily accessible tabulations, show survey data separately by family income, then program participants can be compared to the subgroup in the survey whose incomes are most similar to theirs.

Forecasting the Situation without the Program   Another way that statistical techniques can be used is to extrapolate past trends into the future, as a way of estimating the counterfactual—that is, the condition that would have occurred if no program had been operating. Thus, for example, an evaluation of a dropout prevention program can use past school data to project the rate of future school dropouts, on the assumption that past trends continue into the future. Then the evaluator compares the actual rate of school dropouts with the projected rate at given points in time and assumes that any observed difference is due to the program.

A more sophisticated form of this procedure was used to evaluate a nutrition assistance program in Puerto Rico (Beebout & Grossman, 1985). Data were taken from two food intake surveys carried out in 1977 and 1984. Changes in the food stamp caseload were modeled before the program was implemented. After the program, the evaluators compared current estimates of food expenditures to the expenditures that would have occurred, based on the model, if there had been no program. Similarly, Garasky (1990) projected the welfare caseload in Massachusetts based on data from 1976 to 1983, when a state employment and training (ET) program went into effect.

In another study (Holder & Blose, 1988), simulation was used to model the effects of a complex of factors on alcohol-related traffic accidents in a community. The simulation took into account such factors as the consumption of alcohol in the population by age, sex, and drinking practices, vehicle miles driven, legal age limit for purchase of alcohol, enforcement of driving-under-the-influence statutes and conviction rates, and disposable income. The effects of each of these factors on alcohol-related traffic accidents was modeled on the basis of the best available research. The simulation yielded projections of the frequency of injuries and fatalities for the years ahead under a range of different assumptions—all assuming the absence of any programmatic intervention.[10] Once an intervention was implemented, projected

---

[10]Such a simulation model could be used to estimate the effects of an intervention before it is implemented in order to figure out whether it is likely to make a positive difference. Computer simulations can be a planning tool (Holder & Blose, 1988).

injuries and fatalities could be compared to actual injuries and fatalities, with the simulation in effect providing the comparison group.

One of the key limitations to this approach is one that we have met before: outside events. Events outside the program that are not accounted for in the statistical model can be responsible for changes in welfare cases or food expenditures or dropouts. For dropouts, for example, availability or unavailability of jobs might lead to changes in leaving school. Or changes within the schools may be involved, such as alterations in curriculum, school administration, or teaching staff. This procedure can be supplemented with other techniques, such as comparison groups, to try to identify and deal with changes due to outside events.

Statistical Adjustments for Preexisting Differences between Program Participants and the Comparison Group

Whether a comparison group is constructed of similar people or from data in existing surveys, their nonequivalence to the program population is a constant affliction. This is selection bias, which we have met before.

A common method for seeking to equate program participants and members of nonrandom comparison groups is to control statistically for the variables on which they differ. The idea is simple: Identify the variables that are likely to affect program outcomes and then remove the differences between the groups on those variables by analysis. For example, if participants are more likely than the constructed comparison group to be new arrivals in the company at the start of the executive training program, control for length of time in company.

Regression analysis is one of the statistical techniques that can be used for this purpose. In effect, it controls for differences between the program group and the comparison group. The variables may be measures of health status, income, length of employment, severity of crime committed, or whatever else there is reason to believe differentiates the groups. Regression analysis can be used to estimate the extent to which each of these variables predicts program outcomes, and once these have been taken into account, differences in the outcome that remain are assumed to be due to participation in the program. It is a method for equalizing the two groups on those factors that the evaluator knows about, has measured, and has entered into the analysis.

In multiple regression, large numbers of factors can be controlled simultaneously, and additional terms can control for the interactions among them. If the evaluator has identified and appropriately measured the relevant differences between the two groups, the end result is to leave the two groups much the same for analytic purposes. Any differences in outcomes can then be ascribed to the effects of the program.

That is the general idea of statistical adjustment. In practice, more complex procedures are usually used. The problem of noncomparable groups does not yield readily to solutions, and statisticians incorporate a variety of procedures into their quest for comparability. The key is good knowledge or theory about which variables matter for gauging the effects of the program.

Many studies have used these kinds of techniques (e.g., Ashenfelter, 1978; Dobson, Grayson, Marshall, O'Toole, Leeder, & Schureck, 1996; Kiefer, 1979; Lee & Loeb, 1995), either alone or in conjunction with other statistical procedures, such as selecting comparisons from existing datasets. Controlling for differences through statistical controls has proved to be highly useful. However, a recurrent limitation is the inability to account for *all* the factors that distinguish the two groups. Those who do and do not enter a program differ in a variety of ways, not all of which are known or measured. Still, with increasing experience and with increasingly sophisticated statistical methods, much progress has been made. In some fields such as job training, hundreds of evaluations have been conducted, and a good deal of knowledge has accumulated. Increasingly, complex statistical methods have been introduced, and continued discussions and debates among analysts lead to further refinements in method.

Modeling the Selection Process One of the currently popular analytic refinements has been to model the selection process itself. That is, the evaluator develops a regression equation that includes all the elements presumed to affect the decision to enter the program. These become the independent variables. The dependent variable is participation in the program. The solution to the equation is a predicted probability that each case will be in the program group. This prediction score for each individual is then entered as a control variable into the overall regression (Heckman, 1980; Heckman & Hotz, 1989).

Many evaluators have adopted the technique. It has staunch supporters but critics as well. Its value rests on good knowledge of the characteristics that are predictive of participation in the program and on the availability of good data that measure those characteristics. Inventive statisticians have developed other correction techniques. Donald Rubin, for example, has developed a procedure using what he calls propensity scores (Rosenbaum & Rubin, 1983, 1984).

Before we leave this section, let me note that the evaluator who attempts to use these statistical methods has to have a full understanding of the techniques and of the assumptions on which they are based. She also needs the technical training to use appropriate statistics wisely. In addition, she has to understand the measures that were used in the evaluation, their statistical properties, and distribution. Consultants can solve some of the problems, but it is important for the evaluator to understand what the consultant is doing. Fortunately, a good statistician can often explain the logic of the procedures in terms that are accessible to people with a modest level of statistical expertise.

One final note: An issue of the *Journal of Educational Statistics* (Wainer, 1989) dealt with problems of interpretation created by nonrandom samples, and the authors suggested several solutions. After pages of text, equations, graphs, and unexpected sprightly prose, the organizer of the issue, statistician Howard Wainer, listed a set of conclusions. Among them were the following:

> Statistics can't work magic.
>
> Without information, the best we can do is to characterize our ignorance honestly.
>
> It is important to know the subject area so that we can better model selection.
>
> The only consensus we can hope for among competing analysts is the kind of testing any proposed adjustment strategy has to successfully undergo prior to acceptance. (p. 188)

The testing continues.

When to Use Nonequivalent Control Group Designs

Now that I've discussed methods for constructing and adjusting comparison groups, let's consider when it is beneficial to rely on them. Obviously, there are times when the evaluator has little choice. It's either a nonequivalent (nonrandomized) comparison group or no comparison at all. Evaluators agree that some comparison is better than none. The more similar the comparison group is in its recruitment and the more similar their characteristics on pretest measures, the more effective they will be as controls. To repeat, any differences between the groups should be measured and reported, and the evaluator should indicate the likely direction of bias stemming from noncomparability, noting whether it tends to underestimate or overestimate program effects.

Comparisons with nonequivalent groups are useful, but several studies urge that such comparisons be used with caution. Evaluators have studied cases where both nonrandom comparison groups and randomized control groups have been available. When they compared the results, they found that nonrandom comparisons often gave misleading results. This has been true even after statistical adjustments were introduced to control for known differences between the groups. Boruch and his colleagues reviewed results where experimental evidence on program effects was collected alongside evidence from quasi-experiments or econometric modeling. They conclude on the basis of a series of studies that the procedures can yield results that are very wide of the mark (Dennis & Boruch, 1989; National Research Council, 1989). Using data from evaluations of training programs, two sets of investigators (Fraker & Maynard, 1987; Friedlander & Robins, 1994; La Londe, 1986; La Londe & Maynard, 1987) compared the results of randomized experimentation, quasi-experimentation, and econometric modeling. They relied on the randomized experiment for providing the true estimate of program effects; in contrast, the other procedures ranged from overestimating effects by 50% to underestimating them by 2,000%. Similarly, evaluations of the Salk polio vaccine were undertaken by both randomized experiments and by an early quasi-experiment in which second graders received the Salk vaccine and first and third graders were used as the comparison group. The quasi-experimental results differed considerably from those of the experiment (Dennis & Boruch, 1989). Shadish and his colleagues compared randomized and nonrandomized evaluations of marital and family therapy (Shadish & Ragsdale, 1996) and education and drug abuse prevention programs (Heinsman & Shadish, 1996). They found sizable differences in results, but when crucial design features were taken into account, nonrandomized studies more closely approximated randomized results. Further comparisons of randomized and nonrandomized designs will be useful in understanding the conditions under which nonrandomized designs produce results that are similar to those of experiments.

In conclusion, let me recommend an important strategy. If the evaluator can determine the selection of even a fraction of the program recipients, she can assign them randomly to program and control conditions. At least for this subset of recipients, she will be able to make valid estimates of the difference that program participation makes.

Summary

This chapter reviews a variety of research designs for evaluating the process and the outcomes of social programs. Informative data can be obtained by asking people on the scene about their experiences. Experts can be called in to render judgments based on their experience and knowledge of programs of the same type.

These sources offer useful information, particularly on inputs and processes of program implementation. When the evaluation is meant to apprise directors, sponsors, and funders about outcomes, the evaluator will want to use designs that are less vulnerable to bias and incompleteness.

In a more formal mode, the evaluator can collect outcome measures on the program group *after* the program has been in operation and seek to impute participants' status prior to entry. This design is likely to be used when the evaluator is called in too late to collect *before* data herself. Better is a before-and-after design, where comparable data are collected pre- and postprogram. The design can be strengthened by adding *during* measures while the program is in midstream. Following the tracks of program theory improves the design further by investigating whether the hypothesized links between process and outcome materialize.

Time-series designs add additional data points. Starting long before the program begins, continuing "during-during-during" the program, and going on for several years after the program ends, time series indicate whether the pattern of outcome measures supports the conclusion that the program is responsible for observed effects. Time-series data also show whether positive effects are sustained over time, accelerate, or fade away. Multiple time series add comparisons with sites that did not receive the program. Such comparisons are a way to rule out the threat that outside events, rather than the program, caused observed outcomes.

Existing longitudinal data series are an excellent source of time-series data. Thousands of such series are available at local, state, and national levels. Where no source covers the topics required for the evaluation, the evaluator can seek to collect appropriate data over time by repeated interviewing of panels of respondents. The longer the interviewing can continue, the more suitable will the data be for time-series analysis.

One-group before-and-after designs can be strengthened by the addition of comparison groups who do not receive the program. One way to create comparison groups is by matching nonparticipants to participants on characteristics that are related to desired outcomes. Thus, the evaluator often seeks people of the same age, race/ethnicity, gender, socioeconomic status, severity of condition, or other key attributes. In order to avoid differences in other unmeasured attributes, such as motivation, the evaluator will try to find people who had not heard about the program, who live in communities where the program was unavailable, or who were on the waiting list.

Evaluators can create artificial comparison groups by using available data sets containing similar people who were not served by the program. They can try to select out the subset of respondents most similar to program participants for comparative purposes. Before-and-after comparisons with these respondents offer clues about whether exposure to the program was the key factor in change.

Statistical methods can be used to try to equate participants and comparisons, whether the comparison groups are developed by matching procedures or from existing datasets. The most common statistical techniques involve controlling for variables that are expected to affect outcomes. When their effects on outcomes are accounted for, any remaining difference between participants and comparisons is assumed to be the result of participation in the program. A cautionary note: The effect of any variables that are not measured and not included in the analysis is not controlled. Since evaluators often cannot identify all the variables that influence outcomes, and since they do not have measures of some variables even when they can identify them, statistical corrections can lead to under- or overestimating program effects. Another statistical procedure is to identify the factors that differentiate those who enter the program from those who do not and to model the selection process. When this can be validly done, the effects of selection bias can be controlled.

The purpose of these increasingly complex designs is to rule out the possibility that things other than the program are causing whatever outcomes are observed. They seek to counter threats to the validity of the causal conclusion and improve internal validity. In evaluation a number of threats to validity have been identified, such as maturation, outside events, testing, and instrumentation, but the most pervasive and serious problem is selection: Those who enter a program are usually unlike those who do not enter on a number of measured and unmeasured characteristics.

Evidence about which variables are implicated in desired outcomes comes from research and prior evaluations, and better knowledge is accruing over time. Measurement of the appropriate variables depends on the state of the measurement art and the availability of well-measured variables in existing datasets. Measurement progresses, but with cutbacks in federally supported data series, less data are likely to be available and intervals between collection points are lengthening. Statistical techniques are advancing to cope with discrepancies between program and comparison groups, and more studies are comparing the results of nonequivalent comparison groups and random-assignment control groups. From these efforts, evaluators are getting a better understanding of which techniques work well to equate experimental and comparison groups and where further progress is required.

Although the informal and quasi-experimental designs in this chapter do not control against all threats to causal attribution, many of them provide sufficient information to size up the situation. Where serious ambiguities remain about the causal link between the program and observed outcomes, the evaluator can patch on further investigation. The key is to recognize what the weaknesses are and to compensate for them through parallel—or additional—inquiry.

TABLE 9-1 HYPOTHETICAL FINDINGS OF A TRAINING PROGRAM[a]

A:	PERCENT EMPLOYED AFTER THE PROGRAM		
Chronically unemployed	70		
Single mothers	50		
Released offenders	20		

B:	PERCENT OF PROGRAM GROUP EMPLOYED	PERCENT OF CONTROL GROUP EMPLOYED	PERCENTAGE POINT DIFFERENCE
Chronically unemployed	70	60	+ 10
Single mothers	50	35	+ 15
Released offenders	20	2	+ 18

[a]Thanks go to Robert Granger for the idea for the table.

received. The evaluator does not have the same command over the situation and must make adaptations to the busy program world. Nevertheless, when circumstances are propitious, she can control the assignment of people into the program and control groups, and take readings of their status at the beginning and end of the program (and during the program and on into the future, where possible).

The main purpose of the randomized experiment is to answer the question: Was it the program or something else that caused the changes observed between the before and after periods? Because the individuals were almost surely the same at the beginning and lived through the same events and experiences, the only thing that distinguishes them is the receipt or nonreceipt of the program. The question of whether change can be attributed to the intercession of the program is an important one in evaluation, and the experiment is geared to answering it with a high degree of authority.

Randomization When Program Spaces Are Limited

Randomized experiments are possible under a variety of circumstances. If the evaluator has a say in how program participants are chosen, she can opt for random assignment. Sometimes program staff object to this procedure on the grounds that it denies service to needy people. But if the program is unable to serve everyone who needs service anyway, then somebody is going to do without. Random assignment is a fair way to allocate scarce resources and is arguably fairer than choosing applicants on a first-come, first-served basis or on the basis of who people know (Boruch, 1997).

The practitioner's counter to this argument is that staff should make the decisions. They would choose people who are most in need or on the basis of some other professional criterion. They would not leave selection to the vagaries of chance. However, the program is still of uncertain value. If consensus existed that it was beneficial, there would be little need to evaluate it. It would be introduced systemwide everywhere (or as far as budgets allow). Inasmuch as the program is still something

of an unknown quantity, there is no certainty that enrollment will benefit its participants. As Boruch, Dennis, and Carter-Greer (1988) have written:

> Examples of programs that have generated detectable and unambiguous effects
> are in the *minority* in human services. They are also in the minority in research
> on medicine, business, criminal justice, education, and elsewhere. (p. 412)

A program might even harm clients. In medical research that tests new drugs,
this is well known to be true. In the New Jersey Negative Income Tax experiment in
the 1970s, one of the findings was that the husband and wife families that received
a guaranteed income had an unusually high rate of marital breakup.[3]

It is also possible that people who are most in need are not necessarily helped
the most by a given program. People with the most serious problems may have
grown apathetic, unmotivated, or angry, or have turned to other resources to improve
their lot. Extent of need may not be the optimal selection criterion. Other professional criteria may be little better. Before people enter the program, practitioners
have only superficial knowledge of them or their condition, and they do not necessarily know which applicants would make responsive clients. A lottery (i.e., a randomization procedure) is an eminently reasonable way to enroll cases.

It may be hard to convince practitioners that what they do is not necessarily
advantageous for their clients or that their bases for selection are not ideal. But they
can often be helped to recognize the logic of randomization. With random assignment,
the value of their program will be rigorously tested and demonstrated to the world. An
inducement of this sort, coupled with the logical argument that the program is still
developing and can benefit from better understanding of effects, can help to win cooperation for the procedure. The evaluator can sometimes assure practitioners that after
the study is over, members of the control group can be admitted into the program.

In recent years, as evaluation has become more familiar to people in a whole
range of programs, the plethora of objections to randomization that practitioners
used to raise has diminished. They have become accustomed to the rationale, the reason, and the routines of evaluation, and they seem to raise fewer objections.
Occasionally now, clients object, particularly if they believe that they are being
deprived of something of merit. But when openings in a program are in short supply, there are obviously valid reasons for using a selection strategy that gives everyone an equal chance of entering the program.

Randomization to Alternative Service

One way around the problem of seeming to withhold service is to offer controls
some other kind of service or opportunity. The alternative service has to address a
want or need different from the one addressed by the program. If it were a variant of
the program geared to meeting the same need, it would be a planned variation evaluation, which I discuss a little later. It would be examining which version of the program had better outcomes. But if it is dealing with a different need entirely, the members of the control group can still function as true and legitimate controls. Thus, for

---

[3]Robinson Hollister tells me that the finding was in error, but it caused consternation in Congress
when it was reported, and it was a factor in the congressional decision to abandon the idea of a guaranteed income policy.

example, students who are assigned to the control group for the new math program may receive a special art program. Their ability to function as controls for the math program is unimpeded, but they are not discriminated against. Some may even be happier with the art course than they would have been with math.

In cases where no real treatment can be offered to controls, a placebo program can be devised that gives the aura, but not the substance, of service. It removes the possibility of a Hawthorne effect, a positive response that is due merely to the attention that participants receive.[4] Avoiding Hawthorne effects is a consideration, but it appears unwise for both ethical reasons and those of public policy to provide a service to controls that is patently phony, like the sugar pill of pharmacological experiments. The alternate service should have some likelihood of doing good. One possibility is offering controls a cheap version of the program under study. Thus, Scriven (1967) suggests that controls in a curriculum project might receive a quickie curriculum developed over a summer by graduate students. This can be viewed as a placebo, but it might turn out to be as effective as the master curriculum painstakingly developed by specialists.

Randomization in a Staged Program

Another opportunity for random assignment comes when the program takes place in stages. One set of executives is going to receive a staff development program during the summer, and another group is going to receive the same training six months later. The executives can be randomly assigned to the two groups. The later group can become the control group for the group that first receives the training.

In Figure 9-1, group 1 receives the program first, and the unexposed group 2 serves as controls. The dotted line shows the improvement that group 1 makes. For group 2, which receives the program six months later, the first group (even though now unequal) serves as controls. The solid line shows their progress on the outcome. The third measure taken six months after group 1 has been exposed to the program gives evidence of whether effects for that group persist or fade away.

Even though the groups were randomly selected, there are three problems here: (a) The timing is different enough so that outside events could influence whether the trainees apply their learnings back in the firm. In the time interval between the two executive development programs, conditions in the firm may change sufficiently to encourage or discourage learning and application of program learning; (b) the second group of executives, knowing that their program is coming up, could fail to take steps that they might otherwise take to improve their knowledge or skills; and (c) six months is a short time for follow-up of the effects of a development program that presumably has aspirations to create long-term improvements in job performance. Yet at the end of six months, the control group loses its unsullied status.

Thus, the staging, or sequencing, of sessions of a program often creates the opportunity for random assignment, but such a procedure has limitations. One is the

---

[4]The term comes from a series of studies made at the Hawthorne Works of the Western Electric Company between 1927 and 1932. Researchers found that when management paid attention to workers, no matter what shape it took, output increased. For example, decreasing the illumination, as well as increasing it, led to higher output. Although recent reexamination of the data has thrown some doubt on the interpretation in this case, the Hawthorne effect is a phenomenon that has been observed in many situations.

FIGURE 9-1   EXPECTATIONS FOR EFFECTS OF PROGRAM ON TWO STAGED GROUPS

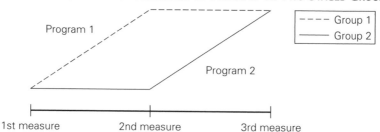

Note: This figure portrays a situation similar to that in Figure 8-2. The two figures look different because this one shows the expected *change* in outcomes for the groups, whereas Figure 8-2 shows only the comparisons that were being made. Also, this figure includes two groups while Figure 8-2 included four groups. But there is one important difference that lands the figures in different chapters: This figure depicts groups that have been randomly assigned, whereas the groups in Figure 8-2 were not randomly assigned but were natural groups that entered the program voluntarily at different times.

problem of the waiting list. That is, people who are on the waiting list can be designated as controls, but they know that they will be admitted into the program at some future time. Their behavior is likely to be different from what it would otherwise be. As we noted in Chapter 1, smokers who are on the waiting list and in the control group for a smoking cessation program do not generally try to quit smoking on their own. If they had not been promised admission at some later time, many of them might have enrolled in some other cessation program, or enlisted a friend who also wants to quit cigarettes and make a concerted collective effort to kick the habit, or bought some of the aids now on the market. Evaluation should compare the behavior of program participants with the natural behavior of those who don't receive the program, not with some artificially modified behavior.

Of course, similar problems can arise when people apply for admission to a program and are assigned to a control group, without being promised later admission. The situation of controls, with or without waiting lists, suggests a general caution. People assigned to control groups don't go off to Never-Never Land. They don't receive the program, but they have many other experiences, and some of them may actively seek analogous help elsewhere. Currently, dozens of programs are available from a wide variety of sources for teachers' professional development, prevention of family violence, weight control, community development, homework assistance, and so on. Members of a control group for any one program may seek or wander into equivalent service somewhere else. It is not possible, nor would it be ethical, for the evaluator to stop them. Furthermore, the evaluation should discover whether the program adds something of value to what people would ordinarily get on their own.

Any experiment does not pit the program against nothing. It compares the program with the usual run of experience. Therefore, evaluators have to interpret the results of the randomized-assignment study (and studies with nonequivalent comparison groups) with recognition that controls have options, live lives, and undergo change. Evaluators use control groups because they want to find out whether the program provides benefits beyond those of common experience.

Randomization of Sites

Another opportunity for randomized assignment arises when a program is being introduced in spatially separate locations. For example, a chain of health clubs may decide to introduce new Nautilus equipment in some sites and not others. Provided it has enough locations, it may choose the sites randomly and use the sites without the new equipment as controls. Then it can examine such outcomes as increase in number of members. With enough cases, it is reasonable to assume that customers and prospective customers at the program sites have characteristics similar to those at the control sites, at least with regard to their propensity to join or rejoin the club.

The reason for the emphasis on spatially separate locations is the concern about possible communication between program people and controls. When the program is providing information (e.g., to new mothers), a program mother who lives near a mother in the control group is likely to talk to her, and the conversation may well include the new information that she is receiving. The control group is thus contaminated—that is, it is receiving the program surreptitiously, innocently enough but undercutting the evaluative comparison. All random-assignment evaluations have to guard against the possibility that members of the control group learn about, or experience, elements of the program. If they do, they have a chance to gain program benefits, and the contrast between the two groups is reduced. The evaluation then underestimates the effect of the program.

Another opportunity for randomization arises when a new facility is being built. People can be randomly assigned to different locations in the facility. Some maternity patients can go to the quarters with extensive self-care arrangements and others to traditional hospital rooms. Ward and Kassebaum (1972) report on the opening of a new correctional facility in California. Before the prison opened, they prevailed upon the Department of Corrections to assign inmates randomly to three of four quadrangles. (The fourth was reserved for especially difficult prisoners.) Because the quadrangles were physically separate, one group could receive group counseling, one could experience a community living program, and the third could serve as a control group, all without fear of communication or contamination. Randomization ensured comparability of the populations at the start.

Agencies that sponsor programs are providing opportunities for random-assignment evaluations by mandating them for their grantees. When the Department of Labor, for example, requires the job training programs it funds to undergo random-assignment evaluation as a condition of funding, it is awesome how rapidly propitious conditions materialize. Perhaps even more conducive is the funding of the evaluations themselves. Some government agencies and foundations have put sizable sums of money into random-assignment evaluations so that they can have valid estimates of the effectiveness of their programs.

Planned Variations

One feasible strategy for introducing random assignment is to give different versions of the program to the experimental and control groups. Nobody is denied service; nobody has to wait. Each group receives a variant that is believed to have some efficacy.

This kind of design is applicable even when a program serves everyone who meets eligibility standards and there are no extra cases to serve as a control group. People in the program can be randomly assigned to different versions of the program. Considering the purpose of the evaluation and the use that is likely to be made of study results, this is an eminently sensible procedure. When a program has been universally adopted, only in extraordinary cases will the real question be whether to continue or scrap it entirely. The question is much more likely to be *which version* of the program will be instituted.

In this case, the control group then is not without *some* program. That is a fruitful comparison only if decisions to be made involve a choice between this program and none at all. Often, the choice will be between the innovative program and the usual treatment for the group. A new curbside recycling program can be compared with recycling at central collection points, the current procedure. Total Quality Management (TQM) practices can be compared with standard management practices. The control group in this case receives the standard treatment. Or the pending choices are among several versions of a new program and the evaluation randomly assigns people to different versions of the innovation. There can be more than two groups. Where the situation allows, the evaluator can study two (or more) versions of a new program *plus* a control group that receives routine treatment or nothing at all.

Just as evaluators can randomly assign people to different versions of a program, they can assign people to different intensities of service. Variation in the intensity of treatment is a dose-response design, named after the practice of testing different dosages of medication in the trial of new drugs. We met dose-response in Chapter 8 when it was applied to quasi-experimental design. It is equally applicable to random-assignment studies.

When the program is a full-service program and serves everybody, there can be variations in the amount of service each person receives. All eligible people in the program area are entitled to receive home health care, but some can be randomly assigned to receive more frequent visits from health aides than others. A Population Council study of the provision of contraceptive services in Lima, Peru, randomized clinics to provide doctors' visits either one, two, or four times a month. Prior demonstration had showed that the program was effective, and the experimental evaluation at this point was dedicated to finding out how much service made a difference (Dennis & Boruch, 1989). Similarly, a hospital in Barbados offered first-time mothers counseling designed to help them delay a second pregnancy. After they left the hospital, the women were randomly assigned to receive either one or three visits from a nurse to reinforce the counseling message (Bertrand et al., 1986).

Often special demonstration programs are set up to test a variant of the usual service. The health center program may go on as usual, while new enrollees are randomly assigned to a project in which case managers have overall responsibility for coordinating all appropriate services for the family.

Thus, the unlimited availability of service for everybody does not preclude the use of random assignment. The only constraint is that the service cannot be compared with receipt of no service. The questions that evaluation can answer have to do with how much, what kind, how often, and under what conditions.

Procedures for Random Assignment

Random assignment to the program and the control group can be accomplished in a variety of ways. Where the program is provided to individuals, such as psychotherapy, *individuals* can be randomly assigned to treatment and control. Where the program is provided to *groups*, such as fifth grade classrooms, the groups can be randomly assigned. Some get the program and some do not. Or program *staff* can be randomly assigned to different strategies. For example, half of all welfare workers are provided with computerized records on their clients and half are not. In some cases, *sites* are randomly assigned to program and control conditions, with some sites offering the new program and others offering the standard fare. For public information campaigns or other programs that attempt to reach a whole city or county, such as telecasts of messages to reduce fat intake or increase exercise, *geographic areas* can be randomly assigned to receive or not receive the broadcasts. Another ingenious method of randomization is to randomize *time periods*. Thus, in the evaluation of a criminal court diversion program, Hillsman-Baker and Rodriguez (1979) had lawyers accept into the treatment group the first cases that came up in a time segment (e.g., between 9 A.M. and 11 A.M.), until the quota for that period was filled and then assign the next intakes to the control group. The evaluators varied the length of the time segments and randomly arranged them across lawyers and work hours.

As a general rule, evaluators prefer to randomize at the level of the individual. Such a procedure gives more cases (larger Ns), and more independent cases are statistically desirable because they give more statistical power. But some programs deal with groups, like organizational units, classrooms, or hospital services, and individuals within those groups cannot be randomly assigned elsewhere. For example, a summer institute to give elementary school teachers special skills for teaching science cannot randomly assign some students out of the teacher's class. Every student he teaches will receive whatever enhanced benefits the summer institute has provided. If the evaluation wants to find out how much difference the summer institute makes for students' science knowledge, it will have to randomly assign teachers to the summer science institute and to a control group and then compare their *classes'* knowledge of science. In the planned variation mode, it might give teachers in the control group a different institute, perhaps one on teaching reading, on the assumption that better reading skills won't affect students' knowledge of science. Then classes whose teachers studied reading become the controls for the classes whose teachers studied science (and vice versa).

When programs are provided to intact groups, such as housing projects, even if hundreds of people are sampled in each housing project, the evaluator does not necessarily have hundreds of cases. Individuals within each project are affected by the same selection criteria, history, and swarm of conditions and events, inside and outside the program. They are not independent units in a statistical sense. Let's say there are four housing projects with 500 people sampled from each. If every person in a project were a clone of the others in the same project, the analyst would have not 2,000 cases but four. On the other hand, if every individual were completely unique, she would have 2,000 cases. In practice, the situation is somewhere in between. The more homogeneous the residents within a project are, the fewer independent cases there are, and therefore the less statistical power there will be to detect program effects. One solution is to increase the sample of housing projects, perhaps sampling fewer residents from each one.[5]

Usually when dealing with large aggregates, such as housing projects or cities, sponsors select a relatively small sample into the program. For example, foundations are likely to fund only five or six cities to undertake major neighborhood revitalization initiatives. With such small samples, random assignment to program and control conditions is not likely to yield comparable groups. There is no purpose to selecting cities randomly, since no six cities will be representative of cities at large. And a random procedure can introduce a lot of practical drawbacks. The cities may be widely scattered across the country, making the evaluation difficult and time-consuming. The cities sampled may already have equivalent programs; they may vary widely in history and culture; their populations may differ demographically and economically. Comparisons between them and generalizations across them will not make particular sense. The laws of probability don't work well with samples of fewer than 30 or 40. With large enough samples, the odds are very high that members of the two groups will be similar on all measured and unmeasured characteristics, but with small samples they can differ egregiously.

To reduce such problems, one useful procedure is to stratify the population from which the program and control groups will be assigned. Cities, for example, can be divided into strata by population size (over 500,000, 300,000–500,000, etc.) and the evaluator randomly selects cities from each stratum. Two or three stratifiers can be used (eastern cities with over 500,000 population, western cities with over 500,000, etc.). Without increasing the sample size, this procedure improves the comparability of the groups and increases the precision of estimates. A simple variant is to *pair* units that are alike on characteristics relevant to outcomes. Then *randomly* one member of each pair is assigned to the program group and the other is the control.

Each individual group or unit should have a known probability of winding up in the program or the control group. They don't have to have an equal probability, because the program and control groups do not need to be the same size. There can be more people or groups in the program, or more people or groups in the control condition. Statistical computations are a little easier and more efficient when the numbers are equal, but there are few other compelling reasons to make the sizes equal. Sometimes there are good reasons to have more people in one condition. For example, if staff members are reluctant to deny service to needy people, the evaluation can make the program group twice as large as the control group (Boruch et al., 1988). Cronbach and Associates (1980) argue against wasting evaluation resources on studying large control groups that are not exposed to any program services, and therefore also (for different reasons) suggest a larger program group. On the other hand, when the capacity of the program is limited and can serve only a modest number of people, the control group can be larger.

A common way to carry out random assignment is to make a list of all poten-

---

[5]Another procedure is to use multi-level analysis. Multi-level modeling allows the analyst to include individual-level variables in the calculations, thus taking account of the degree of similarity among residents. It adjusts estimates of program effect to take non-independence into account.

tial candidates for the program. The evaluator gives each name on the list a number. She then goes to a table of random numbers or has the computer generate random numbers. She lists the numbers generated in the order they come up. If she wants a program group of 100 cases, she matches the first 100 random numbers to the names on the list and takes them into the program and the next hundred random numbers into the control group.

Another way is systematic sampling, which involves randomly selecting the first unit and then every nth unit after that. If n is 10, then the proportion of the total population that will fall into the sample is 1/10. Systematic sampling is iffy when the list from which units are drawn is ordered in some ways. For example, if the names of individuals are alphabetical and there are bunches of O names (O'Casey, O'Hara, O'Rourke), those people may not have a fair chance of being chosen. If names of husbands and wives are listed alternately, either men or women may be left out almost entirely.

Other ways of random assignment are rolling dice or writing names on pieces of paper and pulling them out of a hat. In each case, care has to be exercised that the procedure doesn't go awry. If you roll dice (even numbers go into the program and odd numbers are controls), don't make exceptions as you go. If you put names into a hat, be sure the pieces of paper are well mixed, or else the last names to go in will cluster near the top and stand a better chance of being chosen.

Staff can be randomly assigned to program strategy when the control group receives some program variant such as the ordinary type of service. It is important that staff not have a chance to select the modality they prefer. If they do, their skill or enthusiasm or motivation to do well can get mixed in with the type of service. The study will find out only whether people who *choose* the strategy perform well, and such results may not generalize to staff who are reluctant or indifferent. On the other hand, an argument can be made that only staff who are experienced and enthusiastic about a particular type of treatment can give it a fair test. If this is so, random assignment of staff is not a reasonable procedure.

It is often more workable to assign each staff member to one particular treatment than to expect each one to vary what he does depending on whether the client is a member of the program or control group. It is difficult for staff to implement two or more different treatments with different recipients—and to keep track of who gets which.

Nevertheless, in the Minneapolis domestic violence experiment, Sherman and Berk (1984) did just that. The program required police to provide one of three treatments to the violent spouse: advice, which could include informal mediation, ejection from the home for eight hours, or arrest. The evaluators considered randomizing days, precincts, cases within individual officers, officers within treatment, and officers across treatment (Boruch & Wothke, 1985). They chose to randomize case handling methods within each officer. They gave officers a pad of report forms color coded for the three different actions. Each time the officers encountered a situation that fit the experiment's criteria, they were to take the action indicated by the top form on the pad. Although the evaluators took several steps to monitor that the police adhered to the randomized actions, they found that many officers failed to fully follow the design.

Coping with Difficulties That Arise

Singing the praises of randomized experiments is one thing, but actually running one is something else. It requires constant vigilance. Things can go wrong from the initial assignment of cases to program and control groups all the way to differential dropouts (attrition) from the two groups. Some matters are under the evaluator's control, but on other matters she has to rely on the goodwill and good sense of staff at the sites. For example, in one study the program began losing clients, so staff took clients from the control group and enrolled them in the program. In another study staff who served clients in the control group became so aggrieved and dispirited about being left out of the banner program that they almost gave up trying.

Where program staff have important responsibilities for assigning clients and maintaining the integrity of the experiment, the evaluator has to keep good relationships with them. She should remind them of the requirements for which they are responsible at intervals and keep an informal (or even a formal) check on what is going on.

Refusal to Participate

Some people randomly assigned to a program may find the program uncongenial or threatening and refuse to attend. Some people assigned to the control group may be angry that they are denied the program or annoyed to be asked to supply data when they receive no benefits. For these and other reasons, people may refuse to fill their allotted slots. The situation would be all right if "refuseniks" in the two groups were alike on important dimensions and left the remaining groups still equivalent. But that is never the case. Those slated to be participants and controls have different grounds for refusing to participate, and are therefore different kinds of people. The remaining groups are no longer equivalent.

What the evaluator can do is delay the randomization procedure until after preliminary agreements have been reached. She can first check the eligibility of every individual for the program and ask for their cooperation in providing data for the study. At that point she can randomize among those who have agreed to cooperate in data collection. Or she can go further and explain the program and control options, ask for agreement to accept either option, and randomize among those who agree to accept whichever status they are assigned. The later the randomization occurs, the less likely are people to refuse to participate. The people who did not agree to give data in the first case or to give data and accept either the program or control condition in the second case are already gone, so there is less likelihood that people will refuse to participate. Constantine et al. (1993) recruited a sample of low-birth-weight premature infants for an infant health and development program. They received parental consent to include 1,028 infants. After consent was obtained, they assigned one-third to the intervention and two-thirds to a control group. Only 17 families withdrew their infant from the study because they objected to the group assigned.

Results of an evaluation that randomizes only among people who accept randomization procedures will apply only to people who would voluntarily remain. Randomizing among cooperative people may limit the generalizability of the study's findings. But the alternative, the loss of many people from the study entirely, may have an even worse effect.

When the study is comparing the effects of the regular treatment and an innovative program, potential participants are not being denied service; they are just not being invited into the innovative program. They are probably more likely to agree to participate. Even more attractive to prospective participants is an evaluation that studies two or more versions of a program. Many people will probably participate in a randomization procedure when they know that they will receive one version of the program or another.

Nonattendance

An allied problem is that some of the randomly assigned participants in the program, while not refusing to participate, will show up rarely, if at all. The evaluator may be tempted to drop them from the study. They are not being exposed to the program's services and can hardly be expected to benefit. Nevertheless, the proper conservative procedure is to continue to include them as participants in the analysis. The rationale is that some members of the control group, had they been offered the program, would also have failed to attend, so the appropriate comparison is between the two total groups. Further, in any subsequent replication of the program, some clients will be similarly refractory. They, too, will stay away. The evaluation should produce evidence on how the whole population of expected beneficiaries will fare in the program, not just those who actively participate. The evaluator can always do a sub-analysis of outcomes for those who attended regularly.

Attrition

While random assignment effectively precludes selection bias, it is still susceptible to selection's evil cousin, differential attrition. People will *drop out* of both the program and control groups. Their reasons for dropping out are apt to differ. People who receive services they value are more likely to stay with the study; controls have less commitment and are more likely to drop out. When attrition is high, the initial equivalence of the two groups is compromised.

The evaluator can take a number of steps to reduce the effect of attrition on the study. One is an all-out effort to remain in contact with controls at frequent intervals so that the study has their current addresses. (Because program participants show up at the program site, their addresses are likely to be on record.) Another step is to offer incentives for consenting to interviews or filling out forms. The evaluator can make nominal payments, give wanted information (unrelated to the program), or offer attractive tokens of some kind. (I once gave respondents lottery tickets.) The evaluator should also try to impress on both groups the social importance of the data they provide, and use whatever persuasion, cajolery, or blandishments will work.

After people disappear or refuse to give further information, the evaluator can compare their before data with the data of those remaining in the study. Such analysis will reveal whether dropouts differ from those who stay, and if so, in which ways. If those who drop out of the control group are more able than most controls, comparison of outcomes between participants and controls has to take this difference into account. At the end participants are being compared to controls who can be expected to do less well than the full control group would have done. Similarly, dropouts from the program group should be compared to those who remain in order to understand whether the program group remains representative of the original sample, or whether some particular segment of participants has defected. Analysis of outcome data has to take account of attrition. The evaluator can use data collected earlier from the dropouts to adjust the groups statistically. She uses statistical techniques to bring the two groups back to their original equivalent condition. If she does not have sufficient information, at the least she should indicate the direction of bias in results that the losses create.

Interference from Outside

Sometimes other agencies come along and provide controls with the same kinds of services that program participants are receiving. The New Jersey Negative Income Tax (NIT) experiment, which was providing a guaranteed income to poor families in New Jersey, almost collapsed when the state changed its system of welfare payments to the control group right in the middle of the experiment. The new payments were close to the higher payments that the program was providing to participants. The researchers added families in Pennsylvania in order to maintain a reasonable control. Similarly, a changing economic or political climate can make services available to the presumably sheltered controls that are equivalent in many respects to the program being studied. About changes in outside conditions, like changes in law and the economy, the evaluator can do little, except try to respond as quickly and creatively as the NIT researchers, but sometimes she lacks adequate resources. In that case, the best she can do is keep scrupulous records and report exactly what happened, where, and when—and perhaps try to add new control cases in the next round of programming (Pechman & Timpane, 1975; Watts & Rees, 1977).

Conditions That Make Randomized Experiments Problematic

Random assignment is the design of choice in evaluation when questions concern the attribution of outcomes to the intervention of the program. But there are situations when it is probably not desirable.

One is when a program is not well developed and well specified. Without a reasonable degree of stability, a program may not be a promising candidate for any kind of evaluation. Given all the extra bother and expense of experimentation, random assignment makes even less sense. The program should have at least a modicum of coherence and predictability.

Similarly, programs that depend on local initiative and opportunistic interventions do not make desirable random-assignment candidates. Community-level interventions are often of this type. A group of local residents, social service staffs, and/or government officials are funded to promote healthful conditions, prevent crime and violence, improve housing, integrate social services, and revitalize the community economy. What they do depends on their planning process and on the opportunities in the community. The program is unstructured, designed to take shape as community leaders define and respond to local needs and as they see openings for productive action. It is possible to think of reasonable evaluation strategies for such programs, including qualitative investigation or the tracking of program theory and collection of data on interim outcomes. But random-assignment strategies are difficult in this context.

Another case when random assignment is not the preferred strategy is when time is of the essence. If a particular type of intervention is being considered for immediate adoption, the policy community wants a reading on its effectiveness in short order. Experiments take time, usually lots of time. A less protracted design may be in order.

More importantly, experiments usually should not be undertaken unless there is good reason to believe that the program has a chance of success. It is wasteful to do a random-assignment evaluation for a shoddy or marginal program. Early reconnaissance should be undertaken first. Only if there are favorable indications is it time to haul out the experimental machinery.

Criticisms of the Randomized Experiment

The experimental model has come under attack in some quarters not only because it is unwarranted but because it can be counterproductive.

In a review of experimentation in education, Smith (1994) notes that she was raised on Campbell and Stanley (1966) and honed her skills on Cook and Campbell (1979) but has come to believe that experiments decontextualize action and distort effects. While the experiment controls certain kinds of bias, such as the assignment of the least disturbed patients to the treatment group, it cannot control the bias of the agency's decision to evaluate at time 1 rather than time 2, the evaluator's bias of reporting results in the best possible light, or the agency's attempt to censor study findings. She quarrels, too, with the experiment's tendency to regard the program as a single molar entity that can be introduced and manipulated.

Behn (1991) reviews the evaluation of Massachusetts' Education and Training program for families receiving public assistance and discusses the major difficulties that would have attended any attempt to design it as an experiment. It was impossible to standardize the treatment that welfare recipients received. The quality of service varied markedly across welfare workers. Moreover, an important part of the program was to change the attitudes of welfare workers and potential employers and make them believe that welfare recipients *want* to work—"They're winners." If the welfare workers and employers experienced such a change in attitude, it would affect members of the control group, too. In fact, by the logic of the program, it *should* affect them. But then they would lose their credentials as controls.

Critics have listed an array of charges, not all of which are well founded, even in principle. Here are the most frequent complaints:

1. The experiment requires holding the program constant rather than facilitating its continual improvement. Managers want to improve the program on the basis of what they learn, but evaluators insist on maintaining the treatment intact over a long enough period to collect before and after data.
2. Even if the program is nominally held stable, the quality of the staff differs markedly, they provide different kinds and quality of service, and the program is *not* uniform. What the aggregated results mean is not clear.

3. Experimental results help the program community make decisions only after a project has run full cycle and not during its implementation. There is a long hiatus before anything useful accrues to the program.

4. Experiments tend to test program components one at a time for the sake of manageability, whereas a combination of services may be necessary for success.

5. The random-assignment process leads to an inequitable distribution of power between evaluators and program staff (Conrad & Conrad, 1994). Evaluators have too much say and place practitioners in a subordinate position. Program concerns are short-changed. For example, when programs have to make extraordinary efforts to persuade clients to sign up, the assignment of half of them to a control group undercuts the enterprise.

6. An experiment tries to control too many conditions, making the program so aseptic that it is ungeneralizable to the real world.

7. The experiment doesn't investigate how and why effects appeared or help people understand which components were key to success. It is good at addressing questions of causal inference but diverts attention away from more important questions about how to understand and improve the system.

8. Things change. Knowing that a program worked at one period doesn't necessarily mean that it will work later under different conditions.

That is an impressive list of charges, and in view of the way evaluations are done, some of them have point and weight. Most of them are not inevitable elements of randomized assignment and can be overcome through better planning and design. Some of them are endemic to all, or almost all, evaluations, not the special bane of the experiment.

Conceptually, random assignment is relevant to the question of whether the program caused the outcomes observed. It highlights, but does not create, problems about holding the program constant, fielding one-component-at-a-time programs, differences in quality of implementation across sites and staff, long time periods before results are available, or the fact that the world moves on and programs that are found successful (or unsuccessful) at one time may have different effects at a later time. All evaluations have to confront these kinds of issues. They are part of the game. Inventive evaluators have to devise inventive solutions to make their studies relevant, practitioner friendly, responsive to potential users of results, and as valid as possible.

Randomized design, like all other designs, is most comfortable with a stable program. Only when it is clear what the program consists of does the evaluator know what the findings are a result of. When the program is in development and changes over its course, it is hard to interpret the meaning of evaluation results. Would effects have been better (or worse) if the program had stuck to the original concept? But randomized assignment does not require a stable program any more than do other designs. In principle it can be used even when the program meanders. If there is interest in the effects of a program under developmental conditions or in its non-standardized form, randomized designs are perfectly suitable for studying outcomes.

Can anything be done to keep the program on a reasonably steady course? Some authors recommend that when innovative programs are being evaluated, the evaluator should be in control of the entire operation. Then the program will be conducted with evaluation requirements in the forefront, and random changes will be fended off. But holding the program steady, let alone controlling it, is beyond the authority of most evaluators. If programs are under strong pressure to change, neither the evaluator's cajolery nor imprecations can hold back the tide.

Another suggestion is to develop programs in a carefully staged developmental process. Stage 1 would be a trial-and-error period in which the program tests and modifies components. Stage 2 would take the tested program and, without allowing further shifts, subject it to random-assignment evaluation. If stage 2 yielded good results, stage 3 would provide a field trial under realistic operating conditions. Only stage 2 requires a stable program; at other stages, variation is not only tolerated but expected. If an agency were committed to such a rational course of action, it could effectively resolve the issue of program shifts. But such a situation is exceedingly rare.

In the real world, programs almost inevitably evolve, for better or for worse. If the program and the drift are described and classified, evaluation can still cope with the disorderly world. The following are some suggestions for studying a shifting program:

1. Take frequent periodic measures of program effect (e.g., monthly assessment in programs of education, training, therapy), rather than limiting collection of outcome data to one point in time.

2. Encourage a clear transition from one program approach to another. If changes are going to be made, try to see that A is done for a set period, then B, then C.

3. Clarify the assumptions and procedures of each phase and classify them systematically.

4. Keep careful records of the persons who participated in each phase. Rather than lumping all participants together, analyze outcomes in terms of the phase(s) of the program in which each participated.

5. Suggest a recycling of earlier program phases. Sometimes this happens naturally; on occasion, it can be engineered. If it is possible, it provides a way to check on earlier conclusions.

6. Seek to set aside funds and get approval for smaller scale evaluation of (at least) one program phase or component that will remain stable for a given period.

7. If the question is a comparison between the original model program and a naturally evolving version of it, it is possible to divide the program into two subunits, one of which remains stable and the other of which is encouraged to improve continually on the basis of best opinion.

Randomized design does not require a simple one-strand program. Experiments can cope with whatever program is implemented. It is certainly easier to manage the evaluation of a simple program and try to hold it to its script. The evaluator can readily monitor activities to see the extent to which they adhere to what they were supposed to be. It is also easier to interpret the results of a single-strand program because it is obvious which strand caused the effects. But an experiment can also come up with results about a complex intervention and demonstrate whether or not the program caused the effects observed. To figure out which *components* of the intervention had the most significant impact is not the experiment's raison d'être. For that task the evaluator can turn to other techniques. She can disaggregate outcomes by the program components to which participants were exposed and find out which program activities were associated with good outcomes, and she can track the unfolding of the assumptions about change that were embedded in program theory. Both of these strategies are compatible with random-assignment designs.

Variation in quality of program implementation across sites and staff is no more a problem to random-assignment studies than to other evaluations. If any evaluation has a sufficiently large number of cases, the variations will tend to cancel out. The experiment is actually in a better position to cope with such variations by the sheer fact of randomization. Through operation of the laws of probability in a reasonably large study, participants in the innovative program and controls receiving the standard fare are likely to get just about the same distribution of good and poor service.

Randomized assignment has been faulted because of the shift in authority from practitioners to evaluators, and that is largely true. But the power imbalance is a political issue, rather than an evaluation issue. If the evaluation sponsor wants to know the outcomes of the program and whether the program caused the outcomes, and insists on high precision of results, some shift in authority over assignment is required. Evaluators ought to be able to negotiate with practitioners to devise methods of assignment that do not interfere unduly with their work.

Random-assignment procedures may lead to the loss of some hard-to-recruit clients. The enrollment time frame may create conditions where the program scrambles to fill treatment and control slots. In the scramble, it sacrifices careful recruitment and explanation to clients of what they can and cannot expect from the program. A consequence may be a high dropout rate from the program. These are unfortunate consequences, but they are not attributable to random assignment per se, and they are usually remediable through better planning. The time period for enrollment can be extended; better recruitment strategies can be developed. If clients are in very short supply, random assignment is probably unwarranted.

The most serious complaint is that many randomized experiments try to control so many conditions that results don't readily generalize to other sites, times, or populations. One of the common restrictions in random-assignment studies is strict eligibility criteria for program participants and controls. The experimenter doesn't want a lot of oddballs of varying stripes in either group, because their idiosyncrasies are likely to reduce the comparability of the groups. Certain entry characteristics may be fixed, such as age, severity of disability, or test scores. The advantage of a carefully defined and controlled population is that the evaluator can confidently specify the universe to which her findings are applicable. However, limitation on the characteristics of participants and controls reduces the generalizability of the findings. No one can say whether experimental findings apply to all the groups who were excluded from the study, groups whom other programs must serve.[6]

Random-assignment studies may also try to standardize the treatment, to make it uniform across staff, sites, and times. The reason is clear. If the evaluator goes to all the effort to conduct a randomized experiment, she wants to be sure that she can

---

[6]The experimenter does not have to control participant characteristics or treatment conditions. To qualify as an experiment, she has to control only one thing, assignment. "All the rest can be uncontrolled and even unmeasured and the experimental results are internally valid" (Shadish, 1997).

specify the nature of the program with precision. She wants no fogginess about what it was that caused the outcomes. But critics such as Conrad and Conrad (1994) claim that "strict standardization of the treatment in multi-site applications will restrict its generalizability and adaptability" (p. 12). Because the program is narrowly standardized, it may not generalize well to other sites now and in the future. Because it is confined to one set of operating procedures, it is not allowed to learn from experience and adapt to its several environments. However, the effort to standardize program operation is not an intrinsic characteristic of random-assignment studies. It represents a means to increase the interpretability of study results.

It is true that many experiments leave important variables out of account. When results converge across sites and circumstances, evaluation becomes confident that it has located a trustworthy effect. But sometimes outcomes vary across sites and situations, and if the evaluation doesn't have data that can explain the variation, it can report only the overall impact of the program and results at each site. Many random-assignment studies are so busy concentrating on the mechanics of experimentation that they forgo opportunities to include data on program activities, staff, or recipients. Few random-assignment studies attend to context or to the program's theories of change. But there is no reason, except exhaustion, why they could not.

Critics tend to blame random assignment for unfortunate conditions that it is not designed to deal with. Although some experiments exacerbate limitations common to almost all evaluations, they are not uniquely responsible for these limitations. Almost every evaluation—quantitative or qualitative, experiment, quasi-experiment, survey, or case study—would be subject to many of the same problems. The source of the complaint seems to be that random assignment is expected to be a magic bullet that cures all ills. Evaluators have to realize that experiments cope very well with the question of causal agency but do not solve all the other problems in evaluation.

In a review of evaluation experience, Cook and Shadish (1994) conclude that "random assignment is already common in social science and could be even more widely used if researchers were better informed about how to circumvent objections to it" (p. 556). Federally supported evaluations of job training programs have often been conducted as randomized experiments, and many federal programs for welfare recipients have also used experimental methods (Friedlander & Hamilton, 1993; Martinson & Friedlander, 1994; Riccio, Friedlander, & Freedman, 1994; Stevens, 1994). Given its very real attractions, the issue is how to realize its advantages without bogging down in its implementation problems and limitations. Some evaluators who used to at least kowtow to the experimental gods before settling on a less onerous strategy have now abandoned the preliminary ritual and turned to other designs. But for its primary purpose, the randomized experiment remains the best instrument in the evaluator's tool kit.

Summary

The experimental model for evaluation depends on random assignment of units to the program and the control group. With randomization (and a sufficient number of cases), the groups are similar on just about all dimensions at the start. Whatever differences emerge at the end are attributable to the program; it can be confidently assumed that the program caused the changes.

Program and control groups do not have to be equal in size. There are often good reasons to assign more cases to one group or the other. Nor should there necessarily be only one program group. Several versions of a program can be evaluated, varying in type of service, frequency of service, intensity of service, or other features.

Randomized experiments are so demanding to manage that they should not be undertaken unless there is evidence that the program is likely to be successful. A first go-round with soft techniques (correlational, one-group before-and-after) can indicate whether a program warrants experimental evaluation.

Randomization to treatment and control can be accomplished by assigning individuals, or groups, or staff, or sites, or geographic areas. When the evaluator confronts a small potential population (e.g., school districts or cities), she can stratify the population and select randomly from each stratum, or create matched pairs and randomly select one unit from each pair.

Random-assignment evaluation, for all its appeal in establishing causal attribution, is still vulnerable to problems. Among them are sabotage of the assignment procedure, client refusals to participate, attrition, and outside interference. Attrition is a particularly thorny problem, because despite the evaluator's meticulous care in maintaining the experiment, the loss of cases reduces the comparability of the program and control groups at the end. Statistical adjustments, much like those discussed in Chapter 8 to make program and comparison groups more similar, can be introduced to compensate.

Some evaluators criticize the randomized experiment on a number of grounds: It tries to keep the program unnaturally stable, tests a narrowly defined program strategy, tries to control too many conditions, and is so artificial that findings do not generalize to the real messy world. It is true that randomized experiments tend in these directions, but most of the complaints are *not inherent limitations* of the experiment; it need not accept such shriveled conditions.

Management of random assignment studies does indeed make heavy demands on the evaluator's attention and energy and may deflect her from other concerns. She may also seek to simplify program conditions and constrain a number of variables, such as program strategies, in order to be able to draw crisp conclusions about a well defined intervention. But much experience has shown that with good planning, random assignment is compatible with even complex, realistic, and untidy programs.

What random-assignment evaluation is uniquely suitable for is ensuring that the program *caused* the outcomes. For that mission, no other design approaches its power. When other questions are more salient, the evaluator may find that the less arduous quasi-experimental designs described in Chapter 8 are adequate for her purposes.

10

EXTENSIONS OF GOOD DESIGN

Now that the evaluation has been suitably designed, the evaluator has an opportunity to consider extensions of the design. This chapter discusses three possible elaborations: replication, meta-analysis, and cost-benefit and cost-effectiveness analysis.

Replication

Replication is a useful tool. Repeated investigation is vital for confidence in the validity of evaluation results. As the noted statistician R. A. Fisher said, the standard of firm knowledge is not one extremely significant result but repeated results of statistical significance. Repetition of results is the basis of scientific generalization. It is also the basis of political confidence in the utility of evaluation findings. Through repeated investigation, we can increasingly specify the conditions under which programs succeed or fail and the processes by which success and failure come about.

Thousands of evaluations have been carried out on programs of job training for the chronically unemployed, the effects of class size on student achievement, the effectiveness of psychotherapy, weight control, and delinquency prevention programs and many others. As study findings became available, program designers modified the next round of programs to profit from the lessons learned. Then new evaluations were conducted.

Replication has led to incremental improvements in programming. But a byproduct of repeated evaluations has been the emergence of inconsistent, and in some cases conflicting, findings about the same kind of program. Some studies show positive effects from programs for police foot patrols; other evaluations show no measurable effects. Some studies show that bilingual education improves the achievement of students with little knowledge of English; other evaluations show little effect on achievement. Members of decision-making communities become confused by the variations in results. One response has been to question the veracity of all evaluations. If evaluators can't agree among themselves, why should anybody take them seriously? Or the response has been more cynical: If you don't like the results of the current study, wait a few months and another study will come along with different conclusions. When evaluators have been unable to specify the sources of disagreement across studies (e.g., whether the differences were due to variations in activities, participants, or community contexts), audiences become more skeptical about evaluation.

Into the breach comes a technique for combining results across many studies to observe the overall effect of programs of a particular type. This is meta-analysis.

Meta-Analysis

Once a number of quantitative studies have been done evaluating the same kind of program, it is possible to combine their results to get better and more generalizable estimates of program effects. The single program (and program evaluation) is the prisoner of its setting. Evaluation results hold for the special place, time, staff, participants, and external conditions that were on the scene when the study was done. Pooling results of many evaluations shows the nature of outcomes of many similar programs across a range of settings. Thus, for example, Wortman and Bryant (1985) report a synthesis of the effects of school desegregation on the achievement of black students; Lipsey (1992) combines data from many studies that examine the effectiveness of programs to treat juvenile delinquents; Lou and colleagues (1996) synthesize the effects of small-group instruction on achievement.

Cook et al. (1992) define meta-analysis as

> a set of quantitative techniques that permit synthesizing results of many types of research.... In meta-analysis the investigator gathers together all the studies relevant to an issue and then constructs at least one indicator of the relationship under investigation from each of the studies. These study-level indicators are then used (much as observations from individual respondents ...) to compute means, standard deviations, and more complex statistics. For most intents and purposes, study-level data can be analyzed like any other data, permitting a wide variety of quantitative methods for answering a wide range of questions. (pp. 4–5)

As this definition states, evaluations that deal with a particular kind of program are collected, and each of the original studies becomes one case in a new analysis. The batch of cases is then analyzed to yield generalizations about this type of program.

When the studies that are analyzed are evaluations, meta-analysis is sometimes called meta-evaluation. However, that term is properly reserved for a different concept, the evaluation of evaluations. Meta-analysis is the preferred term.

For researchers, meta-analysis is a logical extension of the qualitative literature review. Researchers and evaluators have long looked at previous studies to see what earlier researchers have found. Such information helps them decide which issues are well settled and can be laid to rest and which are still salient and deserve priority in their new study. When they have completed the study, they want to place the findings in the context of earlier research, demonstrating how they amplify, support, contradict, or diverge from what was previously known.

As the literature has proliferated, reviewers cannot read every study reported; they have to exercise selectivity. They have to decide which studies to include and how to interpret them. Then they have to integrate evidence that derives from different theories, different time periods, different variables, different measures of variables, and so on, and to keep their own preconceptions from skewing their conclusions. They have to decide which studies to give the most credence and how much weight to give them.

Meta-analysis provides a quantitative procedure for the literature review. It does not solve all the problems by any means, but it provides a systematic and reproducible technique for taking earlier results into account.

Purposes of Meta-Analysis

In evaluation, meta-analysis can be used for three major purposes. The first is to combine evidence to find out the overall direction of effects. While individual studies come out with varying results on the effectiveness of a program, meta-analysis takes into account the whole body of studies in reaching conclusions.

A second purpose is to find out the conditions under which better outcomes are realized. Provided that the original studies include sufficient information about program features, the meta-analyst looks across the body of evaluations to distinguish the types of program activities, participants, and settings where positive outcomes are reached. She can precipitate out of the data those characteristics that are associated with desired outcomes and thus have more to say about program components that work. For example, meta-analyses in education have looked at the effect of such components as class size, level of resources, and preparation of teachers. With many studies to draw on and much diversity in the nature of programs to analyze, meta-analysis can provide explanation of effects more effectively than can one evaluation of one program alone.

A third purpose for meta-analysis is to examine the characteristics of *evaluations* that influence the kind of effects they find. For example, for some time it was believed that quasi-experimental studies were more likely to show positive outcomes than were random-assignment studies. Quasi-experiments, in this view, were relatively squishy and perhaps vulnerable to intentional or unintentional manipulation, whereas experiments provided hard evidence, and hard evidence would be *less* apt to show a positive program effect. The implication was that readers should apply a discounting factor to results of quasi-experiments, mentally reducing the size of the effect. Recent investigations give little support to that supposition. Comparisons of experimental and quasi-experimental studies show that they often differ, but they differ in both directions. One meta-analysis of 74 meta-analyses found that randomized studies had higher effect sizes than nonrandom studies (Lipsey & Wilson, 1993).

But other study features may be implicated in the direction of results. Perhaps studies with short periods of follow-up artifactually show better outcomes or studies that use program record data rather than original data collection. Meta-analysts can examine the research procedures used in the original studies to see whether certain procedures are consistently associated with more positive findings and are artificially generating spurious findings. Such information would help evaluators to improve their craft.

Techniques of Meta-Analysis

Following Cooper and Hedges (1994b), we can divide the meta-analysis process into five stages: (1) formulating the question that the meta-analysis will be called upon to answer; (2) collecting previous studies (searching the literature); (3) evaluating the studies and coding them; (4) analyzing and interpreting the evidence; and (5) presenting the results of the meta-analysis. The following paragraphs explain the fundamentals of each step.

1. *The question* that most commonly drives meta-analysis in evaluation is: What are the overall results of this kind of intervention? This is the kind of information that interests policymakers, and it engages social scientists who seek to understand and theorize about the consequences of various interventions. Simultaneously, meta-analysis can ask: What are the effects of components of the program or of the research features of the studies themselves?

2. *Searching the literature* for relevant studies may look like plain donkey work, but it is a critical phase of meta-analysis. A recurrent problem is the inability to collect a comprehensive set of studies. In particular, analysts come across the problem of publication bias—that is, the likelihood that studies accepted for publication are more likely than unpublished studies to find significant relationships. Journals favor papers with significant results, and evaluators do not submit articles for publication when there are no significant results to report. (Rosenthal [1991] calls this the file-drawer problem. Evaluators shove nonsignificant results into the file and forget them.) Wortman (1994) demonstrates that published studies show greater effects than unpublished studies. Relying only on published studies, therefore, tends to overestimate the frequency and magnitude of positive outcomes.

Accordingly, the analyst has to go beyond the journals in a search for the fugitive literature. She has to examine a wide range of sources, including data systems like PsycINFO, ERIC, and Medline, and supplement the computer search with personal inquiries to evaluators and evaluation funders in the field. Otherwise, the synthesis starts off with a biased tilt.

3. *The evaluation of studies for inclusion* presents problems that bedeviled literature reviewers before the onset of meta-analysis and confronts meta-analysts as well. Almost all studies have some design and measurement flaws, but if the analyst rules out all flawed studies, she is left with only a handful of studies to consider. Therefore, the question is where to draw the line. How good does a study have to be to be worth including? What criteria for inclusion should be established? Some analysts believe that studies of mediocre or marginal quality should be rejected. Others hold that all but the worst studies should be included and that the flaws of individual studies will tend to cancel each other out. Some of the include-them-all group urge analysts to code the design features of all studies they include. Then they will be able to investigate whether studies with specific flaws show better or worse outcomes than studies of higher quality. The analyst will have the data to study the influence of design features on the direction and magnitude of evaluation results.

However, in fields where thousands of evaluations have been done, the analyst can hardly include them all. There are good arguments for eliminating the most egregiously flawed. The important thing is to make the criteria explicit, clear, objective, and open to readers.

The analyst's next task is to decide which information to extract from the studies. She has to choose variables and develop specific coding categories. Just as she needs an admission rule to decide what kinds of studies should be included, she needs a measurement rule to decide which outcomes and program features should be studied and how to measure them. She has to decide what to do if the original study does not give enough information about the treatment provided to participants or about outcomes or if it has a great deal of missing data. The life of a meta-analyst is full of judgment calls. Only slowly are some of the rules being codified.

4. *Analyzing and interpreting meta-analytic data* raises a host of technical issues. Among the questions that arise are which versions of the variables to use, whether to weight studies differentially, which statistical model to apply, how to go about the statistical analysis, what comparisons and estimates to produce, and so on. A variety of techniques are available to characterize and combine data. The literature on meta-analysis is full of highly technical procedures, advice, and debates. One recommendation is that whenever there is uncertainty about the original study, the analyst should go back to the primary data in the study to be sure that the data from every study are analyzed by the same rules.

A good synthesis is not complete without sensitivity analysis—that is, an exploration of how well results hold up under different assumptions (National Research Council, 1992). The analyst does the analysis a number of times, varying the assumptions she makes, to see how consistent the conclusions are when the parameters are changed. A strong form of check is predictive validation—that is, predicting what the conclusions of the next study will be, and checking if the prediction is correct. Another check is retrospectively predicting what results would have been found on the basis of current conclusions. Where assumptions are not confirmed by such checks, the analyst has to carefully consider which assumptions have the best empirical support. Whenever shifts in assumptions lead to widely different conclusions, such information is important to report.

5. *Presenting analytic results to both technical and nontechnical audiences.* When the audience is other analysts, researchers, and evaluators, the conventional format of the journal article is usually appropriate. The procedures of analysis are spelled out, and findings are displayed and interpreted within the customary framework of the field. When the intended audience is members of the policymaking community or other laypeople, much more attention has to go into making both the procedure and the results intelligible.

Requirements for Meta-Analysis

The usual expectation is that the analyst starts with a set of evaluations of programs of a similar type. If the programs have common goals, it makes sense to combine their results and find out how well this kind of programming attains the desired goals. It is usual to require that the studies report outcomes on similar measures, such as scores on achievement tests or school attendance or percentage of students who graduate. When programs have much the same aim, provide similar activities, and measure common outcomes, meta-analysis makes eminent sense.

However, depending on the aims of the meta-analysis, each of these requirements can be relaxed. For example, if the analyst wants to examine the consequences of a wide array of programs that provide psychological help, she may want to include therapy programs, counseling programs, training programs, educational programs, and so on. Lipsey and Wilson (1993) included all those kinds of programs and more. Or she may want to look at all programs that aim to benefit handicapped persons, to see whether any of them—and which kinds especially—make a difference in their ability to be productive and self-sustaining. She can examine evaluations of vocational education, physical rehabilitation, changes in laws regarding public access to buildings and transportation, and so on. The range of programs can be wide, but there need to be at least some common indicators of outcome.

Similarly, the analyst may make use of an array of different outcome measures. In a meta-analysis of a preschool program she may include not only measures of cognitive achievement but also measures of socioemotional status, health status, and attitudes toward school. Giaconia and Hedges (1982) meta-analyzed 153 open education programs, summarizing the results of existing evaluations on 16 outcome measures, such as attitude toward school and reading achievement. One reason for incorporating a melange of outcome measures is that different studies don't always use the same indicators, and in order to collect enough evaluations to work with, the analyst has to accept whatever measures are available. Another reason is that the analyst wants to gather together the evidence on a wide array of outcomes, combining as many cases on each outcome as she can find, in order to report the evidence in one place under one conceptual umbrella.

Combining Results

There are three basic ways of combining data from different studies. One technique is to count up the number of studies that show positive results, the number that show no difference, and the number that show negative results. This vote counting was the earliest numerical technique used. It is a quick and relatively easy way of summarizing a great deal of information, and it has intuitive appeal. However, it does not make use of most of the original data, and even when it suggests whether a relationship exists in the data between receiving the program and having good outcomes, the procedure does not give an indication of the magnitude of the relationship. It also typically has low power to detect effects (Hedges, Laine, & Greenwald, 1994). Furthermore, by counting only the direction of the relationship, it doesn't attend to whether the original studies showed that the program was a roaring success or whether it barely squeaked into the positive column. Nor does it take account of different sample sizes, even though studies with large samples are more likely to show significant effects than small studies. What is good is that it takes account of the range of available studies, but it discards a large part of the evidence. Analysts currently recommend that it be used only when the original studies do not give enough information to use more sophisticated techniques.

A second technique of synthesis takes account of more of the available data and examines the significance level of the effects in the original evaluations. A significance level is the probability that relationships in the data (say, between a measure of program input and a measure of participant outcomes) are *not* the result of chance but represent a real relation. (Statisticians cavil with this definition and give a more accurate but much more complicated definition. For our purposes, this will serve.) Meta-analysis based on combining significance levels uses more of the information in the original studies than vote counting, and it is relatively easy to do if you know statistics. Typically the analyst looks at the significance of the relationship between a measure characterizing the program and a measure of outcome. As Hedges et al. (1994) write:

> A combined significance test is a way of combining statistical significance values (p values) from studies that test the same conceptual hypothesis but that use different designs ... or that may measure the outcome variables differently (e.g. standardized tests that differ in subject) to obtain an overall level of significance for the collection of studies under consideration. (p. 8)

When significance levels are the best data available, combining significance values is an acceptable option. But wherever possible, meta-analysts prefer to use it as an adjunct to more informative techniques.

The third procedure is to combine "effect sizes." An effect size is the magnitude of the relationship between two variables. The original evaluations frequently report effects in a variety of different ways—raw mean differences, standardized mean differences, correlation coefficients, regression coefficients, and many others. An example would be that the correlation found in one study between the average socioeconomic status of students and the likelihood of heterogeneous grouping in classes was -.15 (Lee & Smith, 1993). In meta-analysis, the analyst translates all the different measures into one standard metric. Once she has converted effect sizes into a common unit, she can pool and manipulate the data in much the way that evaluators and researchers analyze raw data in a regular study—by calculating means and analyzing variance in effect sizes across studies.

Advantages and Limitations

A major advantage of the meta-analytic enterprise is the ability to improve the estimate of outcomes of a particular type of program. By pooling information from many different evaluations, meta-analysis in effect increases the size of the sample and improves the precision of estimates of program effect. It also takes account of different realizations of the program and a range of different settings, participants, staffs, and historical periods. Thus, it improves both internal validity (the soundness of conclusions about the relationship between inputs and outcomes) and external validity (the generalizability of conclusions to other places and people).

Synthesis of evidence leads to a better estimate of the size of effects yielded by a particular type of program. The findings of any one evaluation typically show small program effects. If the sample of people studied is small, the results often fail to meet the level of statistical significance; if the sample studied is large, results of the same magnitude are more likely to be statistically significant. In either case, given the variability that different evaluations generally display, it is usually not obvious how seriously policymakers and practitioners should take the evidence. Meta-analysis brings a measure of precision and reliability to the enterprise. It helps to show whether observed changes, even if small, are real and consistent.

One of the unexpected outcomes of meta-analytic work has been to show that many kinds of social programs actually have beneficial effects. Although results of the original studies tended to be marginal and often not statistically significant, meta-analysis has frequently displayed positive cumulative outcomes. Lipsey and Wilson (1993) reviewed 302 meta-analyses of programs in mental health, psychotherapy/behavior modification, counseling (family, offenders, meditation, therapies), health-related psychological or educational treatments (e.g., for medical patients, biofeedback, treatment for pain), organizational interventions, education (e.g., computer-based instruction, audio and visual instruction, cooperative tasks, student tutoring, behavioral objectives), classroom organization, feedback to teachers, test taking, content-area instruction, preschool education, special education, language and bilingual instruction, teacher training, and other programs. Given the variability of results in the original studies, there has been considerable uncertainty about their effectiveness. In the analysis, all but 6 of the 302 programs showed positive effects, and the size of effects was often dramatic.

In the past a common evaluation finding was that the program made no significant difference. In fact, in 1985 Rossi posited a law of evaluation that said: "Only those programs that are likely to fail are evaluated.... [I]f a social program is effective, that characteristic is obvious enough and hence policy makers and others who sponsor and fund evaluations decide against evaluation" (cited in Shadish et al., 1991, p. 387). (Rossi has backed away from this statement in recent years.) But meta-analyses are disclosing strong patterns of positive results that can't be explained away as artifacts of meta-analytic techniques. The lack of significant effects in the original studies may well have been due to small sample sizes; meta-analysis in effect increases the sample size. It is yielding results that have important implications for practice and for policy.

Another advantage is that pooling results from a series of small studies that have already been completed is less costly than mounting one large study, and it has the additional advantage of increasing the range of conditions to which the results apply.

Meta-analysis also makes explicit the statistical reasons that may explain discrepancies in evaluation findings. According to Taveggia (1974), the outcome of each study can be viewed as a single data point in a distribution of data points. By the laws of probability, results are expected to be inconsistent. What appear to be contradictions can be seen as data from different points in a single distribution, including the positive and negative tails of the distribution. This is an explanation that may sing more sweetly to statisticians than to the policy community, but it is consistent with the logic of statistics and sampling theory.

But meta-analysis does not always achieve one important result that people looked forward to: the resolution of disputes about program outcomes and the arrival at consensus. A notable controversy between Hedges and others (Greenwald, Hedges, & Laine, 1996a, 1996b; Hedges et al., 1994) and Hanushek (1994, 1996, 1997) shows that meta-analyses, too, can lead to conflicting findings. Hedges and his colleagues and Hanushek have done several meta-analyses of the effects of educational spending on student achievement. To a large—but not total—extent they used the same body of studies. Yet because of different models and different statistics, they came out with divergent conclusions. Hanushek's analysis concluded that school inputs made no across-the-board difference in achievement, whereas Hedges and his colleagues concluded that higher inputs were related to better achievement.

Techniques of meta-analysis are still undergoing development, but even with new developments, meta-analysis will never be a paint-by-the-numbers procedure. As in all evaluation, the role of judgment remains central, and the possibilities for divergent findings endure.

Another concern sometimes voiced about evaluation synthesis is that the analyst is remote from the field. The first-level evaluator has more or less exposure to the day-to-day workings of the program; the meta-analyst almost inevitably has none. All she knows is what she reads in other people's reports—and, where possible, in the raw data. Any palpable sense of the program in action is lacking. The program is usually over, so there is not even a retrospective opportunity to see what went on. The analyst must depend for program knowledge on descriptions in evaluation documents. If these are sketchy or missing, she has to characterize the program as "an essentially nondescript variable" (Cronbach, 1982, p. 311).

Other criticisms, once plausible, have now generally been superseded by improvements in the craft. Meta-analysis used to lump studies together, usually without regard for the historical dimension. It combined evaluations done 20 years earlier with those just completed, and thus did not take account of the evolutionary development of this type of program over time. Now meta-analysts generally code the year of the study and enter the time of the evaluation into the analysis. Meta-analysis also tended to ignore program context. The nature of the program environment went unnoticed. Now whatever data the original studies contain about context (e.g., whether the program took place in a public sector, nonprofit, or private setting) are usually included in the analysis.

But meta-analysis is still limited by the intrinsic limitations of the original studies. If some of the evaluations included in the synthesis have incomplete data or inappropriate statistics or sparse descriptions of the program and its participants, the meta-analysis inherits the disabilities. One recourse is to contact the original authors to obtain further information.

Meta-analysis is a demanding craft. The analyst has to deal with many technical issues and make judgments about such questions as what to do about missing data, whether to eliminate outliers (i.e., studies whose results are much higher or much lower than all the others), what to do about programs that serve special categories of recipients (Hauser-Cram, 1983), and so on. As with other kinds of analysis, sophisticated knowledge of statistics is necessary.

Nevertheless, it has made considerable headway. The 1990s have seen marked development of "meta-evaluation for explanation" (Cook et al., 1992)—that is, the use of meta-analytic techniques to examine the association between specific program features and the direction and size of program effects. This kind of analysis extends the reach of the single study and shows how a wide variety of implementations affect program outcomes. Meta-analysis can also examine the relationship between the research features of the study and the direction and size of effects to find out whether evaluators' design decisions affect what they find out.

Statistical approaches to data synthesis have marked a real advance. Meta-analysts have made the review of the literature a research endeavor in its own right. They have adopted higher standards for question formulation, systematic collection of original studies, assessment of studies for inclusion, and analysis of data. In so doing, they have improved the craft, and the field keeps undergoing dynamic and enthusiastic development. Their work is yielding much important information about the efficacy of programs and policies.

Cost-Benefit and Cost-Effectiveness Analysis

Once an evaluation has answered questions about the process and outcomes of a program, another question can emerge: Is the program worth its cost? Even if outcomes are good, do the benefits outweigh the costs that the program incurs? This is the domain of economic analysis. It is familiarly known by the names of two of its common forms, cost-benefit and cost-effectiveness analysis.

The basic idea is to add up all the costs, not only direct expenditures but also indirect and intangible costs, and compare them with the value of program benefits. This is conceptually easy to imagine, but in practice, it is difficult to do.

Cost-benefit analysis was originally used as a prospective technique—to help decision makers decide among courses of action for the future. Inasmuch as the alternative policies and programs had not yet been implemented, there was little data on which to base assumptions about cost or benefit. The analyses were often based on assumptions that were stronger in logic than in data. Much economic analysis is still done as a prospective technique, to help people in decision-making positions consider the attractions of options for program and policy.

As programs and policies go into operation and as evaluation yields data on their outcomes, the comparisons of benefit and cost become more accurate. Without evaluation, cost-benefit analysts have to assume what program effects will be. Good evaluation data make the assessment of alternatives more persuasive. But inasmuch as the focus is on the future, many uncertainties exist, and many estimates and surmises enter in.

Categories of Efficiency Analysis

The whole field of analysis that relates the benefits of programs and policies to their costs is called economic analysis or efficiency analysis. Four subtypes can be identified. (1) *Cost-minimization analysis* seeks to find the least expensive way to accomplish some defined outcome. If the goal is to reduce alcohol-related automobile deaths, cost-minimization compares a range of policies that will presumably be effective in that regard and seeks the least expensive alternative. (2) *Cost-effectiveness analysis* compares the costs and consequences of different methods for achieving the same outcome. A cost-effectiveness analysis will look at several options of varying probable effectiveness, such as driver education, regulation of closing hours of bars and taverns, and increased police highway patrols, and compare the costs associated with each option in reaching the same level of reduction in deaths. (3) *Cost-benefit analysis* translates costs and consequences into the same metric, usually dollars, so that they can be expressed in a simple term, such as a ratio of benefits to costs. (4) *Cost utility analysis* adds the notion of utility—that is, the value or worth of a specific outcome for an individual or for society. It asks not only what it costs for alternative programs to extend a person's life by two years but also confronts the question of how much utility an increase in life has when it is accompanied by pain or disability (Drummond, Stoddart, & Torrance, 1987). Cost-utility analysis has given rise to measures like "healthy days of life" of "quality-adjusted life-years (QALY)." Quality adjustments give a lower value for years of life that are accompanied by morbidity or negative side effects (Johannesson & Jonsson, 1991). Although cost utility analysis is still controversial, it has become fairly common in health analyses.

The two most common forms in practice are cost-effectiveness and cost-benefit analysis. Cost-effectiveness analysis is "a truncated form of cost-benefit analysis that stops short of putting an economic value on ... outcomes of programs" (Klarman, 1982, p. 586). One overriding reason for not trying to put a monetary value on benefits is that it is exceedingly hard to decide what many social benefits are worth. What is it worth, for example, to teach a child to do math? To save a human life? To provide housing for a homeless person? There are certain cost savings that can be estimated, such as the cost of holding a student back a grade for an additional year and providing another student-year of schooling. But what is the worth of a student's feelings of competence and self-confidence, or a formerly homeless person's sense of reintegration into the social world? The difficulty of quantifying benefits such as these makes it more attractive to select a given level of achievement (say, passing grades in math) as the criterion and to compare alternative means for achieving that criterion level—that is, to do cost-effectiveness analysis.

A concept that is central to efficiency analysis is perspective. Every analysis has to be done from a particular perspective, whether the perspective is that of the individual, a specific institution, a target group for services, a federal department, the government's overall budget, or society at large (Drummond et al., 1987). Outcomes that are satisfactory from one perspective may look far different from another perspective. What is good for General Motors, to reverse a famous phrase, is not necessarily good for America.

The perspective that the analyst takes determines which items are to be considered costs and which are to be included as benefits. If the individual's perspective is taken, then the costs that count are only those that the individual pays for. Since most programs supply a large fraction of the inputs, often the individual's major cost is his time. Accordingly, since the costs are borne by some other entity, such as government, efficiency analyses that assume the individual's perspective tend to show higher net benefits than other analyses.

When the analysis assumes the perspective of the organization sponsoring the program, then the costs to the organization are its out-of-pocket expenditures and the forgone opportunities to do other things with its staff and facilities, and benefits include the grants that it receives from the government or foundations (as well as such intangible benefits as enhanced reputation or access to new clienteles). If a unit of government is the sponsor, then it will count as benefits all the monies it does not spend for other purposes. For example, if a training program reduces the amount of money it has to pay for welfare benefits, then welfare savings are a benefit. If city government installs a new system of street lighting and the lighting reduces crime, then benefits include the savings in police time, court processing, and correctional costs.

Probably most often analysts take the perspective of the whole society. This is the most comprehensive perspective but also the most complex. It has to take account of the consequences of the program for all groups in the society, including those who are not participants in its activities. From a societal perspective, moving costs from one function to another does not represent either a net cost or a net benefit. For example, farm price supports are both costs (to government) and benefits (to farmers) and so cancel each other out from a societal perspective.

Analysis from a societal perspective has to take an interest in the *distributional effects* of the program—that is, whether the program transfers resources from one segment of the society (say, taxpayers) to another segment (say, students in private schools, as in a school voucher program). The distributional consequences of policies and programs are not generally stated in quantitative terms, but they should be reported in text. Some consequences are less acceptable to a society than others.

An important feature of the perspective from which analysis is undertaken is that items that are costs in one perspective can be benefits in another. For example, stipends paid to program participants are a benefit from the participants' perspective but a cost to the program. So the analytic result—the difference between costs and benefits—will be different depending on the perspective taken.

All efficiency analysis has the useful feature of requiring attention not only to the program benefits that evaluation generally emphasizes but also to the costs, both expenditures and intangible costs that running a program incurs. It is sometimes easy for evaluators to forget that demonstration of a positive result, even one that is statistically significant and causally linked to the program, is not sufficient in itself to logically justify continuation of the program. The program may be so costly that costs exceed benefits, or alternative programs may achieve the same benefits at lower cost. So economic analysis is a useful conceptual corrective.

It is probably worth saying at the outset that although efficiency analysis is a logical follow-on from evaluation, it is a specialized craft that few evaluators have mastered. Undertaking a cost-benefit or cost-efficiency analysis gets quickly into highly technical areas about which controversy rages—well, if "rages" is too emotional a term for these arguments about quantification, controversy at least continues. So it is important to obtain expert assistance before going very far.

Some Key Terms

Before we go much further, key terms need to be defined:

> *Marginal cost:* If a program served only one individual, the cost would be astronomical. But when the program serves more people, costs are spread over many individuals. To serve one more individual costs less. That additional individual incurs the marginal cost. However, costs don't necessarily continue going down for every additional unit. Expansion of the program may call for more expensive recruitment strategies or bring in more disadvantaged cases; it may necessitate the recruitment of more staff and perhaps less qualified staff. The marginal cost (i.e., the incremental cost of serving an additional unit) has to be calculated from available data.
>
> *Average cost:* The average cost is the total cost of the program divided by the number of units served.

Discount rate: The discount rate is a correction factor introduced into the calculation of benefits and costs to account for the fact that people prefer to have money now. Future benefits are worth less, on the principle that a bird in the hand is worth two in the bush. Even if the bird in the bush is sure, it won't be available for some time, and therefore has lower value. Analogously, costs that have to be paid in the future are less onerous. To correct for lags in time, a discount rate is applied, something on the order of 4% or 5% a year, to calculate the current value of future amounts.

Estimating Costs

It would seem that the easy part of the analysis would be figuring out what it costs to run a program. And it is fairly easy to estimate direct costs—salaries, rent of facilities, supplies, and so on. But in order to do an inclusive accounting of direct costs, the analyst should define the pathways of delivering the service and examine all the resources consumed along the paths. It is important to remember that charges do not equal costs. For example, the value of the services provided by volunteers needs to be counted. So, too, does the cost of participants' transportation to the program site.

A basic concept of efficiency analysis is *opportunity cost*, the value of alternative activities that might have been undertaken with the same resources. It is the cost of things forgone. So part of the cost of a program is the value of participants' time that might have been spent on other endeavors. This would include, for example, the money they might be earning at work, but it also includes the value of their leisure time, time with their families, and time maintaining their households.

The simplest and therefore most common method of estimating the forgone opportunity for participants' time (i.e., what they might have done with their time if they had not been in the program) is to use prevailing wage rates. The assumption is that in the absence of the program they would have been earning wages. However, the procedure is not so defensible when the program deals with the very old, the very young, homemakers, the disabled, or other populations who either do not work or who earn considerably less than others. If they are not in the labor force or earn very little, the analysis seems to say that their time has little value. There is something ethically unsettling about such assumptions.

Opportunity costs, like all costs in efficiency analysis, are estimated by market prices wherever this is practicable. Sometimes, market prices are obvious, such as the cost of travel for staff and participants. But sometimes market prices require extensive calculation or are lacking, such as for the value of homemakers' time. In such cases, shadow prices are used. Shadow prices are estimates based on costs for analogous activities. Thus, homemakers' time is apt to be costed at the wage they could have earned if they were working. Where good experience has accumulated, shadow prices represent reasonable cost estimates, but sometimes they are little more than good guesses.

Other problems arise when costs are being projected into the future. The analyst may assume that costs will go down as the program learns to be more efficient through experience, or if it obtains economies of scale, or if it serves a larger population and so spreads costs over more participants. On the other hand, costs of continuing a program could increase. This would be likely, for example, if more difficult cases entered the program and required more intensive services.

Another problem in measuring costs arises when a program provides several services jointly and the analysis seeks to abstract the costs of just one component. A hospital, for example, might provide both in-patient and out-patient care, or both services and education. The same staff members often offer several kinds of service, and the same facilities and equipment are employed. In this kind of case, the analyst can generally calculate the marginal cost of adding an additional unit of service, although she has difficulty calculating the average cost of out-patient service alone.

In a work-site health education program, Erfurt, Foote, and Heirich (1991) conducted their analysis from the perspective of the companies providing the program. They included the costs of the health educator, wellness counselors, classes, and initial screening to identify employees with health risks. However, they did not include the costs associated with each site's wellness committee which was composed of representatives of labor, management, and the medical department; they did not include administrative or overhead costs for operating the program, or out-of-pocket costs of participating employees. Their report gives their reasoning for these inclusions and exclusions, so that others can consider how reasonable the claims are and what adjustments they would make in order to make the results more plausible to them.

Overhead costs are usually omitted in the calculation of costs, because of the difficulty of parceling them out and allocating them to one specific activity of an organization. Capital costs may or may not include depreciation of equipment. When a demonstration program is run, the costs are often greater than they would be for routine practice. Is the analyst justified in assuming a lower cost for a regular program? These are among the many judgments facing cost estimation.

Estimating Benefits

One of the challenges in efficiency analysis is deciding which benefits to include in the analysis. To make a program look good, it is obviously useful to include as many benefits as possible. In an analysis of a smoking-cessation program undertaken from the perspective of the firm sponsoring the program, the analysts included such benefits as reductions in absenteeism and disability and reduced costs for fire, life, health, and workers' compensation insurance (Weiss, Jurs, Lesage, & Iverson, 1984). Even with a success rate of 16% and counting employees' time off the job, the calculations showed substantial net benefits.

What is it reasonable to include in calculating benefits from the prevention of a case of drug abuse? Should the analyst include the increase in the participant's probable lifetime earnings, or these *plus* the costs saved to society for welfare payments, hospital treatment, police enforcement, incarceration in prison, injury to potential victims, and so on?

To move from evidence of outcomes to dollar benefits, analysts often posit theories of amazing grandeur. Translations of achievement test scores in grade school into increases in lifetime earnings make heroic assumptions: that raising a child's achievement by one grade in a short period has the same implications for future earnings as the completion of another grade in school; that test score gains will not erode with the passage of time; that the value of additional time spent in school can be inferred from census data on the average earnings of people with differing years of schooling. This last assumption may be particularly suspect, since there is ample evidence that years of schooling and earnings are both related to the antecedent factor of family social class (Rivlin, 1971). To ascribe earnings solely to schooling (and inferential schooling at that) ignores the importance of social class background on both variables.

Intangible benefits are always a problem. The ultimate example is the saving of a human life. If an automobile seat belt policy saves lives, what is each life worth? The analyst can look at jury awards for death in negligence or malpractice suits. The analyst can look at state legislatures' appropriations for compensation in cases of wrongful death or average life insurance amounts or other surrogate valuations. But obviously different sources will yield different amounts, and no consensus emerges. Some people even question the ethics of trying to turn a life into a monetary amount.

One interesting procedure for valuing intangible benefits is to ask people what they would be willing to pay for the particular benefit. The willingness-to-pay (WTP) procedure was developed in environmental economics as a means for measuring environmental benefits (Johannesson & Jonsson, 1991) and involves running a survey to pose the question of what people are willing to pay for a benefit. Obversely, the survey can ask how much money a respondent would be willing to accept to forgo a benefit. Some practitioners challenge the validity and reliability of willingness-to-pay surveys, and others worry that high-income respondents are willing to pay more for the same benefits. In practice, WTP methods have yielded as much as 200-fold differences in valuations of a human life (Luce & Elixhauser, 1990). Still, in some cases WTP enables the analyst to find a seemingly objective measure, or at least a measure other than his own estimate, for difficult-to-measure entities.

When monetarizing intangible benefits becomes too complex and difficult to justify, the analyst can shift to cost-effectiveness analysis, where a given level of outcome is used as the criterion (say, the saving of 20 lives) and alternative policies are compared in their costs for reaching that objective. However, cost-effectiveness analysis takes account of only one outcome, and many programs and policies bring about an array of outcomes. Ingenious schemes have been proposed for developing ratings scales and weighting schemes to combine outcomes, but each procedure involves more judgments and more challengeable assumptions.

Another bypass of the quantification problem is to report outcomes in their natural units—for example, number of students admitted to college or number of foster children returned to their natural parents. The decision-making community can consider the information and assign their own weights in arriving at policy choices.

Appropriate discount rates are another concern. Different analyses use different discount rates, and therefore lead to varying results. Some analysts recommend standardizing the discount rate across all analyses for purposes of comparability, but most analysts seek a true discount rate appropriate for the program or policy with which they are engaged. The consequence: another set of judgments.

When to Undertake Efficiency Analysis

Cost-benefit and cost-efficiency analysis raise the important issue of relation of program benefits to the investment that society (or an organization) makes in the program. It asks the kinds of questions that many policymakers need to raise: Are the outcomes worth what they cost? Can the same level of benefit be obtained at lower cost? Efficiency analysis is not a competitor to evaluation. It is a logical follow-on that takes program costs into account.

As noted, the technique is awash in judgments. With increasing experience many procedures are becoming standardized, but analysts still face issues of the perspective they should take, which costs and which benefits to consider, how costs and benefits should be measured, how they should be valued, what groups should be compared, and what discount rate should be applied. Depending on the answer to those questions, results can differ by orders of magnitude. Problematic assumptions are probably inevitable (Lewis, Johnson, Chen, & Erickson, 1992). Readers of cost-benefit and cost-efficiency analysis have to read the fine print.

Efficiency analysis makes good sense only if evaluation has found the program to be effective. It is fruitless to go through all the *sturm und drang* unless there is good reason to expect the program to yield positive returns. When evaluation has determined the *extent* of positive consequences, efficiency analysis is in a much better position. It also helps if outcomes can be readily translated into monetary terms. Training programs are probably the most often studied because it is relatively easy to calculate probable future earnings of successful trainees.

Cost-benefit and cost-efficiency analysis are also easier to conduct when program costs are separate from other organizational expenditures. If funding streams are intermingled, disentangling them introduces extra complexities into the estimation of costs.

In sum, efficiency analysis is a valuable method of study because it asks a vital question and marshals evidence systematically to answer the question: Do the program's benefits outweigh its costs? Efficiency analysis takes evaluative findings about program effectiveness and puts them into a larger framework, and in so doing, it provides information in a form that appeals to policymaking communities. However, efficiency analysis entails involved technical detail, which makes it the province of qualified analysts. It also entails extensive sets of judgments, which call for solid reasoning and careful explanation of the reasoning applied. The reader has to be able to understand how the analyst conducted the analysis, so he can decide how much credence to give it and whether, from his point of view, it represents an over- or underestimate of benefits, an over- or underestimate of costs, or whether in the words of Goldilocks and the Three Bears, it is "just right." Consumers of efficiency analysis also have to be educated to read reports carefully so that they understand all the assumptions built into the analysis and do not assume that one final figure represents the unvarnished truth.

Summary

This chapter has discussed three possible ways to enrich evaluation design. Replication is important. Repeated evaluations of a similar type of program help to crystallize the main direction of outcomes, establish the conditions under which the program is effective, and identify the limits to its effectiveness. However, when evaluations come up with divergent findings without being able to account for the discrepancies, they leave audiences perplexed. Into the breach comes meta-analysis.

Meta-analysis is a procedure for synthesizing the results of a body of evaluations. It essentially treats each study as a case in a "super-study" and analyzes study-level data like any other data with a variety of quantitative methods. In so doing, it can serve three purposes: reach conclusions about the overall effects of programs of a given kind, identify the conditions under which the program is more or less likely to be effective, and discover which if any research methods are associated with (and perhaps spuriously generating) better or poorer outcomes.

A main advantage of meta-analysis is its ability to improve estimates of program outcomes. One side benefit that has emerged is a finding that many social programs that the original evaluations found to have little if any positive effects in fact have significantly positive effects when their results are combined. This finding is a boost for program practitioners and for evaluators who are weary of being the bearers of bad tidings.

A limitation is that meta-analysis does not resolve all discrepancies. Meta-analysts can disagree. The procedure is so complex that different analysts, using different studies, models, and statistics, can still reach variant conclusions. Another limitation is that the meta-analyst must rely on the data in the original studies. If the original studies lack detailed descriptions of the program, use inappropriate statistics, and are riddled with missing data, meta-analysis falls heir to the problems.

Nevertheless, meta-analysis is making considerable headway. It is giving single-program evaluations the opportunity for a second career. It is leading to the discovery of important effects. As its procedures undergo continued improvement, it promises to be an increasingly useful addition to the evaluation repertoire.

Economic (or efficiency) analysis adds a further dimension. It examines the costs of a program and compares them to the benefits the program produces. Cost-benefit analysis and cost-effectiveness analysis are the two most common forms of efficiency analysis. While their logic is easy to comprehend, conducting the analyses is technically challenging. As is true of other modes of evaluation, judgment calls have to be repeatedly made.

Efficiency analysis uses evaluative evidence of outcomes to estimate program benefits. On the cost side, it includes not only direct outlays for the program but also indirect costs and opportunity costs (i.e., opportunities that were given up in order to run and participate in the program).

Efficiency analysis asks vital questions: Do the program's benefits outweigh its costs? What does it cost to reach a given level of effectiveness? It mobilizes evidence to answer these questions and provides answers in a language that appeals to many members of the policy community. But audiences have to learn not to take the dollar numbers as gospel. They should read reports carefully and understand the assumptions built into the analysis. When viewed with an appropriate dose of skepticism, cost-benefit and cost-effectiveness analysis provide valuable conclusions about program pay-offs.

11

QUALITATIVE METHODS

Society needs less to be told what it is doing wrong than to be shown what it is
really doing.

—Lester Ward (1918)

Our main goal is to connect the traditions of what are conventionally denoted
"quantitative" and "qualitative" research by applying a unified logic of inference
to both.... The same underlying logic provides the framework for each research
approach.

—Gary King, R. O. Keohane, and Sidney Verba (1994)

The most striking development in evaluation in recent years is the coming of age of
qualitative methods. Where once they were viewed as aberrant and probably the
refuge of those who had never studied statistics, now they are recognized as valuable additions to the evaluation repertoire. Qualitative methods accomplish evaluative tasks that were previously done poorly or entirely scanted.

It took a long time for qualitative researchers to achieve recognition. They
waged an uphill struggle against the quantitative establishment in evaluation. Their
writings were often argumentative and strident as they strove to gain legitimacy.
They are now comfortably ensconced in the evaluation field, although to judge by
recent articles, some of them continue to see themselves as underappreciated under-
dogs. I for one see them as full partners in evaluation, with very special contributions to make.

This chapter discusses several styles of qualitative evaluation, ranging from
the long-term in-depth immersion that characterizes ethnography to intermittent
short-term spells of informal interviewing. I mention data sources, strategies of
analysis, and ethical issues that are particularly pungent when the evaluator is a
longtime inhabitant of the program scene.

Qualitative research studies people and events in their own context. As Kirk and Miller (1986) write, qualitative research "fundamentally depends on watching people in their own territory" (p. 9). It maintains a holistic approach, not abstracting individual variables for study but seeking to understand the whole interaction within its natural setting.

Some people write about qualitative methods as though they were all of a piece. But there are many varieties, and they differ from each other as much as controlled experiments differ from interview surveys. Some are intensive and time-consuming; others can be used in short-term low-investment studies. What they have in common is that they rely on words and narrative rather than counts and statistical analysis.

In Chapter 4, I discussed the advantages and disadvantages of qualitative evaluation. In a nutshell, the following are the main advantages:

Greater awareness of the perspective of program participants, and often a greater responsiveness to their interests

Capability for understanding dynamic developments in the program as it evolves

Awareness of time and history

Special sensitivity to the influence of context

Ability to enter the program scene without preconceptions or prepared instruments, and to learn what is happening

Alertness to unanticipated and unplanned events[1]

General flexibility of perspective

Design of Qualitative Evaluations

The qualitative evaluator usually enters the program scene with a sense of openness and receptivity to experience. But she does not go in unprepared. She begins the evaluation with an understanding of the questions that the study is expected to address and a knowledge of the key issues surrounding the program. She has at least the rudiments of a study design and has to develop it further.

To talk of the research design of a qualitative study sounds to some like an oxymoron. These people think that the researcher goes in, watches and talks to people, and figures out what to do next. The design, in this view, is visible only after the study is over.

In some qualitative studies, that is indeed the case. But evaluation studies are commissioned with an end in view. Study sponsors want to know something. The evaluator is usually asked to address a given set of issues or, if she has more independence, has had to specify in advance which issues she plans to pursue. Moreover, evaluations usually run on a strict time schedule and often with limited funds, and they cannot afford a leisurely pace or a totally improvisational style of work. Under the circumstances, the evaluator needs a plan.

---

[1]William Foote Whyte (1984), one of the outstanding anthropological researchers of the past 50 years, quotes Joshua Lederberg, a biomedical scientist and then-president of Rockefeller University, on the subject of research: "Research has to be opportunistic because you don't know what you are going to discover. The things you discover may not be the things you set out to do" (p. 20).

Which sites will she go to? How long will she (or her team) stay at each site? Which people will she talk to? About how many people in which positions is she likely to need to interview? Which kinds of activities will she try to observe? What central question does she intend to answer, and what kind of information does she need to answer it?

Her choices of design are roughly similar to those discussed in Chapters 8 and 9—after-only, before-and-after, before-and-after with comparison group, and so on. However, in qualitative evaluation, the main emphasis is generally on the "during" phase, as in "before-during-during-after." Its comparative advantage is its ability to make sense of things as they happen and to begin analysis while events are still in progress.

If the evaluator has a good deal of information about the program or about other programs of the same type, she may be able to narrow in on design issues fairly fast. Although she will not settle all matters up front, she can make general plans. For example, she can decide the basis on which to choose the site or sites she will study. When she is evaluating a multi-site program, she has a number of choices. She might select sites randomly, but since she will usually be able to study only a few sites, that is rarely a preferred choice. She can seek to locate representative sites. That strategy often has good pay-off. She can sample for maximum diversity in order to understand the full range of experience within the program. Or she can first study what she believes is a typical case and follow that investigation with a site that she thinks will differ drastically; such a strategy will show the limits of the conclusions reached in the first case. Some mix of typical sites with discrepant or exceptional sites will provide a basis both for indicating variations in program experience and for qualifying the conclusions that would be reached if only typical sites were studied.

Miles and Huberman (1994) list 16 types of sampling methods that can be employed. They include *opportunistic sampling,* taking advantage of opportunities that open up; *convenience sampling,* going to the sites that are easiest to get to and perhaps have the most cooperative staffs; and *snowball sampling,* starting with one site and learning from people there which other sites would be relevant to the study and continuing to use new information to select the later sites.

Some evaluation sponsors are interested in finding out whether a particular program model *can* work under exceptionally good conditions. They therefore want to sample exemplary cases—that is project sites that have a reputation for excellent operation. There may be a tinge of self-servingness in this approach. The agency may want to show itself and its grantees in the best possible light. But there are also good reasons to inquire whether a particular program approach has the capability of succeeding, given the right context and talent. Sampling on the basis of quality or reputation is therefore another strategy.

Silverman (1993) suggests that even if the researcher is limited to one site, she should get information describing the population of sites and explicitly compare the site she studies to the whole set of sites. A comparison with other sites enables the evaluator to locate her project within the distribution of projects, and it resolves concerns about the representativeness of the site studied.

Perhaps the most important advice in selecting sites is to have a careful and explicit justification for the choice. There should be theoretical grounds for choosing particular locations over others. Since qualitative evaluation does not have the large samples common to quantitative approaches, the evaluator has to make sure that she deploys her resources to the places where she will learn the most. But qualitative evaluation also has the advantage of being able to shift course in midstream. If one site proves uninformative, or if exciting new events develop elsewhere, she can capitalize on new information and move the site of her data collection or expand to additional sites.

The evaluator also has to decide whom to talk to. How much attention should she give to opinions and experiences of administrators, of staff, of recipients, and of people outside the program? She can decide *who* is the best source for *which* kind of data. She can allot her time according to the primacy of the information each group is likely to give and make at least a rough approximation of how many people she will talk to. She needs to decide the basis on which she will select informants and respondents (to seek a wide range, by following cues from previous informants, to represent a specified set of positions or roles, etc.). Guba and Lincoln (1989) suggest selecting for maximum variation so that the broadest possible scope of information is collected. As in the choice of sites, different criteria jostle for attention. The evaluator needs to think the issues through. Again she has the advantage of flexibility and can add new respondents as she learns more.

Resources and time schedules for the evaluation will largely determine how long she can stay in the field, whether she will do sustained fieldwork spending months at a single site or whether her work in the field will be transitory. Depending on types of questions to be studied and resources available, she can provisionally decide to spend one day at the project site every week, or spend two weeks there at the beginning, middle, and end of the project, or whatever frequency makes sense. Many large qualitative evaluations visit sets of sites every 6 to 12 months and spend perhaps a week at each doing interviewing and observation. In the interim, they keep in touch by phone and fax.

Another design issue is the time period for observation and interviewing. If she is studying school programs, for example, she needs to understand the school calendar. Some seasons are good for observing classrooms and talking with teachers. Other times are scheduled for school holidays, administration of standardized tests, class trips, major assemblies, staff development activities, and so on. The evaluator has to work around the program calendar.

Although this is not general practice, the qualitative evaluator can decide to include control sites—that is, sites that do not offer the program although similar to program sites in other respects. Such a design is likely to be especially relevant when the evaluation is dealing in program outcomes, rather than process alone. There is no reason why the qualitative evaluator cannot adopt design options that have stood quantitative evaluators in good stead. The important point is that the design be appropriate for the questions that are being addressed and the purposes that the evaluation is expected to serve.

All the initial choices are subject to change as the qualitative evaluator learns more about is happening. But the more specific are the questions the study is addressing, the more useful is thoughtful planning in the early weeks and months.

For all kinds of design choices, there are benefits in carefully specified criteria and systematic design. The well-planned study will have more comprehensive coverage and be more credible. Audiences are likely to have more faith in evaluation findings when the evaluator has made an effort to sample with system and consistency and can justify the choices she has made.

Collecting Data

All types of qualitative inquiry are not the same. The qualitative field encompasses a range of different traditions and methods of investigation. I give a brief overview here, but my account of methods is stubbornly practical and omits the rich philosophical and theoretical premises that underlie them. In a following section, "But More Than That...," I give a glimpse of the world view that generally animates qualitative approaches.

As we will see in a later part of the chapter, qualitative methods can be combined with quantitative approaches, often with good effect. Just as a combination of data collection strategies within a single tradition provides benefits, with the strengths of one compensating for the weaknesses of another, so qualitative and quantitative approaches can prop up each other's frailties and contribute their own special advantages.

Ethnography

The prototypical qualitative method is ethnography. Ethnography is the approach that anthropologists use in studying a culture, whether on a remote Samoan island or among large-city police. Anthropologists usually spend a long time in the field, participating in activities with the people whom they are studying, observing what they do, talking with them about what they think and mean, and over time coming to absorb the norms and ideas of their subjects. Some of the classics of American social science of the past 60 years are ethnographic studies, among them *Street Corner Society* by William Foote Whyte (1955), *The Urban Villagers* by Herbert Gans (1962), and Elliot Liebow's *Tally's Corner* (1967).

Ethnographic methods make heavy demands on the researcher. They require a willingness to suspend all that one believes in an effort to see the world through other people's eyes. They require a firm grasp on methods, from the initial conceptualization of the project and the negotiation of entry into the site to the analysis and interpretation of the vast quantities of information collected. There are also heavy time demands, as the ethnographer immerses herself in the local environment and culture. Ethnography is not a part-time diversion. When you read the books that ethnographers have written about their experiences in the field, such as Whyte's *Learning From the Field* (1984), Rosalie Wax's *Doing Fieldwork: Warnings and Advice* (1971), or Van Maanen's *Tales of the Field* (1988), you gain an appreciation of the intellectual, social, and physical demands that they must meet.

Ethnographic methods have been used in a number of evaluations. For example, Logsdon et al. (1988) used ethnography to study the implementation of a parent-child activities project in a low-income elementary school. They found that although teachers were positive about the worth of the activities, the distribution and collection of materials represented one more thing to do, and the activities did not connect directly to the curriculum. Some of the students, realizing that the materials were external to the school and did not represent teachers' assignments, did not take them seriously. Many parents were enthusiastic about the activities, but their responses were so much more positive than the rate of return of the completed materials that the evaluators discounted them.

In a national ethnographic evaluation of a program for dropouts and potential dropouts, Fetterman (1988) reports an extensive system of observation and review of written records. Two-week visits were made to each program site every three months, usually by two-person teams, for a period of three years. Fetterman's evaluation also makes use of quantitative data on such variables as staff terminations, student graduations from the program, and their subsequent college attendance and employment. The ethnographic data elaborate and explain the quantitative indicators. One finding, for example, was that failure of staff to enforce rules regarding lateness and proper dress contributed to repeated student tardiness and absences and led to inappropriate apparel for the workplace (p. 270).

Participant-Observation

Similar to ethnography but drawn from a different set of theoretical principles, participant-observation is just what it sounds like: observation of a scene by a researcher who takes part in the activities and events. She engages in the activities that she is studying, but her first priority is the observation. Participation is a way to get close to the action and to get a feel for what things mean to the actors. It provides an occasion for small talk and gossip with real participants and other windows into the meaning of the happenings being observed. It gives the participant-observer a tangible sense of what it is like to be a policeofficer on the narcotics squad or a single parent in public housing or a clerk in the motor vehicle bureau. She learns from direct as well as vicarious experience.

Participant-observation can be a long-term technique, or it can be used for a shorter period of time. But it can't be a hit-and-run operation like interviewing. The researcher has to stay long enough to earn acceptance and trust from the permanent players if she expects to learn things that are not obvious on casual inspection. Perhaps a short involvement in a methadone maintenance center or a court mediation program is enough to give a researcher material to write about, but for responsible evaluation of a program, a measure of time is needed.

The participant-observer does not usually whip out her notebook on the spot, just as an ethnographer does not. She is wary of calling the attention of others to her dual loyalties—to the group and to her research. She often wants others to see her as one of them, so that they level with her about their beliefs and feelings. After an observation, she tries to get to a private place quickly so she can take notes before she loses the flavor of the happening with all its emotional aura.

Observation

Another technique, not the opposite of participant-observation but an alternative to it, is nonparticipant-observation. The nonparticipant comes to the site with no intention of taking part in events. Perhaps a program serves a population that she cannot blend into, such as members of the military. Perhaps the events she wants to know about are illegal or immoral, such as gang activities, and the researcher doesn't want any truck with them. Or perhaps her experience is so foreign to what is happening that group members would not want her to try to participate. This exclusion is often true when she is literally foreign to the culture. In any case, she arrives with the explicit intent of observing. By remaining in contact with the group over an extended time, she gradually comes to be familiar. Members of the group forget about her research purpose and go about their business much as they would if she were not there. At least she hopes so.

Observational techniques enable the researcher to gather information that often would be unavailable by other means. Members of the group might not be likely to talk about activities for any of a number of reasons. They might not want outsiders to know what they were doing. They might be wary of threat if word leaked out. Or they might be so accustomed to the group and its culture that they took it for granted as the way things are; they would have no sense of perspective on its activities and could not articulate what made it distinctive. Or they might lack the self-awareness or the linguistic gifts to describe and explain. Observational techniques let the researcher see for herself, and into the bargain she gets palpable experience of what the world is like for the people she is studying. David Cohen (1988) sat in a classroom (at a student-sized desk) day after day, week after week, to watch a teacher, to whom he gave the pseudonym of Mrs. Oublier, implement a new science curriculum.

Observational techniques can be short term as well. A researcher or evaluator can go into a department store and watch a salesman fresh from a training program try to put his new learnings into practice. An evaluator can observe what participants do at a senior citizen center or in a juvenile court. She will take careful field notes, just as the ethnographer and participant-observer do, and she will continuously describe and analyze the meaning of what she is seeing. She is interested in describing events and understanding their meaning in the unique context.

Informal Interviewing

Along with all the observational procedures goes conversation with the people on the scene. Part of the advantage of hanging out is being able to talk to people as things happen. But interviewing can be done as a stand-alone technique, too. The evaluator, after locating relevant people to talk to (more about locating people later), gains their agreement for an informal interview.

The qualitative interview doesn't rely much on pre-formed structured questions, as does the survey interview that quantitative researchers use. Rather, the interviewer has a general sense of what she wants to find out from the person—and maybe one or two items that she wants to ask everybody in the same way in order to have comparable information. She usually starts out the study with some general questions to orient her to the situation, and as she goes along and learns more, she hones more specific questions.

Generally she will ask different questions of different people for several reasons. For one thing, respondents have different sorts of information. A program manager knows about relations with the national office. An old-time employee will know the history of the agency. An intake worker will know about the criteria that are actually being used to accept clients into the program. She capitalizes on the unique perspective that each person brings.

With qualitative methods the interviewer doesn't necessarily stick to the topic she began with. In the course of the conversation the respondent may tell her something that she realizes is of vital importance to the study, maybe something the evaluator had not heard before. At that point she is likely to put aside her earlier plans and follow up on the new information. She will ask the person to tell her everything he knows about it, and she will probe with further nondirective questions ("And what happened then? Who else was there?") until she has heard the story in the respondent's own words.

The qualitative evaluator on occasion tape-records the interviews and has them transcribed for further analysis. More often she takes notes during the interview, writing down the main points of the discussion and using the respondent's own words when possible. As soon afterward as she can, before her memory dims, she fills in much of the rest of the interview. Separately she also notes her reactions to the interview and her ideas or conjectures about the meaning of what was said. The elaborated field notes become a main form of qualitative data.

The interviewer attends not only to the respondent's words but to nonverbal cues as well, such as facial expressions and body language—for example, the way the respondent covers his mouth or glances away when discussing a particular subject. I remember doing an interview with a colleague who was a nurse by training. After the interview, she said to me, "When we asked him about X, did you see the way the pupils of his eyes dilated?" It had never occurred to me to look at the pupils of anyone's eyes. The qualitative interviewer is sensitive to the physical setting, too. In a respondent's home, she looks at the furnishings and pictures on the walls; in a classroom, she notes the ways that desks and chairs are arranged. These observations become part of the field notes.

Informal interviewing aims to get the respondent's story from his own unique perspective. The interviewer does not suggest answers or answer categories. She lets the respondent talk about the situation in his own words and at his own pace. *Probing* is the key technique—that is, asking further open-ended questions to pursue a topic, until the interviewer believes she has learned what she needs to know. If she gets more information later from someone else, she can come back to the first respondent and ask further questions.

Sometimes the interviewer will receive conflicting reports from different people she talks to. In such a case, she may decide to confront them with the contradictory account. "You told me that nurses never turn on the XYZ equipment without a doctor's order, but nurses in Maternity say they do that all the time. How is that?" The interviewer does not inject her own opinions on what is good and right, but she does try to make sense of what she is hearing.

Informal interviewing can be an iterative process. The interviewer can keep collecting information until she believes she understands the situation. Then, especially in evaluation studies, she may leave the scene until time comes for a follow-up. She may return several times during the course of the program and then again after the conclusion of the program for several further rounds of data collection.

Focus Groups

The focus group is a technique that was developed in market research to learn about consumers' reactions to a new product or service. It has been successfully acclimated to social science and evaluation research (see Chapter 7). Its basic feature is that a number of people are brought together, and the researcher raises a question for them to discuss. The focus group allows the researcher or evaluator to observe the cross-talk and interactions in the group.

Group process can be illuminating. For example, staff members at a juvenile detention facility may tell an interviewer about the democratic climate and egalitarian relationships among the staff. During the course of focus-group discussion, on the other hand, the researcher may observe that everyone defers to the assistant director; when he speaks, no one contradicts him. The focus group provides the researcher with a mini-organization to observe. Even though it is an artificial and short-lived organization, it provides a window onto interactions and relationships.

Furthermore, in the course of focus-group discussion, participants will often voice divergent sentiments or different versions of the facts of the case. Sometimes they will attempt to resolve the discrepancies among themselves. The evaluator can observe what the disagreements are and what the basis is for the differences. She will see how participants go about resolving them, and, of course, she will learn what resolution they come to. The procedure may effectively reconcile differences, or if it does not, it illuminates the fault lines along which differences persist.

The focus-group technique is good at stimulating interaction and revealing the nature of public discourse and representation, probably better than the individual interview. It is not as effective in tapping individuals' personal beliefs, attitudes, or even their idiosyncratic interpretations of experience. Focus groups probably work better when participants are relatively equal and not involved in hierarchical work relationships. Equals are more comfortable talking to each other and less likely to censor their statements. But when work relationships are central to the evaluation, the evaluator can organize a hierarchical focus group; then she has to interpret the data in light of the constraints imposed by the members' ongoing relationships.

Documents

Another source of data is the documentary material that programs inevitably generate—laws, regulations, proposals for funding, contracts, correspondence, minutes of meetings, reports, brochures for the public, and similar offshoots of program operation. Reading through the archives can be deadly, but for certain kinds of questions, documents are a good place to search for answers. They provide a useful check on information gathered in interviews. Also, when other techniques fail to resolve a question, documentary evidence can provide a convincing answer.

A major advantage of documents is that they were written contemporaneously with the events they chronicle, and thus are not subject to memory decay or memory distortion. A main disadvantage is that they were written for other purposes. For example, an application for funding was written to impress the potential funder with the merit of the program and to mask its problems. Minutes of a meeting were written to record decisions taken, not reveal disagreements or frictions among attendees nor, necessarily, to mention issues on the agenda about which no agreement could be reached. As historians know, contemporary documents have to be read with their original purposes and intended audiences in mind. Nor are documents necessarily complete. All kinds of mishaps can intrude, from absent secretaries to agency self-censorship. Not infrequently, archival material is missing, because files are lost, misplaced, or discarded. Few people have an interest in maintaining a record for the record's sake.

Extracting information from documents can be a qualitative operation. It can also be done in quantitative fashion, by categorizing data items, coding, and counting. In qualitative evaluation, the description and analysis of documentary material follow much the same rules as analysis of other narrative accounts.

Other Techniques for Collecting Information

Much other material can be drawn upon in evaluation. Physical evidence, the signs and artifacts that people leave behind, can offer insights. Sometimes newspaper stories provide pieces of the puzzle. Quantitative researchers may do a content analysis of news stories, using procedures of coding and counting. Qualitative researchers will use them much as they do other documents. In evaluations of classroom projects, children's drawings, essays, or homework papers can give relevant information. Photographs and pictures are sometimes illuminating (Bogdan & Biklen, 1992, pp. 101–104; Harper, 1994). In odd cases, the evaluator can draw on letters (Kirkup, 1986) and journals and biographies (Smith & Kleine, 1986). The qualitative evaluator should think creatively about where significant information might reside and then follow its tracks. Then she will use techniques of description, analysis, and interpretation to make sense of the information for evaluative purposes.

Case Study

People sometimes talk about qualitative studies as case studies. Unless we want to blanket all qualitative research under the label of case study, it is hard to think of a case study as a particular design. Rather, it is a way of organizing data so as to keep the focus on the totality. It tries to consider the interrelationships among people, institutions, events, and beliefs. Rather than breaking them down into separate items for analysis, the case study seeks to keep all elements of the situation in sight at once. The watchword is *holistic.*

Yin (1994, p. 13) defines the case study as an empirical inquiry that investigates a phenomenon in a natural setting when the boundaries between the phenomenon and its context are not clear, using multiple sources of evidence. There can even be quantitative case studies, such as the study of organizational dynamics through use of psychometric scales. The defining feature is the exploration of complex real-life interactions as a composite whole.

But More Than That ...

I have listed a number of techniques and information sources that qualitative evaluators use in their work. But qualitative approaches to evaluation are more than a collection of techniques. Embedded in the qualitative framework are a number of assumptions about reality, about human groups and organizations, about research, knowledge, and evaluation.

The most basic assumption in most of these approaches is that the researcher seeks to understand experience from the perspectives of participants in the action. Experiences may be different for different actors, and differing cultural and occupational groups will have their unique take on events. So the researcher does not aim for a single version of the truth but rather for a carefully modulated account of events as seen from multiple points of view. She may see her job *not* as adjudicating among participants' competing versions but as understanding the contexts in which participants are situated and the way in which these contexts give rise to divergent accounts (Silverman, 1993).

Some modes of qualitative inquiry adopt a constructivist orientation. Constructivism has many faces, but in a common guise, it questions whether there is such a thing as a real reality out there. Evaluators who accept constructivist ideas suggest that everybody constructs his own vision of the world. The reason we think there is a single hard reality is that we have been socialized to accept a common interpretation of experience. In fact, each person sees different facets of events, experience, and the world.

If there is no single reality, then the validity of an evaluation cannot be assessed by its correspondence with reality. The evaluation has to represent the varied interpretations of the multiple actors on the scene. The evaluator cannot reach "conclusions" but can only develop her own view of the program out of her many-sided inquiry. She then has to negotiate her view with program actors who have their own claims, concerns, and views. In this tradition, the evaluator's aim should be to develop a joint construction of the program based on consensus among stakeholders (Guba & Lincoln, 1989; Kirkup, 1986; Reinharz, 1981).

In place of validity as a criterion for a successful evaluation, these qualitative evaluators offer different criteria. They speak of authenticity, which is rooted in the fairness of open discussion. They speak of credibility and illumination. They mention responsibility to the needs and values of the program.

On the other hand, there are qualitative researchers who pay considerable attention to validity in the traditional sense (Kirk & Miller, 1986; Maxwell, 1992; Silverman, 1993), and provide useful discussions about ways to think about and try to ensure it. In their view, qualitative work remains within the domain of science, and it must seek to reach responsible conclusions that other researchers can replicate.

Adherents of qualitative approaches characterize their methods in a host of impressive and often poetic terms. Qualitative methods are collaborative, interactive, hermeneutic, intuitive (Guba & Lincoln, 1988), authentic, illuminative (Parlett & Hamilton, 1976), responsive (Stake, 1986), improvisational (Agar, 1986), meaningful (Kirkup, 1986), naturalistic (Hammersley & Atkinson, 1983), holistic, humanistic (Maxwell et al., 1986). These terms, for all their variety, highlight several additional features.

One certainly is interest in collaboration with the people who are the "subjects" of the study. Qualitative evaluators tend to abhor the notion of subjects. Most of them, but not all, want their studies to empower people on the scene, to give them voice and expression, to represent *their* knowledge and beliefs as well as those of the evaluator. There is also a concern with the effects of evaluation reports on the lives of people studied and a desire, as in the Hippocratic Oath in medicine, to "first do no harm."

These evaluators uphold humanistic values. They want their work to advance their beliefs in egalitarianism and justice (House, 1990). They are uncomfortable with the usual arrangements that seem to give the evaluator a large measure of control over the fate of program staff and program recipients. They want the study process itself to be microcosm of a fairer society, with everyone involved being accorded respect and dignity, and with everyone having a say about the conceptualization and conduct of the evaluation. They seek to level the playing field and move toward equality of influence over the evaluation report. Since there is no single truth, all perspectives deserve a hearing, and everyone's construction should be represented.

This characterization is a broad-brush outline of the belief structure underlying much qualitative research and evaluation, but it does not by any means apply to all. Within the qualitative tradition, voices are raised against turning over to others the evaluator's responsibility to derive meaning from her study. The evaluator has knowledge and skills, and a resolute focus on the study, that the other people involved almost always lack. Some qualitative evaluators object to substituting the explanations offered by respondents for the evaluator's own analysis. There is also strenuous objection to the unremitting relativism of the extreme constructivist position.

Nor should these descriptions of the qualitative orientation set up a stereotypical contrast with quantitative evaluation. Probably most quantitative evaluators also have a deep concern for the people they study and hold abiding humanistic values. The profession of evaluation tends to attract people who want to do research that advances the lot of people in need. And as we will see later in the chapter, many evaluators combine qualitative and quantitative methods in their studies. So the notion that qualitative and quantitative evaluators inherently line up in opposing camps is not only exaggerated but misguided.

Fieldwork and Analysis

The procedures of qualitative evaluation begin with negotiating entry to the site, making contacts with people, and gathering data. The evaluator takes extensive notes of the information that she learns through observation, interviewing, casual conversations, and other data collection procedures. These field notes are the stuff of qualitative work. She usually adds her own impressions of each interview and each observation to the record. At irregular intervals she records emerging ideas and insights about the meaning of the information. Thus, she begins analyzing data as she collects it and continues analysis on an ongoing basis. Basically, the job is to find the main themes in the data, to see where the evidence leads. The aim is to gain an understanding of what is happening and why it is happening.

To corroborate information she obtains from different sources, she triangulates the data. Triangulation is a cross-check through different modes of inquiry. If interviews, observations, and documents agree, the evaluator gains confidence that the information is right. It is usually assumed that the different data collection methods are biased in different ways, and if they agree, the evidence is strong, and if they don't fully agree, their idiosyncratic biases will cancel each other out. Combining them in a thoughtful way will lead to a more authentic story. However, all methods of inquiry may incorporate similar biases, and in this circumstance triangulation does not necessarily move to a more illuminating story. Where the evaluator encounters discrepancies, she will want to look searchingly at the sources of disagreement and probably undertake further investigation.

Over time, she develops increasingly firm hunches, or what quantitative researchers might call hypotheses, about the meaning of the data. She reviews the information she has collected to see how well it supports her hunches and where and how often the ideas are contradicted. She modifies the hypotheses to accommodate the discrepant information, qualifying some of her earlier hunches and extending others. In order to increase the validity of her conclusions, she then goes out of her way to try to disprove the hypotheses. She purposely looks for information that would tend to disconfirm them. If her insights hold up under this kind of test, she has a sense that she is on the right track.

Toward the end of the study, she will analyze and interpret all the information she has collected. Having collected stacks of interviews, tapes, abstracts of documents, observational records, and field notes, the evaluator has to figure out what it all means. As the recent crop of books on analysis of qualitative data (e.g., Miles & Huberman, 1994; Silverman, 1993; Strauss, 1987; Strauss & Corbin, 1990; Wolcott, 1994) make clear, this is no trifling task.

In recent years, computer programs have been developed to help in the analysis of qualitative data. Narrative transcripts are entered into the program, and the analyst can sort the data in a variety of ways. She can organize segments of the data by theme, by respondent type, by event, etc., without losing sight of the larger context in which the data are embedded. Weitzman and Miles (1995) have written a helpful sourcebook about the relative advantages of different computer programs for qualitative analysis.

When the time comes to write the report, some qualitative evaluators believe that they should negotiate its content with the people in the program. They feel a sense of responsibility toward the people they study and an obligation to consult with them on interpretation of results and presentation of conclusions. If they seek to reach a *consensus* about the description, interpretation, and implications of the study, they have to be prepared for lengthy negotiations. The resulting account will probably be richer and more illuminating, but there is likely to be a time lag before the report is ready for release. However, if controversy continues and consensus cannot be reached, there is a temptation to eliminate the topic from the report. Such exclusion would represent a loss of information and insight, even a kind of censorship by those who refuse to reach a reasonable accommodation. It is better to present variant views and try to explain the context and meaning structure from which the different interpretations arise.

Near the end of a study the evaluator may face a major uncertainty in interpretation. She may have come to certain explanations on the basis of the data, but outspoken participants disagree with her interpretation. Or she may be undecided in her own mind about what to make of contradictory accounts or changes over time that veer off the expected trajectory. For example, a nutrition program seemed to be going well for a long time and then abruptly fell into decline without any plausible explanation. The evaluator can call upon people at the site to help her craft new insights. They may assist her in understanding facets of the situation that eluded her earlier. Or she can capitalize on the flexibility of qualitative approaches and undertake new investigation. Just as in quasi-experimental designs for quantitative study, the strategy is to rule out plausible rival interpretations of the data. She can pursue inquiries of specific issues to find out whether alternative interpretations are more or less convincing.

Engaged as it is with participants, qualitative evaluation tends to take a participant-eye view of the dissemination of study results. Sometimes qualitative evaluators interpret *participants* to refer only to program managers, project directors, and staff. They are concerned about the possible harm the evaluation reports can do to the interests of staff (e.g., Simons, 1989) and therefore take a gingerly approach to reporting shortcomings. They pay less attention to whether clients are receiving the best and most relevant help for their needs as they interpret them. But some qualitative evaluations take account of the perspectives and interests of clients as well.

The longer the evaluator spends in fieldwork, the stronger her sense of responsibility to participants is apt to be. Although a few qualitative evaluators try to behave in much the same detached way as do quantitative evaluators, on the whole the qualitative approach values its involvement in the field perspective and its engagement with the point of view of the people studied.

Qualitative evaluators are likely to report periodically and iteratively to program people to keep them abreast of what the evaluation is finding out. They may also play an active role in disseminating the report to those in higher positions who make decisions about the program, so that staff will derive real benefits from the study.

In reporting and disseminating study findings, the evaluator aims to transmit to others a palpable description and interpretation of program experiences and their meanings to participants. By using stories of actual events, dramatic episodes, and respondents' own words, she vividly illustrates her findings. She wants readers to gain a vicarious experience of the events studied, so that even if the specific findings do not generalize to other places and times, the insights will inform their understanding and interpretation of subsequent events.

Qualitative Evaluation and Program Theory

Qualitative evaluation is highly compatible with the idea of program theory, as I have been discussing it. Program theory refers to the chain of assumptions that explain how program activities are going to lead step by step to desired outcomes. In its early articulation, it is a set of guesses, or hypotheses, about the mechanisms that will operate to bring about success. When enough data have been collected, the evaluator can determine what the program theory is in action—that is, which expectations are being *acted upon* for connecting program processes to participants' achievement of program goals.

Qualitative methods are well suited to the explication of the program's theory in action. Qualitative evaluation seeks explanations of what the program is doing, why it follows the course that it does, how recipients respond, and why they act in the ways they do. If the study is concerned with outcomes, qualitative evaluation generally seeks to understand the steps by which those outcomes are realized. It concentrates on the mechanisms that *mediate* between program services and client responses.

In earlier chapters I talked about developing a set of program theories early in the study and then collecting data to see which chain or chains of theories are supported by the evidence. In qualitative work, program theory tends to be discovered in the course of the study. It emerges from the data. However, there is no reason why the qualitative evaluator cannot develop early hunches about the steps through which outcomes are expected to be realized. In fact, in the normal course of fieldwork, that is usually one of the things she does implicitly. Her initial explorations with people at the site often lead her to a preliminary understanding of staff's assumptions about how program activities will lead to outcomes. With her mandate to reach conclusions about the program, she may find it useful to formalize early versions of program theory and use them as a basis for investigation. As the evaluator learns more, she will progressively modify and improve the assumptions with which she began. Because of her commitment to involving program people, she will often develop her growing understanding of the program's theory in collaboration with program practitioners and perhaps clients.

Qualitative evaluation has a special advantage for finding out when program operations depart from expectations and new theories are needed. Because of its closeness to the scene, it generally sees what is going on and is alert to discrepancies between the rhetorical theories that people espouse and the actions and mechanisms that are visible in program action. Where events diverge from original expectations, qualitative methods are fluid enough to capture an account of what is really going on. They can provide information to help in the development of an alternative model of how the program is working and what its consequences are for the people it serves.

Ethical Issues

Qualitative approaches to evaluation run especially heavy risks of violating ethical boundaries, and anthropologists as the vanguard of the qualitative research movement have written feelingly about the ethics of investigation (e.g., Punch, 1986). I have already discussed some of the ethical issues that arise in evaluation. Fieldwork raises additional issues.

One thing that occasionally happens in qualitative evaluation is that the evaluator enters the program venue without making clear to staff and participants what her role there really is. Often the intent is kind: not to upset or offend program people by telling them that she is evaluating what they do. But the result is deception, which has no place in evaluation under any circumstances. Still worse, of course, would be a lie. An evaluator who claimed to be doing research for her doctoral dissertation when she is actually evaluating the program (even if she plans to use the data for her dissertation) is perpetrating an unacceptable deceit. Candor is essential. It is not only honest to tell people at the beginning of the study that they are being questioned and observed for evaluative purposes; it is also wiser politically. If they find out at the end, the whole study—and the evaluator—may be in for trouble.

Another ethical issue arises when the evaluator hears information that reflects badly on individuals. I talked about this in Chapter 7, but in qualitative evaluation, the opportunities are multiplied. If the information has nothing to do with the program, its processes, or outcomes, then she must hold it in strictest confidence. Suppose the evaluator finds that some staff are perennially absent or off the premises when they should be at work. Is that something she has an obligation to tell the director of the program, or should she save the information for the report she will write a year from now? Evaluators might have a difference of opinion on questions like this. Much depends on the specific promises of confidentiality that the evaluator made to respondents at the beginning (which suggests that such promises need to be carefully framed at the beginning). As a rule, standards for what is reportable should be discussed frankly. Only with open discussion among evaluators and between evaluators and program staff will the field of evaluation make headway in developing and implementing ethical standards of behavior.

Another issue is the possibility of bias that arises from the qualitative evaluator's relationships on the site. Having spent a good deal of time with staff and program recipients, the evaluator grows attached to those who have been articulate in helping her to understand the meaning of submerged events. She begins to see the world through their eyes, gets angry at things that harm them, rejoices at things that make their days better. She begins to worry about how the findings of the evaluation are going to affect the project and their lives. Is she going to report observations fairly, or is she going to bury unpleasant findings and overemphasize findings that put people she cares about in a sunny light? Is she, for example, going to suppress information that might lead officials in the central office to reduce their commitment to the project?

Some qualitative evaluators believe that any bias that arises in favor of program staff and clients is a healthy corrective. Most evaluators pay much more attention to the concerns of higher level administrators and policymakers. Somebody should take the welfare of staff and clients into account. Other qualitative evaluators seek ways of counteracting such biases, usually through strategies of systematic sampling, triangulation of evidence, and independent investigation at multiple sites or in multiple studies.

Combining Qualitative and Quantitative Approaches

Qualitative evaluation, as I have emphasized, has special strengths, and these strengths often complement the strengths of quantitative approaches. Therefore, there are many occasions when an evaluator is well advised to consider combining the two approaches to improve the quality and interpretability of the study.

At the simplest level, the evaluator can incorporate some quantitative techniques into a qualitative study. For example, after conducting a number of qualitative interviews and observations, the evaluator can count. She need not restrict herself to reporting about *some* or *many* but can calculate what proportion of elderly tenants raised the subject of fear of crime in the interview or the length of time that patients she observed waited at the clinic before they saw a physician. Elementary counting can help the evaluator to check on patterns she thinks she sees in the data and help her reexamine her impressions. It can also provide evidence that convinces readers of her report that she has not selected only those quotes or anecdotes that support her argument. More advanced statistics can be used, too. Although such a position may sound like heresy to the devout, it is being embraced in some ethnographic circles today.

The evaluator can also add comparison sites to the study. Knowing how precincts without the innovative program are dealing with the homeless and the theories with which they operate, she can better understand the theories and actions of the program site she studies. The contrast with experience at nonprogram sites can highlight the changes that the program introduced both in process and in outcomes. Such imports from the quantitative tradition can strengthen qualitative investigation without sacrificing its advantages.

At a deeper level, the evaluator can run separate substudies. She can conduct a qualitative evaluation of program process to describe and analyze how the program is operating and a quantitative study of outcomes to examine such things as rate of recidivism of offenders, birth weight of newborns, or earnings of trainees. Sometimes the qualitative study is conducted first for formative purposes, so that the evaluator can feed back information to help in the improvement of services. Then a quantitative outcome evaluation is conducted. In other cases, the qualitative and quantitative studies are contemporaneous, with one team investigating program process and the other collecting data on outcomes. If the two parts of the evaluation are linked, the evaluator has an opportunity to use knowledge of the nature and intensity of program inputs to understand the kind of outcomes that are reasonable to expect.

Some evaluation theorists, notably Guba and Lincoln (1989), hold that it is impossible to combine qualitative and quantitative approaches responsibly within an evaluation. They believe that the two methodologies rest on different epistemological and ontological principles. Quantitative evaluation has a neopositivist or rationalist basis, with assumptions that there is a real reality out there and that scientific methods can approximate it. On the other hand, qualitative methods (as they define them) rest on constructivist beliefs that each person constructs his own reality, and that research can identify only the perceptions of participants and the meanings they ascribe to their experiences.

However, most writers on the subject find that the two approaches are highly complementary (e.g., Cook & Reichardt, 1979; Fetterman & Pitman, 1986; Greene & Caracelli, 1997; House, 1992; Jick, 1983; Kidder & Fine, 1987; Maxwell et al., 1986; Smith, 1986). Cronbach (1982) writes that however elegant a quantitative design may be, narrative information drawn from observation of the sites plays a major role in understanding and interpreting it. Such information also makes an interpretation persuasive "because it can convert statistics into a down-to-earth story" (p. 303).

There are a number of specific ways that the approaches can be combined:

1. *To study different parts of the program,* such as a qualitative study of program process and a quantitative study of program outcome. Mark and Shotland (1987) call this complementarity.

2. *To study different stages of the program.* In the early developmental stages when a pilot demonstration of the program is being run, qualitative methods can pro-

vide formative information that will help practitioners craft the standard version. Once the final standard version is implemented, quantitative evaluation can be conducted.

3. *To help develop the evaluation design and measures.* Here a qualitative study is run to find out the lay of the land. From the information it provides, evaluators can develop appropriate measures and an appropriate research design for quantitative study.

4. *To study the same phenomena through multiple methods.* The aim is to check information acquired by one method against information acquired by other methods in order to corroborate findings. Such a multi-method approach (e.g., with survey interviews, observation, and document analysis) is the ultimate in triangulation. If different approaches, methods, and theoretical perspectives yield convergent stories, confidence in the validity of results is increased.

5. *To aid in the interpretation of the results.* This can work both ways. If a qualitative evaluation comes up with vague conclusions, a quantitative component can be added in an attempt to nail down some firm results. Or a quantitative evaluation yields results that are hard to understand. For example, why did only one segment of the physicians in the health maintenance organization reduce their use of diagnostic tests? A qualitative component can be added to answer questions that the quantitative evaluation failed to explore.

All of these combinations extend the breadth and range of inquiry. They allow the evaluation to say more and to speak more confidently.

Summary

Qualitative evaluation has come of age. It makes important contributions to the evaluation of social programs, including a focus on the perspectives of program staff and participants, an awareness of context and history, and ongoing documentation of how the program works. It has particular value for discovering phenomena that were not originally anticipated. Whether it involves intensive on-site inquiry over a lengthy period or brief visits at intervals, it gives a running account of the program in operation and the responses and actions of its clients. It provides systematic understanding of complex interactions and insight into the processes of change.

In a qualitative study, design choices have to be made. The evaluator has to decide which sites to study and the criteria by which to select them. Shall she select sites for representativeness? To maximize diversity? To show exemplary operation? To disconfirm the prevailing wisdom about programs of this kind? There can be arguments for each of these strategies—and others. The significant point is that the evaluator has to have a conceptual basis for making her choices, and she has to be able to justify them by reference to the purpose of the study. Similarly, she has to choose respondents for interviewing and locations for observation. Again, she needs a conceptual basis and defensible criteria.

In qualitative evaluation, many methods are available for data collection. Among the usual techniques are ethnographic investigation, participant-observation, nonparticipant-observation, short-term observation, informal interviewing, casual conversation, and review of documents. We met many of these data collection methods in Chapter 7, but qualitative evaluators give them a special spin. They are sensitive not only to words but also to meanings. They try to understand the norms and value systems that underlie the words, and in order to do so, they attend to the physical setting, concrete artifacts, gestures and body language, and anything else on the scene. The aim, as in all evaluation, is to answer the central evaluation questions, but qualitative evaluators do so in dynamic terms and probe into the why of what they find.

The qualitative perspective rests on philosophical and theoretical assumptions about the nature of reality and knowledge. Although the schools and traditions of qualitative inquiry differ among themselves, generally they question the existence of a single reality. They believe that people construct their own versions of the world based on their own identities and experience. Therefore, they do not expect evaluation to produce truth, but rather they seek to reflect the multiple experiences of the participants in the program. Some qualitative evaluators give program people a strong say in the interpretation of data and in the writing of the report.

Qualitative work raises particular ethical issues. Probably the most significant is a tendency to go native, to accept the positions and perspectives of program people as their own. Many qualitative evaluators tend to be inattentive to concerns of administrators and policymakers, such as efficiency, cost containment, or the relative worth of this program as compared with other programs that serve the same clientele. The evaluators' sense of responsibility is to the people she studies, and she may downplay their shortcomings and overemphasize matters that concern them. But this tendency is by no means universal, and where it does exist, it is perhaps a corrective to the common bent in quantitative studies to place policy and management concerns first.

Qualitative evaluation meshes well with theory-based evaluation. In the normal course of qualitative work, the evaluator often surfaces the assumptions and theories underlying the program. In the theory-based mode, she can develop hypotheses about program theory early in the study and organize the fieldwork to test the theory in action.

Qualitative and quantitative approaches can profitably be combined. Each is strong where the other tends to be weak. As Dabbs (1982) has written, "Quality is the what; quantity the how much. Qualitative refers to the meaning, the definition ... characterizing something, while quantitative assumes the meaning and refers to a measure of it" (p. 32). Among the many possible combinations of the two methodologies are a qualitative study of program process coupled with a quantitative study of outcomes; a qualitative pilot study to learn the lay of the land followed by the development of measures and design for a quantitative study; a formative qualitative study of the demonstration phase of the program in order to aid in program improvement and a quantitative study of the resulting program; follow-up of a quantitative study that yielded confusing findings with the conduct of a qualitative study in order to understand what was going on. Such combinations extend the range of evaluation and its ability to provide useful data and interpretation.

ANALYZING AND INTERPRETING THE DATA

Unobstructed access to facts can produce unlimited good only if it is matched by the desire and ability to find out what they mean and where they lead. Facts are terrible things if left sprawling and unattended.

—Norman Cousins (1981)[1]

[E]ventually, of course, our knowledge depends upon the living relationship between what we see going on and ourselves. If exposure [to knowledge] is essential, still more is the reflection. Insight doesn't happen often on the click of the moment, like a lucky snapshot, but comes in its own time and more slowly and from nowhere but within.

—Eudora Welty (1971)[2]

Introduction

The aim of analysis is to convert a mass of raw data into a coherent account. Whether the data are quantitative or qualitative, the task is to sort, arrange, and process them and make sense of their configuration. The intent is to produce a reading that accurately represents the raw data and blends them into a meaningful account of events.

This book is no place to learn the techniques of data analysis in either tradition. Many books exist to induct novices into the inner sanctums of analysis and to update "adepts" on the latest analytic developments. The quantitative tradition has 100 years of statistical progress to draw upon. Textbooks are available to explain whether and when to use analysis of variance, analysis of covariance, regression analysis, multi-level analysis, survival analysis, event history analysis, structural equation modeling,

---

[1]From Norman Cousins, *Human Options: An Autobiographical Notebook.* Copyright © 1981 by Norman Cousins. Reprinted by permission of W. W. Norton & Company, Inc.

[2]From Eudora Welty, *One Time, One Place* (New York: Random House, 1971). Reprinted by permission of Random House, Inc.

and other multi-syllabic analytic techniques. Books on data analysis can be supplemented by excellent journals, university courses, consultants, and conferences.

The qualitative approach, where texts used to concentrate almost solely on field methods for collecting data, has recently seen an explosion of books on analyzing the data collected (e.g., Maxwell, 1996; Miles & Huberman, 1994; Silverman, 1993; Strauss, 1987; Wolcott, 1994). Here, too, there are courses, journals, conferences, and workshops. Much specific advice is available, but the instruction is not (and probably never will be) as detailed or explicit as for quantitative analysis. Despite the plethora of resources, I want this book, unlike other books on evaluation, to say something about data analysis. It is too important a subject to go unremarked.

Analysis grows out of all the preceding phases of the evaluation. It is heavily dependent on the central questions that the study has chosen to address, the research design, and the nature of the measures and data collected. At the point of analysis, the evaluator brings another set of skills to bear in deriving meaning from the design and the data in order to answer the central questions.

In this chapter, I first set out the central tasks of analysis in evaluation. Next I outline a set of analytic strategies common to both qualitative and quantitative analysis, although I go on to point out key differences in the two approaches. Finally, I consider the use of information beyond that collected in the study.

This is a short chapter. It does not try to tell the reader *how* to analyze research data, how to use computer programs or perform statistical calculations, or how to make sense of sprawling descriptions. Libraries are full of books that do just that. At the end of the chapter, I list texts on analytic methods. What this chapter tries to do is provide the *logic* of data analysis in evaluation. Anyone, with or without training in research techniques, ought to be able to follow the logic of the analytic task.

Analytic Tasks in Evaluation

The basic tasks of evaluation are to provide answers to the questions listed in Figure 12-1. An evaluation study can go about answering these kinds of questions in a limited number of ways. Evaluators will follow strategies such as those listed in Figure 12-1. The list presented follows the sequence more common in quantitative than qualitative work. I discuss the qualitative spin on the analytic task in the next section.

No one study will seek to answer all the questions in Figure 12-1, but the figure sets out the range of questions that evaluative analysis can address.

Question 1 calls for descriptions of the program in operation. This is often called process evaluation. The basic task is description. The description can be either quantitative or qualitative in nature, or a mix of both. The quantitative evaluator will rely on counts of various aspects of the program. The qualitative evaluator will develop narratives. Her emphasis is likely to be on the dynamics of the operation and the environment surrounding the program (such as the structure of the program organization or the neighborhood and community environment). As question 1d suggests, she is also apt to be interested in the recipients' interpretations of the program and their participation in it: What does it mean to them in their own terms?

As question 2 notes, the implicit question in a process evaluation may be

FIGURE 12-1   LOGIC OF ANALYSIS IN EVALUATION

1. What went on in the program over time? Describing.
   a. Actors
   b. Activities and services
   c. Conditions of operation
   d. Participants' interpretation
2. How closely did the program follow its original plan? Comparing.
3. Did recipients improve? Comparing.
   a. Differences from preprogram to postprogram
   b. (If data were collected at several time periods) Rate of change.
   c. What did the improvement (or lack of improvement) mean to the recipients?
4. Did recipients do better than nonrecipients? Comparing.
   a. Checking original conditions for comparability
   b. Differences in the two groups preprogram to postprogram
   c. Differences in rates of change
5. Is observed change due to the program? Ruling out rival explanations.
6. What was the worth of the relative improvement of recipients? Cost-benefit or cost-effectiveness analysis.
7. What characteristics are associated with success? Disaggregating.
   a. Characteristics of recipients associated with success
   b. Types of services associated with success
   c. Surrounding conditions associated with success
8. What combinations of actors, services, and conditions are associated with success and failure? Profiling.
9. Through what processes did change take place over time? Modeling.
   a. Comparing events to assumptions of program theory
   b. Modifying program theory to take account of findings
10. What unexpected events and outcomes were observed? Locating unanticipated effects.
11. What are the limits to the findings? To what populations, places, and conditions do conclusions not necessarily apply? Examining deviant cases.
12. What are the implications of these findings? What do they mean in practical terms? Interpreting.
13. What recommendations do the findings imply for modifications in program and policy? Fashioning recommendations.
14. What new policies and programmatic efforts to solve social problems do the findings support? Policy analysis.

whether the program did what it was supposed to do. Did it continue to operate as its designers intended, or did it shift over time? The analytic strategy is comparison. The descriptive data about the program (e.g., frequency of home visits, content of curriculum) are compared to the blueprints of program designers. The answers can indicate the ways in which the program diverged and perhaps why it diverged from the original plan.

Question 3 asks whether recipients of the program prospered. Here the analytic mode is comparing the recipients' situation before and after exposure to the program. If data have been collected several times prior to the program, at several times during the program, and/or at multiple times after the conclusion of recipients' exposure, all those data are included in the analysis. With intermediate data points, the evaluator can assess or calculate the rate of change.[3] For example, did recipients improve rapidly during the early part of their encounter and then level off? Did they improve all across the course of the program so that their immediate postprogram status was much better, only to see the improvement fade out in the succeeding months? Such analysis can be performed either quantitatively or qualitatively.

Question 3c asks about the meaning of program participation to its beneficiaries and how they construed their improvement or lack of improvement. For example, a youngster who barely improved his reading score on a standardized test may still be delighted that he can now read a few simple words and write his name. That may mark tremendous achievement to him. This question is the home turf of qualitative methods.

Question 4 asks how recipients compared to nonrecipients. If the groups were randomly assigned, then their status on key variables was probably very similar at the outset. Any difference at the end represents a gain due to the program. If the groups were not selected randomly, it is useful to find out how their initial status compared, particularly on the critical variable that will be used as the outcome indicator (e.g., frequency of illegal drug use, knowledge of geography). Their status on other factors that might be expected to influence outcomes should also be compared (such as the length of time that they have been using drugs, their IQ scores). If the groups differ in significant ways, this differential has to be taken into account in subsequent analyses.

Question 4b calls for comparing the amount of change in the program and nonprogram groups. If the program group went up considerably on the outcome variable while the comparison group did not change at all, the evaluator has a basis for beginning to make judgments about the value of the program. When the comparison group was chosen through randomization, the evidence seems pretty convincing that the program had some degree of success. But for nonrandom comparison groups, many other possible explanations will have to be tested before reaching that conclusion. Even with randomized controls, additional checks may be required. These kinds of concerns will take us to question 5.

Question 4c is the multi-wave analog to question 3b. It asks for comparison of the rates of change of the two groups. Answers will give an indication of the relative trajectories.

---

[3]John Willett points out that the term *rate of change* seems to imply linear change, whereas much change is nonlinear. I acknowledge the point but retain the term because the alternative—*growth trajectory*—is less familiar to nontechnical readers. Keep in mind that change need not be linear over time.

Question 5 asks whether the program was the cause of whatever changes were observed. The analytic strategy is ruling out plausible rival explanations. As Campbell (1966) has written:

> It is the absence of plausible rival hypotheses that establishes one theory as "correct." In cases where there are rival theories, it is the relative over-all goodness of fit that leads one to be preferred to another. (p. 102)

Could something else *plausibly* have led to the situation found at follow-up? If so, then it is worthwhile examining whether such conditions or events were operative. For example, were the program group and the comparison group different at the outset and could that have been responsible for differential success? *How* did the two groups differ, and is it reasonable to think that differences on *those* characteristics led to different outcomes?

The randomized experiment is the design best suited to ruling out competing hypotheses. Even with random assignment, it is possible that slippage occurred. The seemingly superior performance of program recipients might be due to the fact that the poorer risks dropped out of the experimental group and better risks dropped out of the control group. That would suggest that had it not been for the differential attrition, the program group would not look so good. The basic analytic task is to consider what other influences might have caused the pattern of data observed and then see whether those possibilities can be rejected.

For comparison groups constructed without randomization, many more checks will need to be made. As noted in question 4, the groups might have been dissimilar to start with on the key criterion variables and on variables that affected their ability to do well. If they were located in different communities, they might have been exposed to different influences, which affected their outcomes. In cases such as these, analysis cannot totally compensate for the original inequalities. However, additional analyses can narrow down the list of possible contaminants and help the evaluator reach an estimate of program effects—perhaps not a point estimate but an estimate of the *range* of effects that are probably attributable to the program. The evaluator needs to think hard about all the ways in which the program and nonprogram groups differed not only at the beginning of the program but all through its course and into its aftermath. Then she has to find data that allow her to test the extent to which each factor was implicated in the outcomes.

I remember reading some time ago about an airline crash that occurred because the runway was too short and the plane could not stop before crashing into the barrier. It turned out that the runway had been built to the appropriate length, but over the ensuing months little things happened that chipped away at its size. A new hangar was built that needed extra room. A small part of the runway was diverted to accommodate parked vehicles. The paving at one end was cracking and was removed until it could be replaced. Each of these decrements was small and by itself did not compromise safety. Cumulatively, however, they led to disaster.

That seems to me a good analogy to analysis of evaluation data, especially in cases without randomized assignment. The evaluator has to find each of the small discrepancies that might vitiate the conclusions about the effects of the program. No one of the small problems is important enough to cancel out the first-order effects, but cumulatively they may undermine the evaluation conclusions—unless taken into account.

Question 6 is the cost-benefit question. It asks for a comparison of the costs of the program with the benefits that accrue to participants and to the larger society. Costs of the program include not only out-of-pocket expenditures for running the program but also opportunity costs—that is, benefits that were forgone because of the program. For example, trainees in a job training program could have been working and earning wages. Because of their enrollment in the program, they lost those wages. That is a program cost.

Program benefits were calculated in answering questions 4 and 5. The analysis there indicated how much and what kind of improvement was the result of the program. For example, an emergency hotline to the police might have increased the number of crimes for which arrests were rapidly made and reduced residents' fears about their safety. The costs of the program can be fairly readily calculated; costs include the personnel staffing the hotline, the phone costs, and the diversion of officers from employment on other police work. What about the benefits? How can the analyst quantify the worth of higher arrest rates and reduced fear? Data are available to estimate the cost of police investigation of a crime, so a decrease in the number and length of those investigations can be costed out. If early arrests are more likely to lead to convictions, then the analyst has to seek data on the benefit to society of placing a criminal behind bars for a given period of time. (The additional costs of prosecuting the cases and of incarceration need to be deducted.) The worth of a decrease in residents' fears is harder to quantify. Analysts have developed methods to quantify the value of such intangible benefits, although as we saw in Chapter 10, much depends on the analyst's judgment.

Question 7 asks which characteristics of the program or the people in it are associated with better or poorer performance. The analytic strategy is disaggregation. The evaluator looks at the data to see if there are apparent relationships between some characteristics of the program and the outcomes. Question 7a asks about participant characteristics (a program input). Did men or women do better? Question 7b asks about program components (program process). Did prison inmates who attended group counseling do better than those who received individual counseling? Question 7c asks about conditions in the environment. Were welfare mothers in low-unemployment states more successful at getting jobs than those in high-unemployment states? The evaluator can look at one variable at a time to see whether any of them proves to be significantly related to outcomes. With regression analysis, she can find out which of a set of variables are associated with good outcomes, when other variables are held constant.

Qualitative evaluators can also examine the relationship between characteristics of clients and the services they received and the characteristics of their progress in the program. Miles and Huberman (1994), for example, provide guidance for constructing matrices that reveal this kind of relationship.

Question 8 asks whether there are clusters of services, conditions, staff, and clients that tend to go along with better outcomes. This question goes beyond the investigation of single variables to examine the effect of combinations of variables. With the use of interaction terms in regression analysis, the analyst can discover the extent to which the effect of one variable on outcomes is increased or decreased depending on the levels of another variable. For example, single-variable analysis may show that better outcomes are obtained when patients receive service from medical specialists and also when they stay in the hospital for shorter stays. If an interaction term is entered into the regression equation, the results may show that disproportionally better results are obtained when service from medical specialists and short stays are combined. Other statistical techniques allow for investigation of complex relationships in data sets of different types. Similar analyses can be done by qualitative evaluators who systematically factor and cluster the narrative data they have. Ragin (1994) presents a procedure to facilitate such analysis.

Question 9 inquires about the processes through which change takes place. This has traditionally been the domain of qualitative analysis, notably the case study. However, with the development of new methods of structural modeling and growth curve analysis, quantitative methods are catching up to the demands of the task. The evaluator who isn't familiar with these methods can consult a good applied statistician.

One relatively simple way of analyzing the processes of change is though comparison of observed events with the ways in which program actors expected change to occur—that is, comparing events with program theory. The evaluator has laid out expectations for the microsteps by which change will take shape, and she examines evolving events in relationship to that theoretical model. This gives some suggestion about whether the program works in the way that program people anticipated.

If the evaluation data show that most of the assumptions of the program theory were met (e.g., police foot patrol made the police presence more visible to gang members, gang members became more wary of apprehension and reduced the frequency of illegal activities, incidence of crime by juveniles went down), the analysis of why the program worked is fairly well specified. The study may also shed light on other mechanisms at work. For example, another component of program theory may have anticipated that police foot patrol would encourage adults in the neighborhood to take stronger protective action, such as auxiliary neighborhood policing, which would make gang members reduce their criminal activity. Did this chain of events take place? *Why* questions may also be addressed. For example, did gang delinquency simply shift to other neighborhoods that were not being patrolled? Of course, one study is hardly likely to find answers to all the questions that can be asked. But to the extent that data are available to *explain* program outcomes, they can be exploited—to give at least provisional guesses, or new hypotheses, about what processes the program sets in motion.

When the program theory with which the evaluation began proves to be a poor rendition of events, the evaluator has more work to do. Why didn't nutrition supplements to pregnant women improve the birth weight of their newborns? The theory was perfectly straightforward. Nutrition supplements would improve the women's health and nutritional status, and their babies would be born at normal weights. If the data show that this outcome was not reached for most women in the program, do data give clues to the reason? Maybe not. Then further inquiry is required. In one study further investigation showed the women did not take the supplements themselves but instead added them to the family's meals—put them in the common pot. Therefore, the supplements had little effect on the woman's health or the birth weight of the child. Unless the quantitative evaluator had foreseen some such eventuality and developed measures to capture such behavior, she might not know why things came out as they did. The qualitative evaluator would have a better chance of finding out, but even she could miss the actions of women back in the privacy of their own kitchens. It might take a follow-on study to track down the mechanisms that led to observed effects.

In using program theory as a guide to analysis, a possible limitation is that the data are not thoroughly accommodating. They may not line up in clear-cut patterns that shout yes, this is the way it is, or no, that's all wrong. The associations are usually going to be partial, and the evaluator will have to exercise careful judgment in figuring out the extent to which they support the theory. One concern that she will have to attend to is whether a plausible theory that has not been tested would fit the data even better. If time allows, she will often want to test several alternative theories to see whether the data fit one of these theories more snugly than the one she started with.

While I have suggested that basing evaluation on programmatic theories of change spins off multiple advantages, it is not a panacea. When the data spraddle in indeterminate ways, they do not allow for clear-cut testing of program theories. The evaluator has to exercise judgment in interpreting how well the program adheres to the posited theories. Statistical tests alone are not going to resolve the issue. Judgment is an indispensable component in the analysis.

Program theory has many benefits for the evaluation enterprise. Even when it does not lead to *crisp* conclusions about the processes and mechanisms of change, it will provide more information and more useful kinds of knowledge than are currently available. Further, its widespread use will encourage analysts to develop and apply new statistical methods to the analysis of the fit between theory and events. Qualitative analysts can hone their own brand of analytic skills on the exercise.

The tenth question focuses on unanticipated (and usually undesired) effects of the program. This question actually has more to do with data collection than analysis. For qualitative evaluators, it suggests that they remain alert to possible undesired side effects throughout the fieldwork. For quantitative evaluators, it suggests that they devise measures of possible unwanted effects early in the game and collect the requisite data. When time comes for analysis, the data of either stripe are analyzed according to the same procedures used for more desirable outcomes.

Question 11 looks outward to the generalizability of study findings. It asks what the limits of the data are, and an analytic strategy for addressing the question is the examination of deviant cases. Let's take an example. An evaluation of a home-care program for the aged finds that most of the clients were maintained in their own homes and were happier there; although their physical condition continued to deteriorate, the deterioration was not as profound as in aged patients in a nursing home. For this program, the results were positive.

The next question is how generalizable these results are to other programs. There may be several features of the study that suggest caution. For example, in one nursing home evaluation, the study population was all under the age of 80; it is not obvious that results will be the same with older populations. Any limiting condition such as this needs to be specified in the evaluation report. Second, some of the elderly people in the study did not do well. When the evaluator examines these deviant cases, she finds that they tended to be people with serious chronic health problems like diabetes and emphysema. Based on deviant-case analysis, the evaluator may want to limit her conclusions and not claim across-the-board success.

Question 12 asks about the implications of evaluation findings. Putting together everything the study has revealed, the evaluator has to interpret their meaning. She has to decide which among the many data items are important and worth highlighting, and which findings, even if statistically significant, are less noteworthy. She has to combine individual findings into coherent bundles and in some cases disaggregate findings to show the subcategories of which they were composed. For example, Friedlander and Burtless (1995) examined the impact of welfare-to-work programs on participants' earnings. Increase in total earnings was important, but the analysis was more revealing when it isolated the separate effects of a number of components: shorter initial joblessness, faster job finding, increased proportion of people finding employment, earnings on the job, and duration of employment.

Interpretation is the phase of analysis that makes sense out of the varied strands of data. It turns data into a narrative, a story. It identifies strengths and weaknesses and highlights conditions that are associated with both.

The evaluator inevitably comes to the task of interpretation with certain preconceptions. Sometimes the preconceptions take the shape of support for the program, for the general idea behind the program, or for the program's clientele. The evaluator may believe that early childhood education is a very good thing or that job development for adults with disabilities is vitally needed or that adoption of Total Quality Management will make firms better and more productive environments for their workers. Sometimes her preconceptions are more general, taking the shape of perspectives on life, people, research, intervention, justice, and equality. They come from her life experiences and stock of knowledge. At the interpretation stage, they influence the way she proceeds. In the old unlamented positivist world, it was assumed that the facts should speak for themselves and the investigator should be totally neutral. She should do everything she could to expunge her own knowledge and beliefs from the analytic task, to become a cipher while she ciphered. In these postpositivist days, we recognize the futility of such advice; we can't erase the essence of what we are and know from the research process. But we can seek to be conscious of our biases and of the way they affect interpretation, and we can even state our biases up front in evaluation reports.

Much of the knowledge that will influence interpretation is knowledge of prior evaluations of the program or programs of the same type. The evaluator can show the extent to which the current program has been similarly or divergently implemented and the extent to which findings about outcomes support or disagree with earlier findings. The analysis will also seek to answer questions left unanswered in earlier work—in effect, to fill in missing parts of the program puzzle.

Beyond this type of information, the evaluator will bring to bear knowledge from social science research and theory. Concepts and theoretical generalizations about, say, ego defenses or organizational gatekeeping, can inspire creative ways of interpreting evaluation data. Nor can (or should) the analyst ignore the whole realm of "ordinary knowledge" (Lindblom & Cohen, 1979) that tends to define what we all believe simply because we live in the United States around the turn of the millennium. As Cronbach (1982) has written:

> Experience used in interpreting a summative finding comes partly from supplementary sources. Some of these sources may speak of the program itself, but observation of other programs, tangentially related social research and theory, and commonsense views (community experience) all may carry weight. A study gains authority insofar as it is translated into a story that fits with other experience. (p. 303)

But it is the analyst's job not to accept unquestioningly the everyday assumptions that are part of our workaday lives. She should try to surface them, turn them around in her mind, look at them from a new angle, probe them, and see if the process generates new insights. For example, Schon and Rein (1994) discuss the tenacity of familiar metaphors in structuring how we see the world. They offer the example of fragmented services, a common diagnosis of the problems involved in delivery of social services. This metaphor limits attention to only a subset of the phenomena involved in the problem. It also implicitly contains the outline of the logical solution. If the problem is fragmentation of services, the obvious remedy is integration, making them whole. A commonsense way of looking at the problem thus forestalls other approaches that might have greater chance of success. The evaluator should not settle for facile explanations even when (especially when) they are part of the current orthodoxy.

A dilemma that evaluators may face when they reach the stage of interpretation is what do when the findings show that the program has had little effect. Although, strictly speaking, this is a political rather than an analytic problem, findings of this sort tend to merge the political with the analytic. Especially when the evaluators are being paid by program people and/or have been working closely with them, there is a strong temptation to soft pedal poor results and emphasize positive findings. If the aim is to encourage program managers and practitioners to listen to results rather than reject them and to modify activities rather become defensive, such an approach is understandable. However, when it does violence to the data, it runs the risk of becoming the whitewash that Suchman warned us against in Chapter 2. It is not obvious that downplaying serious flaws will benefit program people in the long run. More helpful will be sensible and practical advice on how to cope with poor results.

Which brings us to the next phase, task 13: developing recommendations for change in program or policy. Evaluators are not always expected to develop the implications of their results into recommendations for action. Sometimes they are asked to be the purveyors of straight evidence, what Sergeant Friday on the old *Dragnet* program called "just the facts, ma'am," while program and policy people see it as *their* responsibility to review the evidence in terms of changes needed. Program people understand the program in its historical setting, its management, the political climate, and the options available, and they can best consider what adaptations should and can be made. They can use evaluation findings as one guide to change, if change seems called for, but they have much other knowledge that they can bring to bear.

In other cases, however, the evaluator is expected to offer her judgment of the types of action that should be taken. The evaluator has an intimate understanding of the details of the information in the study, and she has worked long and hard to comprehend it in all its complexity. Program and policy people often want the evaluator to take the next step and recommend the kinds of changes they should make. When she is called upon to do so, the evaluator has to take full advantage of all the evidence. For example, if she has identified conditions in the program that are associated with better outcomes, she has leads to the kind of recommendations that are well supported in the data. If she has examined the fit of the data to the program's theory of action, the data provide suggestions on steps to take next. If she has data from observation and informal interviewing, she will have ideas about the kinds of changes that make sense.

However, some evaluations are black box evaluations. They have collected data only on outcomes and do not know what went on inside the program box, treating it as though it were totally opaque. The studies may have been after-only, before-and-after, before-and-after with comparison groups, time series, or before-and-after with randomized controls, but the focus was on outcomes, with little attention to the operation of the program. When outcomes are less than satisfactory, the evaluator has little sense of the conditions that led to the outcomes. She is in a bind when it comes to recommendations. Clearly something is wrong now, but what would make it better? Some evaluators have specialized in a programmatic area for years—say physical rehabilitation, child abuse prevention, or teaching English as a second language. Out of their years of evaluating such programs and their other substantive knowledge in the field, they have developed a stock of knowledge. They have a base on which they can draw to make recommendations.

However, many evaluators are not topic-area specialists. They evaluate programs of many different kinds and thus do not have deep knowledge about any one subject area. If the study doesn't provide information about factors that influence program effectiveness, they have to make do with common sense in developing recommendations for change. They are sometimes driven to recommending the opposite of whatever the unsuccessful program is currently doing—especially if the report is almost due and they have little time left to think about the kinds of recommendations that would be sensible.

Needless to say, this is not good practice. Even in this bind, the evaluator has a responsibility to think about the recommendations she is making with the same critical faculty that she devotes to current practices. Are the recommended changes likely to achieve desired effects? Is there experience elsewhere that suggests that they will be practical, feasible, and effective? What program theory would they represent? Are they consonant with other conditions in the environment, such as level of budget or staff capabilities? To find out if the changes she is thinking of recommending are likely to work, she can turn to social science theory and research, past evaluations of similar programs, and the judgment of experts in the field. Collecting information about the likely effects of recommendations is worthwhile, even if it involves only consultation with program managers and staff. In effect, she would be doing something approaching an evaluability assessment on the prospective recommendations. If there is enough time, a wise course of action would be to collect some data on the recommended practices in action, but except on the smallest scale, this is not likely to be feasible in a time-bound study.

In all cases, however much data the study provides and however substantively expert the evaluator is, the act of making recommendations requires the evaluator to extrapolate beyond the evidence at hand. She has to think about the future world into which any recommended change will enter. If the federal government is going to give states more authority to set rules, if school districts are going to devolve more authority to schools, if budgets are going to be under continued stress, what do these conditions mean for the program in the future? And what kind of recommendations make sense under the coming conditions? If the evaluator has been foresightful, she will have data on some sites that are similar to the conditions that are likely to prevail, such as a state that has been allowed to allocate federal transportation funds across different modes of transportation or a school district that has decentralized decision making to the schools. She can examine these cases carefully as she develops ideas for recommendations.

No one expects the evaluator to be Nostradamus (and how well did all his predictions work?). But the point is that the evaluator cannot assume that tomorrow's world will be the same as today's. Training programs for displaced workers (displaced by shifts in technology) will be affected by changes in economic activity and the employment rate; court-ordered programs of community service for adjudicated delinquents will be affected by changes in laws, sentencing guidelines, and community sentiment. The possibility—even the probability—of relevant change has to be taken into account in the recommendation-making enterprise.

Evaluators rarely recommend the total eradication of a program. Even if data show that the program is totally ineffective, the usual recourse is to try to patch it up and try again. But policymakers will also welcome insights about alternative strategies, and findings from the evaluation can inform the formulation of new interventions. This is the subject of question 13: When new policies and programs are under consideration, what lessons does this evaluation offer to the venture? Here we are in the domain of policy analysis, but we take a distinctively evaluative slant.

The analysis of future policies and programs usually starts with a problem—such as the inaccessibility of public transportation to handicapped people. The policymaker, bureaucrat, or analyst interested in the problem generates a list of possible solutions, such as wheel-chair-accessible elevators in train stations, kneeling buses, and subsidized vans that pick up handicapped customers on call. The analyst has the task of investigating which, if any, of these proposals would be operationally practical, conceptually logical, and empirically supported by past experience. The contribution of evaluation is to supply empirical evidence about the effectiveness of these practices.

The person undertaking analysis of this sort is likely to be a policy analyst rather than an evaluator. But he needs to know a good deal about what evaluation has to say. In analyzing the likely effectiveness of alternatives, he seeks the sum total of evaluation evidence on each topic. Meta-analysis is of particular use. By combining results of dozens or hundreds of evaluations of similar programs, meta-analysis contributes state-of-the-art knowledge to the forecast. The synthesis of evidence is applied to the analysis of future policies and this extends the reach of evaluation beyond the individual program to the future of programming generally in an area.

Although question 14 takes us beyond the terrain of the individual evaluator, it has been addressed by evaluators. The General Accounting Office's former Program Evaluation and Methodology Division essentially reinvented aspects of policy analysis on a distinctly evaluative base. It published a paper on what it called prospective evaluation, an attempt to formalize a method for extrapolating from existing studies to future times and places (U.S. General Accounting Office, 1989). Because GAO works for the Congress, it is often confronted with requests to examine proposals and bills that would set up new programs, and the paper illustrates the ways in which the staff goes about synthesizing past evaluation findings to judge the likely efficacy of future proposals. An interesting sidelight of the GAO paper is the emphasis it places on surfacing the "theoretical underpinnings of prospective programs" (GAO, 1989, p. 60, see also pp. 30–33). Explicit program theory as well as evaluative evidence help to determine the potential of a proposal for successful operation.

General Strategies of Analysis

The tasks of analysis of quantitative and qualitative data have much in common, but evaluators will go about the tasks in different ways. There are two basic reasons for the difference in strategy: the nature of the data and the analytic intent. First, quantitative and qualitative analysts have different kinds of data in hand. The quantitative evaluator is working with measures that yield numerical values, such as years of schooling or scores on tests of knowledge. Even those data that started out as narrative responses to interviews or notes from observations have been coded into a set of categories to which numerical values are assigned. The qualitative evaluator, on the other hand, is working with sheaves of field notes—narrative accounts of conversations, interviews, observations, fieldworkers' reactions and tentative hunches, school documents, and so on. Therefore, the task that each confronts is different.

Quantitative studies usually have a large number of cases. The large size of the sample helps to ensure that oddities of individual cases cancel each other out, and the data will show the main effects of the intervention. If the sample has been chosen through random sampling, results will generalize to the population from which the sample was drawn. However, quantitative studies often have a limited number of descriptors about each case. A local evaluation can have data on 300 science teachers, and a national study can have data on 2,000, but both have relatively little information about each teacher—perhaps length of time he has been teaching, grade(s) taught, scores on capsule science tests before and after the staff development project, and perhaps one or two more items. Although there is limited information on each participant, the large number of cases makes statistical analysis appropriate.

A qualitative evaluation of the same project would have data on a small subset of the teachers in the staff development project, maybe 8 to 15. If the evaluation team has several members, they might have studied three or four times that many people, but not so many that they could not remember each individual in his own social and historical context. The study would probably have a large amount of data about each one: notes on conversations over time, observations of the person's participation in the staff development project, transcribed interviews, and so on. The information would cover scores of topics, from each person's background and views on teaching to the physical setting of the staff development project, from the actions of the staff developer to the character of the schools to which the science teachers will return. By narrowing down to a relatively small number of cases, qualitative evaluators are able to bring into focus all the details, idiosyncrasies, and complexities in the individual case. However, it is often not apparent how representative these cases are nor how generalizable they are to all science teachers in the program.

The second and more important reason that quantitative and qualitative evaluators undertake different modes of analysis is that their intentions are different. Qualitative evaluators aim to look at the program holistically, seeing each aspect in the context of the whole situation. They are concerned about the influence of the social context. They try to understand prior history as it influences current events. Their emphasis is dynamic, trying to gain a sense of development, movement, and change. In essence, they aim to provide a video (a few years ago we would have said a moving picture) rather than a series of snapshots at time 1, time 2, and time 3. In addition, they are concerned with the perspectives of those involved with the program and the meaning of the experience to them. Rather than impose the evaluator's assumptions and definitions, they seek to elicit the views of participants.

Quantitative analysts traffic largely in numbers. Much of the work that they have to do at this stage they have already done through the development and/or selection of measures and data collection. They have defined the variables of interest and the ways they are measured, and now is the time to focus on locating significant relationships among them. Through statistical techniques, they identify associations among variables and the likelihood that associations are real and not mere chance fluctuations. Their aim is to model the system of cause and effect.

To put the distinction in a more general way, quantitative evaluators tend to focus on whether and to what extent change in x causes change in y. Qualitative evaluators tend to be concerned with the process that connects x and y.

A third difference can be mentioned, the time ordering of analytic tasks. Quantitative evaluators generally wait until the data are in before they begin analyzing them. They need not wait until *all* the data are collected, but they usually wait until all the data *from one wave* of data are collected, coded, checked, entered into the computer, and cleaned. Qualitative evaluators, on the other hand, generally begin their analysis early in the data collection phase. As they talk to people and watch what goes on, they begin to develop hunches about what is happening and the factors in the situation that are implicated in events. They can use subsequent data collection to test their early hypotheses. Analysis is an ongoing process.

Despite the differences in the two traditions, they have common features. Quantitative analysts don't throw numbers unthinkingly into a computer and swear by the results that come out the other end. Qualitative analysts don't read the entrails of animals to figure out what the data mean. They share commitments to systematic and honest analysis. They also confront common tasks, as outlined in Figure 12-1.

Furthermore, only a limited number of strategies are available for data reduction and interpretation. Listed below is a set of these basic strategies. Most analysts make use of them, whether their proclivities are qualitative or quantitative.

Basic Analytic Strategies

Describing
Counting
Factoring (i.e., dividing into constituent parts)
Clustering
Comparing
Finding commonalities
Examining deviant cases
Finding covariation
Ruling out rival explanations
Modeling
Telling the story

Describing

All evaluators use description to evoke the nature of the program. They describe the program, its setting, staff, structure, sponsorship, and activities. The qualitative analyst is likely to provide narrative chronicles; the quantitative evaluator will provide summary statistics on a series of measures. But in order to give a fair accounting, they all have to engage in description.

Counting

Counting is a part of description and of most other analytic strategies. Counting helps to show what is typical and what is aberrant, what is part of a cluster and what is unique. Even the hardiest qualitative analyst will talk about "more," and "a few," and in order to be sure that she is right, judicious counting is in order. Counts also help to show the extent to which program participants are representative of the larger population to which results might be relevant.

Factoring

I use factoring in the algebraic sense of breaking down aggregates into constituent parts. Quantitative evaluators have already factored aggregates into components in the process of measurement. They have constructed measures to capture different facets of inputs, process, and outcomes. Qualitative evaluators prefer not to abstract people and events into parts but to deal with them holistically. Their emphasis is on gestalt and the natural context. Nevertheless, the human mind, for all its grandeur, is too limited to hold dozens of thoughts simultaneously. Even devout qualitative evaluators break out separate aspects of experience and deal with them in sequence—while trying to keep the larger context in mind.

Coding is an example of factoring. The coding of narrative material into categories is a common practice in evaluation. It splices up a narrative into a set of categories that have common substantive content. The procedure allows the analyst to examine the content and frequency of each category, and the covariation among categories.

Clustering

Clustering is the procedure of putting like things together. It identifies characteristics or processes that seem to group, aggregate, or sidle along together. Factor analysis, principal components analysis, cluster analysis, and multi-dimensional scaling are among the statistical techniques for accomplishing this kind of aggregation. Qualitative evaluators tend to cluster cases through iterative reading, grouping, coding, or data displays (Miles & Huberman, 1994). Glaser and Strauss (1967) suggest a systematic procedure called analytic induction for developing categories and models. (I describe it in the section Examining Deviant Cases.) Ragin (1994) describes an explicit way to array qualitative data along a set of dimensions to figure out which cases belong together, what he calls the comparative method. Many qualitative analysts who deal with a small sample of cases rely on their immersion in the materials and repeated rereading of their data to arrive at appropriate clusters.

A concomitant task is deciding what each cluster is a case of. As the analyst develops clusters, she uses intuitive or explicit concepts to group cases together; each case exemplifies the concept that unites them into a category. But as she goes along, she refines and redefines the concepts. Some cases will not fit her original definition of the concept and the concept must be altered or narrowed down, or the case must be dropped from the category and another category found for it. Some concepts will turn out to be useless for making sense of the data. New classifications will be needed. Conceptual clarification is an ongoing task.

Comparing

Comparison is the heart of the evaluation enterprise. The analyst compares the situation before, during, and after the program. She compares program participants with those who did not receive the program. She compares participants with one another to see whether there is a great deal of variability within the program group. Sometimes there is as much variability among the program participants as there is between them and the members of the comparison or control group. In that case, the difference between program and control groups may not be significant, either statistically or practically. Analysis of variance and regression analysis are statistical techniques for finding this out.

Qualitative evaluators, who usually analyze a small number of cases, can compare individuals directly. When they have comparison groups, they, too, have to guard against the possibility that differences within each group are as large as differences between the groups. Rather than make a series of comparisons on single characteristics, they craft multi-dimensional portraits that show similarities and differences.

Finding Commonalities

A basic strategy of the analytic task is to locate common trends and main effects. What are the common experiences that groups of program participants have? What are the common elements that characterize successful participants? Much of the statistical repertoire is geared toward identifying such similarities.

Qualitative analysts who face the same task are often advised to find patterns in the data. Without more specific guidance, I've always thought that that advice is as useful as Michelangelo's advice on how to carve a marble statue: Chip away all the marble that is not part of the figure. One of the specific ways of finding patterns is to look at the frequency of *clusters* of events, behaviors, processes, structures, or meanings, and find the common elements. Brilliant insights arise from finding commonalities among phenomena that were originally viewed as totally unconnected.

Examining Deviant Cases

In statistical analysis, the deviant case is far from the body of the distribution. Analysts may sometimes drop such cases to concentrate on the central tendency and simplify the story. But at some point it is often worthwhile to take a hard look at them and what makes them so unusual. Qualitative analysts, too, may ignore aberrant cases, but important information may lurk at the extreme ends of a distribution. Qualitative analysts can use systematic techniques to incorporate the information into their analysis. One such technique is analytic induction (Bogden & Biklen, 1992; Glaser & Strauss, 1967) which requires analysts to pay careful attention to evidence that challenges whatever constructs and models they are developing. With analytic induction, they keep modifying their concepts and introducing qualifications and limits to their generalizations until the conclusions cover all the data. Cases that are different from the mainstream, outliers in statistical terms, can also give important clues to unanticipated phenomena and may give rise to new insights into what is happening and why.

Finding Covariation

It is one thing to find out whether the values of one phenomenon are related to the values of another. This is the strategy that I have called comparison. Another question is whether *changes* in a phenomenon are related to changes in other phenomena. Does increasing the number of hours of classroom training for disturbed adolescents over the course of the school year lead to better adjustment? Does improving the social relationships among staff in the program lead to improving relationships among participants? Again, statistics has tried and true procedures for making estimates of covariation. Qualitative evaluation has to handcraft such techniques on a study-by-study basis.

Ruling out Rival Explanations

Both quantitative and qualitative evaluators want to be able to ascribe results to the program intervention. They need to separate those changes that the program brings about from changes caused by extraneous circumstances. Even the so-called cadillac of designs, the randomized experiment, may leave loopholes and uncertainties about causation. The analyst must rule out the possibility that something other than the program was responsible for observed effects.

To go about this step, the analyst identifies plausible alternative explanations. Were successful outcomes brought about by the new math curriculum or by new computing facilities in the schools or the school restructuring that empowered teachers and raised their morale and enthusiasm? Were unsuccessful outcomes the result of the curriculum or were they due to the poor quality of curriculum implementation, insufficient class time devoted to it, or competing demands on students' attention? Whatever factors might *plausibly* be held responsible for observed results—noncomparability of program and comparison groups, outside events, the pattern of dropouts from the program, inappropriate measures, changes in the conduct of the program over time—may need to be examined.

If the evaluator locates a potential explanation that seems reasonable, she has several options. She can collect available data to see whether the rival explanation can be ruled out; she can collect new data to try to disprove it; she can mount a small substudy to investigate its cogency. If the data do not contradict it, she should acknowledge it as a possible explanation for the results and perhaps tag it for further investigation.

Modeling

Modeling is a procedure for putting all relevant information together to create explanations of important outcomes. Here is where all the prior steps come to fruition. The analyst characterizes the nature of program effectiveness. She identifies the elements that were implicated in program effectiveness and assesses the relative weight of their contribution. She notes which elements worked together synergistically to enhance success and which elements were incompatible with each other. To the extent possible, she explains how the program achieved the observed results. She notes which program components and theories were supported in the analysis and which were not. At the end she has a rounded account of what happened and, at least to the limit of her data, how it happened.

Telling the Story

Come the end of the analytic phase, all evaluators have to communicate their findings to readers. Communication requires putting the data into understandable form. Nobody has a monopoly on techniques for making evaluation results clear, putting them in context, pointing out the limits of their applicability, and interpreting them in light of likely developments in program and policy. Writing is where the rubber hits the road. Good writing is not only a matter of style and grace; it is actually a test of the extent to which the writer fully understands what she is talking about. If she can't communicate it well, perhaps she hasn't fully grasped it herself.

An Example of Program Theory as a Guide to Analysis

Program theory can provide a structure for analysis of evaluation data. The analysis can follow the series of steps that have been posited as the course that leads from the intervention through to the achievement of goals.

Let's take an example. A group at Stanford evaluated an education program for asthma patients to enable them to gain increased control over their symptoms and reduce their suffering from asthma (Wilson et al., 1993). The underlying theory was that education would increase their understanding of their condition and therefore their confidence that they could control it, which in turn would lead to their adherence to a treatment regimen, and thus to better control of symptoms. Because the theory guided the evaluation design, the evaluators had measures on each of the steps posited in the theory. The study included 323 adult patients with moderate to severe asthma. There were two treatment groups, one receiving group education and one receiving individualized education, and a control group.

The evaluators monitored participation and found that 88% of the patients assigned to group education attended all four sessions. Observation of the sessions indicated that "educators adhered closely to the program outlines and script, and used the handouts and homework assignments as intended" (p. 569). Notice the importance of this component of the evaluation. Without the monitoring of content, there would be no way of knowing what actually went on in the group education session—that is, whether the program in action was the same as the program design.

The evaluators compared the treatment and control groups on before-and-after measures to see if there were any changes. If not, the thing to explain would be where the theory stalled out and why the program failed. If there were changes, and there were, then the analysis would concentrate on how much change there was, how the program worked, who benefited the most, and which components of the treatment were most effective.

Following the training, patients who received education showed improvements in their test scores on understanding and knowledge about asthma.[4] They also adhered to the regimen of care, which included both cleaning their living quarters and self-care. They showed significantly greater improvement in their bedroom environment (absence of allergenic furnishings, better dust control and cleaning practices) and much better technique in use of a metered-dose inhaler. However, the program group did not significantly improve in getting rid of pets to whom they were allergic or (for the 10% who smoked) giving up smoking, but the number of patients in these categories was small.

Final outcomes for the group-education group were positive. They were less likely to report being bothered by asthma than they had been originally and less likely than the controls; they had fewer days with symptoms than controls; physicians were more likely to judge them improved; their visits to clinics for acute care declined significantly.

However, the article reports the outcomes for the treatment and control groups as a whole and does not link outcomes to earlier stages in the program, such as attendance at group education sessions or adherence to regimen. It is likely that sample sizes would get too small to find significant differences if the group were partitioned along the lines of the theory. Still, it would be informative to know whether those who did everything right (i.e., attended sessions, cleaned up their home environ-

---

[4]The data about test scores on knowledge about asthma do not appear in the article mentioned. I talked to Sandra Wilson in 1994 and obtained this information.

ments, and used the inhaler properly) turned out to have better outcomes than others, or whether there were some features that didn't link to outcomes. One statement in the article notes that improvement in inhaler technique was associated with reduction in patients' bother with symptoms of asthma, but improvement in inhaler technique "could not account for all of the observed improvement in symptoms" (p. 575). Thus, most of the how and why questions about the program were answered through statistical analysis because the evaluation included appropriate measures to track the unfolding of outcomes.

One rival hypothesis that the evaluators explored was that physicians might have changed patients' medications over the course of the program, which could account for some of the positive results. However, they found that people in the education and control groups did not differ at the outset or at follow-up in intensity of medication (typically four or five daily drugs), and there were no significant changes in the proportions receiving specific types of medications. So medication was not the explanation for change in condition.

A finding about the superiority of group education over individual education led to further exploration of why the group program was more successful. Evaluators interviewed and learned that patients valued and benefited from the opportunity for peer support and interaction, and educators believed that the group setting encouraged patients to express fears and concerns, which the educator could then address. Also, educators were typically more comfortable in group than individual teaching. So here, the why questions were answered through reports from participants.

This report is a fine example of analysis that follows the logical progression of expected effects. It shows that qualitative evaluation doesn't have a monopoly on insight into the processes of program operation. The quantitative evaluator can do just as well if she has savvy about the program, good program theory, measures of inputs and outcomes, and appropriate measures of intervening processes along the lines of the program theory. And good statistical know-how—and the opportunity to add on further inquiry when results are puzzling.

Books on Analytic Methods

It is not possible to shoehorn a description of analytic methods into this book without terminal oversimplification. Many good books already provide the help in this arena that evaluators can use with profit. Here are a few titles.

For Quantitative Evaluation

Linear Models (Regression/ANOVA)

Afifi, A. A., & V. Clark. (1990). *Computer aided multivariate analysis* (2nd ed.). New York: Chapman and Hall.

Lunnenberg, C. (1994). *Modeling experimental and observational data*. Boston: PWS-Kent.

Neter, J., M. H. Kutner, C. J. Nachtschein, & W. Wasserman. (1996). *Applied linear statistical models* (4th ed.). Homewood, IL: Irwin.

Multi-Level Modeling

Bryk, A., & S. Raudenbush. (1992). *Hierarchical linear modeling*. Beverly Hills, CA: Sage.

Goldstein, H. (1995). *Multilevel statistical models* (2nd ed.). London: Edward Arnold.

Structural Equation Modeling

Bollen, K. A. (1989). *Structural equations with latent variables*. New York: Wiley.

Loehlin, J. C. (1992). *Latent variable models: An introduction to factor, path, and structural analysis*. Hillsdale, NJ: Erlbaum.

Event History Analysis

Allison, P. D. (1984). *Event history analysis*. Quantitative Applications in the Social Sciences, no. 46. Beverly Hills, CA: Sage.

Blossfeld, H. P., A. Hamerle, & K. U. Mayer. (1989). *Event history analysis*. Hillsdale, NJ: Erlbaum.

Yamaguchi, K. (1991). *Event history analysis*. Beverly Hills, CA: Sage.

Categorical Data Analysis, Log-linear Modeling, Logistic Regression

Agresti, A. (1990). *Categorical data analysis*. New York: Wiley.

Hosmer, D. W., & S. Lemeshow. (1989). *Applied logistic regression*. New York: Wiley.

Meta-Analysis

Cooper, H., & L. V. Hedges. (1994). *Handbook of meta-analysis*. New York: Russell Sage Foundation.

Cook, T. D., H. Cooper, D. S. Cordray, H. Hartmann, L. V. Hedges, R. J. Light, T. A. Louis, & F. Mosteller. (1992). *Meta-analysis for explanation: A casebook*. New York: Russell Sage Foundation.

For Qualitative Evaluation

Strauss, Anselm L. (1987). *Qualitative analysis for social scientists*. Cambridge: Cambridge University Press.

Silverman, David. (1993). *Interpreting qualitative data: Methods for analyzing talk, text, and interaction*. London: Sage.

Wolcott, Harry F. (1994). *Transforming qualitative data: Description, analysis, and interpretation*. Thousand Oaks, CA: Sage.

Miles, Matthew B., & A. Michael Huberman. (1994). *Qualitative data analysis: A sourcebook of new methods* (2nd ed.). Thousand Oaks, CA: Sage.

Maxwell, Joseph A. (1996). *Qualitative research methods*. Thousand Oaks, CA: Sage.

Ethical Issues

Two new ethical issues can arise somewhere around here. One has to do with ownership of the data. The evaluator often thinks that the raw data and analyses belong to her. The study sponsor may believe that his agency owns the data. The disagreement doesn't become contentious until one or the other wishes to release the data to other investigators for possible reanalysis. If a federal agency is the sponsor of the study, it is almost always willing to release data. In some large studies, the government agency will even fund the preparation of public use disks and documentation to make further analysis of the raw data easy. Other sponsors, such as foundations, national associations, and service agencies, can be less disposed to release. The best treatment for this problem is prevention. In the early phases of the study, perhaps even before the contract is signed, the evaluator and sponsor should draw up guidelines about ownership and release (and publication) of the data.

The other problem is the safeguard of confidentiality of the raw data. Even with all the protections that the evaluator has introduced (removal of names and other identifiers), computerized databases are becoming less secure. New technologies are making it easy to access databases, which can lead to the identification of sites and individuals. When databases reach the World Wide Web, the possibilities for data misuse will multiply. The problems are new, and creative people are working on solutions.

Summary

This chapter has discussed analytic strategies for making sense of data. Not seeking to duplicate textbooks devoted to methods of quantitative and qualitative analysis, it tries to reveal the logic of analysis. It sets out a range of questions that an evaluation may be called upon to address and suggests the basic technique that analysis of each question requires.

The basic questions that can be answered in analysis are: (1) what happened in the program; (2) how faithfully did the program adhere to its original plans; (3) did recipients improve: (4) did recipients fare better than nonrecipients of program service; (5) was observed change due to the program; (6) did benefits outweigh costs; (7) what characteristics of persons, services, and context were associated with program success; (8) what combinations or bundles of characteristics were associated with success; (9) through what mechanisms did success take place; (10) what were the unanticipated effects; (11) what limits are there to the applicability of the findings; (12) what are their implications for future programming; (13) what recommendations can be based on the findings; (14) what new policies and programs do the findings support.

In setting out the logic of analysis, I call attention to the commonalities between quantitative and qualitative approaches to evaluation. Both approaches make use of such basic strategies as describing, comparing, disaggregating, combining and clustering, looking at covariation, examining deviant cases, ruling out rival explanations, modeling, and interpreting and telling the story.

The evaluator's analytic priorities are determined by the purpose of the study. The purpose of the study determines the questions asked, the design used, and the analysis conducted. Take a project that offers clean needles to drug users in order to prevent their contracting AIDS. If the issue in contention is whether drug users will come to the needle exchange project and accept needles from a city agency, then the analysis concentrates on counting and describing those who come to the project and comparing those who attend with the number and characteristics of drug users in the community (from external data sources). If the burning issue is whether rates of new HIV-positive cases go down, then the analysis compares the incidence of cases before and after the initiation of the project.

The chapter also suggests that the evaluator make use of data from sources outside the project to supplement the data collected explicitly for evaluation. Such data can include data from other evaluations, data from social science research, data available in city records or agency files, and even new investigations to follow up anomalies or puzzles that the evaluation reveals. By the end of the analysis, the evaluator should have answers to the questions with which she began.

The chapter concludes with the example of an analysis of a program to educate asthma patients in techniques of self-care.

13

WRITING THE REPORT AND DISSEMINATING RESULTS

What a splendid pursuit Natural History would be if it was all observing and no writing!

—Charles Darwin (1868)[1]

The crucial remaining intellectual task is to shrink the complexity down to a relatively small number of dimensions.

—Mark H. Moore (1988)

[This] is a plea for calling shots as they really appear to be (on reflection and after weighing all evidences), even when this means losing popularity with the great audience of men and running against "the spirit of the times."

—Paul A. Samuelson (1962)

[C]alls were increasingly heard to expand the researcher's role so that he or she was made increasingly responsible, not only for producing relevant and valid results, but also for acting to bring the results to the attention of relevant parties and to help them interpret the results in terms of their interests.

—Thomas D. Cook (1985)[2]

This chapter covers three topics: writing the report of evaluation results, dissemination to prospective users, and the uses made of the results in program and policy.

---

[1]From Charles Darwin, "Letter to J. D. Hooker" (1868), quoted in Harry F. Wolcott, *Transforming Qualitative Data: Description, Analysis, and Interpretation* (Thousand Oaks, CA: Sage Publications, 1994), p. 152. Copyright © 1994 by Sage Publications, Inc. Reprinted by permission of Sage Publications, Inc.

[2]From Thomas D. Cook, "Postpositivist Critical Multiplism," in *Social Science and Social Policy*, ed. R. L. Shotland and M. N. Mark (Beverly Hills, CA: Sage Publications, 1985), pp. 21–62. Copyright © 1985 by Sage Publications, Inc. Reprinted by permission of Sage Publications, Inc.

Reporting

Putting the Report Together

The time has come to write. Questions have been posed, data collected, information analyzed and interpreted, and the output now has to be put down on paper. Soon perhaps paper will be obsolete, and the report will be electronically composed and distributed. But the report will still require composition—words, numbers, and interpretation.

Some people who thrive on the earlier phases of evaluation—framing the problem, designing the study, collecting and analyzing data—become anxious when faced with the necessity of writing the report. The quote from Charles Darwin in the epigraph above gives the texture of their lament. Writing well is as difficult a task as any of the more technical tasks in evaluation, but it is learnable and doable. Several sources of help are available. Becker (1986) offers good advice. Even more useful may be an article by Krieger (1988). It is short, knowledgeable, and full of gems like these: "Your aim is to get done. First, a draft. Then you can fix it. Try not to worry about your career or God's judgment. Just get done" (p. 410). "Outlines can be in any form. Alter them as you go along, adding in bits and pieces, elaborations, working out the next section as you need to" (p. 411). "Don't look back. Keep on writing. You can always cut and paste *later.... *Edit *later.* Look up things *later.* Footnotes *later*" (p. 411). "Theory works in the same way that comparative cases do. It gives you a baseline from which you can be surprised. It helps you make sense of what you are doing. You always have a theory, perhaps an unarticulated one, but you always do" (p. 413). "Working it out makes it work. Writing leads to a making sense of the world you did not know you possessed" (p. 409). The main theme is that the secret to writing is to keep on writing. Get help from your friends, if you need it, but don't allow yourself to get bogged down. Just keep going until you have told the story that your data indicate.

Contents of the Report

What should the report look like? The answer to that question, as to many questions in evaluation, is: It depends. It depends primarily on who the audience is. It also depends on how many separate versions of the report will be prepared for different audiences. And it depends on what the audiences expect.

A comprehensive report is usually required by the study sponsor and is of interest to program managers. But it may be overkill for other audiences. Staff, clients, policymakers, and the public are likely to toss aside a big heavy document that tells them too much, however brightly it is written. Briefer, more modest versions can be custom made for audiences that want capsule versions of the central findings.

By and large, the report for evaluation sponsors should be addressed directly to the questions underlying the evaluation. Give the main findings up front. An evaluation report is not a mystery story where the reader is kept guessing until the denouement at the end. Neither is it like an academic paper that begins with a history of the question, a review of previous research, and a description of methodology. In an evaluation report, the findings come first. That's what people want to know.

FIGURE 13-1 POSSIBLE OUTLINE FOR EVALUATION REPORT

I. Summary of Study Results
   A. Questions addressed
   B. Brief description of program
   C. Main findings
      1. Concise summary of findings
      2. Implications
      3. Recommendations for the particular audience (program improvement, policy action, etc.)
II. Problem with Which the Program Deals
   A. Size, scope, seriousness, trends over time
   B. Prior efforts to deal with it
III. Nature of the Program
   A. Goals and objectives
   B. Activities
      1. Original plan of activities
      2. Actual program activities
         a. Content
         b. Frequency
         c. Intensity
         d. Changes over time
         e. Consistency with, changes from, original program design
   C. Context
      1. Sponsorship of the program
      2. Setting(s)
         a. Community
         b. Site
         c. Facilities
      3. History of the program
      4. Funding
   D. Beneficiaries
      1. Number and characteristics
      2. How recruited
      3. Length of stay in program
      4. Dropouts
      5. Other relevant data
   E. Staff
      1. Number and characteristics
      2. Length of time with program
      3. Other relevant characteristics

IV. Nature of the Evaluation
    A. Central questions
    B. Conduct of the study
        1. Study design
        2. Time period covered
        3. Methods of data collection (brief; detail in appendix)
        4. Methods of analysis (briefer; detail in appendix)
    C. Results
        1. Findings
        2. Limitations to the findings
        3. Conclusions
        4. Interpretation
    D. Recommendations for action
V. Comparison with Evaluations of Similar Programs (optional)
VI. Suggestions for Further Evaluation (optional)
VII. Acknowledgments
    Appendices
    A. Methodology
    B. Tables of data
    C. Transcripts of selected narrative material

Figure 13-1 presents an outline of what a full-scale report of an evaluation might cover. For people who want to know all the details, and for documentation and archival purposes, the full report will contain a discussion of the problem with which the program deals, a description of the program, perhaps illustrative anecdotes about significant happenings, and full discussion of the data. Study methods will also be described in detail, often in an appendix.

The first section is an executive summary. It is designed for readers who want a rapid overview of findings. Most people will read little more than this section, so make it good. Select the most important findings and present them cogently. Explain the evidence that supports the conclusions, but without much technical detail. The paragraph on implications should discuss the meaning of the findings for the future. In Chapter 12, I discussed whether or not the evaluator should include recommendations in the report. If the evaluator is qualified to do so and expected to do so, a summary of the recommendations belongs in this section. She should explain the evidence on which the recommendations are based.

The executive summary can also be issued as a separate report for a wide audience. In fact, because different sets of readers have somewhat varying interests, perhaps several versions of it will be prepared. The findings that interest program staff probably deal with the aspects of the program over which they have some control. They are likely to want to know about recruitment of participants, their retention in the program, how well activities are being implemented, the kinds of service that work more or less effectively, program rules that help or hinder, clients' eye views, and similar things. The summary written for them can give overall findings but then focus on issues that fall within their purview.

A summary report for program clients and the public should be shorter and focus on highlights. By and large, these audiences are not as interested in particularities as are the people whose work lives are bound up in the program. They want to know what the evaluation can tell them that affects *them*, their choices, and their future. The language in the report should be simple and straightforward but not condescending.

Policy audiences are likely to want a different order of information. Federal program managers, foundation executives, school board members, and others of their ilk have to make decisions not about specific clients in a particular setting but for larger publics (e.g., all families receiving nutrition supplements, all special education students in the school district). They want to know the broad picture. Some of them also need to know the patterns that suggest possible changes in eligibility rules, levels of funding, types of staffing, and types of services. The summary for them needs to be short and crisp, highlighting the main results and the basis for them.

Preparing separate reports for different audiences is expensive and time-consuming. However, if the evaluator hopes that the report will have an influence on the future of policy and program, it is important that people know about and understand the evaluation results. People in decision-making communities need to understand what the study did and did not find out, and any subsequent action that they propose on the basis of the findings needs the support of clients, staff, and the public. Without an informed public, reformative action stands much less chance of enactment.

The rest of the report can follow the outline in Figure 13-1. None of the sections needs to be long. The description of the problem and earlier efforts to cope with it draws on information that was probably available when the program began operation. This section puts the program into the larger social context. The section on the program is meant to clarify what went on. It discusses the program's goals, the intended plan of action, the actual activities that were implemented and how they changed over time. If the evaluator has conducted a process evaluation, she will have a great deal of information to report here, but even without a concerted study of implementation, the report should give the reader a picture of the program in action.

Also useful is a description of the context within which the program operated. Here mention might be made of the sponsor, the setting, any prior history of the program that is relevant, and something about funding. It is not necessary to give dollar amounts of funding, although something might be said about its general level, and note can be taken of whether the program grant is expected to continue indefinitely or is time-limited, with or without the possibility of refunding.

Short sections can describe the participants and staff in the program. Readers will understand outcomes much more readily if they know how many people participated, what their characteristics were, how long they received program service, how many dropped out (and if it is known, why they dropped out), and anything else that is relevant to outcomes. Description of staff members can help the reader put flesh on the outline of program activities: who it was who delivered program services, what their educational levels were, how continuous their tenure with the program was, and so on. If the management of the program was relevant to program success, that may be important to note.

The next section is the big section of the report. It goes into much more detail than the executive summary about the findings of the study. It discusses the main questions the study addressed, the time period it covered, and the methods used for data collection and analysis. The methodological paragraphs should be short; only researchers like to read discussions of methodology. Other readers want to know enough to be assured that the study was conducted with high competence. Full discussion of data collection and analysis belongs in the appendix. Here the main emphasis is on the findings.

In describing study results, give the conclusions first and then support them with data. Novices sometimes go through their analysis step by step to explain how they proceeded and present conclusions only at the end. This is not the place to display your thinking processes or analytic legerdemain. Be forthright. You're the evaluator. Explain what you found, and then give the supporting evidence. If the data are qualitative, this will usually mean providing themes that emerged from the data, buttressed by quotes from respondents and stories of observations. If there was diversity of opinion or divergent evidence, it is wise to report it and indicate how rare (or common) it was.

The section on interpretation considers the meaning of the findings in context. It describes the evaluator's view of the implications for action and indicates which stakeholder groups were consulted and agreed. If some groups offered interpretations with which the evaluator did not agree, she may want to incorporate their ideas as an alternative perspective. She can marshal evidence and logic and present her reasons for not agreeing, but she gives their views a hearing. Whatever limitations exist to the study's conclusions (short time period, low response rate, loss of cases, etc.) deserve an important place in the report as well.

A recommendations section, if there is one, can go into more detail here than in the executive summary. The section should explain the basis for the recommendations and the reasons that the evaluator believes they would lead to improvement. If she has done preliminary analysis of how the recommended changes might work out, the information belongs here. She can also present whatever she knows (and can justify) about circumstances that may make recommendations easy or hard to implement and the level and kind of resources that would be required to put them in place. If she knows the agency well enough, she can discuss where responsibility for making the changes should lie.

The report might also include a section on how the findings of this evaluation fit with findings from prior evaluations of similar programs. If this study marks a change from previous experience, the reader will be interested, especially if the evaluator has evidence or good hunches about the reason why. Given the harried schedule of many evaluators, such a section is a luxury that they may have to forgo. But if the evaluator has been evaluating similar kinds of programs over the years, she probably knows enough to write the section without a lot of extra work.

Another optional section is a discussion of questions still outstanding. No evaluation settles all the questions in the field, even provisionally, and the evaluator may have found some tantalizing bits of evidence that cry out for further investigation. Or she may have discovered much more (or much less) success than evaluations of similar programs without being able to pinpoint the reasons. An additional study could follow up. It is worth recording whatever direction the evaluator sees for productive work.

Although it has not been common practice, the evaluator should usually include somewhere in the report a statement about the sponsorship of the evaluation. Unless there are compelling reasons to the contrary, the reader should be told who paid the bills and whether there is any possibility of a conflict of interest. A well-known study of violence on television and its effects on children was sponsored by the NBC television network. The study concluded that there was little evidence to believe that television violence stimulated violent behavior in children. Although it was a methodologically sound study, it differed from other research on the topic, and the study's sponsorship was relevant information. In the spirit of open disclosure, the evaluator may want to include information about her own affiliations, too. For example, if she is on the staff of a consultant organization that also provides technical assistance to the program, readers might well be informed.

Characteristics of the Report

Clarity   The report should be clear. It should be written in language that speaks to program and policy people. Save the abstruse statistics and sociological theory and the references to Foucault for the academic paper published in professional journals. (Later I give an outline for an academic paper.)

Graphics   Charts, diagrams, and graphs can lend visual appeal. They should be self-explanatory, with all the information necessary for interpretation included. The familiar pie charts and bar charts can be expanded to show comparisons between different sets of data, and line graphs offer a versatile technique for showing changes over time. (See Henry, 1995.) A wonderful source of ideas on graphic presentation by Tufte (1983) offers a wide array of ingenious charts.[3] Simple tables can also tell a story economically and clearly (Moses, 1987). For reports to a nonresearch audience, it is usually advisable to avoid complex tables and equations, but visual displays, like stem and leaf plots or scatter diagrams, can convey a great deal of information fairly painlessly and add visual spice to the report.

Program Theory   Where in the report does the discussion of program theory go and who gets it? To the extent that the evaluation has examined the underlying assumptions on which the program is based, it will have much to say about which assumptions are supported in the present instance and which did not appear to work. For example, a community-wide program to coordinate all social services that serve a set of high-risk families was based on a theory that better coordination among service professionals would lead to better assistance to the families. The evaluation had little to say about that theory because it was never put into practice. Professionals from different agencies were so hamstrung by the rules and procedures of their own agencies and their own professional beliefs that they could not achieve effective coordination. The evaluation thus puts into question another assumption underlying the program, namely that convening a group of high-level agency managers and

---

[3]Tufte has written two subsequent books. In one (1990), he concentrates on design strategies for portraying substantive (largely non-numerical) information, with special attention to maps, transportation schedules, and dance and musical notation. The other (1997) describes graphic designs that give a sense of three dimensionality and motion. In all of his books, Tufte provides examples of poor chart work, designs that obscure more information than they reveal.

gaining their assent to coordination will actually result in coordination. Where does the examination of this theory belong in the reporting process?

First of all, it is not necessary to label this assumption a theory, or even a hypothesis. Those words sound pretentious to some readers (sometimes even to me). But the finding is obviously of importance to a wide range of audiences—policymakers, managers, service staff, clients, program designers, social scientists, and other evaluators. Each of them has an interest in knowing how difficult it was to bring about coordination. They should know, too, that if the program failed to bring about improvement in the target families, it was not because coordination was a bad idea. As G. K. Chesterton said about Christianity, it hasn't failed; it just hasn't been tried. For those who seek to understand what it takes to make programs succeed, the main theoretical insight is the failure of the convert-and-command assumption. Evidently agency executives were not converted enough to promote coordination in their agencies, and/or top-down commands from agency executives to their staffs to coordinate could not overcome the bureaucratic pressures that maintained the status quo.

Theory can help to structure the report and make it more understandable, but it needs to be phrased in ways that fit the interests and style of the audience.

Timeliness   Timeliness is a useful quality in an evaluation report. When the report is available *prior to* the making of decisions about the program, it has a greater potential for impact. A report that comes out after the future of the program has been decided is obviously of lesser value to decision makers. On the other hand, if the report is not ready in time for the next legislative vote or budget authorization, it does not necessarily lose all chance for influence. Sometimes these milestones do not take place when they were originally scheduled. The legislature postpones hearings, and voting is delayed. The agency is diverted to new issues. The evaluation report that was rushed through to be on time for the April decision sits around until November when the policy community gets around to the matter.

Furthermore, questions about the program, if they are important enough, do not get settled once and for all. They surface again and again. A program is reauthorized and funds are allocated repeatedly. Rules and regulations are changed periodically. People will still want to know each time which groups are reached and not reached, which kinds of clients are best served, and which services have the best record of success. Inasmuch as many uses of evaluation are not direct and immediate, but take place over a longer period in a variety of indirect ways, the report that comes out after the current decision still has an opportunity to make a difference—especially if the study has been done with scrupulous care and has something significant to say.

Still, it is a decided advantage to meet decision deadlines. Promptness demonstrates the reliability of the evaluators and their intention to be of help. Promptness increases the number of opportunities to make a difference. But it is probably not wise to be prompt if it means sacrificing the trustworthiness of results. Sometimes if time is very short, you may be able to give an interim report on matters of immediate concern to the program community and include only those results you can fully justify, saving a fuller analysis for a later report.

Candor about Strengths and Limitations   The evaluation report should always indicate the degree of confidence that readers can have in its findings and the limitations on its applicability. There is an ethical dimension in acknowledging where the report falls short (representativeness of its respondents? number of cases? special conditions under which the program operated?) and how far the results can be generalized. It is also smart strategy. Readers, especially savvy readers who have been through evaluations before, are more likely to trust a report when the authors acknowledge its shortcomings. They also have a better idea of which findings to rely on, which are likely to be questionable or controversial, and how far out on a limb they should go in following the guidance the report provides.

Generalizability   One of the limitations of the study is likely to be that it was a captive of a particular time and place. The program and policy communities want to know whether the findings about five projects in Tennessee will generalize to their states, and whether they should try to fix the flaws identified in Tennessee before importing the program model. The evaluator should provide explicit information about the projects evaluated (what they did, with what staffing and level of resources, for which kinds of recipients) and about the sample of participants whom she studied. Such information will help prospective users of the evaluation decide how well the findings fit their situation. Because program and policy communities are looking toward the future, they are also interested in how the finding will apply in different time periods. Anything the report can say about the environments in which the evaluated projects operated and how closely the circumstances resemble conditions looming ahead will assist readers to judge the study's generalizability.

Inclusion of the Program Organization's Views   Some organizations, like the U.S. General Accounting Office, send their draft reports to the agencies whose work they are reviewing. GAO policy is that the "report should include the pertinent views of responsible officials of the organization, program, activity, or function audited [i.e., evaluated] concerning the auditors' findings, conclusions, and recommendations, and what corrective action is planned" (U.S. General Accounting Office, 1992, p. 14.1–6). GAO asks for written critical comments, and then revises the report to the extent that it believes the agency's criticism is justified. Where it does not agree, it explains its position and the reasons for it. An official GAO (1991) manual gives advice to its staff:

> Critical comments must be effectively rebutted or GAO's position must be presented more persuasively; that is, do not restate the same position but phrase it differently and provide factual support to convince the reader.... Where an agency presents persuasive arguments that validly refute the draft or aspects of it, GAO should modify its position and may want to consider dropping the portion in question.... An entire copy of the agency's comments may be included as an appendix to the report. (pp. 12.11–10,11)

In practice, GAO often binds the agency's full critique into the final report. Readers thus have full access to alternative views.

Since GAO works in a highly visible and political environment, it takes special pains to represent the views of the agencies whose programs it has evaluated. While most evaluators do not go this far, the GAO example is an important model.

Reporting to an Academic Audience

It often makes good sense to report study results to academic audiences as well. If knowledge about the effectiveness of programs and program approaches is to cumulate, the study must reach the relevant professional and academic groups. These are the people who plan programs, evaluate programs, teach the next generations of practitioners, managers, and policymakers, and serve on advisory groups at all levels. It is important that they hear the lessons of evaluation.

The appropriate channel for reaching these groups is an article in a professional journal. But there are several different academic audiences—social scientists who study human and organizational behavior, evaluators of social programs, and scholars in relevant professional fields, such as education, public health, or social work. Each group reads different journals. The evaluator has to figure out the important things she has to say and then choose a journal that reaches the relevant audience. When the evaluation has information useful to professionals, she has to select the specific findings that would matter for program design, professional education, or social policy. For an evaluation audience, she needs to select the findings that would appeal to their interests, either substantive or methodological. For social scientists, such as psychologists, sociologists, or economists, the emphasis might be on the theoretical learnings of the study and its insights into how people and organizations function.

Journal articles have their own logic of presentation. Most evaluators learn that tradition during their graduate training. It is quite different from the form of presentation that appeals to other audiences but serves its own purposes. Figure 13-2 is a possible outline for a journal article.

FIGURE 13-2 POSSIBLE OUTLINE FOR JOURNAL ARTICLE

I. The Issue Addressed
  A. The question this article deals with
  B. What makes the question problematic
  C. Review of prior evaluation, research, and theory on the topic
II. Description of the Study
  A. Methods of study
  B. Description of data
  C. Methods of analysis
III. Results
  A. Findings related to the question in I.
  B. Discussion/interpretation of findings
IV. Implications
  A. For theory and knowledge
  B. For policy or programmatic action
  C. For further research
V. References

Perhaps the most important point is that this kind of reporting doesn't attempt a comprehensive review of the study's results. Rather, it requires careful selection of evidence to make an argument. The purpose is likely to be to extend the existing literature, challenge prior knowledge, or add to theory.

Sponsor's Right to Demand Changes in the Report

In Chapter 4, I recommended that the evaluator and the study sponsor work out an agreement during the planning stage of the study about whether the evaluator has full control over the study report. The agreement should indicate whether she has the right to include what she believes is appropriate in the report or whether the sponsor can insist on changes. The agreement should include provisions about the right to release and distribute the report and the right to publish in academic and professional journals. That may have seemed like picky advice back in Chapter 4, but here is where it comes home to roost.

Sometimes an evaluation report turns out to be highly critical of a program or of its implementation in a particular locale. The manager and/or staff can find the report disturbing, and they may honestly believe that it is incorrect. They may assume that the evaluator doesn't understand the dismal conditions under which they work or the much worse record of other programs that confront the same kinds of problems. They call for changes in the report.

The evaluator should listen with an open mind. Being a good listener is not only nice, it can be rewarding. The sponsor or the staff have insights to offer. Perhaps their interpretation should lead to a softening of certain conclusions or a recasting of others. If so, the evaluator can profit from their suggestions. But if she listens and considers and then decides that the changes they want violate the meaning of the data, she should have the right to say no. She can include their objections in an appendix to the report, which may satisfy most of the critics. But autonomy is an important value in evaluation. The evaluator should not be coerced or cajoled into being an apologist for the program when her data tell her otherwise. A major contribution of evaluation is to provide an independent assessment, so that informed publics can trust the findings.

If no agreement was reached in advance about who has rights to change and to release reports, and the program agency insists on revisions, the time for a donnybrook has arrived. Study sponsors may threaten to hold up payment for the last part of the evaluation unless the evaluator capitulates to their demands. Life can become intensely irksome. My advice to the evaluator is to stand by her principles. She can cite the research codes of the American Evaluation Association or such other professional associations as the American Sociological Association or the American Psychological Association. If there is one universal research rule, it is: Do not distort the data.

Similar precepts apply to the release of a report. If the sponsoring agency cannot force changes, it may seek to delay release of the report until after its salience has faded. A year from now interest may have died down in the agency and elsewhere. The evaluator is in a tenuous position when refused permission to send out copies. If she does so against a clear directive, she may be in for sorry times.

The best remedy for these ills is advance agreement, preferably in writing. The agreement should specify the degree of autonomy that the evaluation staff will have. It should indicate the procedures to be followed if disputes about interpretation of the data arise. It should specify the conditions under which the report will be released and who has the right to control release dates, reporting modes, and audiences. Again, should disagreements arise, there needs to be a predetermined appeals procedure. While recognizing the rights of the agency to monitor the quality of the evaluation and to protect itself against irresponsible work, the evaluator should not bargain away the independence of the study from politically motivated pressure.

Dissemination

Reports are one kind of dissemination device. They alert a variety of stakeholders to the fact that the study has been completed and has something to report. If stakeholders actually read the report, they can learn the lessons that came out of the study. The large comprehensive report that goes to the study's sponsor serves a number of other useful functions. It fulfills the contractual obligation for reporting that usually accompanies evaluation funding. It is also a repository of information to which people can refer for specifics about data, method, and interpretation. When different people remember divergent messages from the study, the report is the place they can turn to resolve the conflict.

But it is probably unrealistic to rely heavily on the report (even on the separate carefully tailored reports) to get the word out. Only a few dedicated or concerned individuals are apt to read reports with much care. They are either hungry for guidance, or worried about the effect of the report on the program and their own career, or zealous about doing the necessary spadework for some political policy initiative—or they are professionals whose job it is to keep up with the literature. Most other people will learn what the study had to say through *talk*. Interpersonal communication tends to be more powerful than written documents.

Strategies for Dissemination to Practitioners

Intensive Interaction   There is a body of research on knowledge utilization, which examines the communication of research results to such direct-service staff as teachers, nurses, physicians, parole officers, and judges. Although the lessons derive mostly from inquiry about research studies, there is good reason to believe that they apply to evaluation as well. Some knowledge utilization studies have found three key requirements for successful communication of research messages.

1. *Inclusion of potential users of new research knowledge in the process of the research.* The researcher gives practitioners an opportunity to help shape the research questions at the outset, giving them feedback of early results, encouraging them to participate in interpretation of data, and so on. When time comes for dissemination of the final report, the audience has come to understand and have a sense of ownership of the findings.
2. *Making the communication between researchers and practitioners truly two-way communication.* Researchers often want to do all the talking. They have the word, and they want to pass it on to the uninitiated. They need to listen to, and respect, what practitioners have to say. They have to recognize that they do not

have a monopoly on knowledge and can learn from the wisdom of practice. Practitioners want to be heard as well as harangued, and when they feel like equal partners, not passive receivers of messages, they are more likely to take research results seriously.

3. *Sustained interaction over time.* As the two previous points have suggested, personal contact between researchers and practitioners is important through the course of the research. It is just as essential, perhaps more essential, after the report is finished. Then is the time when practitioners have to wrestle with questions of whether and how to apply the findings in their own organizations and their own practice. When the researcher continues to meet and talk with them over a year or more, the research results remain in the forefront of their attention. They have an opportunity to discuss alternative interpretations of the data with the researcher, and together they may come to greater insight about the meaning of the data. Opportunities multiply for rethinking practice in the light of the findings and for creatively crafting new directions that build on the results of the research (Fullan, 1991; Huberman, 1989).

These lessons from studies of knowledge utilization probably apply in full measure to the use of evaluation results. If the evaluator can follow the precepts, chances are good that practitioners with whom she interacts will hear about the findings, accept them as credible and relevant, and even begin to use them as a basis for thinking and acting differently. However, there are some obvious limitations to this dissemination strategy.

Limitations to Intensive Interpersonal Strategies   For one thing, this degree of involvement with program people is expensive in both time and cost. Very rarely do evaluators have sufficient funding to support ongoing meetings with practitioners and to continue disseminating the results of their study for lengthy periods after study completion. They usually have to go on to the next study.

Another limitation is that they reach only the subset of practitioners who can be readily identified as stakeholders. They probably miss a great many people who would be interested in using evaluation results if they had a chance to learn about them—people in other agencies who run programs similar to those that were evaluated or who are considering initiation of such programs. For example, if the evaluation dealt with an innovative bilingual program in one school district, there are probably 1,000 other districts that could profit from the information if they knew about it. But these strategies do not reach them.

Furthermore, agency staffs are not always constant over time. Some people lose interest, or are distracted by other obligations, and fail to attend meetings. Moreover, staff members change jobs—and agencies. Practitioners come and go, and the people with whom the evaluator worked at the beginning are not there at the end when results are ready to be implemented. Not infrequently, a new manager comes in who has little interest in the old evaluation and has a very different agenda for action.

Finally, these kinds of strategies do little to reach policy actors. No congressman or state legislator is going to sit through a series of sessions with evaluators no matter how concerned he is about bilingual education. There are just too many other demands on his time. Heads of federal agencies, directors of national organizations, foundation executives, and other key actors in the policy process cannot devote the time to continuing contacts that high involvement strategies demand. For these kinds of audiences, alternative strategies are needed.

Other Direct Strategies   To reach audiences beyond the immediate project, evaluators can seize opportunities in the wider professional milieu. They can give speeches to organizations of practitioners, present findings at conferences where relevant audiences congregate, participate in professional development workshops, and generally make concerted efforts to reach people who can put evaluation findings to use.

One of the advantages of talking to professional audiences in this way is that the message becomes amplified. One professional who hears a speech or participates in a roundtable with the evaluator takes the story home. He tells his colleagues and friends. They discuss the ideas, argue about them, pass them along. Although much of the detail is lost, and some of the findings may even be distorted in the re-telling, a widening circle will hear about evaluation results.

Gaining a personal interview with an important policymaker can be useful, but it is well to remember that he is bombarded with requests for his time from scores of people who want to sell him something. Unless the evaluator has a special "in," arrangements for this kind of audience probably require more effort than they are worth.

Written modes can be effective if tailored to the audience. Where people are not apt to read a report on the study, no matter how short and snappy, they can often be attracted by a news item or a column in a publication they routinely read. Thus, the evaluator can try to place a column or interview in a publication for practitioners. She needs to know which journals and magazines the relevant practitioner groups read. She can contact editors to find out how to place a short piece on nutrition or parole or preschool care.

Special pamphlets or newsletters can be crafted to appeal to a particular public. Sometimes the research organization for which the evaluator works circulates newsletters describing its work, and a summary of study results belongs there. The evaluator can submit copies of reports to bibliographic services, clearinghouses, and on-line databases.

Dissemination through Intermediaries   Reaching distant program audiences and actors in the policy process is a difficult task for an evaluator to accomplish on her own. Fortunately, there are a number of intermediary institutions that can be pressed into service. They are not foolproof carriers of the evaluation message, but when they work, they help to get evaluation results into professional conversation and policy discourse.

THE MASS MEDIA   Some evaluations produce newsworthy findings. They contradict long-accepted beliefs. Or they touch upon a subject that a mass audience cares about, such as health care or children's well-being. Or they deal with issues on the political agenda, like education reform. Or they generate conflict among professionals or organizations. Or they uncover a paradox. Or they just happen to be on a particular reporter's agenda. When an evaluation coincides with journalistic values—such as public concerns, the explosion of myths, timely political news, conflict, paradox, or reportorial agenda—it may be possible to interest reporters in its coverage (Weiss & Singer, 1988). Thus, the *New York Times* (Chira, 1993) covered a study of day-care centers that showed the shortage of care available to working-class families, and it identified the dilemma that these families faced—too poor to pay for care and too rich to get subsidies. It was a human interest story. Evaluation results can sometimes be modeled into stories of human interest, a genre that appeals to reporters.

When the mass media report an evaluation, it gets widespread attention. The story reaches professionals, potential clients, and members of the public. It also reaches policy actors, who are more likely to pay attention because they know that their constituents and colleagues have access to it, too. They cannot sweep the findings under the rug. If the subject is within their jurisdiction, they may be asked about the study. They had better be informed.

If the sponsor of the evaluation is a government agency, a large foundation, or a national association, the sponsor may hold a press conference and invite reporters from many papers to attend. The evaluator will be invited to make a brief presentation, pointing up facets of the data that have appeal for a mass media audience. She also has a chance to answer questions and give more information. Without this type of sponsorship, the evaluator herself can send a press release to local newspapers highlighting findings that appear to be newsworthy. She can follow up with phone calls, and if she receives expressions of interest, she can talk to reporters in person. These kinds of initiatives are sometimes successful in getting journalistic notice, less often with television, which wants pictures, than with the press. I did a study of the reporting of social science, including evaluation, in the mass media, and the book contains tips from successful social scientists on how to attract media attention (Weiss & Singer, 1988).

STAFF AIDES   Whereas securing a private audience with a policymaker or getting him to read even a one-page summary is a difficult feat, his aides are more accessible. They are the ones who are expected to be well informed about details, to keep up with the professional literature, and to be knowledgeable enough to write detailed legislation, regulations, or policy memos. They have more of a stake in finding out the latest news about the programmatic area in their bailiwick. With responsibility for the specifics of policy action, they are often the best people to make use of evaluation findings directly. For conveying the big picture, they have the ear of their principals.

If the evaluator has connections with people in appropriate offices, a few strategic phone calls may secure an appointment. If she doesn't, she can try calling anyway. Some staff members are very accessible.

CONSULTANTS, TRAINERS, AND ADVISORS   In almost every area of social programming, an army of specialists offers consultation and advice to operating agencies. Some of these specialists are individuals whose expertise arises from their many years of practice in the field. Sometimes they are academics who reach beyond the walls of the academy to influence the direction and quality of programming. An evaluator who convinces such specialists of the salience of her findings may be able to influence the nature of the advice they purvey to a large number of agencies and programs.

INTEREST GROUPS   The notion of disseminating evaluation results to interest groups strikes some people as verging on the unethical. The interest group has already made up its mind. It knows which interest it wants to advance. It is not likely to change its mind on the basis of evaluative evidence. If it uses evaluation, it will press it into the service of a predetermined cause.

Nevertheless, if the interest group does not distort the evidence, they are a perfectly respectable audience. When the evaluation supports the position the group is already taking, they will take the results and run with them. Since they are usually experts in the ways of the policy world, they almost ensure the results a hearing in important circles.

Of course, interest groups will attend to the findings selectively, amplifying those data they find congenial and ignoring those they dislike. However, evidence suggests that they do not generally distort the evidence (Rosenthal, 1993; Weiss, 1989). Their influence among policymakers depends on their credibility. If they are found to be lying, they forfeit all access to higher circles and essentially end their careers. The evaluator who can tolerate a certain selectivity in the reporting of her findings (which is easier when she is in sympathy with the group's basic position) will find that the interest group represents a pre-sold audience that may give the findings high visibility in the course of their lobbying activity.

POLICY NETWORKS   The policy network is an informal aggregation of specialists who keep in continuing contact around developments in a particular substantive field (Heclo, 1977; Sabatier & Jenkins-Smith, 1993). There are networks around school financing, energy conservation, AIDS treatment, and many other topics. Participants select themselves into a network largely on the basis of their jobs and interest. They tend to come from federal and state agencies, legislatures, the media, universities, research organizations, and interest groups. They maintain contact largely by telephone, and they hold continuing conversations about what is happening and what should happen next. Since some of the participants are analysts, they are receptive to analytic information, and they share the information in the course of their talk. When evaluation information and ideas enter such a network, if they are believed, they can be incorporated into the ongoing conversation—and perhaps ultimately into action that the network has supported.

These are some of the intermediary institutions that can assist in the dissemination of evaluation results. An evaluator with an important and interesting message can make efforts to get her message heard in these venues. None of them is in business to disseminate evaluation knowledge. They are busy with their own concerns. The media aim to inform and entertain mass publics. Interest groups want to secure favorable action for their cause from executive and legislative agencies. Nevertheless, each of them on occasion adopts evaluation findings and incorporates them into persuasive messages for key audiences.

Utilization of Evaluation Results

Given her efforts at dissemination, the evaluator often finds that the organization begins to make changes in practice and in policy. The changes may be slow in coming, but in time the organization takes the lessons of evaluation to heart and alters the way it works. However, in other cases, nothing much seems to change. She has heeded all the injunctions in the text: gained commitment from administrators, geared the study to agency purposes, involved practitioners, conducted a methodologically competent study, completed it in time for decisions, and disseminated results briskly, and still the results seem to be ignored. How can this happen? How can an organization that has gone to the trouble of engaging an evaluator and paying for a study proceed to ignore it?

The reasons fall into two general categories: characteristics of organizations and politics.

Organizational Resistances

Organizations tend to find the status quo a contentedly feasible state. Changing organizational practices takes money, a factor often in short supply. It requires management effort and time. Often it requires changing the accustomed practices and habits of staff, who are satisfied with things as they are and believe in their present way of working. If new skills are needed, this will take retraining of old staff (again time, money, a break in comfortable routines) or the employment of new people (who must be found, attracted, paid, and kept).

In short, an organization is a complex social system. It has built up a pattern of staff role behaviors and a system of motivation and rewards for compliance with existing roles. It is not sure that it will be successful in instituting new patterns. Small wonder that the organization wants to be convinced that new practices will have significantly better outcomes than old ways before it disrupts existing arrangements.

Further, organizations have concerns other than achieving their goals. They are interested in survival. Program managers are out to protect their programs and their organizations. They want to generate support, maintain their position in the political and interorganizational environment, and satisfy their constituencies. Evaluators tend to assume that accomplishing the objectives for which the program was established is the overriding imperative. But for program managers, the priority is to keep the agency—and the program—going. If they ignore evaluation results, it is for the larger good, as they see it—to maintain a functioning agency with its capacity to give important services to clients who need the services.

Nor should these survival concerns necessarily be viewed as antithetical to the achievement of goals. Although they can contribute to organizational rigidity, they are also in one sense preconditions for effective activity. The organization is building up strength and credits for the future. Managements sometimes fear that too much change, too frequent or too drastic, will lead to instability, a lack of direction, and a loss of confidence in the organization's capabilities. These are authentic concerns.

Another set of issues has to do with the acceptability of new practices to outside groups. Revisions in program may cause changes in relationships to funders, clients, agencies that refer clients, agencies that receive clients, and other community organizations. There is a chance that the changes will not be acceptable. If they conflict with current expectations and fail to satisfy the interests of these groups, the organization may be in for a period of struggle and chaotic adjustment.

Further, new practices may not fit in with prevailing social values or the interests of one segment of society or another. For example, a recommendation to reduce the number of children in special education classes can run into objections from parents who want the services for their children. Even if proposed changes would help to improve achievement of program goals, it is perfectly possible that they will have deleterious side effects and create new kinds of problems. Lack of certainty about the acceptance of the recommendations outside the agency can be an effective inhibitor of change.

Organizations also tend to believe in a set of values and in particular methods of work. Any conclusions that threaten their basic allegiances are likely to receive short shrift. Thus, studies that discount the effectiveness of traffic safety courses or graduate fellowships or that suggest alternatives to individual psychotherapy meet with resistance from agencies committed to these values and procedures. When one evaluation showed that a group work program for potentially delinquent high school girls was ineffective in preventing delinquent behavior, the agency response was to suggest an increase in the number of group sessions per week. Wherever strong ideological commitments are involved (particularly to basic beliefs), even totally negative results will not lead to abandonment of programs; evaluation must offer guidance for improving the way programs meet their goals.

Evaluators may think of the program as an intervention, constructed so that they can study its effects, but to policymakers and program staff, the program is something else. It is often their cause, something they believe in, something in which they have a big psychological and political stake. They may feel a strong bond to the clients with whom they deal—victims of spouse abuse, schizophrenics, special-needs children. For some, the program is also their job, their livelihood, their route to advancement. The program has little resemblance to the antiseptic experiments of the psychological lab.

Organizational constraints on the use of evaluation results come into play primarily when study results disclose shortcomings in program performance. When the evaluation demonstrates high success, the program agency is likely to celebrate, but there is little there to use in instrumental fashion to improve the state of the art. The agency can publicize the results to policy actors in order to bolster support of the program and increase its budget. If the program agency is a nonprofit organization dependent on philanthropic contributions, donors should expect circulars in the mail trumpeting the effectiveness of activities and asking for increased donations. Inasmuch as enhancing support for effective services is an appropriate goal for evaluation, these are appropriate uses. But the negative report is tossed into the basket between "In" and "Out" that is marked "Stalled."

Certainly, conscientious administrators want to do good as well as do well, but they can find cheerful rationalizations for persisting in an unproductive course

("The poor showing is temporary"; "It's the result of outside conditions"; "All we need is more money"; "The evaluation isn't very good anyway").

Political Constraints

Political considerations can also inhibit attention to evaluation. Evaluation is not only a scientific enterprise; it is also an exercise in politics. It derives its political overtones from two basic sources. It is dealing with real-world programs that are created and maintained by political forces through political processes. Second, people in higher echelons of government, who will make decisions about the future of the programs, are embedded in politics.

Programs do not just happen. Programs come into being through political processes, through the rough and tumble of political support, opposition, and bargaining. Because evaluations are likely to be requested when the programs are relatively new, the political origins are fresh and warm. Legislative or agency sponsors have attached their reputations to the program. Clients, some of whom may have been mobilized to help secure funding for the program, often have high expectations for what it will accomplish for them. A support structure coalesces around the program, composed of bureaucrats, program delivery staff, supportive legislators, and clients. But waiting in the wings are potential opponents composed of earlier foes, other agencies competing with the program's turf and mode of service, professional guilds whose members are not being employed, reporters looking for a muckraking story, and people with other priorities for the money the program is spending.

In such an environment, program directors often view evaluation as more of a threat than a help. Whereas a largely favorable evaluation might give some help in pointing out possible improvements, a basically negative report could have more serious consequences: It could lower staff morale, reduce legislative or bureaucratic commitment and funding, or reopen struggles with contending agencies. Program directors are wary.

Second, evaluations get embroiled in the politics of higher level policymaking. Officials at levels beyond the immediate program, such as legislators, foundation executives, and federal program directors, have less allegiance to the program as it is than do the staff on the site. They have a wider range of options than just the program under review. And by the nature of their jobs, they are often more aware of public expectations and more concerned with seeing that the public gets its money's worth in program results. So they are less likely to reinforce the stockade against an unfavorable report.

But they respond to the imperatives of their own systems. For legislators, a prime motivation is getting reelected, and in pursuit of that aim, they need to satisfy constituents. They also want to remain members in good standing in their party, earn the support of the legislative leadership, and respond to the concerns of important interest groups. Tolerating an ineffective program may make sense if it gains the approbation of a key committee. High administrative officials seek to merit the support of their bosses, maintain the cooperation of the client group with which the agency constantly deals, and avoid controversy and conflict within the agency. Program managers want to ensure continued support of the program by holders of the purse and gain prestige and repute among members of their professional guild.

Much of policymaking work involves negotiating compromises among powerful competing factions. Evaluation evidence is only one input into the mosaic.

What evaluation can do is demonstrate just what the policymaker is giving up when he settles for a poor program or fails to adopt a successful one. Evaluation indicates what social benefits are being forgone, so that policymakers can judge whether the political gains are worth the social losses. Evaluation helps policymakers make decisions with their eyes wide open to programmatic consequences. But evaluation is never the sole basis on which policy decisions are made. Policymakers inevitably, and legitimately, take a variety of factors into account.

The endemic sensitivity to political concerns irks many evaluators. They believe that sound evidence about process and outcome should be heeded and that improvements based on evidence should preempt political issues. But before they deride others, they should recognize that evaluation itself takes a political stand. Evaluators make a series of political statements simply by agreeing to undertake a study. The message is twofold: that the program is problematic enough to need evaluating and that the program is a serious enough effort to be worth the time and effort to evaluate.

A political statement is implicit in the selection of some programs to undergo evaluation and others to escape scrutiny. The evaluated program has all its linen, clean and dirty, hung out in public; the unanalyzed program can tuck its secrets away in the bureau drawers. Generally three kinds of programs are subjected to a mandate to evaluate: new programs, such as environmental cleanup or new science curricula; programs that serve marginal populations, such as AIDS patients or the homeless; and innovative programs that are trying out new approaches or techniques of service, such as cooperative learning in the classroom or devolution of authority over education in Latin America to local municipalities.

The evaluator who agrees to study a new program in effect agrees that the program's viability is in doubt. Otherwise there would be no point in evaluating it. On the other hand, the evaluator is also saying that the program is plausible enough to be worth study. For some programs, where intensity of service is so low that they can make little headway or where they are replicas of programs that evaluations have already found wanting, there is little point in yet another evaluation. Yet the evaluator's willingness to sign on gives the program legitimacy.

Furthermore, the evaluator almost inevitably limits the study to the effects of the few things that the program changes. She evaluates the introduction of housing vouchers or new strains of rice, thus suggesting that all other elements in the situation are either unimportant or fixed and unchangeable. The intervention is the key variable, and other conditions that may give rise to and sustain the problems facing the client population are given short shrift. Evaluation tends to ignore the social and institutional structures within which problems of the client population are generated and sustained. This position has obvious political overtones.

When it comes to the specification of the evaluation questions, those who have the most say are likely to be the organization that finances the program or the agency that runs the program. Rarely are direct-service staff or clients consulted. Yet they might ask different questions from those the top brass asks. Similarly, at the end of the study, when drawing implications from the results, the evaluator may consider only steps that are practical from the standpoint of agency management. If she wants the findings to be used, she takes account of the managers' options and constraints. She is less likely to think long and hard about the practicalities of clients' lives or what makes sense in terms of the options that are open to teachers or nurses or staff in the college financial aid office.

Each study builds in certain values and assumptions. Values are built into the study through the choice of questions, the choice of respondents, the choice of sites, even the selection of one methodological approach over another. It makes a difference whether the underlying question is: Is the agency running as good a program as it can given all its constraints? or Are the clients of the program getting all the help they need to lead constructive and satisfying lives?

Most of the political implications of evaluation have an establishment orientation. They accept and support the status quo. They take for granted the world as defined in the existing social structure, the organization of agencies, official diagnoses of social problems, and the types of ameliorative programs provided. But while it accepts the world as given, the basic tendency of evaluation is reformist. Its whole thrust is to help improve the way that society copes with social and economic problems. At the same time that evaluation accepts program assumptions, it subjects them to scrutiny. It not only accepts; it tests and challenges.

Evaluation conclusions usually identify a gap between expectations and outcomes. The assumptions often are that relatively modest adjustments will be sufficient. Few recommendations look to basic changes in agencies, programs, or the surrounding structure. The political stance of evaluation is unremittingly incrementalist.

Proposed Remedies for Nonuse of Evaluation Results

A variety of remedies have been proposed for the neglect of evaluation results, particularly results that disclose flaws and shortcomings. They include (1) making the study more cogent, (2) redoubling dissemination efforts, (3) taking politics out of program decision making, (4) revising expectations for what constitutes adequate use of results, and (5) meta-analysis.

More Cogent Studies   In terms of making the study forceful and compelling, a number of characteristics will help. I did a research project some years ago about the kinds of research that are likely to be used (Weiss, with Bucuvalas, 1980). One thing that made a difference was the quality of the study as research.[4] Potential users were more likely to heed a study's findings when they believed that the study was methodologically sound. (Not all subsequent research on knowledge utilization has affirmed the finding, but many studies agree.) The reason that prospective users care about research quality is not that they are methodological purists. They care because, if they rely on the study for direction and support, they want to be sure that the findings are right. They do not want opponents in the inevitable debates to be able to challenge the credibility of the study. If they base their case on invalid evidence, they

---

[4]This study examined the usefulness of research studies, including a modest number of evaluations. The results appear to apply to evaluation studies.

are likely to lose face, lose the policy debates, and/or embark on poorly designed change. They don't want to go through the travail of implementing change if the study is sending them off in the wrong direction.

Evaluation has to be credible to its potential users. They have to believe the findings and they have to believe that the findings will withstand attack.

Another characteristics of research that increases attention to results is basic compatibility with potential users' sense of the situation; the research is consonant with their view of how the world works. A third characteristic is that the research presents some challenge to the agency status quo. It does not affirm that all is well; rather it shows where shortcomings lie. As these two features indicate, prospective users find it important for research to be congruent with their own beliefs but not necessarily with current agency practice. To warrant attention, research has to present unfinished business for the agency to consider, even though the agency may not do anything about the situation in the near term. The final two features of useful research revealed in the study were the provision of clear direction for action and relevance to the organization's particular situation. Evaluation with these attributes is not guaranteed to carry the day, but it stands a better chance of influencing the organization.

Increasing Dissemination   Another remedy is to intensify efforts to communicate results. This chapter has suggested a range of strategies. Forceful pursuit of them can help to diffuse evaluation results within the program organization and in attentive outside communities.

Taking Politics out of Decision Making   Evaluators often long for a world where rationality holds sway and decisions are made on the basis of evidence, not politics. What can be done to lessen the pressures to protect the agency, the program, and the staff's own careers? Probably not much. Politics in the broad sense is pervasive. In one famous exhortation to reduce the influence of politics and increase the influence of rationality, Campbell (1969) wrote:

> One simple shift in political posture which would reduce the problem is the shift from the advocacy of a specific reform to the advocacy of persistence in alternative reform efforts should the first one fail. The political stance would become: "This is a serious problem. We propose to initiate Policy A on an experimental basis. If after five years there has been no significant improvement, we will shift to Policy B." (p. 410)

Attractive as the proposal is, it does not appear simple. All our experience suggests that groups engaged in reform have to *believe* in what they advocate if they are to weather the political struggles, and that decision makers have to be *convinced* that the plan is good and right and worth the investment. Rivlin (1971) notes:

> The Office of Economic Opportunity might have told Congress: "We don't know whether preschool programs will work, or what kind would be best, but we have designed a program to find out." But would they then have gotten the money? (p. 85)

Further, administrators and program staff become committed to the programs to which they devote their energies. Such dedication is probably important for their success as practitioners; a skeptical wait-and-see posture might well hobble their effectiveness in action. They, and sometimes program participants as well, develop vested interests in the program. Other political interests, too, congregate around things as they are. They tend to cling to what they know and do. Legislative politics, bureaucratic politics, and professional politics are pervasive.

But this is a fast-moving world. Community conditions and aspirations change. New people come into leadership positions in agencies. Outside review stimulates organizational self-analysis. What was once immutable becomes the subject for debate. Evaluation evidence may be taken down from the shelf and gather partisans; new studies may be commissioned. Thus, when President Clinton opened a national debate on health care reform in 1993, the findings of the health insurance experiment that had been conducted in the 1970s and early 1980s became grist for the analytic mill, and its findings influenced the proposals that were introduced and debated in the Congress (Newhouse & Insurance Experiment Group, 1993). However, the whole health care proposal went down in political flames.

Rather than yearning to free evaluation from the pressures of politics, a more fruitful course would be to undertake and report evaluation with full awareness of the political environment. A study will be more useful and more likely to be used if it addresses the issues that are in contention and produces evidence directly relevant to political disputes. This is true at the organizational level and in higher level policymaking. In relation to federal policy, advice comes from Chelimsky (1996), who headed the General Accounting Office's Program Evaluation and Methodology Division for many years. She has said:

> If research is done within a political environment, then researchers [and evaluators] need not only to understand that environment, but also to construct some sort of roadmap or framework that can serve to organize the consideration of political issues within the research process. (p. 40)

Revising Expectations for Evaluation Use   It may be that evaluators are expecting too much. One problem is the time frame. Evaluators expect change to happen right away, but it usually takes a period of time before results come into currency and gain support and even longer for organizations to mobilize resources for action. In the interim, the organization seeks out other data and advice and stirs them into the pot. Evaluation findings are intermingled with practitioner experience, political know-how, and ideological commitment, and the melange crystallizes into action when political opportunities open. By that time, the evaluator has long since gone on her way, and people in the organization may lose sight of the findings that started them on the road to reform in the first place.

Just as our time frame has been too short, our implicit conception of use has been too mechanistic. Many evaluators expect program and policy communities to accept findings completely and implement them forthwith. This expectation disregards the experience and knowledge that people on the scene already have from their long-term immersion in the issues. It doesn't take account of the contending priorities that they face, the concerns with feasibility, acceptability, costs, value structures, political advantage, and the need for political support.

When we look at how officials in executive agencies and legislatures actually use research information, we find four main types of use (Weiss, 1989):

1. *Guidance for action.* Evaluators usually assume that users will use their work to gain direction for changes in program and policy. Such use certainly happens, perhaps most often when community-level projects engage their own evaluator. But it appears to be the least common kind of use of the four.

2. *Reinforcement of prior beliefs.* Many evaluation conclusions affirm what people already know and believe about shortfalls in the program. The use of such knowledge is not dramatic—or even visible. But it bolsters the confidence of those who want to press for needed change.

3. *Mobilization of support.* Evaluation findings can be used to mobilize a coalition of support for change. The findings become ammunition in organizational debates. Proponents use them to convince waverers and contend with opponents. This kind of use is especially frequent in legislative settings, where reference to evidence gives a semblance of rationality to political contests. Thus, members of Congress repeatedly referred to positive findings from long-term follow-up evaluations of the Perry Preschool program to support reauthorizations of Head Start (Schweinhart et al., 1993).

4. *Enlightenment.* Much of the use of evaluation results, like the use of social science research generally, is a general increase in understanding. People learn more about what happens in the program and afterwards. They gain a better idea of program strengths, fault lines, opportunities for improvement. Old myths are punctured, issues previously unrecognized come to the fore. As a result, people think differently. They reorder their priorities, dismiss some earlier concerns as unimportant, begin thinking along different tracks. Although they may not *do* anything different for a while, the shift in thinking can in time have important consequences for the eventual actions they take.

   The ultimate in enlightenment would come when new (and perhaps surprising) evaluation findings are absorbed into professional lore and the common wisdom. People would come to take them for granted and accept them as simply common sense.

Use of evaluation for reinforcement of beliefs, mobilization of support for change, and general enlightenment are probably more common than instrumental use for direct action. These uses are not as obvious, dramatic, nor as satisfying to the evaluator, but they may be equally important.

Meta-Analysis   Except for people linked to the program directly evaluated, most potential users of evaluation results want to know more than what one study said. They want to know the weight of the evidence. Program people at other sites and people who participate in the policy process realize that dozens, scores, even hundreds of studies have been done in some program areas and that studies often come up with discrepant findings. Rather than accept one study as gospel, they want to know where the study fits within the rubric of research on programs of the same type.

Here is where meta-analysis can increase the use of evaluation findings. When results are synthesized across evaluations, potential users of the information have more information, and they have greater confidence in the results. With greater confidence, if other conditions are favorable, may come heightened willingness to apply them.

Conclusions about Use of Results

Many decision-making communities use evaluation results to improve the effectiveness of what they do. They learn where failings occur and then seek ways to overcome them. However, other agencies apparently sit on the results, citing the difficulties of the task they do, the inadequacy of resources, and the lack of public support. Even evidence of serious shortcomings seems to leave them unmoved.

But when resources are scarce, or when the pro and anti forces are finely balanced (and out of expediency as much as rationality), policymakers sometimes allow trials of an innovative program and provide for appropriate evaluation of effects before they embark on a major reform. The large social experiments of the 1970s, with negative income tax, health insurance, housing vouchers, and other experimental programs, came about largely because there was considerable support but not enough to enact the reforms on a national basis. Although the social experiments produced a great deal of important learning, they did not lead to full-scale enactment of the reforms. By the time their results became available, reform energies had waned and the political climate had changed. The reformist impulse had been replaced by the more conservative posture of the Reagan years. Experimentation and evaluation take time, and in the interim, in T. S. Eliot's words, "between the idea and the reality, between the motion and the act, falls the shadow."

When organization personnel are dissatisfied with things as they are, they are more receptive to the implications of evaluation results. It is a state of puzzlement and dissatisfaction that sometimes leads to evaluation in the first place, and under these conditions, the results are apt to be taken seriously. In conditions of acute crisis, when a program is perceived to be a glaring failure, people will seek help from many sources, including evaluation, to provide guidance for next steps. Sublime discontent with the welfare system's failure to move recipients off the welfare rolls led to a long series of programs in training, education, and job search. Each national program was evaluated, and the findings informed development of the next set of programs (e.g., Bloom, Fellerath, Long, & Wood, 1993; Friedlander & Hamilton 1993; Quint, Polit, Bos, & Cave, 1994). Now that much authority for welfare has been devolved to the states, it remains to be seen if states will heed the lessons of previous evaluations.

With more understanding of what evaluation is and what it can and cannot tell, decision makers are probably more receptive to its information than they were in earlier days. They have worked with evaluators. They are savvy about the process of evaluation. They are not so shocked when evaluation reveals shortcomings in a program that they thought was wonderful. They have come to realize that even good programs rarely fulfill *all* the expectations that people invest in them. When evaluation shows shortfalls in the program, they are less likely to circle the wagons in defense or to volley off antagonistic buckshot. Evaluators who specialize in the evaluation of community-level projects report recurrent success in helping organizations implement the findings (Patton, 1990).

The program community has come to realize that a critical evaluation is not going to be used to close down the program. Even when results are below expectations, society has made a commitment to deal with the problem and is unlikely to withdraw the commitment precipitously on the basis of evaluation. Managers and staff have enough experience now to realize that they can often improve their programs by attending to the findings of evaluation. Evaluation gives them a basis to make changes that will bring the program closer to what public officials, clients, and they themselves want it to be. If they drag their heels a bit, that is not necessarily a bad thing. It is wise to make sure that the study represents sound research and good judgment before embarking headlong on major reform.

With the current emphasis on accountability of agencies to their publics, managers often look upon evaluation as a way of fulfilling their obligations to account for their stewardship. It provides a means for reporting back to funders, sponsors, and attentive publics.

Evaluation will never provide all the answers. What it can do—and this is no minor contribution—is help to rally support for effective programs, identify innovative programs that are making advances over current service, and expose the failings of existing programs—along with indications of the kinds of change that would make them work. Evaluation can sometimes get publicity for program successes and failures, help to generate interest in program effectiveness outside the narrow confines of the agency, and provide support for those reformers who seek to improve program operations. Maybe the most practical use of evaluation findings is to provide hard evidence to support the proponents of change within the decision-making system—the people within and outside the agency who have been seeking to alter present modes of programming. Study data legitimate their cause and give them chapter and verse to cite. Another major contribution is raising new issues and altering the nature and climate of discussion. Over time, a recurrent pattern of evaluation findings can gradually work changes in public and professional opinion.

At one point I bemoaned this slow and indirect approach to social change and yearned for bolder contributions (Weiss, 1973). In recent years, however, I have come to appreciate how difficult social change is and how resistant social problems are to intervention. I am more impressed with the utility of evaluation findings in stimulating incremental increases in knowledge and in program effectiveness. Over time, cumulative increments are not such small potatoes after all.

14

*E*VALUATING
*W*ITH *I*NTEGRITY

Now this is not the end. It is not even the beginning of the end. But it is, perhaps, the end of the beginning.

—Winston Churchill (1942)

This book has presented a view of evaluation as an art as much as a science, directed both toward practical reform and to accumulation of knowledge, with responsibilities to an array of audiences that include—but go beyond—the study sponsor. This chapter offers a reprise of the major themes.

Evaluation, as I have defined it, is the systematic assessment of the operation and/or the outcomes of a program or policy. Intrinsic to evaluation is a set of standards that (explicitly or implicitly) define what a good program or policy looks like and what it accomplishes. The purpose is the improvement of the program or policy, either by encouraging the elimination of unsuccessful interventions or by giving guidance for how the existing intervention can be modified.

Evaluation is a marvelously versatile enterprise. Evaluation can look at programs and policies that aim to change knowledge, opinions, attitudes, and/or behavior, whether they are targeted at individuals, families, work groups, organizations, communities—or even public opinion and community norms.

Evaluation can examine the processes by which programs[1] are implemented, the outcomes for participants, or both. It can evaluate a single project, a group of projects, or a whole regional, national, or international program. It can evaluate components within a project, such as the nature of the program recruitment process or the techniques taught to case managers to prepare them for their jobs. The scale differs, but much the same kinds of methods are used to examine implementation and outcomes at every level.

---

[1]To avoid repeating the phrase programs or policies, I talk about programs from here on, but I mean to subsume policies as well.

The aim in each case is to understand what is happening and with what consequences. In this chapter I reprise some fundamental ideas about how evaluation should be carried out in a democratic society in the new century.

Know the Program

An evaluator[2] has to understand the program she is studying. She has to know not only what is in official documents and public relations brochures but what actually goes on in the dailiness of program life. This knowledge is essential to help her design an evaluation that is responsive to the real issues facing the program and the concerns of program sponsors and other stakeholders. When the evaluator has close knowledge of the program, she avoids being misled or deflected from core issues.

Knowledge of the program contributes to every stage of the evaluation: defining evaluation purposes, deciding on questions the evaluation will address, selecting an appropriate research design within the constraints of the setting, collecting requisite data without raising hackles, analyzing and interpreting study results in relevant ways, and making responsible efforts to communicate findings and promote their use in subsequent program and policy action.

One important way to gain a deep understanding of the program is to explore the assumptions embedded in it. How do program designers assume that the program is going to lead to desired outcomes? What are the mechanisms they expect to mediate between implementation of activities and the emergence of desired end results? These expectations, whether they are carefully articulated or tacit, represent the program theory. Program theory includes the processes of program implementation (how the program is carried out) and the desired outcomes (the anticipated consequences for program beneficiaries), and then hypothesizes about the mechanisms that link processes to outcomes.

Often evaluation is called upon to show not only how the program was implemented and what its outcomes were but also how and why it obtained the observed results. To answer questions about *how* and *why*, the evaluator can use the program theory as scaffolding for the study. She tracks the expected sequence of events to see whether each step takes place as the theory hypothesizes. If so, she can say a great deal about the how and why of program success. If things do not work out as anticipated, she can point to the assumptions that went unrealized and the stage in the sequence at which the theory broke down. Such information gives guidance for program improvement. Thus, explication of the program's theory of change can provide a framework for identifying key junctures and points of articulation that can become the focus for evaluation.

Maintain High Technical Quality and Relevance

Technical quality in research is usually defined in methodological terms, relating to the excellence of design, measurement, fieldwork, and analysis. In evaluation, all of these elements are highly important. In addition, the evaluator has to ensure that the study has high relevance to the local situation.

---

[2]I talk about the evaluator, but in many cases a team of evaluators will be involved in the study.

First of all, the evaluator has to ask the right questions. Knowing what questions are right for the evaluation to address is a challenging task. It runs up against such obstacles as trite and lazy formulations of questions by study sponsors (e.g., "we always have to look at student test scores" no matter what the program); conflicting purposes and questions from diverse stakeholders; the attempt of program managers to shield the more problematical aspects of program operations from view; changing issues and ideologies in the political arena, and so on.

To develop the right questions, the evaluator has a range of resources, chief among them a knowledge of the program and of past evaluations of similar programs. In addition, she usually needs to consult with a variety of stakeholder groups. Stakeholders—funders, managers, staff, clients, collaborating institutions—provide useful perspectives on the problematics and priorities in the field. True, they may each have their own parochial interests and disagree among themselves, and the evaluator is not bound to accept their words as gospel. But she should devote serious attention to the issues that engage them. She may often choose to go beyond their concerns to address issues of more general salience, but she has to be responsive and relevant to the people on the scene.

The evaluator has to match research methods to the questions that have been defined for study. She can use a whole array of research methods—case studies, ethnography, randomized experiments, surveys, reanalysis of existing databases, and so on. She can rely on qualitative or quantitative methods for data collection and analysis; often she will use both methods in order to capitalize on their special advantages. The evaluator chooses the methods that can best address the questions being asked. She may have a preference for certain methods, either because she believes they are stronger and more sophisticated or because she is skilled in their use, but her preferences are not the point. The point is to use methods and techniques that enable her to answer the paramount questions and concerns that have been identified.

Many evaluations focus on outcomes—what the recipients of the program gained from their participation. But even when outcomes are the central focus, the evaluator is often well advised to study the processes of the program, too. She will learn whether the program functioned in the manner it was expected to function (or whether it fizzled, improved, or adapted to changing circumstances), she will learn the kinds of service received by different recipients, and she will come to understand the reality rather than the rhetoric of the program. When it comes time to interpret the evidence on outcomes, she will have more information to work with. She will even be able to disaggregate outcomes in terms of the differential exposure of recipients to different program conditions. This kind of analysis will contribute considerable insight.

An important question involves the *net* effects of the program, over and above what would ordinarily happen to people in the absence of the program. This question requires a research design that allows the evaluator to identify the extent to which the program is the *cause* of observed effects. The evaluator has to be able to disentangle the effects of the program from other operative factors. The randomized experiment is well suited to this task. But in many situations, random assignment to program and control groups is incompatible with program operations, and the evaluator has to seek alternative designs that gain traction on the question. This is one of many circumstances that require the evaluator to balance competing claims, in this case balancing the realities of program life (which, for example, make random assignment impossible) with the need for reaching responsible conclusions about the net effects of the program. But note that randomized experimentation is often more feasible, at least for subsamples of the program population, than the evaluator may initially expect.

Design is also contingent upon the purposes the study is called upon to serve. Sometimes the evaluator's task is to feed back findings to the project under study so that staff can improve their work. In other cases, evaluation is called upon to generalize results to other agencies, auspices, places, staff, client groups, and times. The evaluator has to choose a research design that is responsive to the situation—and its purposes and constraints—and still maintain high technical quality.

Use Balance and Judgment

Evaluation is an art of balance and judgment. Evaluators work in a context where the program takes priority and conditions are not always hospitable to systematic study. They rarely have control over all the conditions that will affect what they can and cannot do. Therefore, they have to make tradeoffs between the requirements for doing high-quality research and the limitations imposed by the program setting and the people who work there. They have to exercise judgment at each phase of the evaluation study.

The choice of study design has to take account of (1) the kinds of information that study sponsors demand; (2) the wishes and viewpoints of other stakeholders, who have their own questions and interests, and who will have a say in the future of the program; (3) the nature of the assumptions (program theory) that underlie the program, and the elements and junctures in the theory that are most uncertain or controversial and in need of study and evidence; (4) possibilities that evaluation will gain a hearing in other locations (the legislature, projects just getting under way, professional education); and (5) opportunities to advance the long-range incorporation of evaluation results into professional knowledge, public opinion, and taken-for-granted common sense.

Evaluation has to make constant efforts to juggle these competing demands and responsibilities. The evaluator has to consider which tradeoffs make sense under current conditions and which demands must take priority.

Therefore, the planning and conduct of evaluation is an iterative process. As conditions change, the evaluator rethinks priorities and choices. She makes some changes in plan because of technical concerns. For example, she has located or developed good measures of program process and outcome, but the necessary data are not available, and new measures have to be designed. Or she has worked out a fine quasi-experimental design, but the communities that were to serve as comparisons suddenly institute their own version of the program and are no longer available for comparative purposes. She now has to rethink appropriate comparisons.

Some of the iteration is also a response to changing program circumstances—changes in personnel, organizational structure, political conditions, or budgets.

Because evaluation takes place in a political environment, it has to respond to changes in that environment. Adaptation to change is part of the task that evaluation undertakes because it deals with real programs and because it aims to influence the future of real programs and policies in a changing world.

Consider Use from the Start

In planning and conducting the study, the evaluator needs to take account of the uses to be made of evaluation results. The evaluator wants to ensure that evaluative conclusions will be heard, respected, and accepted, and that they will become the basis for subsequent thought and action about the program. Accordingly, she lays the groundwork for acceptance of findings from the outset. She tries to plan the evaluation in a way that fits the program and its environment. She addresses questions that potential users of the findings raise, perhaps involves potential users in the study process, reports findings to them early and listens to their interpretation of what the findings mean. She then puts serious effort into getting results reported to various audiences in intelligible ways, and remains in contact with program people for follow-up.

An important responsibility of the evaluator is to work to secure a hearing for evaluation results in arenas of policy and practice. She has to report carefully and graphically to multiple audiences; disseminate information in written, oral, and electronic form; and continue to press for attention over the long term. If she has something important to say, she should work hard at saying it and ensuring that it is heard.

The evaluator usually hopes that the findings of the study will be used to remedy program failings and capitalize on program strengths. Many such uses of evaluation do in fact happen. But first, evaluation findings have to be accepted as accurate and useful. Then the new findings interact with what people already know about the program, their values and beliefs about what is right, their self-interest and the interests of their agency, and the constraints embedded in the structure, standard operating procedures, and culture of the agency.

Program and policy decisions in a democracy do not take place in an autocratic context. There is rarely a single decision maker who can adopt evaluation results and hand down orders. Rather, the evaluator who wants to bring about action has to take account of many different groups, all of whom have a say about the future of the program. She has to see that they all have access to the findings and understand their import. Then the different groups negotiate and accommodate their positions over time.

Even when members of the program and policy communities become convinced by the findings and want to take corrective action, they have to generate support in other constituencies, amass resources, allay suspicions, employ staff with appropriate skills, and see that front-line practitioners endorse and implement the changes. Evaluation becomes part of the politics of program decision making.

Because of the complexities of the decision-making process, only occasionally do evaluation results trigger an immediate and direct response. Such use usually emerges when the findings are relatively noncontroversial, involve few resources or accord with mainstream opinion, and relate to a situation that is widely agreed to be in need of change. The use of evaluation for controversial decisions on a national scale, where strong beliefs and large amounts of money are involved, is often not so swift and direct. But evaluators should not lose heart. Change often comes, but it is apt to be subtle and gradual. Despite the delay, the use of evaluation in such circumstances can be highly important. Evaluation affects the ways in which the program community sees the world—what the issues are and which facets of the issues deserve attention, which of the issues deserve priority, what comfortable assumptions are unfounded, and what alternatives are possible. Shifts in understanding often have significant consequences not only in the program evaluated but in other programs and policies in many locations. Ideas are a major ingredient in policy and program reform.

Behave Ethically throughout the Study

An evaluator has a responsibility to be a fair and honest reporter on the strengths and weaknesses of the program or policy. Her own inclinations and the interests of study sponsors, staff, and clients need to be taken into account, but nothing should deflect her from her primary mission of evaluating with integrity—giving as honest an account as she can with the best tools she can command.

The evaluator has to behave ethically toward all the actors on the program scene. She has to be aware of ethical considerations at every stage of the study. For example, she should tell people who give information exactly what she means when she promises them that their responses will be confidential, and she must abide by the promises. She must take pains to assure that her work does not cause harm to the people she studies, within the limits called for by fair and honest reporting.

The several ethical obligations—to the study sponsors broadly conceived, to the people in the program, and to herself—can come into conflict. Honest reporting may reflect badly on the performance of staff and hurt their reputation and careers. The data may show that a program for a needy group to which the evaluator is strongly committed has little effect, and an honest report will strengthen the legislature's resolve to terminate it. What is the ethical course?

The primary ethical obligations in evaluation can be condensed into two rules: Do not harm the people studied, and do not distort the data. But simple as these rules seem, they can collide with each other. Reasonable people will give priority to one or the other. My belief is that the most important responsibility of the evaluator—ethically as well as technically—is to do a study of the highest quality she and her team are capable of, so that their conclusions are as valid and insightful as they can make them, and then report them candidly. That is the task for which the evaluator was invited into the program arena.

Survive and Reap Rewards

Doing a good evaluation is not a stroll on the beach. It is a demanding job. But with all the demands that evaluators face, they reap special rewards. Like other researchers, they have an opportunity to learn something that nobody else yet knows. The work is never boring; each study is a chance to venture into terra incognita and generate understanding. But evaluators do more. They do research that is more than grist for scholars' cerebrations; they do research that has a chance of improving the well-being of people in need. Whether programs and policies deal with the ill or the poor, victims or abusers, drinking drivers or bored high school dropouts, we evaluators have an opportunity to help policy and program communities to do a better job. We have an opportunity to help society allocate its resources wisely. We have a chance to aid many publics to understand the nature of social problems and appropriate ways for dealing with them. Done well, evaluation is noble work.

GLOSSARY

Note: These terms can have broader meanings. They are defined here in terms of evaluation. For generic definitions, see Vogt (1993).

action research   Applied research that engages practitioners with researchers in the study of organizations or activities. Emphasis is on ongoing improvement of practice by the practitioners themselves.

after-only designs   Evaluation designs in which measures are taken only after the program has been completed.

alpha   *See* Cronbach's alpha.

analysis of variance (ANOVA)   A test to determine if the difference between two (or more) groups on some measure is larger than would be expected by chance alone. It contrasts the variance between groups with the variance within each group.

applied research   Research done with the intent of applying results to a specific real-world problem. Evaluation is a form of applied research.

attrition   The loss of subjects, either from the participant group or the comparison (or control) group over the course of a study. Attrition can be a threat to the validity of study conclusions when participants drop out differentially from the program and comparison groups.

average cost   The total cost of a program divided by the number of units served.

before-and-after designs   Evaluation designs that compare data collected before and after the program.

benchmarks   Interim indicators or markers of progress toward a goal.

bias   Anything that produces a systematic error in a study's conclusion.

black box evaluation   An assessment that collects data only on program inputs and outcomes and pays little attention to what happens during the course of the program or to the mechanisms by which change is brought about.

case study   A research strategy that investigates a phenomenon in its natural setting using multiple sources of evidence.

categorical measure   A measure that sorts data into a limited number of categories. (*See* nominal measure, ratio measure, and interval measure.)

causal attribution   The claim that *x* caused *y*. More specifically, in evaluation the claim that the program was responsible for the observed effect. Statements of causal attribution are generally most cogent when a randomized experiment has been conducted.

central tendency   A single number that best represents a distribution of a set of numbers. Three common measures of central tendency are the mean, or average; the mode, or most common value; and the median, or middle value.

closed-ended question   A question that limits respondents' answers to predetermined response categories. Multiple choice and yes/no questions are examples of closed-ended questions. (*See* open-ended question.)

clustering   The procedure of identifying characteristics that are similar and grouping similar things together.

codebook   A list of the variables in a dataset, their range of possible values, and definitions of codes that have been assigned to these values to facilitate data analysis.

coding   The process of organizing data into sets of categories to capture the meaning or main themes in the data. Coding is usually done in the analysis of qualitative data, but quantitative data can also be grouped into code categories.

comparison group   A group of people or units (classes, work teams, organizations, etc.) that does not receive the program under investigation. In analysis it is compared to the group of program recipients on measures of interest. Comparison groups differ from control groups in that they are not selected randomly from the same population as program participants. (*See* control group.)

composite measure   A measure constructed from several separate measures of the same phenomenon.

confounding   The inability to separate out the individual effects of two or more variables on a single outcome. When the effects of extraneous variables can not be disentangled from the effects of the causal variables (program processes), the result may be the over- or underestimation of program effects. (*See* threats to validity.)

constructivism   The philosophical position that truth is contingent and conditional and that there are multiple perspectives and multiple realities. Constructivist researchers hold that people in different geographic, cultural, or social locations construe knowledge, truth, and relevance in different ways, each of them legitimate and worthy. (*See* positivism.)

construct validity   The extent to which a variable captures the concept it is intended to measure.

contagion effects   Positive effects of the program that are picked up by others. If contagion spreads to the control or comparison group during the study period, *see* contamination.

contamination   The absorption of elements of the program by members of the control or comparison group during the study. Contamination is a threat to validity because the group is no longer untreated for comparative purposes.

control group   A group chosen randomly from the same population as the program group but that does not receive the program. It is a stand-in for what the program group would have looked like if it had not received the program.

control variable   Any variable used to adjust for differences in subgroups or settings, especially differences between the program and comparison groups.

convenience sample   A nonrandom sample drawn from the target population because of ease of access.

correlation   The extent to which two or more variables are related to each other.

cost-benefit analysis   A type of economic evaluation in which both costs and consequences of a program or set of programs are expressed and compared in monetary terms.

cost-effectiveness analysis   A type of economic evaluation in which costs and consequences of a program or set of programs with similar aims are compared. Costs are expressed in monetary terms while program consequences are expressed in their natural units such as number of lives saved.

cost-minimization analysis   A type of economic evaluation that weighs costs of a variety of programmatic approaches to determine the least expensive alternative to accomplish a defined outcome.

cost-utility analysis   A type of economic evaluation that compares costs and consequences of a set of programs. The program consequences are expressed in terms of utility—the value or worth of a specific outcome for an individual, group, or society.

counterfactual   The situation under investigation as it hypothetically would have been if the same participants had not been exposed to the program intervention. The counterfactual situation would answer the question: What would have happened to this exact same set of individuals were they not affected by the program? An evaluator attempts to simulate the counterfactual with control and comparison groups.

covariation   The relation of changes in one phenomenon to changes in another phenomenon.

Cronbach's alpha   A measure of internal reliability or consistency of items in a test, index, or inventory. It ranges from 0 to 1, and indicates the extent to which the items are measuring the same construct.

cross-sectional survey   A survey conducted at a single point in time.

dataset   A collection of related information items that an evaluator or researcher uses to answer the research question(s).

dependent variable   A measure of the presumed effect in a study. In evaluation it is a data item that represents an expected outcome of the program. Its values are predicted by other variables, called independent variables, whether or not it is caused by the independent variables. (*See* independent variable.)

design   The plan or structure a researcher develops to guide the study. The design specifies which groups to study, how many units in a group, by what means units are selected, at what intervals they are studied, and the kinds of comparisons that are planned.

discount rate   A correction factor used in economic analyses to adjust future costs and benefits to their present monetary value.

dosage   A measure of the amount or intensity of service received by participants in a program.

dose-response designs   An investigation in which the effects of different quantities or intensity of services are compared.

ecological fallacy   False conclusions reached by trying to apply findings at one level of analysis to another level. Concluding that each student in a particular class was absent for 10% of the semester when the classroom absentee rate was 10% is an ecological fallacy.

economic analysis   A field of analysis that compares consequences of programs to their costs. Also known as efficiency analysis. Four subtypes of efficiency analysis are cost-minimization analysis, cost-effectiveness analysis, cost-benefit analysis, and cost-utility analysis. (*See* cost-minimization analysis, cost-effectiveness analysis, cost-benefit analysis, and cost-utility analysis.)

effect size   The magnitude of the relationship between two variables. In evaluation, usually the measure of the magnitude of the relationship between program variables and outcomes.

efficiency analysis   *See* economic analysis.

empirical research   Research that relies on quantitative or qualitative data drawn from observation or experience.

empowerment evaluation   Evaluation that gives practitioners and/or program participants control of the design and conduct of the evaluation, in order to "legitimize community members' experiential knowledge, acknowledge the role of values in research, empower community members, democratize research inquiry, and enhance the relevance of evaluation data for communities" (Fawcett et al., 1996, p. 162).

ethnography   A method of qualitative data collection associated with anthropology. Typically long term, the ethnographer immerses herself in the local environment and culture, participating in activities with the people whom she is studying, observing what they do, talking with them about what they think and mean, and, over time, coming to understand their norms and ideas.

evaluation   The systematic assessment of the operation and/or outcomes of a program or policy, compared to explicit or implicit standards, in order to contribute to the improvement of the program or policy.

executive summary   A condensed version of a research or evaluation report that provides an overview of the results.

experiment A study in which the evaluator has control over some of the conditions in which the study takes place and some aspects of the independent variables being studied, including assignment of study participants. The criterion of a true experiment is random assignment of participants to experimental and control groups.

experimental group The group assigned to receive the program, whose outcomes are compared with those of the control group. Experimental and control groups are randomly assigned.

expert judgment The opinion of a knowledgeable outsider.

external validity The extent to which evaluation findings can be applied to cases, settings, and times beyond the scope of the study. (*See* generalizability.)

factoring The process of breaking down aggregates into constituent parts.

field notes A written record of observations, notes of conversations and interviews, and emerging ideas and preliminary insights maintained throughout the study period.

focus groups A method of data collection in which 6 to 12 respondents are brought together to discuss and provide data on a particular issue(s).

formative evaluation A type of evaluation conducted during the course of program implementation whose primary purpose is to provide information to improve the program under study. (*See* summative evaluation.)

full-coverage programs Programs that serve everyone who meets the eligibility requirements. Medicare, Social Security, and public schooling are full-coverage programs.

generalizability The extent to which the findings of a study can be applied to other populations, settings, and times. (*See* external validity.)

goal A program's desired outcome.

goal-free evaluation An evaluation that does not proceed from a program's official goals but examines outcomes that are broadly conceived to be consequential for the lives of participants.

Hawthorne effect A change in an outcome measure that is the result of the attention that participants receive during an intervention rather than a result of the program under study.

history *See* outside events.

hypothesis The researcher's firm hunch, arising from theory or experience, that a particular predictor (in the evaluator's case, a program or aspect of a program) causes an outcome. Hypotheses are confirmed or denied using empirical analysis.

impact The net effects of a program (i.e., the gain in outcomes for program participants minus the gain for an equivalent group of nonparticipants). Impact may also refer to program effects for the larger community. More generally it is a synonym for *outcome*.

implementation theory The theory that if activities are conducted as planned, with sufficient quality, intensity, and fidelity to plan, they will attain desired results.

Implementation theory does not deal with the processes that mediate between program services and the achievement of program goals but deals exclusively with the delivery of program activities. (*See* program theory.)

independent variable   The presumed cause of some outcome under study; changes in an independent variable are expected to predict a change in the value of a dependent variable. (*See* dependent variable.)

index   A composite of related measures that can be used to characterize a phenomenon.

indicator   A measure that consists of hierarchically ordered categories arranged in ascending or descending order of desirability.

informed consent   A written or verbal agreement in which potential participants agree to participate in the study after receiving adequate information about the study to make a reasoned decision.

inputs   The resources used to conduct a program.

instrument   A means used to measure or study a person, event, or other object of interest. Examples include an interview form, test, or questionnaire.

instrumentation bias   Bias introduced into a study when an instrument used to collect data is changed over the course of the study; what appears to be a program effect is due to a change in the measuring instrument.

internal consistency   The extent to which items in a scale or test measure aspects of the same thing.

internal validity   The extent to which the effects found in a study can be unambiguously attributed to the presumed causal variables, such as program activities.

interrater reliability   Agreement among raters; a measure of the consistency in judgments of several evaluators or researchers rating, ranking, or coding phenomena.

interval measure   A measure consisting of mutually exclusive, exhaustive categories arranged in a hierarchical order. The intervals between numbers that represent categories are equal, but there is no true zero on the scale.

intervening variable   A variable that provides a link between other variables. In evaluation, an intervening variable usually describes a process or near-term effect that occurs between the inputs of a program and its long-term outcomes.

longitudinal study   A study design in which data are collected at several points in time from the same individuals, groups, or organizations.

marginal cost   The incremental cost of serving one additional participant.

matching   A method to create a comparison group. Individuals, schools, communities or other units are matched to the units participating in the program on characteristics assumed to affect their reaction to the program. Or if the evaluator has some control over participant selection, she can create sets of matched pairs and assign one of each pair to the program group and to the comparison group.

maturation   Natural change or growth in study participants over time. Maturation is a potential threat to the validity of study conclusions if it is confused with the effects of the program.

measure Data expressed quantitatively to characterize a particular phenomenon; numbers assigned to objects or events according to rules.

mediating variable An intervening variable that represents the mechanism through which an independent variable is expected to influence a dependent variable. For example, an increase in participants' knowledge may represent the pathway by which behavioral outcomes are realized.

meta-analysis The systematic analysis of the results of a body of evaluations of similar programs to produce an estimate of overall program effect.

moderator variable A variable that distinguishes between subgroups that have different outcomes. The moderator variable divides the study population into subgroups that respond differently to the program.

monitoring An ongoing assessment of program operations conducted during implementation, usually by sponsors or managers, to assess whether activities are being delivered as planned, are reaching the target population, and are using resources appropriately.

mortality *See* attrition.

N Number of cases. Upper-case *N* refers to the number of cases in a population, while lower case *n* usually refers to the number of cases in the sample studied.

net outcome The change in outcomes for program participants minus the change for an equivalent group of nonparticipants.

nominal measure A measure that consists of descriptive categories. A nominal measure assigns a number to each category (e.g., 1 = female, 0 = male); the numbers represent different categories in the set but have no mathematical meaning.

nonequivalent comparison group designs Also known as quasi-experiments, these evaluation designs rely on nonrandomized comparison groups to evaluate program effects.

null hypothesis The hypothesis that two or more variables are not related. Research looks for evidence that the null hypothesis does not hold, thus indirectly demonstrating that the opposite is true. In evaluation, the null hypothesis frequently is that program participation is not related to desired outcomes.

objectives The specific, desired program outcomes.

observation A data collection method in which the researcher watches and records events and processes.

one-group designs Evaluation designs that examine a single program only; these designs employ no comparison group.

open-ended interview A form of interviewing that does not use preformed, structured questions but rather allows the respondent to shape the direction and focus of the interview. Open-ended interviewing aims to get the respondent's story from his own perspective.

open-ended question   A question that asks for narrative responses and allows respondents to respond in their own words. (*See* closed-ended question.)

operationalize   To translate general program inputs, processes, and goals into specific, measurable variables. More generally, to define a concept in a way that can be measured.

opportunity cost   The value of benefits that would have accrued from other activities if resources had not been allocated to the program under study. More generally, an opportunity cost is whatever participants, organizations, or society at large have to give up to do something else.

ordinal measure   A measure consisting of categories arranged in a hierarchical order. The intervals between numbers that represent categories are not equal.

outcome   The end results of the program. Outcomes may be intended or unintended and be positive or negative.

outcome evaluation   A study of whether or not the program produced the intended program effects. Outcome evaluation relates to the *phase* of the program studied—in this case, the end result of the program.

outlier   An aberrant case that differs from almost all other cases on some measure.

outside events   Happenings or conditions that take place during the course of the program that may affect outcomes. If outside events are confounded with the effect of program processes, they pose a threat to the validity of conclusions. Cook and Campbell (1979) call them "history."

panel interviewing   The process of conducting repeated interviews with the same set or panel of respondents over time.

partial coverage program   A program that does not serve all of the population eligible to receive the program.

participant-observation   A method of data collection in which the researcher takes part in the activities under study while observing and recording what occurs.

patched-up design   A study that controls only those sources of error (or threats to validity) likely to appear in a given situation.

peer review   An assessment, often of a proposal or report, conducted by people with expertise in the author's field.

pilot   A small, preliminary test or trial run of an intervention or segment of an evaluation such as an instrument or sampling procedure. The results of the pilot are used to improve the program or evaluation procedure being piloted before it is used on a larger scale.

planned variation evaluation   An investigation that compares two or more versions of a program to determine which version produces better outcomes.

population   The whole group about which the evaluator wants to draw conclusions. A sample is a subgroup drawn from the population that is often meant to be representative of the population.

positivism   The philosophical position that a rational truth exists, that there is a single reality, and that scientific methods can approximate it.

posttest   A measure taken after a program ends.

pretest   A measure taken before a program begins.

probability sampling   *See* random sampling.

probing   The asking of successive open-ended questions to pursue a topic and encourage respondents to talk further about an issue or clarify their meaning.

process evaluation   A study of what goes on while a program is in progress. Process evaluation relates to the phase of the program studied—in this case, program implementation. (*Compare* outcome evaluation.)

program   A structured intervention to improve the well-being of people, groups, organizations, or communities. Programs vary in size, scope, duration, and clarity and specificity of goals.

program failure   A failure to implement program activities according to the program plan.

program group   The group that receives the program (which is often compared to a comparison or control group that does not). Also known as the treatment group or, in an experiment, the experimental group.

program model   A diagram of the assumed causal linkages among program inputs, activities, intervening variables, and program outcomes.

program theory   Assumptions about the chain of interventions and participant responses that lead to program outcomes.

proximate measures   Measures of a program's immediate effects that are assumed to be linked to desired ultimate outcomes. Program theory may be used to construct these expected intermediate measures. (*See* benchmarks.)

proxy measure   An indirect measure of a variable used when the variable of interest is difficult to measure directly.

publication bias   Journals' tendency to favor publication of studies that find statistically significant results.

purposive sample   A sample chosen deliberately by the researcher for some specified research reason.

p-value   A statistic measuring the probability that the results found could have been due to chance. The smaller the p-value, the greater the probability that the result was not due to chance alone. By convention, a relationship is judged statistically significant when the corresponding p-value is .05 or less.

qualitative research   Research that examines phenomena primarily through words and tends to focus on dynamics, meaning, and context. Qualitative research usually uses observation, interviewing, and document reviews to collect data.

quantitative research   Research that examines phenomena that can be expressed numerically and analyzed statistically.

quasi-experiment   A class of research designs in which program (or treatment) and comparison groups are selected nonrandomly but in which some controls are introduced to minimize threats to the validity of conclusions. Quasi-experiments are often used when conducting research in the field under real-life conditions in which the evaluator cannot assign groups randomly. (*See* experiment.)

randomize Selection according to the laws of chance. A sample can be randomly selected from a population to be representative of the population. Individuals eligible for a program can be randomly assigned to program and control groups in order to make the groups equivalent at the outset. Randomization is a rigorous procedure that seeks to avoid human bias.

random sampling A sampling strategy to select units from a population that gives every unit a known probability of being selected into the sample. A random sample is the aggregate of units so chosen.

ratio measure A measure consisting of categories arranged in hierarchical order that has equal intervals between categories (i.e., any two adjoining values in a ratio measure are the same distance apart). The scale of a ratio measure is anchored by a true zero.

regression line A graphic representation of a regression equation. The regression line best summarizes the relationship between a predictor (on the x-axis) and an outcome (on the y-axis). It represents the predicted value of y (the outcome) at every possible value of x (the predictor).

regression to the mean The tendency of extreme scores at any one occasion to move closer to the population mean on the next try. In evaluation, regression to the mean can be misinterpreted as a consequence of the program and is thus a threat to the validity of conclusions.

reliability The consistency or stability of a measure over repeated use. An instrument is said to be reliable if repeated efforts to measure the same phenomenon produce the same result.

results-based accountability Holding programs accountable not only for the performance of activities but also for the results they achieve.

RFP Request for Proposal; a notice, usually from a governmental agency, stating the nature of the study desired and inviting interested evaluators to submit proposed study plans.

sample A group of units selected from a population for study; a subset of the population. (*See* random sampling, stratified random sampling, and convenience sample.)

sampling The act of selecting units from a population. In evaluation, sites may be sampled to deliver the program, individuals may be selected to participate in the program (and often to be in a control group), and individuals in the program and control groups can be selected for inclusion in the study.

sampling error The difference between the true results in the population and the estimate of results derived from a sample because the sample studied is not perfectly representative of the population from which it was drawn. In general, sampling error is lower as sample size increases.

scale An aggregate measure constructed by combining a group of related measures of a variable. Often interchangeable with index, but may also arrange items in order of intensity or importance. (*See* index.)

selection bias   The bias resulting from preexisting differences between program participants and the comparison group. Effects found at the conclusion of the evaluation may be due to the fact that different types of people were selected or selected themselves into the program and comparison groups.

self-evaluation   Self-assessment of program processes and/or outcomes by those conducting the program.

sensitivity analysis   An exploration of how well results hold up under different assumptions or conditions.

shadow prices   Estimated costs of goods and services that are not accurately valued in the marketplace. A shadow price, based on the cost of an analogous activity or good, can be used to impute a cost in economic analysis.

sleeper effect   An effect that is not manifested early (e.g., immediately after the program) but emerges over time; a delayed reaction.

stakeholder evaluation   A study in which stakeholders participate in the design, conduct, and/or interpretation of the evaluation.

stakeholders   Those people with a direct or indirect interest (stake) in a program or its evaluation. Stakeholders can be people who conduct, participate in, fund, or manage a program, or who may otherwise affect or be affected by decisions about the program or the evaluation.

statistical control   A statistical technique used to subtract out variance in dependent variables attributable to extraneous sources. In evaluation, such controls are often used to reduce selection bias by adjusting data for program and comparison groups to make them equivalent on characteristics the evaluator deems critical.

statistical power   A gauge of the likelihood that a true effect will be detected. In general, statistical power is increased by including more cases in the sample.

statistical significance   The degree to which a value or measure is larger or smaller than would have been expected by chance alone. By convention, a relationship is judged statistically significant when the probability of obtaining the sample result (or a more extreme result) by chance is 5% or less if there is no relationship between the predictor and the outcome.

statistical weighting   A technique used to adjust for over- or underrepresentation of certain groups in the sample. Data for underrepresented cases are weighted to compensate for their scarcity in the sample and thus make the sample a better reflection of the underlying population.

stratified random sampling   A sampling strategy that divides the population into subgroups or strata and draws random samples from each stratum.

stratify   The division of a sample into discrete segments or strata based on some descriptive characteristic of relevance to the study.

structured interview   A type of formal interview that covers a set of specific questions and asks each respondent the same questions, with the same wording, in the same order.

summative evaluation   A study conducted at the end of a program (or of a phase of the program) to determine the extent to which anticipated outcomes were produced. Summative evaluation is intended to provide information about the worth of the program. (*See* formative evaluation.)

systematic sample   A sample drawn by selecting every nth case from a list of potential units.

testing bias   Change in responses due to the experience that respondents gain from repeated use of the same measuring instrument. Such changes in response due to experience may be confounded with the effects of the program and thus represent a threat to the validity of conclusions.

test-retest   A procedure to estimate the reliability of test instruments. Test-retest examines the consistency of answers given by the same people to the same test items, or a parallel set of test items, on two different test administrations. If the answers are very consistent, reliability is high.

theories of change   The assumptions that link a program's inputs and activities to the attainment of desired ends; it includes both implementation theory and program theory.

theory-based evaluation   Evaluation that tracks the anticipated sequence of linkages from inputs and activities to outcomes.

theory failure   The failure of the underlying theory of cause and effect on which the program is based.

threats to validity   Conditions other than the program that could be responsible for observed net outcomes; conditions that typically occur in quasi-experiments and, unless controlled, limit confidence that findings are due solely to the program. Threats to validity include selection, attrition, outside events or history, instrumentation, maturation, statistical regression, and testing, among others.

time-series designs   Designs that collect data over long time intervals. In evaluation, time-series designs take repeated measurements of key variables at periodic intervals before, during, and after program implementation and analyze changes over time.

treatment group   The group that receives the program under study; program participants.

triangulation   Using multiple methods and/or data sources to study the same phenomenon; qualitative researchers frequently use triangulation to verify their data.

unanticipated effects   Program outcomes that were not intended or expected at the start of a program.

unit of analysis   The entity about which data are collected, analyzed, and conclusions drawn.

unit of sampling   The entity that is selected into the program.

validity   In measurement, validity refers to the extent to which a measure captures the dimension of interest. In analysis, validity refers to the close approximation of study conclusions to the "true" situation.

variable   A measured characteristic, usually expressed quantitatively, that varies across members of a population. In evaluation, variables may represent inputs, processes, interim markers of progress (intervening variables), longer term outcomes, and unintended consequences.

variance   A measure of the spread, or dispersion, of the values or scores in a distribution. The larger the variance, the further individual cases are from the group mean.

REFERENCES

Abt Associates. (1993). *Informing the welfare debate: Recent research on policy innovations.* Cambridge, MA: Author.

———. (1995). *Measures of child well-being and family support programs.* Cambridge, MA: Author.

Adams, Paul, Catherine Alter, Karin Krauth, Mark St. Andre, & Martin Tracy. (1995). *Strengthening families and neighborhoods: A community-centered approach: Final report on the Iowa Patch Project.* Washington, DC: Department of Health and Human Services, Administration for Children and Families.

Afifi, A. A., & Virginia Clark. (1990). *Computer aided multivariate analysis* (2nd ed.). New York: Chapman & Hall.

Agar, Michael. (1986). *Speaking of ethnography.* Qualitative Research Methods Series, vol. 2. London: Sage.

Agresti, Alan. (1990). *Categorical data analysis.* New York: Wiley.

American Evaluation Association. (1995). Guiding principles for evaluators. In *New directions for program evaluation,* eds. W. R. Shadish, D. L. Newman, M. A. Scheirer, & C. Wye, pp. 19–26. New Directions for Program Evaluation Series (no. 66). San Francisco: Jossey-Bass.

Ashenfelter, Orley. (1978). Estimating the effect of training programs on earnings. *Review of Economics and Statistics, 60,* 47–57.

Ashenfelter, Orley, & David Card. (1985). Using the longitudinal structure of earnings to estimate the effect of training programs. *Review of Economics and Statistics, 67,* 648–660.

Barger, K., & D. Earl. (1971). Differential adaptation to northern town life by the eskimos and indians of Great Whale River. *Human Organization, 30,* 25–30.

Baron, R. M., & D. A. Kenny. (1986). The moderator-mediator variable distinction in social psychological research: Conceptual, strategic, and statistical considerations. *Journal of Personality and Social Psychology, 51*, 1173–1182.

Barth, Frederik. (1990). The guru and the conjurer: Transactions in knowledge and the shaping of culture in Southeast Asia and Melanesia. *Man, 25* (4), 640–653.

Beals, Ralph L. (1969). *Politics of social research.* Chicago: Aldine-Atherton.

Bearden, William O., R. G. Netemeyer, & M. F. Mobley. (1993). *Handbook of marketing scales.* Newbury Park, CA: Sage.

Becker, Howard S. (1986). *Writing for social scientists.* Chicago: University of Chicago Press.

Beebout, Harold, & Jean Baldwin Grossman. (1985). *A forecasting system for AFDC caseloads and costs: Executive summary.* Princeton: Mathematica Policy Research.

Behn, Robert D. (1991). *Leadership counts: Lessons for public managers from the Massachuetts Welfare, Training and Employment Program.* Cambridge, MA: Harvard University Press.

Bell, S. H., L. L. Orr, J. D. Blomquist, & G. G. Cain. (1995). *Program applicants as a comparison group in evaluating training programs: Theory and a test.* Kalamazoo, MI: Upjohn Institute.

Berdie, Douglas R., J. F. Anderson, & M. A. Niebuhr. (1986). *Questionnaires: Design and use.* Metuchen, NJ: Scarecrow Press.

Berleman, William C., & Thomas W. Steinburn. (1967). The execution and evaluation of a delinquency prevention program. *Social Problems, 14* (4), 413–423.

Berman, P., & M. W. McLaughlin. (1977). *Federal programs supporting educational change* (vol. 7). Santa Monica, CA: Rand Corporation.

———. (1978). *Federal programs supporting educational change: Implementing and sustaining innovations* (vol. 8). Santa Monica, CA: Rand Corporation.

Bertrand, J. T., P. Russell-Brown, E. Landry, D. Murray, S. Norville, & Y. Rotschell. (1986). *A test of two strategies for delaying a second pregnancy in teenage mothers in Barbados: Final report.* New Orleans: Tulane University Medical Center.

Bickman, Leonard (Ed.). (1987). *Using program theory in evaluation.* New Directions for Program Evaluation Series (no. 33). San Francisco: Jossey-Bass.

Blau, Peter M. (1964). *Exchange and power in social life.* New York: Wiley.

Bloom, Dan, V. Fellerath, D. Long, & R. G. Wood. (1993). *LEAP: Interim findings on a welfare initiative to improve school attendance among teenage parents; Ohio's Learning, Earning, and Parenting Program.* New York: Manpower Demonstration Research Corporation.

Bloom, Howard S. (1987). What works for whom? CETA impacts for adult participants. *Evaluation Review, 11*, 510–527.

Blossfeld, H. P., A. Hamerle, & K. U. Mayer. (1989). *Event history analysis.* Hillsdale, NJ: Erlbaum.

Bogdan, Robert C., & S. K. Biklen. (1982). *Qualitative research for education: An introduction to theory and methods* (1st ed.). Boston: Allyn & Bacon.

———. (1992). *Qualitative research for education: An introduction to theory and methods* (2nd ed.). Boston: Allyn & Bacon.

Bollen, Kenneth A. (1989). *Structural equations with latent variables.* New York: Wiley.

Boruch, Robert F. (1997). *Randomized experiments for planning and evaluation: A practical guide.* Thousand Oaks, CA: Sage.

Boruch, Robert F., & J. S. Cecil. (1979). *Assuring the confidentiality of social research data.* Philadelphia, PA: University of Pennsylvania Press.

Boruch, Robert F., Michael Dennis, & Kim Carter-Greer. (1988). Lessons from the Rockefeller Foundation's experiments on the Minority Female Single Parent Program. *Evaluation Review, 12* (4), 396–426.

Boruch, Robert F., & Werner Wothke. (1985). Seven kinds of randomization plans for designing field experiments. In *Randomization and field experimentation,* eds. R. F. Boruch & W. Wothke, pp. 95–113. New Directions for Program Evaluation Series (no. 28). San Francisco: Jossey-Bass.

Bowling, Ann. (1991). *Measuring health: A review of quality of life measurement scales.* Philadelphia, PA: Open University Press.

Bozeman, Barry, & Julia Melkers (Eds.). (1993). *Evaluating R & D impacts: Methods and practice.* Boston: Kluwer.

Brandon, Paul R., B. J. Newton, & J. W. Herman. (1993). Enhancing validity through beneficiaries' equitable involvement in identifying and prioritizing homeless children's educational problems. *Evaluation and Program Planning, 16* (4), 287–293.

Brennan, Robert T., A. Braslow, A. Batcheller, & W. Kaye. (1996). A reliable and valid method for assessing cardiopulmonary resuscitation. *Resuscitation, 32,* 85–93.

Brodsky, Stanley L., & H. O. Smitherman. (1983). *Handbook of scales for research in crime and delinquency.* New York: Plenum.

Brown, Brett V., & Christopher Botsko. (1996). *A guide to state and local-level indicators of child well-being available through the federal statistical system.* Washington, DC: Child Trends.

Brown, Prudence. (1995). The role of the evaluator in comprehensive community initiatives. In *New approaches to evaluating community initiatives: Concepts, methods, and contexts,* eds. J. P. Connell, A. C. Kubisch, L. B. Schorr, & C. H. Weiss, pp. 210–225. Washington, DC: Aspen Institute.

Bruner, Gordon C. II, & P. J. Hensel. (1992). *Marketing scales handbook: A compilation of multi-item measures.* Chicago: American Marketing Association.

Bryant, Edward C., & Kalman Rupp. (1987) Evaluating the impact of CETA on participant earnings. *Evaluation Review, 11,* 473–492.

Bryk, Anthony S., J. Q. Easton, D. Kerbow, S. G. Rollow, & P. A. Sebring. (1993). *A view from the elementary school: The state of reform in Chicago.* Chicago: Consortium on Chicago School Research.

Bryk, Anthony S., P. E. Deabster, J. Q. Easton, S. Luppescu, & Y. M. Thum. (1994). Measuring achievement gains in the Chicago public schools. *Education and Urban Society, 26* (3), 306–319.

Bryk, Anthony S., & S. G. Rollow. (1992). The Chicago experiment: Enhanced democratic participation as lever for school improvement. *Issues in Restructuring Schools, 3,* 3–15.

———. (1993). The Chicago experiment: The potential and reality of reform. *Equity and Choice, 9* (3), 22–32.

Bryk, Anthony S., & S. W. Raudenbush. (1992). *Hierarchical linear models: Applications and data analysis methods.* Beverly Hills, CA: Sage.

Bulmer, Martin, Kevin Bales, & Kathryn Kish Sklar. (1991). *The social survey in historical perspective.* New York: Cambridge University Press.

Burghardt, John, Anne Gordon, Nancy Chapman, Philip Gleason, & Thomas Fraker. (1993). *The School Nutrition Dietary Assessment Study: Dietary intakes of program participants and nonparticipants.* Princeton: Mathematica Policy Research.

Cain, Glen, & Harold Watts (Eds.). (1973). *Income maintenance and labor supply: Econometric studies.* Chicago: Rand McNally College Publishing Co.

Campbell, Donald T. (1966). Pattern matching as an essential in distal knowing. In *The psychology of Egon Brunswik,* ed. K. R. Hammond, pp. 81–106. New York: Holt, Rinehart & Winston.

———. (1969). Reforms as experiments. *American Psychologist, 24* (4), 409–429.

Campbell, Donald T., & H. Laurence Ross. (1968). The Connecticut crackdown on speeding: Time-series data in quasi-experimental analysis. *Law and Society Review, 3* (1), 33–53.

Campbell, Donald T., & Julian C. Stanley. (1966). *Experimental and quasi-experimental designs for research.* Chicago: Rand McNally & Co.

Carey, Martha, & M. W. Smith. (1992). Enhancement of validity through qualitative approaches. *Evaluation and the Health Professions, 15* (1), 107–114.

Carlson, David B., & J. D. Heinberg. (1978). *How housing allowances work: Integrated findings from the experimental housing allowance program.* Washington, DC: Urban Institute.

Carroll, Lewis. (1865). *The adventures of Alice in Wonderland.*

Casswell, Sally, & Lynnette Gilmore. (1989). Evaluated community action project on alcohol. *Journal of Studies on Alcohol, 50,* 339–346.

Center for the Study of Social Policy. (1994). Improved Outcomes for Children Project, Center for the Study of Social Policy, *Finding the data: A start-up list of outcome measures with annotations.* Washington, DC: Author.

Chaskin, Robert J., & M. V. Joseph. (1995). *The neighborhood and family initiative: Moving toward implementation, an interim report.* Chicago: Chapin Hall Center for Children, University of Chicago.

Chelimsky, Eleanor. (1996). From incrementalism to ideology and back: Can producers of policy information adjust to the full spectrum of political climates? *Distinguished Public Policy Lecture Series, 1996.* Evanston, IL: Center for Urban Affairs and Policy Research, Northwestern University.

Chen, Huey-Tsyh. (1990). Issues in constructing program theory. In *New directions for program evaluation: Advances in program theory,* ed. Leonard Bickman, pp. 7–18. New Directions for Program Evaluation Series (no. 47). San Francisco: Jossey-Bass.

Chen, Huey-Tsyh, J. C. S. Wang, & L-H. Lin. (1997). Evaluating the process and outcome of a garbage reduction program in Taiwan. *Evaluation Review, 21,* 27–42.

Chen, Huey-Tsyh, & Peter H. Rossi. (1980). The multi-goal theory-driven approach to evaluation: A model linking basic and applied social science. *Social Forces, 59,* 106–122.

———. (1983). Evaluating with sense: The theory-driven approach. *Evaluation Review, 7,* 283–302.

———. (1987). The theory-driven approach to validity. *Evaluation and Program Planning, 10,* 95–103.

Chira, Susan. (1993, September 14). Working-class parents face shortage of day care centers, a study finds. *New York Times,* A20.

Cohen, David K. (1988). A revolution in one classroom: The case of Mrs. Oublier. *Educational Evaluation and Policy Analysis, 12* (3), 327–345.

Coleman, James S., E. Katz, & H. Menzel. (1957). The diffusion of an innovation among physicians. *Sociometry, 20,* 253–270.

———. (1966). Medical innovation: A diffusion study. Indianapolis: Bobbs-Merrill.

Conoley, J. C., & J. C. Impara (Eds.). (1995). *Mental measurements yearbook* (12th ed.). Lincoln, NE: Buros Institute of Mental Measurements.

Conrad, Kendon J., & Karen M. Conrad. (1994). Reassessing validity threats in experiments: Focus on construct validity. In *New directions for program evaluation: Critically evaluating the role of experiments,* ed. Kendon J. Conrad, pp. 5–25. New Directions for Program Evaluation Series (no. 63). San Francisco: Jossey-Bass.

Constantine, W. L., C. W. Haynes, D. Spiker, & K. Kendall-Tackett. (1993). Recruitment and retention in a clinical trial for low birth weight, premature infants. *Journal of Developmental and Behavioral Pediatrics, 14* (1), 1–7.

Converse, Jean M., & Stanley Presser. (1986). *Survey questions: Handcrafting the standardized questionnaire.* Newbury Park, CA: Sage.

Cook, Thomas D. (1985). Postpositivist critical multiplism. In *Social science and social policy,* eds. R. L. Shotland & M. M. Mark, pp. 21–62. Beverly Hills, CA: Sage.

Cook, Thomas D., & Charles Reichardt (Eds.). (1979). *Qualitative and quantitative methods in evaluation research.* Beverly Hills: Sage.

Cook, Thomas D., & Donald T. Campbell. (1979). *Quasi-experimentation: Design and analysis issues for field settings.* Boston: Houghton Mifflin.

Cook, Thomas D., Harris Cooper, D. S. Cordray, Heidi Hartmann, L. V. Hedges, R. J. Light, T. A. Louis, & Frederick Mosteller. (1992). *Meta-analysis for explanation: A casebook.* New York: Russell Sage Foundation.

Cook, Thomas D., L. C. Leviton, & W. R. Shadish, Jr. (1985). Program evaluation. In *The handbook of social psychology* (3rd ed.), eds. Gardner Lindzey & E. Aronson. New York: Random House.

Cook, Thomas D., & William R. Shadish. (1994). Social experiments: Some developments over the past fifteen years. *Annual Review of Psychology, 45,* 545–580.

Cooper, Harris, & Larry V. Hedges (Eds.). (1994a). *The handbook of research synthesis.* New York: Russell Sage Foundation.

Cooper, Harris, & Larry V. Hedges. (1994b). Research synthesis as a scientific enterprise. In *The handbook of research synthesis,* eds. H. Cooper & L. V. Hedges, pp. 3–14. New York: Russell Sage Foundation.

Cordray, David S. (1986). Quasi-experimental analysis: A mixture of methods and judgment. In *New directions for program evaluation: Advances in quasi-experimental design and analysis,* ed. William M. K. Trochim. New Directions for Program Evaluation Series (no. 31). San Fransisco: Jossey-Bass.

Coulton, Claudia J. (1995). Using community-level indicators of children's well-being in comprehensive community initiatives. In *New approaches to evaluating community initiatives,* eds. J. P. Connell, A. C. Kubisch, L. B. Schorr, & C. H. Weiss. Washington, DC: Aspen Institute.

———. (1997). Measuring CCI outcomes using data available for small areas. Paper prepared for the Aspen Institute's Roundtable on Comprehensive Community Initiatives. Cleveland, OH: Case Western Reserve University.

Coulton, Claudia J., J. E. Korbin, & Marilyn Su. (1995). *Measuring neighborhood context for young children in an urban area.* Cleveland, OH: Center for Urban Poverty and Social Change, Case Western Reserve University.

Cousins, Norman. (1981). *Human options.* New York: Norton.

Cronbach, Lee J. (1951). Coefficient alpha and the internal structure of tests. *Psychometrika, 16,* 297–334.

———. (1982). *Designing evaluations of educational and social programs.* San Francisco: Jossey-Bass.

———. (1984). *Essentials of psychological testing* (4th ed.). New York: Harper & Row.

Cronbach, Lee J., & Associates. (1980). *Toward reform of program evaluation.* San Francisco: Jossey-Bass.

Cross, Ted, & Elizabeth McDonald. (1995). *Evaluating the outcome of children's mental health services: A guide for the use of available child and family out-*

come measures. Boston: Technical Assistance Center, Judge Baker Children's Center.

Cullen, M. J. (1975). *The statistical movement in early Victorian Britain: The foundations of empirical social research.* New York: Harper & Row.

Cumming, Elaine, & John Cumming. (1957). *Closed ranks: An experiment in mental health education.* Cambridge, MA: Harvard University Press.

Dabbs, James M. Jr. (1982). Making things visible. In *Studying organizations: Innovations in methodology: Varieties of qualitative research* (no. 5), eds. J. M. Dabbs, Jr. & R. R. Faulkner, pp. 11–63. Beverly Hills, CA: Sage.

Darman, Richard. (1996, December 1). Riverboat gambling with government. *New York Times Magazine,* pp. 116–117.

Darwin, Charles. (1868). Letter to J. D. Hooker, quoted in *Transforming qualitative data: Description, analysis, and interpretation,* Harry F. Wolcott, p. 152. Thousand Oaks, CA: Sage, 1994.

Dennis, Michael L., & Robert F. Boruch. (1989). Randomized experiments for planning and testing projects in developing countries. *Evaluation Review, 13* (3), 292–309.

Dentler, Robert. (1959). *The young volunteers: An evaluation of three programs of the American Friends Service Committee.* Chicago: National Opinion Research Center.

Desai, Arand, & Min-Bong You. (1992). Policy implications from an evaluation of seat belt use regulation. *Evaluation Review, 16* (3), 247–265.

Deutsch, Stuart J., & C. J. Malmborg. (1986). A study in the consistency of stakeholder preferences for different types of information in evaluating police services. *Evaluation and Program Planning, 9,* 13–24.

Devaney, Barbara, Linda Bilheimer, & Jennifer Schore. (1991). *The savings in Medicaid costs for newborns and their mothers from prenatal participation in the WIC Program,* vols. 1 and 2. Princeton: Mathematica Policy Research.

Dickinson, Katherine P., Terry R. Johnson, & Richard W. West. (1987). An analysis of the sensitivity of quasi-experimental net impact estimates of CETA programs. *Evaluation Review, 11,* 452–472.

Dillman, Don A. (1978). *Mail and telephone surveys: The total design method.* New York: Wiley.

Dobson, Matthew, D. A. Grayson, R. P. Marshall, B. I. O'Toole, S. R. Leeder, & R. Schureck. (1996). The impact of a counseling service program on the psychosocial morbidity of Australian Vietnam veterans. *Evaluation Review, 20,* 670–694.

Drummond, Michael F., G. L. Stoddart, & G. W. Torrance. (1987). *Methods for the economic evaluation of health care programmes.* Oxford: Oxford University Press.

Dwyer, Florence P. (1970). *Report to the people, 14* (1). 12th District, New Jersey.

Edwards, Ward, & J. Robert Newman. (1982). Multiattribute evaluation. *Sage*

University Paper Series on Quantitative Applications in the Social Sciences (no. 07-026). Newbury Park, CA: Sage.

Eisner, Elliot. (1991). Taking a second look: Educational connoisseurship revisited. In *Evaluation and education: At quarter century*, eds. M. W. McLaughlin & D. C. Phillips, pp. 169–187. Chicago: National Society for the Study of Education.

Elmore, Richard F. (1996). Getting to scale with good educational practice. *Harvard Educational Review, 66* (1), 1–26.

Enterprise Foundation. (1993). *Community building in partnership: Neighborhood transformation demonstration, Sandtown-Winchester, Baltimore* (progress report). Baltimore, MD: Enterprise Foundation.

Erfurt, John C., Andrea Foote, & Max A. Heirich. (1991). The cost-effectiveness of work-site wellness programs for hypertension control, weight loss, and smoking cessation. *Journal of Occupational Medicine, 33* (9), 962–970.

Farquhar, John W., S. P. Fortman, J. A. Flora, C. B. Taylor, W. L. Haskell, P. T. Williams, N. Maccoby, & P. D. Wood. (1990). Effects of communitywide education on cardiovascular disease risk factors: The Stanford Five-City Project. *Journal of the American Medical Association, 264*, 359–365.

Fawcett, Stephen B., Adrienne Paine-Andrews, Vincent T. Francisco, Jerry A. Schultz, Kimberly P. Richter, Rhonda K. Lewis, Kari J. Harris, Ella L. Williams, Jannette Y. Berkley, Christine M. Lopez, & Jacqueline L. Fisher. (1996). Empowering community health initiatives through evaluation. In *Empowerment evaluation: Knowledge and tools for self-assessment and accountability*, eds. David M. Fetterman, Shakeh J. Kaftarian, & Abraham Wandersman, pp. 161–187. Thousand Oaks, CA: Sage.

Fetterman, David M. (1988). A national ethnographic evaluation: An executive summary of the ethnographic component of the Career Intern Program Study. In *Qualitative approaches to evaluation in education: The silent scientific revolution*, ed. David M. Fetterman, pp. 262–273. New York: Praeger.

Fetterman, David M., & Mary A. Pitman (Eds.). (1986). *Educational evaluation: Ethnography in theory, practice and politics*. Beverly Hills, CA: Sage.

Fetterman, David M., Shakeh J. Kaftarian, & Abraham Wandersman (Eds.). (1996). *Empowerment evaluation: Knowledge and tools for self-assessment and accountability*. Thousand Oaks, CA: Sage.

Flook, Emma Evelyn, & Paul J. Sanazaro (Eds.). (1973). *Health services research and R & D in perspective*. Ann Arbor, MI: Health Administration Press.

Flora, June A., N. Maccoby, & John W. Farquahar. (1989). Communication campaigns to prevent cardiovascular disease. In *Public communication campaigns* (2nd ed.), eds. R. Rice & C. Atkin. Newbury Park, CA: Sage.

Foddy, William H. (1993). *Constructing questions for interviews and questionnaires: Theory and practice in social research*. New York: Cambridge University Press.

Fraker, Thomas, & R. Maynard. (1987). The adequacy of comparison group designs for evaluations of employment-related programs. *Journal of Human Resources, 22,* 194–297.

Friedlander, Daniel, & Gary Burtless. (1995). *Five years later: The long-term effects of welfare-to-work programs.* New York: Russell Sage Foundation.

Friedlander, Daniel, & Gayle Hamilton. (1993). *The Saturation Work Initiative Model in San Diego: A five-year follow-up study.* New York: Manpower Demonstration Research Corporation.

Friedlander, Daniel, & P. Robins. (1994). Estimating the effect of employment and training programs: An assessment of some nonexperimental techniques. Working paper. New York: Manpower Demonstration Research Corporation.

Friedman, J., & D. H. Weinberg (Eds.). (1983). The great housing experiment. *Urban Affairs Annual Review, 24.*

Fullan, Michael G. (with S. Stiegelbauer). (1991). *The new meaning of educational change* (2d ed.). New York: Teachers College Press.

Galvin, Patrick. (1989). Concept mapping for planning and evaluation of a Big Brother/Big Sister program. *Evaluation and Program Planning, 12,* 53–57.

Gans, Herbert. (1962). *The urban villagers.* New York: Free Press of Glencoe.

Garasky, Steven. (1990). Analysing the effect of Massachusetts' ET choices program on the state's AFDC-basic caseload. *Evaluation Review, 14* (6), 701–710.

Giaconia, R. M., & L. V. Hedges. (1982). Identifying features of effective open education. *Review of Educational Research, 52* (4), 579–602.

Gilligan, Carol. (1982). *In a different voice: Psychological theory and women's development.* Cambridge, MA: Harvard University Press.

Ginsberg, Alan, Maureen McLaughlin, Valena Pusko, & Ricky Takai. (1992). Reinvigorating program evaluation at the U.S. Department of Education. *Education Researcher, 21* (3), 24–27.

Glaser, Barney G., & Anselm L. Strauss. (1967). *The discovery of grounded theory: Strategies for qualitative research.* Chicago: Aldine Publications Co.

Glass, Gene V., & Mary Lee Smith. (1979). Meta-analysis of research on the relationship of class size and achievement. *Educational Evaluation and Policy Analysis, 1,* 2–16.

Goodman, Robert M., Abraham Wandersman, Matthew Chinman, Pam Imm, & Erin Morrissey. (1996). An ecological assessment of community-based interventions for prevention and health promotion: Approaches to measuring community coalitions. *American Journal of Community Psychology, 24* (1), 33–61.

Green, Lawrence W., & M. W. Kreuter. (1991). *Health promotion planning: An educational and environmental approach.* Mountain View, CA: Mayfield.

Greene, Jennifer C. (1988). Stakeholder participation and utilization in program evaluation. *Evaluation Review, 12* (2), 96–116.

Greene, Jennifer C., et al. (1989). Toward a conceptual framework for mixed-method evaluation designs. *Educational Evaluation and Policy Analysis, 11* (3), 255–274.

Greene, Jennifer C., & V. J. Caracelli (Eds.). (1997). Advances in mixed-method evaluation: The challenges and benefits of integrating diverse paradigms. In *New directions for evaluation*. New Directions for Program Evaluation Series (no. 74). San Francisco: Jossey-Bass.

Greenwald, Rob, L. V. Hedges, & R. D. Laine. (1996a). The effect of school resources on student achievement. *Review of Educational Research, 66* (3), 361–396.

———. (1996b). Interpreting research on school resources and student achievement. *Review of Educational Research, 66* (3), 411–416.

Guba, Egon G. (Ed.). (1990). *The paradigm dialog.* Newbury Park, CA: Sage.

Guba, Egon G., & Yvonna S. Lincoln. (1986). The countenances of fourth generation evaluation: Description, judgment, and negotiation. In *Evaluation studies review annual* (vol. 11), eds. D. Cordray & M. Lipsey, pp. 70–88. Newbury Park, CA: Sage.

———. (1989). *Fourth generation evaluation.* Newbury Park, CA: Sage.

Hamilton, Gayle, & Daniel Friedlander. (1989). *The Saturation Work Initiative Model in San Diego* (final report). New York: Manpower Demonstration Research Corporation.

Hammersley, Martyn, & Paul Atkinson. (1983). *Ethnography: Principles in practice.* London: Tavistock.

Hanushek, Eric A. (1994). Money might matter somewhere: A response to Hedges, Laine and Greenwald. *Educational Researcher, 23* (4), 5–8.

———. (1996). A more complete picture of school resource policies. *Review of Educational Research, 66* (3), 397–409.

———. (1997). Assessing the effects of school resources on student performance: An update. *Educational Evaluation and Policy Analysis, 19*, 141–164.

Harper, Douglas. (1994). On the authority of the image: Visual methods at the crossroads. In *Handbook of qualitative research*, eds. Norman K. Denzin & Yvonna S. Lincoln, pp. 403–412. Thousand Oaks, CA: Sage.

Hauser-Cram, Penny. (1983). Some cautions in synthesizing research studies. *Educational Evaluation and Policy Analysis, 5* (2), 155–162.

Heckman, James J. (1980). Sample selection bias as a specification error. In *Evaluation studies review annual, 5*, ed. E. W. Stromsdorfer & G. Farkas, pp. 13–31. Newbury Park, CA: Sage.

———. (1989). Causal inference and nonrandom samples. *Journal of Educational Statistics, 14* (2), 159–168.

Heckman, James J., & J. Hotz. (1989). Choosing among alternative nonexperimental methods for estimating the impact of social programs: The case of manpower training. *Journal of the American Statistical Association, 84* (408), 862–880.

Heckman, James J., J. Hotz, & R. Dabos. (1987). Do we need experimental data to evaluate the impact of manpower training on earnings? *Evaluation Review, 11*, 395–427.

Heclo, Hugh. (1977). *A government of strangers: Executive politics in Washington.* Washington, DC: Brookings Institution.

Hedges, Larry V., R. D. Laine, & Rob Greenwald. (1994). Does money matter? A meta-analysis of studies of the effects of differential school inputs on student outcomes. *Educational Researcher, 23* (3), 5–14.

Heinsman, Donna T., & W. R. Shadish. (1996). Assignment methods in experimentation: When do nonrandomized experiments approximate answers from randomized experiments? *Psychological Methods, 1* (2), 154–169.

Heisenberg, Werner. (1958). *Physics and philosophy: The revolution in modern science.* New York: Harper.

Henry, Gary T. (1995). *Graphing data: Techniques for display and analysis.* Thousand Oaks, CA: Sage.

Henry, Gary T., K. C. Dickey, & J. C. Areson. (1991). Stakeholder participation in educational performance monitoring systems. *Educational Evaluation and Policy Analysis, 13* (2), 177–188.

Hillsman-Baker, S. B., & O. Rodriguez. (1979). Random time quota selection: An alternative to random selection in experimental evaluation. In *Evaluation studies review annual* (vol. 4), pp. 185–196. Beverly Hills, CA: Sage.

Holder, Harold D., R. F. Saltz, A. J. Treno, J. W. Grube, & R. B. Voas. (1997). Evaluation design for a community prevention trial: An environmental approach to reduce alcohol-involved trauma. *Evaluation Review, 21* (2), 140–165.

Holder, Harold D., & James Blose. (1988). Community planning and the prevention of alcohol involved traffic problems: An application of computer simulation technology. *Evaluation and Program Planning, 11*, 267–277.

Hollister, Robinson G., & Jennifer Hill. (1995). Problems in the evaluation of community-wide initiatives. In *New approaches to evaluating community initiatives,* eds. J. P. Connell, A. C. Kubisch, L. B. Schorr, & C. H. Weiss, pp. 127–172. Washington, DC: Aspen Institute.

Homans, George C. (1949). The strategy of industrial sociology. *American Journal of Sociology, 54*, 330–337.

Hosmer, David W., & Stanley Lemeshow. (1989). *Applied logistic regression.* New York: Wiley.

House, Ernest R. (1980). *Evaluating with validity.* Beverly Hills, CA: Sage.

———. (1988). *Jesse Jackson and the politics of charisma.* Boulder, CO: Westview Press.

———. (1990). An ethics of qualitative field studies. In *The paradigm dialog,* ed. Egon G. Guba, pp. 158–164. Newbury Park, CA: Sage.

———. (1992, November 5). Integrating the quantitative and qualitative. Speech to American Evaluation Association. Seattle.

———. (1993). *Professional evaluation: Social impact and political consequences.* Thousand Oaks, CA: Sage.

Huberman, A. Michael. (1989). Predicting conceptual effects in research. *Knowledge and Society, 2* (3), 6–24.

Hyman, Herbert, & Charles Wright. (1967). Evaluating social action programs. In *The uses of sociology*, eds. P. F. Lazarsfeld, W. H. Sewell, & H. L. Wilensky, pp. 741–782. New York: Basic Books.

Jick, Todd D. (1983). Mixing qualitative and quantitative methods: Triangulation in action. In *Qualitative methodology* (2nd ed.), ed. John Van Maanen, pp. 135–148. Beverly Hills, CA: Sage.

Johannesson, Magnus, & Bengt Jonsson. (1991). Economic evaluation in health care: Is there a role for CBA? *Health Policy, 17*, 1–23.

Joint Committee on Standards for Educational Evaluation. (1994). *The program evaluation standards: How to assess evaluations of educational programs* (2nd ed.). Thousand Oaks, CA: Sage.

Jones, Reginald L. (Ed.) (1996). Handbook of tests and measurements for black populations (2 vols.). Hampton, VA: Cobb and Henry.

Judd, Charles M., & D. A. Kenny. (1981). Process analysis: Estimating mediation in treatment evaluations. *Evaluation Review, 5* (5), 602–619.

Kallen, David J. (1966, January 10). Personal letter.

Kaufman, Herbert. (1976). *Are government organizations immortal?* Washington, DC: Brookings Institution.

Kelvin, Lord (William Thomson). (1894). *Popular lectures and addresses, 1891–1894*. London: Macmillan & Company.

Kennedy, Stephen D. (1980). *The final report of the Housing Allowance Demand Experiment*. Cambridge, MA: Abt Associates.

Kershaw, David, & Jerilyn Fair. (1976). *The New Jersey income-maintenance experiment: Operations, surveys and administration* (vol. 1). New York: Academic Press.

———. (1977) *The New Jersey income-maintenance experiment* (vol. 2). New York: Academic Press.

Kessler, R. C., & J. A. McRae, Jr. (1982). The effect of wives' employment on the mental health of married men and women. *American Sociological Review, 47*, 216–227.

Kidder, Louise H., & Michelle Fine. (1987). Qualitative and quantitative methods: When stories converge. In *New directions for program evaluation: Multiple methods in program evaluation*, eds. M. M. Mark & R. L. Shotland. New Directions for Program Evaluation Series (no. 35). San Francisco: Jossey-Bass.

Kiefer, N. (1979). *The economic benefits of four employment and training programs*. New York: Garland.

King, Gary, Robert O. Keohane, & Sidney Verba. (1994). *Designing social inquiry: Scientific inference in qualitative research*. Princeton, NJ: Princeton University Press.

Kirk, J., & M. L. Miller. (1986). *Reliability and validity in qualitative research*. Qualitative Research Methods Series, no. 1. Newbury Park, CA: Sage.

Kirkup, Gill. (1986). The feminist evaluation. In *New directions in educational evaluation*, ed. Ernest R. House, pp. 68–84. London: Falmer Press.

Klarman, Herbert E. (1982). The road to cost-effectiveness analysis. *Health and Society, 60* (4), 585–603.

Kostoff, Ronald N. (Ed.). (1994). Special issue: Research impact assessment. *Evaluation Review, 18*.

Kostoff, Ronald N., H. A. Averch, & D. E. Chubin. (1994). Research impact assessment: Introduction and overview. *Evaluation Review, 18*, 3–10.

Krieger, Martin H. (1988). The inner game of writing. *Journal of Policy Analysis and Management, 7* (2), 408–416.

Kubisch, Anne C. (1996). Comprehensive community initiatives: Lessons in neighborhood transformation. *Shelterforce, 18* (1), 8–11.

Labaw, Patricia J. (1980). *Advanced questionnaire design*. Cambridge, MA: Abt Books.

La Londe, R. (1986). Evaluating the econometric evaluations of training programs with experimental data. *American Economic Review, 76* (4), 604–620.

La Londe, R., & R. Maynard. (1987). How precise are evaluations of employment and training programs: Evidence from a field experiment. *Evaluation Review, 11* (4), 428–451.

La Prelle, John, K. E. Bauman, & G. G. Koch. (1992). High intercommunity variation in adolescent cigarette smoking in a 10-community field experiment. *Evaluation Review, 16* (2), 115–130.

Lawrence, J. E. S. (1989). Engaging respondents in development evaluation: The stakeholder approach. *Evaluation Review, 13* (2), 243–256.

Lee, Valerie E., & J. B. Smith. (1993). Effects of school restructuring on the achievement and engagement of middle-grade students. *Sociology of Education, 66*, 164–187.

Lee, Valerie E., & S. Loeb. (1995). Where do Head Start attendees end up? One reason why preschool effects fade out. *Educational Evaluation and Policy Analysis, 17*, 62–82.

Lewis, Darrell R., D. R. Johnson, H.-T. Chen, & R. N. Erickson. (1992). The use and reporting of benefit-cost analyses by state vocational rehabilitation agencies. *Evaluation Review, 16* (3), 266–287.

Liebow, Elliot. (1967). *Tally's corner*. Boston: Little, Brown.

Light, Richard J., & Frederick Mosteller. (1992). Annotated bibliography of meta-analytic books and journal issues. In *Meta-analysis for explanation: A casebook*, eds. T. D. Cook, Harris Cooper, D. S. Cordray, Heidi Hartmann, L. V. Hedges, R. J. Light, T. A. Louis, & Frederick Mosteller, pp. xi–xiv. New York: Russell Sage Foundation.

Light, Richard J., Judith D. Singer, & John B. Willett. (1990). *By design: Planning research on higher education*. Cambridge, MA: Harvard University Press.

Lincoln, Yvonna S., & Egon G. Guba. (1986). But is it rigorous? Trustworthiness and authenticity in naturalistic evaluation. In *New directions for program evaluation: Naturalistic evaluation*, ed. D. D. Williams, pp. 73–92. New Directions for Program Evaluation Series (no. 30). San Francisco: Jossey-Bass.

Lindblom, Charles E., & David K. Cohen. (1979). *Usable knowledge: Social science and social problem solving*. New Haven, CT: Yale University Press.

Lipsey, Mark W. (1989). Drawing toward theory in program evaluation: More models to choose from. *Evaluation and Program Planning, 12,* 317–328.

———. (1992). Juvenile delinquency treatment: A meta-analytic inquiry into the variability of effects. In *Meta-analysis for explanation: A casebook*, eds. T. D. Cook, Harris Cooper, D. S. Cordray, Heidi Hartmann, L. V. Hedges, R. J. Light, T. A. Louis, & Frederick Mosteller, pp. 83–127. New York: Russell Sage Foundation.

———. (1993). Theory as method: Small theories of treatments. In *New directions for program evaluation: Understanding causes and generalizing about them*, eds. Lee Sechrest & A. G. Scott, pp. 5–38. New Directions for Program Evaluation Series (no. 57). San Francisco: Jossey-Bass.

Lipsey, Mark W., & David B. Wilson. (1993). The efficacy of psychological, educational, and behavioral treatment: Confirmation from meta-analysis. *American Psychologist, 48* (12), 1181–1209.

Loehlin, John C. (1992). *Latent variable models: An introduction to factor, path, and structural analysis*. Hillsdale, NJ: Erlbaum.

Logsdon, David M., N. E. Taylor, & I. H. Blum. (1988). It was a good learning experience: The problems and trials of implementing and evaluating a parent participation program. In *Qualitative approaches to evaluation in education: The silent scientific revolution*, ed. D. M. Fetterman, pp. 23–41. New York: Praeger.

Long, David, Robert G. Wood, & Hilary Kopp. (1994). *LEAP: The educational effects of LEAP and enhanced services in Cleveland*. New York: Manpower Demonstration Research Corporation.

Lou, Yiping, P. C. Abrami, J. C. Spence, C. Poulsen, B. Chambers, & S. d'Appolonia. (1996). Within-class grouping: A meta-analysis. *Review of Educational Research, 66* (4), 423–458.

Luce, Bryan R., & A. Elixhauser. (1990). Estimating costs in the economic evaluation of medical technologies. *International Journal of Technology Assessment in Health Care, 6,* 57–75.

Lunnenberg, C. (1994). *Modeling experimental and observational data*. Boston: PWS-Kent.

Lynch, K. B. (1983). Qualitative and quantitative evaluation: Two terms in search of a meaning. *Educational Evaluation and Policy Analysis, 5* (4), 461–464.

Lyons, Gene M. (1969). *The uneasy partnership: Social science and the federal government in the twentieth century*. New York: Russell Sage Foundation.

Majone, Giandomenico. (1988). Policy analysis and public deliberation. In *The power of public ideas*, ed. Robert B. Reich. Cambridge, MA: Ballinger.

Maki, J. E., D. M. Hoffman, & R. A. Berk. (1978). A time series analysis of the impact of a water conservation campaign. *Evaluation Quarterly, 2,* 107–118.

Mangen, D. J., & W. A. Peterson (Eds.). (1982–84). *Research instruments in social gerontology. Clinical and social psychology* (vol. 1, 1982), *Social roles and social participation* (vol. 2, 1982), *Health, program evaluation, and demography* (vol. 3, 1984). Minneapolis, MN: University of Minnesota Press.

Marais, Lorraine. (1996). Message on EVALTALK, LISTSERV.

Mark, Melvin, & Lance Shotland. (1985). Stakeholder-based evaluation and value judgments. *Evaluation Review, 9* (5), 605–626.

———. (1987). Alternative models of the use of multiple methods. In *New directions for program evaluation: Multiple methods in program evaluation*, eds. Melvin Mark & Lance Shotland, pp. 95–100. New Directions for Program Evaluation Series (no. 35). San Francisco: Jossey-Bass.

Marsh, Jeanne C., & M. A. Wirick. (1991). Evaluation of Hull House teen pregnancy and parenting programs. *Evaluation and Program Planning, 14,* 49–61.

Martinson, Karin, & Daniel Friedlander. (1994). *Gain: Basic education in a welfare-to-work program.* New York: Manpower Demonstration Research Corporation.

Massachusetts Department of Public Welfare. (1986a). *An analysis of the first 25,000 ET placements.* Office of Research, Planning and Evaluation, Commonwealth of Massachusetts: Author.

Massachusetts Department of Public Welfare. (1986b). *An evaluation of the Massachusetts Employment and Training Choices Program: Interim findings on participation and outcomes.* Office of Research, Planning and Evaluation, Commonwealth of Massachusetts: Author.

Massachusetts Department of Public Welfare. (1986c). *Follow-up survey of the first 25,000 ET placements.* Office of Research, Planning and Evaluation, Commonwealth of Massachusetts: Author.

Mauser, Gary A,, & R. A. Holmes. (1992). An evaluation of the 1977 Canadian firearms legislation. *Evaluation Review, 16* (6), 603–617.

Maxwell, Joseph A. (1992). Understanding and validity in qualitative research. *Harvard Educational Review, 62* (3), 279–300.

———. (1996). *Qualitative research design: An interactive approach.* Thousand Oaks, CA: Sage.

Maxwell, Joseph A., Philip G. Basbook, & Leslie J. Sandlow. (1986). Combining ethnographic and experimental methods in educational evaluation. In *Educational evaluation: Ethnography in theory, practice, and politics*, eds. David M. Fetterman & Mary A. Pitman, pp. 121–143. Beverly Hills, CA: Sage.

McClintock, Charles. (1990). Administrators as applied theorists. In *New directions for program evaluation: Advances in program theory*, ed. Leonard Bickman, pp. 19–33. New Directions for Program Evaluation Series (no. 47). San Francisco: Jossey-Bass.

McCord, William, & Joan McCord. (1959). *Origins of crime: A new evaluation of the Cambridge-Somerville Youth Study*. New York: Columbia University Press.

McDill, Edward L., Mary S. McDill, & J. Timothy Sprehe. (1969). *Strategies for success in compensatory education: An appraisal of evaluation research*. Baltimore, MD: Johns Hopkins Press.

McDowell, Ian, & Claire Newell. (1987). *Measuring health: A guide to rating scales and questionnaires*. Oxford: Oxford University Press.

McGraw, Sarah A., D. E. Sellers, E. J. Stone, J. Bebchuk, E. W. Edmundson, C. C. Johnson, K. J. Bachman, & R. V. Luepker. (1996). Using process data to explain outcomes: An illustration from the Child and Adolescent Trial for Cardiovascular Health (CATCH). *Evaluation Review, 20* (3), 291–312.

McLaughlin, Milbrey W. (1975). *Evaluation and reform: The Elementary and Secondary Education Act of 1965, Title 1*. Cambridge, MA: Ballinger.

McLaughlin, Milbrey W., & D. C. Phillips (Eds.). (1991). Editors' preface. *Evaluation and education: At quarter century*, 90th Yearbook of the National Society for the Study of Education, part 2, pp. ix–xii. Chicago: NSSE and University of Chicago Press.

Meyers, William R. (1981). *The evaluation enterprise*. San Francisco: Jossey-Bass.

Miles, Matthew B., & A. Michael Huberman. (1994). *Qualitative data analysis: An expanded sourcebook* (2nd ed.). Thousand Oaks, CA: Sage.

Miller, Delbert C. (1991). *Handbook of research design and social measurement* (5th ed.). Newbury Park, CA: Sage.

Moffitt, Robert. (1991). Program evaluation with nonexperimental data. *Evaluation Review, 15* (3), 291–314.

Moore, Mark. (1988). What sort of ideas become public ideas? In *The power of public ideas*, ed. Robert B. Reich, pp. 55–83. Cambridge, MA: Ballinger.

Moses, Lincoln. (1987). Graphical methods in statistical analysis. *Annual Review of Public Health* (vol. 8), pp. 309–353. Palo Alto: Annual Reviews.

Murray, Charles A. (1983). *Stakeholders as deck chairs*. San Francisco: Jossey-Bass.

National Education Goals Panel. (1993). *National education goals report*. Washington, DC: Author.

National Research Council. Committee on AIDS Research and the Behavioral, Social and Statistical Sciences. (1989). *Evaluating the effects of AIDS interventions*. Washington, DC: National Academy Press.

National Research Council. Panel on Statistical Issues and Opportunities for Research in the Combination of Information. (1992). *Combining information: Statistical issues and opportunities for research*. Washington, DC: National Academy Press.

Neter, John, William Wasserman, & Michael H. Kutner. (1990). *Applied linear statistical models* (3rd ed.). Homewood, IL: Irwin.

Newhouse, Joseph P., & Insurance Experiment Group. (1993). *Free for all? Lessons from the Rand health insurance experiment.* Cambridge, MA: Harvard University Press.

Newhouse, Joseph P., W. G. Manning, C. N. Morris, L. L. Orr, N. Duan, E. B. Keeler, A. Leibowitz, K. H. Marquis, M. S. Marquis, C. E. Phelps, & R. H. Brook. (1981). Some interim results from a controlled trial of cost sharing in health insurance. *New England Journal of Medicine, 305,* 1501–1507.

Ohls, J. C., T. M. Fraker, A. P. Martini, & M. Ponza. (1992). *The effects of cash-out on food use by food stamp participants in San Diego.* Princeton, NJ: Mathematica Policy Research.

Olds, David. (1988). Common design and methodological problems encountered in evaluating family support services: Illustrations from the Prenatal/Early Infancy Project. In *Evaluating family programs*, eds. Heather B. Weiss & Francine H. Jacobs, pp. 239–265. New York: Aldine de Gruyter.

Orleans, C. Tracy, V. J. Schoenbach, E. H. Wagner, D. Quade, M. A. Salmon, D. C. Pearson, F. Fiedler, C. Q. Porter, & B. H. Kaplan. (1991). Self-help quit smoking interventions: Effects of self-help materials, social support instructions, and telephone counseling. *Journal of Consulting and Clinical Psychology, 59* (3), 439–448.

Orvaschel, Helen, & Geraldine Walsh. (1984). *The assessment of adaptive functioning in children: A review of existing measures suitable for epidemiological and clinical services research.* Rockville, MD: National Institute of Mental Health.

Ossip-Klein, Deborah J., G. A. Giovino, N. Megahed, P. M. Black, S. L. Emont, J. Stiggins, E. Shulman, & L. Moore. (1991). Effects of a smokers' hotline: Results of a 10-county self-help trial. *Journal of Consulting and Clinical Psychology, 59* (2), 325–332.

Paine, Stanley L. (1951). *The art of asking questions.* Princeton, NJ: Princeton University Press.

Palumbo, Dennis J., & M. Hallett. (1993). Conflict versus consensus models in policy evaluation and implementation. *Evaluation and Program Planning, 16* (1), 11–23.

Parlett, M., & D. Hamilton. (1976). Evaluation as illumination: A new approach to the study of innovative programs. In *Evaluation studies review annual* (vol. 1), ed. G. V. Glass. Beverly Hills, CA: Sage.

Patterson, Blossom H., L. G. Kessler, Y. Wax, A. Bernstein, L. Light, D. N. Midthune, B. Portnoy, J. Tenney, & E. Tuckermanty. (1992). Evaluation of a supermarket intervention: The NCI-Giant Food Eat for Health Study. *Evaluation Review, 16* (5), 464–490.

Patton, George S. Jr. (1947). *War as I knew it.* Boston: Houghton Mifflin Company.

Patton, Michael Quinn. (1980). *Qualitative evaluation methods*. Beverly Hills, CA: Sage.

———. (1989). A context and boundaries for theory-driven approach to validity. *Evaluation and Program Planning, 12*, 375–377.

———. (1990). The evaluator's responsibility for utilization. In *Debates on evaluation*, ed. M. C. Alkin, 185–207. Newbury Park, CA: Sage.

———. (1997). *Utilization-focused evaluation: The new century text* (3rd ed.). Thousand Oaks, CA: Sage.

Pechman, J. A., & P. M. Timpane (Eds.). (1975). *Work incentives and income guarantees: The New Jersey negative income tax experiment*. Washington, DC: Brookings Institution.

Pentz, M. A., E. A. Trevow, W. B. Hansen, D. P. MacKinnon, J. H. Dwyer, C. A. Johnson, B. R. Flay, S. Daniels, & C. Cormack. (1990). Effects of program implementation on adolescent drug use behavior. *Evaluation Review, 14* (3), 264–289.

Peters, Thomas J., & R. H. Waterman, Jr. (1982). *In search of excellence: Lessons from America's best-run companies*. New York: Harper & Row.

Pew Charitable Trust. (n.d.). *The children's initiative: Making systems work, a program of the Pew Charitable Trust*. Philadelphia: Author.

Phelps, Charles E., & Joseph P. Newhouse. (1973). *Coinsurance and the demand for medical services*. Santa Monica, CA: Rand Corporation.

Powers, Edwin, & Helen Witmer. (1951). *An experiment in the prevention of delinquency: The Cambridge-Somerville Youth Study*. New York: Columbia University Press.

Price, James L., & Charles W. Mueller. (1986). *Handbook of organizational measurement*. Marshfield, MA: Pitman.

Punch, Maurice. (1986). *The politics and ethics of fieldwork*. Beverly Hills, CA: Sage.

Quint, Janet C., D. F. Polit, H. Bos, & G. Cave. (1994). *New Chance: Interim findings on a comprehensive program for disadvantaged youth mothers and their children*. New York: Manpower Demonstration Research Corporation.

Ragin, Charles C. (1994). *Constructing social research*. Thousand Oaks, CA: Pine Forge Press/Sage.

Rein, Martin. (1981). Comprehensive program evaluation. In *Evaluation research and practice: Comparative and international perspectives*, eds. Robert A. Levine, M. A. Solomon, G.-M. Hellstern, & H. Wollmann, pp. 132–148. Beverly Hills, CA: Sage.

Reinharz, Shulamit. (1981). Experimental analysis: A contribution to feminist research. In *Theories of women's studies II*, eds. G. Bowles & R. Duelli-Klein. Berkeley, CA: University of California Press.

Reynolds, Kim D., & Stephen G. West. (1978). A multiplist strategy for strengthening nonequivalent control group designs. *Evaluation Review, 11* (6), 691–714.

Riccio, James, Daniel Friedlander, & Stephen Freedman. (1994). *Gain: Benefits, costs, and three-year impacts of a welfare-to-work program.* New York: Manpower Demonstration Research Corporation.

Riggin, J. C. (1990). Linking program theory and social science theory. In *New directions for program evaluation: Advances in program theory*, ed. Leonard Bickman, pp. 109–120. New Directions for Program Evaluation Series (no. 47). San Francisco: Jossey-Bass.

Rivlin, Alice M. (1971). *Systematic thinking for social action.* Washington, DC: Brookings Institution.

Rivlin, Alice M., & P. Michael Timpane (Eds.). (1975). *Planned variation in education: Should we give up or try harder?* Washington, DC: Brookings Institution.

Roberts-Gray, Cynthia, L. F. Simmons, & A. F. Sparkman. (1989). Modular evaluation: The case of the TX Nutrition Education and Training Program. *Evaluation and Program Planning, 12*, 207–212.

Robinson, John P., & Phillip R. Shaver. (1969). *Measures of social psychological attitudes.* Ann Arbor: Survey Research Center, University of Michigan.

Rock, Steven M. (1992). Impact of the Illinois Seat Belt Use Law on accidents, deaths, and injuries. *Evaluation Review, 16* (5), 491–507.

Rog, Debra J. (1991). The evaluation of the Homeless Families Program: Challenges in implementing a nine-city evaluation. In *New directions for program evaluation: Evaluating programs for the homeless*, ed. Debra J. Rog, pp. 47–59. New Directions for Program Evaluation Series (no. 52). San Francisco: Jossey-Bass.

Rosenbaum, P., & Donald B. Rubin. (1983). The central role of the propensity score in observational studies for causal effects. *Biometrika, 70*, 41–55.

———. (1984). Reducing bias in observational studies using subclassification on the propensity score. *Journal of the American Statistical Association, 79*, 516–524.

Rosenthal, Robert. (1978). How often are our numbers wrong? *American Psychologist, 33* (11), 1005–1008.

———. (1991). *Meta-analytic procedures for social research* (rev. ed.). Newbury Park, CA: Sage.

———. (1993). The mediation of Pygmalion effects: A four-factor "theory." *Papua New Guinea Journal of Education, 9*, 1–12.

Rosenthal, Robert, & Donald B. Rubin. (1978). Interpersonal expectancy effects: The first 345 studies. *Behavioral and Brain Sciences, 3*, 377–386.

Rossi, Peter H., & Howard E. Freeman. (1993). *Evaluation: A systematic approach* (5th ed.). Newbury Park, CA: Sage.

Rossi, Peter H., Richard A. Berk, & Kenneth J. Lenihan. (1980). *Money, work, and crime: Experimental evidence.* New York: Academic Press.

Rossman, Gretchen B., & S. F. Rallis. (in press 1998). *Learning in the field: An introduction to qualitative research.* Thousand Oaks, CA: Sage.

Rostow, W. W. (1993). The Austin Project, 1989–1993: An innovational excercise in comprehensive urban development. New Haven: *Seminar on Inner City Poverty*, Institution for Social and Policy Studies, Yale University.

Rubin, Donald B., & N. Thomas. (1992). Characterizing the effect of matching using linear propensity score methods with normal covariates. *Biometrika, 79,* 797–809.

———. (1996). Matching using estimated propensity scores: Relating theory to practice. *Biometrics, 52,* 249–264.

Sabatier, Paul A., & Hank C. Jenkins-Smith (Eds.). (1993). *Policy change and learning: An advocacy coalition approach.* Theoretical Lenses on Public Policy Series. Boulder, CO: Westview Press.

Salmen, Lawrence F. (1989). Beneficiary assessment: Improving the design and implementation of development projects. *Evaluation Review, 13* (3), 273–291.

Samuelson, Paul A. (1962). Economists and the history of ideas. *American Economic Review, 52* (1), 1–18.

Schon, Donald A. (1983). *The reflective practitioner: How professionals think in action.* New York: Basic Books.

Schon, Donald A., & Martin Rein. (1994). *Frame reflection: Toward the resolution of intractable policy controversies.* New York: Basic Books.

Schweinhart, Lawrence J., H. V. Barnes, & D. P. Weikart. (1993). *Significant benefits: The High/Scope Perry Preschool Study through age 27.* Ypsilanti, MI: High/Scope Press.

Scriven, Michael. (1967). The methodology of evaluation. In *Perspectives of curriculum evaluation*, eds. Ralph W. Tyler, Robert M. Gagne, & Michael Scriven, pp. 39–83. AERA Monograph Series on Curriculum Evaluation, vol. 1. Chicago: Rand McNally.

———. (1980). *The logic of evaluation.* Point Reyes, CA: Edge Press.

———. (1991, November). Multiple-rating items. Paper prepared for a workshop on assessing higher order thinking and communication skills in college graduates. Washington, DC.

———. (1991). *Evaluation thesaurus* (4th ed.). Newbury Park, CA: Sage.

Sebring, P. A., A. S. Bryk, S. Lupprescu, & Y. M. Thum. (1995). *Charting reform in Prairie School: Results of student and teacher surveys.* Chicago: Consortium on Chicago School Research.

Sechrest, Lee, & Aurelio Figueredo. (1993). Program evaluation. In *Annual review of psychology* (vol. 44), eds. L. W. Porter & M. R. Rosenzweig, pp. 645–674. Palo Alto, CA: Annual Reviews, Inc.

Shadish, William R. (1997). Personal communication.

Shadish, William R., & Kevin Ragsdale. (1996). Random versus nonrandom assignment in controlled experiments. *Journal of Consulting and Clinical Psychology, 64* (6), 1290–1305.

Shadish, William R., Thomas D. Cook, & Laura C. Leviton. (1991). *Foundations of program evaluation: Theories of practice.* Newbury Park, CA: Sage.

Shadish, William R., D. L. Newman, M. A. Scheirer, & C. Wye (Eds.). (1995). *New directions for program evaluation: Guiding principles for evaluators.* New Directions for Program Evaluation Series (no. 66). San Francisco: Jossey-Bass.

Sherman, L. W., & R. A. Berk. (1984). The specific deterrent effects of arrest for domestic assault. *American Sociological Review, 49*, 261–272.

Silverman, David. (1993). *Interpreting qualitative data: Methods for analysing talk, text, and interaction.* London: Sage.

Simons, Helen. (1989). Ethics of case study in educational research and evaluation. In *The ethics of educational research*, ed. R. G. Burgess, pp. 114–138. New York: Falmer Press.

Smith, L. M., & P. F. Kleine. (1986). Qualitative research and evaluation: Triangulation and multimethods reconsidered. In *New directions for program evaluation: Naturalistic evaluation*, ed. D. D. Williams, pp. 55–71. New Directions for Program Evaluation Series (no. 30). San Francisco: Jossey-Bass.

Smith, Mary E. (1987). A guide to the use of simple process measures. *Evaluation and Program Planning, 10*, 219–225.

Smith, Mary Lee. (1986). The whole is greater: Combining qualitative and quantitative approaches in evaluation studies. In *New directions for program evaluation: Naturalistic evaluation*, ed. D. D. Williams, pp. 37–54. New Directions for Program Evaluation Series (no. 30). San Francisco: Jossey-Bass.

———. (1991). Put to the test: The effects of external testing on teachers. *Educational Researcher, 20* (5), 8–11.

———. (1994). Quality plus/versus quantity: The last word. In *New directions for program evaluation: The qualitative-quantitative debate, new perspectives*, eds. C. S. Reichardt & S. F. Rallis, pp. 37–44. New Directions for Program Evaluation Series (no. 61). San Francisco: Jossey-Bass.

Smith, Mary Lee, & Gene V. Glass. (1979). *Relationship of class-size to classroom processes, teacher satisfaction and pupil affect: A meta-analysis.* San Francisco: Far West Laboratory for Educational Research and Development.

South Carolina State Reorganization Commission. (1989). *An evaluation of the human service integration project, 1985–1988.* Columbia, SC: Author.

Stake, Robert E. (Ed.). (1975). *Evaluating the arts in education.* Columbus, OH: Merrill.

Stake, Robert E. (1986). *Quieting reform: Social science and social action in an urban youth program.* Urbana, IL: University of Illinois Press.

———. (1995). *The art of case study research.* Thousand Oaks, CA: Sage.

Stevens, S. A., S. A. Leiderman, W. C. Wolf, & P. T. McCarthy. (1994). *Building capacity for system reform.* Bala Cynwyd, PA: Center for Assessment and Policy Development.

Stevens, Sally J. (1994). Common implementation issues in three large-scale social experiments. In *New directions for program evaluation: Critically evaluating the role of experiments*, ed. Kendon J. Conrad, pp. 45–53. New Directions for Program Evaluation Series (no. 63). San Francisco: Jossey-Bass.

Stevens, S. S. (1951). Mathematics, measurement, and psychophysics. In *Handbook of experimental psychology*, ed. S. S. Stevens. New York: Wiley.

Stewart, David W., & Michael A. Kamins. (1993). *Secondary research: Information sources and methods* (2nd ed.). Newbury Park, CA: Sage.

Stewart, David W., & P. N. Shamdasani. (1993). *Focus groups: Theory and practice*. Thousand Oaks, CA: Sage.

Strauss, Anselm L. (1987). *Qualitative analysis for social scientists*. Cambridge, MA: Cambridge University Press.

Strauss, Anselm L., & Juliet Corbin. (1990). *Basics of qualitative research: Grounded theory procedures and techniques*. Newbury Park, CA: Sage.

Strickland, O. L., & C. F. Waltz (Eds.). (1988). *Measurement of nursing outcomes: Measuring nursing performance; Practice, education, and research* (vol. 2). New York: Springer.

Sturz, Herbert. (1967, February). Experiments in the criminal justice system. *Legal Aide Briefcase*, 1–5.

Suchman, Edward A. (1967). *Evaluative research: Principles and practice in public service and social action programs*. New York: Russell Sage Foundation.

Sudman, Seymour, & Norman M. Bradburn. (1982). *Asking questions: A practical guide to questionnaire design*. San Francisco: Jossey-Bass.

Taveggia, T. (1974). Resolving research controversy through empirical cumulation. *Sociological Methods and Research, 2*, 385–407.

Thompson, B., & S. Kinne. (1990). Social change theory: Applications to community health. In *Health promotion at the community level*, ed. N. Bracht, pp. 45–65. Newbury Park, CA: Sage.

Thornton, Craig, John Love, & Alicia Meckstroth. (1994). *Community-level measures for assessing the status of children and families*. Princeton, NJ: Mathematica Policy Research.

Toulemonde, Jacques, & Lise Rochaix. (1994). Rational decision-making through project appraisal: A presentation of French attempts. *International Review of Administrative Sciences, 60*, 37–53.

Trochim, William M. K. (Ed.). (1986). *New directions for program evaluation: Advances in quasi-experimental design and analysis*. New Directions for Program Evaluation Series (no. 31). San Fransisco: Jossey-Bass.

Trochim, William M. K. (1989). An introduction to concept mapping for planning and evaluation. *Evaluation and Program Planning, 12*, 1–16.

Tufte, Edward R. (1983). *The visual display of quantitative information*. Cheshire, CT: Graphics Press.

———. (1990). *Envisioning information*. Cheshire, CT: Graphics Press.

———. (1997). *Visual explanations: Images and quantities, evidence and narrative.* Cheshire, CT: Graphics Press.

Tyler, Ralph W. (1991). General statement on program evaluation. In *Evaluation and education: At quarter century*, eds. M. W. McLaughlin & D. C. Phillips, pp. 3–17. Ninetieth Yearbook of the National Society for the Study of Education, part 2. Chicago: NSSE and University of Chicago Press. (Original work published in *Journal of Education Resources*, 1942.)

U.S. General Accounting Office. (1987). *Federal evaluations: Fewer units, reduced resources, different studies from 1980.* Washington, DC: Author.

———. (1989). *Effective school programs: Their extent and characteristic.* Washington, DC: Author.

———. (1991). *Communications manual.* Washington, DC: Author.

———. (1992). *Policies and procedures manual.* Washington, DC: Author.

Van Ryzin, Gregg G. (1996). The impact of resident management on residents' satisfaction with public housing: A process analysis of quasi-experimental data. *Evaluation Review, 20*, 485–506.

Vaughn, Sharon, Jeanne Shay Schumm, & J. M. Sinagub. (1996). *Focus group interviews in education and psychology.* Thousand Oaks, CA: Sage.

Vibbert, Spencer. (1993). *What works: How outcomes research will change medical practice.* Ground Rounds Press.

Villar, J., U. Farnot, F. Barrows, & C. Victora. (1992). A randomized trial of psychosocial support during high-risk pregnancies. *New England Journal of Medicine, 327*, 1266–1271.

Viswesvaran, Chockalingam, & F. L. Schmidt. (1992). A meta-analytic comparison of the effectiveness of smoking cessation methods. *Journal of Applied Psychology, 77* (4), 554–561.

Vogt, W. Paul. (1993). *Dictionary of statistics and methodology: A nontechnical guide for the social sciences.* Newbury Park, CA: Sage.

Wainer, Howard. (1989). Responsum. *Journal of Educational Statistics, 14* (2), 187–199.

Walker, D. K. (1973). Socioemotional measures for preschool and Kindergarten children. San Francisco: Jossey-Bass.

Waltz, C. F., & O. L. Strickland (Eds.). (1988). *Measurement of nursing outcomes: Measuring client outcomes* (vol. 1). New York: Springer.

Ward, David A., & Gene G. Kassebaum. (1972). On biting the hand that feeds: Some implications of sociological evaluations of correctional effectiveness. In *Evaluating action programs: Readings in social action and education*, ed. Carol H. Weiss, pp. 300–310. Boston: Allyn & Bacon, Inc.

Ward, Lester F. (1918). Politico-social functions. In *Glimpses of the cosmos: A mental autobiography comprising his minor contributions now republished, together with biographical and historical sketches of all his writings.* New York: G.P. Putnam's Sons.

Warner, W. Lloyd. (1959). *The living and the dead: A study of the symbolic life of Americans*. New Haven, CT: Yale University Press.

Watts, Harold, & Albert Rees (Eds.). (1977). *The New Jersey income-maintenance experiment* (vol. 3). New York: Academic Press.

Webb, Eugene T., D. T. Campbell, R. D. Schwartz, Lee Sechrest, & J. B. Grove. (1981). *Nonreactive measures in the social sciences* (2nd ed.). Boston: Houghton Mifflin.

Weiss, Carol H. (1972). *Evaluation research: Methods of assessing program effectiveness*. Englewood Cliffs, NJ: Prentice-Hall.

———. (1983a). Ideology, interests, and information: The basis of policy positions. In *Ethics, the social sciences, and policy analysis*, eds. Daniel Callahan & B. Jennings. New York: Plenum.

———. (1983b). The stakeholder approach to evaluation: Origins and promise. In *New directions for program evaluation: Stakeholder-based evaluation*, ed. Anthony S. Bryk, pp. 3–14. New Directions for Program Evaluation Series (no. 17). San Francisco: Jossey-Bass.

———. (1983c). Toward the future of stakeholder approaches in evaluation. In *New directions for program evaluation: Stakeholder-based evaluation*, ed. Anthony S. Bryk, pp. 83–96. New Directions for Program Evaluation Series (no. 17). San Francisco: Jossey-Bass.

———. (1989). Congressional committees as users of analysis. *Journal of Policy Analysis and Management, 8* (3), 411–431.

———. (1995a). Nothing as practical as good theory: Exploring theory-based evaluation for comprehensive community initiatives for children and families. In *New approaches to evaluating community initiatives*, eds. J. P. Connell, A. C. Kubisch, L. B. Schorr, & C. H. Weiss, pp. 65–92. Washington, DC: Aspen Institute.

———. (1995b). The four I's of school reform: Ideology, interests, information, and institution. *Harvard Educational Review, 65* (4), 571–592.

———. (1997). How can theory-based evaluation make greater headway? *Evaluation Review, 21* (4), 501–524.

Weiss, Carol H., with M. J. Bueuvalas. (1980). Social science research and decision making. New York: Columbia University Press.

Weiss, Carol H., & Eleanor Singer. (1988). *Reporting of social science in the national media*. New York: Russell Sage Foundation.

Weiss, Steven J., S. Jurs, J. P. Lesage, & D. C. Iverson. (1984). A cost-benefit analysis of a smoking cessation program. *Evaluation and Program Planning, 7*, 337–346.

Weitzman, Eben A., & M. B. Miles. (1995). *A software sourcebook: Computer programs for qualitative data analysis*. Thousand Oaks, CA: Sage.

Welty, Eudora. (1971). *One time, one place*. New York: Random House.

Wholey, Joseph S. (1979). *Evaluation: Promise and performance*. Washington, DC: Urban Institute.

———. (1983). *Evaluation and effective public management*. Boston: Little Brown.

Wholey, Joseph S. (Ed.). (1987). *Organizational excellence: Stimulating quality and communicating value*. Lexington, MA: Lexington Books.

Wholey, Joseph S. (1994). Assessing the feasibility and likely usefulness of evaluation. In *Handbook of practical program evaluation*, eds. Joseph S. Wholey, Harry P. Hatry, & Kathryn E. Newcomer, pp. 15–39. San Francisco: Jossey-Bass.

Whyte, William Foote. (1955). *Street corner society*. Chicago: University of Chicago Press.

———. (1984). *Learning from the field: A guide from experience*. Newbury Park, CA: Sage.

Wilson, S.R., P. Scamagas, D. F. German, G. W. Hughes, S. Lulla, S. Coss, L. Chardon, R. G. Thomas, N. Starr-Schneiderant, F. B. Stancavage, & G. M. Arsham. (1993). A controlled trial of two forms of self-management education for adults with asthma. *American Journal of Medicine, 94*, 564–576.

Winett, R. A. (1995). A framework for health promotion and disease prevention programs. *American Psychologist, 50*, 341–350.

Wolcott, Harry F. (1994). *Transforming qualitative data: Description, analysis and interpretation*. Thousand Oaks, CA: Sage.

Wortman, Paul M. (1994). Judging research quality. In *The handbook of research synthesis*, eds. Harris Cooper & Larry V. Hedges, pp. 97–110. New York: Russell Sage Foundation.

Wortman, Paul M., & F. B. Bryant. (1985). School desegregation and black achievement: An integrative review. *Sociological Methods and Research, 13*, 289–324.

Wye, Chris, & Richard Sonnichsen. (1992). Another look at the future of program evaluation in the federal government: Five views. *Evaluation Practice, 13* (3), 185–195.

Yamaguchi, Kazuo. (1991). *Event history analysis*. Beverly Hills, CA: Sage.

Yin, Robert K. (1984). *Case study research: Design and methods*. Beverly Hills, CA: Sage.

———. (1994). *Case study research: Design and methods* (2nd ed.). Beverly Hills, CA: Sage.

Zelman, Diane C., T. H. Brandon, D. E. Jorenby, & T. B. Baker. (1992). Measures of affect and nicotine dependence predict differential response to smoking cessation treatments. *Journal of Consulting and Clinical Psychology, 60* (6), 943–952.

INDEX

A

accountability, 28, 51, 119–120
action research, 100
administrative records, 170–171
advisory committees, 91–92
analytic methods, references for, 292–293
autonomy of evaluators, 38–39, 40

B

Barth, Frederik, 46
Baruch, Bernard, 90
Bauman, K. E., 187
Becker, Howard S., 295
Behn, Robert D., 229
benchmarks (*see* intermediate indicators)
Berk, R. A., 225
bias, 149, 153, 267
Bickman, Leonard, 55
Blau, Peter M., 93
Boruch, Robert F., 178, 218
Brandon, Paul R., 102
Brodsky, Stanley L., 137
Brown, Prudence, 98
Bryant, F. B., 236
Burtless, Gary, 279

C

Cabot, R. C., 11
Cambridge-Somerville program, 12
Campbell, Donald T., 67, 88, 149, 183, 216, 229, 315
Carroll, Lewis, 1
Carter-Greer, Kim, 218
case study, 261
Cecil, J. S., 178
Chelimsky, Eleanor, 316
Chen, Huey-Tsyh, 61–62, 137
Chesterton, G. K., 301
Churchill, William, 320
Clinton, Bill, 13, 316
clustering, 286
coding, 168–170
Codman, Ernest, 11
Cohen, David K., 258
commissioning of evaluations, 34–37
comparison groups, 199–205
    constructing, 203–205
    in an existing data set, 207–209
    and selection bias, 210
concept mapping, 104–105
conditions unfavorable for evaluation, 24
confidentiality (*see also* ethical issues), 93–94, 160, 171, 290–291